THE
SEX
BOOK

Author and Designer
SUZI GODSON

Illustrator
PETER STEMMLER

Principle Medical Editors
DR DAVID GOLDMEIER
DR SARAH GILL

Foreword
PROFESSOR ROBERT WINSTON

CASSELL
ILLUSTRATED

First published in the United Kingdom in 2002
by Cassell Illustrated

First published in the United Kingdom in paperback in 2003 by Cassell Illustrated
This edition published in 2006 by Cassell illustrated
Text, design and layout copyright © Unlimited, 2002

A CIP catalogue record for this book is available
from the British Library

ISBN-10: 1-844035-11-5
ISBN-13: 978-1-844035-11-3

10 9 8 7 6 5 4 3 2 1

Printed and bound in Hong Kong

Cassell Illustrated
A division of Octopus Publishing Group
2-4 Heron Quays
London E14 4JP

Contents

Throughout *The Sex Book* you will find sets of yellow pages. These contain practical advice and information on topics like safer sex, contraception, sex toys or sexercises. Yellow pages are cross-referenced in the text by sidebar icons (see example below) that give the relevant pages and page number. Sexual activities that carry a more serious health risk are indicated with a warning sign in the sidebar. If there is a relevant yellow page to read, the warning will be accompanied by a yellow icon.

The quotes in the sidebars have been collected from our own website and through collaboration with other websites.

Safer sex

Warning

Thank You

Sometimes life takes you somewhere that you don't expect and the journey ends up being quite a revelation. This book has been a bit like that. Though I started working on it with my friend Mel Agace, an enormous number of people have helped to make it what it is. The illustrator Peter Stemmler is responsible for its distinctive visual style and I'm pleased to say that The Sex Book is a beard-free zone. Peter draws from life, so all his images are based on photographs of real people. Thanks to Leila, Mark, Natasha, Kelly, Igor and Nicky from JFT models for the fantastic photo shoot. Mel did a lot of research in the US. She met with sex workers at the Bunny Ranch in Nevada, Tantric sex gurus in LA and dominatrixes in New York. They all gave us their unique perspectives on sex and supported the book in its gestation. We were keen to find out what 'regular' people thought about sex too, so Ian Tresman from Knowledge Computing helped us to set up The Sex Book website which was then linked to most major international sexual information sites. Throughout the project we posted hundreds of questions on whatever subjects we were researching, and we have included as many of the replies as we can into the book. Apologies to anyone whose quote didn't make the final draft.

By the time we started writing a weekly sex column in the Independent on Sunday *newspaper, Mel's path had taken her in a different direction. I would have been lost without my two very special assistants, Rose Garnett and Tillie Harris. New friends were the highlight of the project for me, and I can honestly say that without Rose and Tillie this book wouldn't exist. The book has had a huge amount of help and guidance from the medical professions in both the UK and the US. Most notably, I would like to thank Dr David Goldmeier for his heroic, some might say masochistic, attention to the project. Dr Sarah Gill has also been incredibly generous with her time and encouragement. At Cassell, I would like to say a special thank you to the amazing Annabel Merullo who gave this book (and me) her consistent support and attention. Thanks also to my agent Felicity Rubenstein for believing in the project and getting it off the ground. Ben Evans has been very obliging with his 'blokes' perspective'. Nick Coleman, my editor at the newspaper, has been fantastic. His encouragement, grammar tips and general crash course in the English language have helped me to develop my writing skills and find a 'voice'. Thanks also to Jon Summerhill who gave the sex team office space at New Media Industries. His staff had a tough time trying to ignore us discussing nipples and anal sphincters while they got on with some 'real work'. Finally, thanks to everyone at the wonderful Griffin Inn in Felinfach and Llangoed Hall in Wales for looking after me so well during the editing process.*

Medical Editors
Principle Medical Editor: Dr David Goldmeier, Psychosexual Consultant, St Mary's Hospital
Sexual Health Editor: Dr Sarah Gill, Jefferiss Wing GU Clinic, St Mary's Hospital

Consultant Medical Editors
Mr Justin Vale, Dr Simon Barton, Dr Asun de Marquiegui

Principle Researchers
Mel Agace, Rose Garnett, Tillie Harris

Editor
Nigel Perryman

Special thanks
Professor Robert Winston, Professor Anne Johnson, Nana Rausch, Colin Dixon, Dr John Tomlinson, Justin Gaffney, James Agace, Polly Curtis, Dr Tim Dudderidge, John Boylan, John Mitchinson, Claire Marsden, Jessica Cowie, Victoria Alers-Hankey, Patrick Carpenter

Thanks to all those who participated in *The Sex Book* survey: *Anuschka Stephan @ www.rainbownetwork.com, Jane Czyzselska @ www.queercompany.com, Tawanna from www.kuma2.net, Su May @ www.gingerbeer.co.uk, Rufus Griscom @ www.nerve.com, Melinda Gallagher & Emily Kramer @ www.cakenyc.com, www.lovenet.com, www.vavo.com, www.4freedoms@tantra-sex.com, www.jackinworld.com, www.thesite.org, www.skintwo.com.*

Publishers, reviewers and contributors (UK): *Simon Kelner and Tristian Davies at the Independent on Sunday, Roger Alton at the Observer, Dylan Jones at GQ magazine, Lisa Grainger at Elle, Kerry Smith at B magazine, Ilsa Crawford, Simon Blake @ Sex Education Forum, Dr Norma Williams, Steve Lockyear @ The Rainbow Clinic, Jo Pease @ Audre Lourde Clinic, Dr Tuppy Owens @ Outsiders, Angela Phillips @ Goldsmiths College, Kathryn Hoyle and Debbie Green @ Sh-Women's Erotic Emporium, London, Simon Parritt @ SPOD, Howard Del Monte and Colm Keegan @ Pace, Margot Huish @ Barnet Wakefield & Haringey Mental Health NHS Trust, Stephen Whittle @ Manchester University, Dr Katherine Johnson @ UCL medical School, Dr Petra M Boynton @ Royal Free and UCMS, Jean Anderson @ Vavo, John Piper, Dave Hill, Paulene Morphett, Janet Delite, Simon Nelson & David Smith @ St Pancras Hospital, Colin Parker @ Sexware, Claire Taylor and Dr Marianne Parry @ Marie Stoppes, Dr Merryn Gott and Dr Sharron Hinchliff @ Northern General Hospital, Sheffield, Anthony Smith, Leigh Danes and Simon Grey @ Brook Clinics , Dr Gillian Vanhegan @ Brook, Tony Bellfield @ Family Planning Association, Chris Hiley @ The Prostate Cancer Charity, Dr Tim Dudderidge, Peggy Vance, Pascale @ Unit, Nana Rauch, Bernie Gardiner @ Breast Care and Masectomy Association Helpline, Professor Grossman, Society for Endocrinology, John Wadham @ Liberty, Maryon Stewart @ Women's Nutritional Advisory Service, Anthony Haynes @ The Nutrition Clinic, Mercedes Clark-Smith @ Rainbow Network, Joe Lee, Lisa Saffron @ Pink Parents Network, Lisa Sherman @ Skintwo, Ann Taylor, Director @ The Impotency Association, Trudi Norris, @ National Society of Herbalists, Gillian Rodgerson @ Diva, Hilary Critchley @ Centre for Reproductive Biology, James Yeandel @ Human Embryology and Fertilization Authority, Bill Hartnett @ Diabetes Association UK, Alice Charwood @ Active Birth Centre.*

Reviewers and Contributers (US): *Monica Rodriguez @ SIECUS, Wendee Rogerson @ Gay Men's Health Crisis Inc, Michael Roguski @ Callen Lorde, Mistress Delila, Miss Britteny, Miss Ruby, Dennis and all the girls @ The Moonlite Bunny Ranch, Clare Cavanah @ Toys in Babeland, Dr Carol Queen @ Good Vibrations, Lou Paget, Elizabeth McNeff @ New Mobility Magazine, Hanne Blank, Christophe Pettus @ Blowfish, Claudia Varrin SM Mistress, Dale Altrows @ FMT International, Miss Violet (sex worker, sex surrogate), Rosalyne Blumenstein @ Gender Identity Project.*

Thanks to: *Ann Summers, Charlotte Semmler @ Myla, Sam Roddick @ Coco de Mer, Qazi Rahman @ University of London, Ulla Pluggard, Ann Marie Gardiner, Michael Pawson, Dr Jane Pettiffer, Simon Ellis, Andrea Kon @ The Pennell Institute, Daniela Olsen @ The Wellcome Trust, Agent Provocateur, Willliam Spivey @ Outreach Services, Dr Judith Weisz, Janet R Jakobsen, Norma J Leslie, The Baroness, Mitchell Tepper, The Sexual Health Network, The Boston Women's Health Collective, Roni Horn, Dorothy C. Hayden CSW, The Sacred Tattoo Emporium, Al Link & Pala Copeland @ Tantra Sacred Loving Retreats, Eva Norvind (Eva Taurel), Susan Forrest @ Positively Women, Suzi Kruger @ FIST, Becky Torr @ Society for Endocrinology & BioScientifica Ltd, Cindy Jackson @ International Cosmetic Surgery Network, Stephen Conley @ American Association of Sex Educators, Queen Afua, Paul Nevitt @ Outsiders, Jessie Howie, Julian Keeling, Myer Taub, Annie Sprinkle, Betty Dodson, Marty Klein, Gerard Koskovich @ American Society on Ageing, Patrick Hughes @ Greenery Press, Phil Ruhemann @ Age Concern, Condommania, Sadie Allison @ ticklekitty.com, Carli Parker, Syren, Jeff Burton, Eve Ensler, Gemma Barron. Many apologies to anyone or any organisation that we might have forgotten to acknowledge or thank for their contribution to this book.*

Foreword by Professor Robert Winston

Professor Robert
Winston presented
the award-winning
BBC television series
The Human Body,
and his recent BBC
series, Superhuman,
was screened on
ABC TV. The series
explores the body's
amazing capacity for
self repair.

Professor Winston is
a leader in the field
of fertility studies
and he and his team
have carried out
major international
research into IVF.

He is Director
of Reproductive
Medicine at
Hammersmith
Hospital, London
and Professor of
Fertility Studies at
the Imperial College
School of Medicine
in London.

Professor Winston
has been chair of
the House of Lords
Select Committee
on Science and
Technology and he
comments regularly
on medical, ethical
and scientific issues
in Parliament and
the media.

Sex is one of our most basic instincts. Part of this drive, of course, can be explained by our biological need to reproduce, a drive which is inherited from those long-defunct organisms from which we evolved as a species. This instinct is still largely mysterious in many ways. How is it, for example, that experimental science proves we are clearly so often drawn to individuals who are genetically dissimilar from ourselves? And if the sex drive is really about the evolutionary need to reproduce, how is it that homosexual love exists at all? And why is it that humans so often are prepared to risk almost everything for brief sexual contact? But sex is also much more than a basic instinct. At its best, for humans at least, it is often deeply pleasurable and fulfilling – sometimes the best aspect of an otherwise depressing or humdrum existence. At times it contains elements of play and communication, warmth and sometimes sadness, intimacy and the profoundest feelings of satisfaction, even happiness. It is therefore quite frightening how capable we humans are of being sexually unhappy and frustrated, and how frequently we feel unfulfilled by our sexual activity.

In the course of a long career, largely devoted to eliciting the causes of human reproductive failure, I have been acutely aware of the complex problems that arise in relationship to our sexuality. It is truly sad to see so many people who so regularly miss the experience of what a complete sexual relationship can offer. Much learned research has gone into documenting the depressing frequency of human unfulfilled sexual feeling. Rather less has gone into why it is so common. Part of the reason why sexual failure is so frequent is almost certainly due to another prevalent human instinct – that of shame and the difficulty we sometimes have in being open. Certainly, until comparatively recently in our so-called 'advanced' society, sex was usually something referred to with innuendo and more often expressed openly only in pornography and in ways many people found offensive or shocking.

This wonderful book is therefore extremely welcome. It signals a real change in attitudes towards sexuality. It provides a balance between male and female experience and is sensitive but frank. It avoids being a mere manual, but is descriptive and open, and sometimes erotic. It is also, above all, truly open-minded and non-judgemental, as well as full of useful common sense. It seems ironic that perhaps as recently as thirty or forty years ago, it probably could not have been published. Perhaps, after all, it is true that our society is not in such a bad way if books like this can be written and read without embarrassment. As a contribution to human happiness and wellbeing, this book deserves the widest possible readership.

Introduction

Everyone has sex – but not everyone has good sex – and the missing ingredient is usually confidence. Despite the fact that it is potentially the most fantastic, pleasurable (and free) experience available, sex makes many people feel strangely insecure. The myth that it is a 'natural' act which requires no instruction doesn't help. Sure, most people can figure out the basics, but anyone who wants to reach the dizzy heights of multiple climax or get a perfect ten for giving head needs some sex education. And I don't mean school biology or a working knowledge of safer sex methods. In fact, negative sexual health messages can often take the 'sexy' out of sex, when confidence, condoms and co-operation are all that are required.

My experience as a sex columnist suggests that people get much more excited about technical help than emotional guidance. Some readers email me with specific queries, but others give blow-by-blow accounts of their sex lives, and what they really want to know is whether the things they do with their partners are normal or not. They usually are, but because sex is essentially a private act, men and women seem to get very hung up about whether they are 'good in bed'. Thankfully, unlike good looks, waistlines or bank balances, sex is a level playing field. No one has a head start and anyone, anywhere, no matter what their age or persuasion, can have great sex if they are willing to learn.

Knowledge is power and investing in your sexual skills pays huge dividends. Whether your aim is to stimulate yourself, stun your sexual partners or take the monotony out of monogamy, increasing your sexual know-how can transform your sex life. *The Sex Book* is packed with frank, funny and factual details on everything you want to know about sex but are afraid to ask. Checked by a team of doctors, pyschologists and sex experts, it gives step-by-step instructions to techniques your mother never knew existed, yet it looks at sex as an integrated part of everybody's life. Whether you are seventeen or seventy-five, straight, gay, transgendered or in a wheelchair, *The Sex Book* provides solutions to problems you have not even anticipated. With the hottest information on what women want and what men like, it also gives a voice to real people. Throughout the book, quotations from men and women across the globe offer a unique glimpse into other people's personal sexual experiences. When you get to the end of this book you'll realise that everything is 'normal', all things are possible and anything can happen. Enjoy.

Suzi Godson

Suzi Godson runs the successful London-based design group Unlimited.

She has written and art directed several books, including the influential Women Unlimited: The Directory for Life and the popular children's cook book Eat Up.

She currently writes a weekly sex column called 'S is for Sex' in the Independent on Sunday newspaper and she has written features on sex for the Observer newspaper and Marie Claire, Elle and Cosmopolitan.

Peter Stemmler lives and works in New York. He runs Quickhoney, one of New York's leading illustration studios with his partner Nana Rausch.

His clients include Playboy, Cosmogirl, Maxime, Nike, Wired, Harpers Bazaar, Loaded, Talk and The Face.

THE BODY

As a teenager I felt uncomfortable and betrayed by my body. Now, as a confident, voluptuously curved woman of a certain age, I consider it a miraculous altar of beauty and strength. Each woman confident and comfortable enough to enjoy their body as it is helps in the battle against unrealistic body-images and self-hate. **The Baroness, 42, US**

The body

At puberty the body goes through enormous physical and emotional changes. It becomes both sexually active and capable of reproduction, which means that, while you are nervously working out how to develop relationships with the opposite sex, your body is busy sabotaging your confidence by suddenly providing you with periods, big breasts, spontaneous erections, wet dreams etc. All this happens while you freefall down an emotional roller-coaster, trying to ignore the omnipresent media messages telling you that sex is only available to the physically blessed.

There is no doubt that how we feel about ourselves depends on how we compare to others – so, presumably, if we measure up to 'average' we should be happy. Wrong. The average western male is 1.75m (5ft 9ins) tall, weighs 73.5kg (162lbs) and has a 15.25cm (6ins) erect penis. However, most average men admit that they wish they had a bigger penis. The average western female is 1.6m (5ft 3.5ins) tall and weighs 61.25 kg (135lbs), but average women are not happy with their proportions, either. Despite consciously recognising that their physical goals are genetically unobtainable, subconsciously they still measure themselves against yogic celebrities with pneumatic breasts.

Physical dissatisfaction with our external packaging has created multi-billion pound industries in pharmaceuticals, cosmetics, surgery, therapy and fitness. However, we seldom appreciate the intricate beauty of the finely tuned systems that operate beneath the surface of our skins. Anatomy may be deeply unsexy when it is part of the school curriculum, but knowing how your body works is actually a great way of increasing sexual confidence and avoiding some fairly obvious pitfalls. In the UK, 7,700 girls under the age of 16 became pregnant last year and one can't help wondering whether they, or their partners, knew any basic biology.

Besides avoiding pregnancy or STIs (sexually transmitted infections), biological ignorance minimises your sexual pleasure. An incredibly high number of women who don't orgasm have to be shown where their clitoris is and how to masturbate. Men's genitals are external and slightly easier to get a handle on, but internally the prostate gland often remains unexplored, simply because men are completely unaware of both its existence and its sexual potential. The fact is, you can't expect a partner to be familiar with the intimate geography of your sex organs if you haven't come to grips with them yourself. Genitals don't come with a map, and you need to know where you are going – especially when the lights are out.

The mind

I think, therefore I am sexual: Consciousness is what makes us sexual rather than simply reproductive and the mind is a very powerful sex tool. Some people who are physically impaired can even learn to orgasm by mentally transferring sexual sensitivity to other parts of their bodies. Your mind intensifies the experience of sex, but blocking sexual thoughts can do the opposite. In fact, people who cannot orgasm are routinely taught to fantasise as a way of liberating their subconscious.

Nature v. nurture: Most human brains have the same physical components, but their individual responses to stimuli vary. This is because everybody accumulates their own personal history of experiences, and this makes their consciousness unique. We don't develop the ability to remember until we are about two years old, and once this happens we seldom isolate new experiences from previous associations. Memory, opinion, environment and emotion all influence how we interpret new stimuli. The physical 'brain' and the thinking 'mind' are one and the same, but the combination of your individual genetic blueprint (nature) and what happens to you through your life (nurture) determines who you are, including your sexuality, your preferences and your responses. Our capacity for sexual arousal is partly our biological heritage, but our upbringing also conditions many of our sexual responses, especially during the critical period of early adolescence. The way we think is heavily influenced by what is considered to be 'sexual' or even 'appropriate' in the culture in which we live. In the 1970s, in her research into fantasy, Nancy Friday discovered that many young women felt so guilty about their sexual fantasies that they couldn't allow themselves to think about consensual sex and instead fantasised about romanticised rape, during which they were helpless to resist the pleasure they experienced.

Sex on the brain: We think about sex a lot. Psychologist Paul Cameron interviewed over 4,000 people and found that men under 25 think about sex once every two minutes and women under 25 think about it once every five minutes. When it comes to sex, our mind is probably the most eager and athletic part of our anatomy. It can dream, scheme, anticipate and remember. Whether adolescent or octogenarian, we have the capacity to spend hours magnifying remote sexual possibilities or conjuring up fictitious sexual scenarios. The mind can be sexually active at any time or in any place, and it offers a sexual freedom that society or relationships often can't provide. Whatever the reality, in your head you direct the script and you can always organise a happy ending.

I think my biggest erogenous zone is my brain. My imagination, when focused, can arouse any part of my body.
Jan, 53, UK

Sometimes I just wish I could turn my brain off. Even when I want to be in the moment, sometimes I find it hard to focus.
Rach, 29, US

I have secret desires that even I do not know about as I am constantly discovering new ones. I think that secret desires represent the true future, and, what is more, that the true spiritual culture can only be a culture of desires. No desire is blameworthy; the only fault lies in repressing them.
Salvador Dali

I always treated my body and my mind as two distinctively separate elements. As a result I am sure I was only having half the time I could have been having.
Louise, 28, UK

When I fall for a guy my brain goes into overdrive. I can't think about anything else and it lasts for weeks. It affects my whole being.
Martha, 32, US

The brain

The amygdala

The hypothalamus

The pituitary gland

The septum

The thalamus

The cerebral cortex

Me Tarzan, you Jane: The earliest parts of the brain to have evolved are found at the base of the skull, where the spinal cord emerges from the spinal column. This area, known as the hindbrain, is found even in primitive vertebrates, and all our more primitive instincts seem to be governed here.

Sex central: Though it is only about the size of a grapefruit, the brain requires at least 20 per cent of the body's total blood supply and enormous amounts of glucose and oxygen in order to function effectively. No single area of the brain takes sole responsibility for sex. The whole brain is wired by a myriad of nerve connections and, although there is increased activity in specific regions during sexual arousal, the different parts of the brain work in unison. The central region of the brain contains the limbic system. Within it is the amygdala, which controls our emotional state and plays an important part in how we interpret sexual stimuli. It also contains the hypothalamus, which, despite being as small as a marble, manages to regulate sexual behaviour, body temperature, appetite and thirst. The hypothalamus also mediates how we feel pleasure, and is involved with sexual and emotional expression. It monitors the body's internal clock too, so sexual desire is adjusted according to a 24-hour cycle of light and darkness. The hypothalamus exerts control over the pituitary gland, the master gland in the endocrine system that maintains the body's hormonal balance. The septum, contained within the limbic system, is sometimes called 'the pleasure pathway' because it seems to be particularly concerned with sexual pleasure. Pleasure and happiness are thought to depend on the levels of the chemicals serotonin, dopamine and noradrenaline (norepinephrine) in the brain. Indeed, most antidepressant pills work on stimulating the natural production of these chemicals. The septum also contains the thalamus, which acts as the brain's pain centre. It relays sensory information, relating to touch, and is involved in much of our instinctive behaviour, too.

Fantasy factory: The cerebral cortex is the most recently evolved part of the brain, and it is the level of development of this big, bumpy layer that separates us from other mammals. It is the largest part of the brain and the most advanced and complex part of the nervous system. It gives us the ability to speak, to learn, to think, to perceive and to make choices. It is the home of our sexual fantasies, daydreams and good or bad memories. The frontal area of the cortex governs personality and how we understand complex social, moral and ethical issues as well as our ability to solve problems and judge situations.

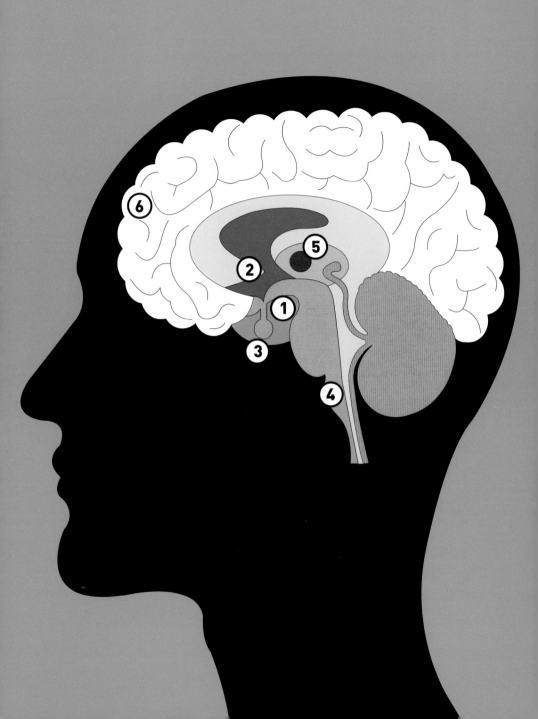

The senses

I feel love: When we are born our senses are already formed. But as we grow, our senses form us. They are our antennae, our awareness, our instinct, the way we meet the world and the way the world meets us. Our senses adapt to different environments. If we are walking down a dark street our eyes quickly adjust to the dark. If we hear footsteps behind us, our ears prick up and our bodies release adrenaline (epinephrine), the fight-or-flight hormone. Our senses adapt and compensate for each other, so blind people, for example, develop better hearing, touch and smell. In an effort to help the rest of us experience the heightened awareness that comes with not being able to see, an entrepreneurial group of blind people have set up a restaurant in Zurich, Switzerland, called the 'Blind Cow'. Diners eat in complete darkness. Unable to see, facial expressions and beauty are all redundant, but the senses of hearing, smell, taste and touch are heightened. It may seem ironic that the venue has become popular for 'blind dates', but, in fact, not being able to see means personality and getting along is the priority. If you can't have a good conversation you end up sitting in silence in the dark.

Sight: Evolutionary theorists believe that subconsciously we still weigh up potential partners' looks in terms of whether they appear to be good 'hunter-gatherers' or good 'child bearers' (though these days that might boil down to collecting takeaways and having elective Caesareans). Usually, eye contact is the first conscious recognition of sexual attraction between two people. It breaks ice, generates smiles and elicits phone numbers. Sexual attraction causes eyes to widen and pupils to dilate, though the onset of arousal causes the eyes to narrow and become less focused. People who like each other maintain far greater eye contact than those who don't, though chimpanzees and other primates gaze at enemies to warn them off.

Touch: The skin is both a protective shield and a sensory organ and it contains nerve endings that are sensitive to touch, pain, pressure and temperature. The receptors for touch and pressure are unevenly distributed, which means that some parts of the body are more sensitive than others. Lips, nipples, hands, fingertips and genitalia contain lots of additional nerve endings. These erogenous zones also have a disproportionate amount of the cerebral cortex allocated to them. Some studies have reported that many women and men consider touch and closeness to be more important than sex. Others have shown that even with proper nutrition and health care, babies deprived of physical contact suffer serious emotional damage, whereas frequent loving touch results in positive changes in brain tissue.

Sound: The sounds a person makes are an important part of the sexual jigsaw. If the face and body are fantastic but the voice sounds wrong, then the chemistry may not work (though you could always consider earplugs). Voice is a signature and, in its natural state, it reveals much about you, your origins and your background. Your tone of voice indicates how interested you are in a person. A gruff, low voice signifies lack of interest, while higher-pitched, lilting tones are more positive. Loving how someone speaks or laughs helps create a vivid mental picture of that person. Even if two people don't speak the same language, sound is still a way of communicating. Whispers, giggles and sweet nothings can be pretty accurately interpreted even if their exact meaning is unclear.

Smell: As newborn infants we cannot see, so initially we recognise our mothers by smell. By the time we grow up, the olfactory centre in our brains can distinguish between the smells of 10,000 different chemicals. Smell plays an important role in helping animals choose a mate and it is thought that humans also manufacture sexual smells, called pheromones. Many Internet sites sell bottled 'pheromones' that are mainly made from non-human pheromones (i.e. from pigs or musk deer), or their synthetic equivalents. Tests show, however, that pheromones are species-specific so if you wear pig, expect to attract pig. Human pheromones are thought to be secreted by the sweat glands in the armpits and pubic hair, and tests have shown that they are responsible for the menstrual cycles of sexually active, heterosexual women who live or work together becoming synchronised. If pheromones work at all they are probably fighting a losing battle against deodorant, perfume or aftershave, but in terms of sexual attractiveness the association of a particular brand of scent with a partner may be just as arousing anyway. Vanilla is believed to be the most universally attractive smell and is also the closest scent there is to breast milk. So a few drops of vanilla essence may be a far more effective way to pull than drenching yourself in Christmas pressie cologne.

Taste: Taste and smell are closely linked together, but taste is the weakest of the five senses. Babies are born with tastebuds all over the inside cavity of the mouth and tongue, making them particularly sensitive to strong flavours. Most of these gradually disappear, though as adults we still have about 10,000 tastebuds left. How someone tastes when you kiss them can influence whether you find them attractive. Skin and body fluids have their own flavours, too. Garlic is not for lovers, though. It may taste great but it gives a pungent smell to your breath and skin and even flavours your semen.

The minute I see someone I usually establish whether I am attracted to them or not. The visual aesthetic of someone is the most important thing for me – that doesn't mean they have to be an oil painting.
Freddy, 22, UK

The ear – talking into it in a very low whisper – and my toes – just sucking on them and running the tongue around them – but hubby never does it!
Mickey Mouse, 29, UK
Lovenet

Smooth skin is a real turn-on for me, I like to caress and run my palm along acres of smooth, soft skin.
Kit, 33, US

When someone kisses my forehead I find it very reassuring and comforting. That kind of care is very erotic to me.
Lilla, 26, UK

Smell is very important, from sweet perfume on women to cologne on men – as well as sweat after exercising.
Sue, 46, UK

Sexual beings

Ch-ch-ch-ch-changes: We are all sexual beings. In the narrowest sense, our sexual anatomy can be defined as purely reproductive, but sex is about much more than biology. We live at a time when attitudes to sex and sexuality are more inclusive and progressive than they have ever been before, and the more we understand about ourselves anatomically, hormonally and intellectually, the less easy it is to stereotype ourselves by gender. There may be pressure to conform when we are younger, but as adults we have the right to individual sexual preferences (as long as they don't harm anyone). Sex may be an instinct, but it is also a desire and a choice. Our inbuilt responses are part nature and part nurture, but our sexuality isn't static. Our bodies are in a continual state of flux as they adapt to age-related or environmental change, and our sexual desires and preferences can be a pretty accurate reflection of our 'self' at any given moment.

Chemical weapons: The delicate balance of our chemical make-up plays a huge part in the changes that take place in our bodies between birth and death. Hormones influence just about everything, including gender definition, the onset of puberty, menopause, body shape, pregnancy, moods and even our ability to enjoy sex. Natural (or even self-imposed) hormonal differences, between one person and another, provide us with endless human sexual variety.

The beginning

Blame the gonads: Both the male and female sexual systems develop from the same building blocks of embryonic tissue, but different hormonal and biochemical pathways develop at a very early stage. Physical differences between the sexes start to appear from around the sixth week of pregnancy, when the gonads, which are initially common to both sexes, start to change into either ovaries (which produce oestrogen) or testes (which produce testosterone). At about eight weeks, levels of oestrogen and testosterone vary, depending on whether the embryo is female or male. In the womb, these hormonal changes lead to the anatomical differences between the sexes, and later in life they bring about and maintain secondary sexual characteristics, such as differences in body shape, voice and hair. During childhood there is little physical difference between girls and boys, apart from in their sexual organs, and both produce the same three sex hormones: oestrogen, testosterone and progesterone. Once puberty begins, differing levels of these hormones cause many physical changes and bring sexuality and the reproductive system to life.

Male puberty

Testosterone: This hormone is the basis of our sex drive (libido). In both sexes, high levels of testosterone can increase sexual thoughts, fantasies and the desire to masturbate and have sex. It can increase self-confidence and it has antidepressant qualities, but too much promotes aggressive behaviour. Extra production of testosterone in the testes triggers puberty in boys, and leads to decreased levels of oestrogen and progesterone. Male levels of testosterone fluctuate over a 24-hour period, rising during the night and reaching a peak in the early morning hours – which is why men often wake with an erection. Testosterone is also responsible for the embarrassing, spontaneous 'trouser tents' that plague adolescent boys.

Growth: Boys usually experience puberty between the ages of 10 and 17. There is an initial growth spurt at around 13, when the arms, legs and penis grow, but the body's main growth starts about a year later, so boys look a bit lanky and awkward for a while. Most boys reach their full height by 18, but bone density and muscle mass continue to increase for several more years. Testosterone increases the ratio of lean muscle to body fat and also causes the skin to thicken and become oilier, which can lead to teenage acne. Some boys develop puppy-fat 'breasts' during puberty, but these only last for a few months until hormone levels settle down.

Hair and voice: Pubic hair (not necessarily the same colour as head hair), first appears at the base of the penis and then spreads towards the stomach and thighs. Underarm hair and coarser body hair generally start growing later. The voice becomes deeper – or 'breaks' – and the Adam's apple develops from the thyroid cartilage. The voice can break overnight (which can be a bit of a shock) but it usually happens more gradually. Facial hair and the voice breaking are often the last signs of sexual maturity to become evident.

Genitals: The penis grows longer and wider and its head becomes relatively larger. The internal sex organs develop and mature. The testes increase in size and production of sperm and seminal fluid starts. Erections can occur even in the womb, but become much more frequent from very early on in puberty, often without any sexual stimulus and at awkward moments. The first ejaculation occurs about a year after puberty begins. It indicates that a boy is producing sperm and may be capable of reproduction. Nocturnal emissions – 'wet dreams' – are a common experience for teenage boys. They are a means of disposing of sperm so that new sperm can take their place. Once a boy starts to masturbate, these dreams become less frequent.

I hated it when my voice broke – one day I was young, free and without a care in the world, the next I became someone who had to help round the house.
Joe, 17, UK

I was about 12 and I was in a jacuzzi in Austria. I had my trunks on and all these naked German people got in and there was one really beautiful woman and her tits were bobbing up and down on the surface of the water. I had to stay in there for hours waiting for my hard-on to go down.
Paul, 22, UK

I am 18 and the last virgin in my class and probably in the world. I have to lie to my mates and I'm not sure they believe me anymore.
Novice, 18, UK

I think there is something wrong with me because I cannot stop thinking about sex. Even old ladies – I imagine them in their bras and what it would be like.
Luke, 17, US

My first wet dream happened when I was staying at my friend's house. I stripped the bedclothes and left.
Blake, 17, US

Female puberty

Oestrogen and progesterone: In girls, puberty is triggered when the ovaries and the adrenal glands begin to increase the production of oestrogen and progesterone. Oestrogen is responsible for maintaining all the main female characteristics, and during the monthly cycle its production peaks just before ovulation to help nourish the lining of the womb and prepare it for a fertilised egg. Progesterone is produced immediately after ovulation until menstruation. It is produced in both men and women, but to a much greater extent by the ovaries in women. It promotes bone growth, plays a part in blood clotting, heightens mood and lowers libido.

Growth: Puberty occurs earlier in girls than boys, sometimes starting as young as eight. One of the first signs is a sudden growth spurt, usually around the age of ten. Fat is laid down beneath the skin (sometimes too liberally), especially on the breasts, upper arms, hips, buttocks and thighs. The sweat glands become more active, sometimes leading to body odour and over-efficient oil-producing sebaceous glands, which can occasionally cause acne. Over time the pelvis starts to widen.

Hair: Hair starts to grow on the pubis, legs and arms, in the armpits, around the nipples and sometimes above the upper lip. Pubic hair is longer, darker and coarser than other body hair. It starts to grow on the vulva before spreading out in an inverted triangle to the pubic mound.

Breasts: The first sign of change is the swelling of the areola (the dark area around the nipple). The nipple then enlarges and the entire breast grows. Breasts are often unequal in size and shape at first. The rate at which breasts grow and their eventual size is partially under genetic control, but hormone levels also play a major role. Men have the potential to grow breasts, but they do not produce sufficient oestrogen to do so. If a man is injected with oestrogen he will develop breasts, and, likewise, when a woman produces extra oestrogen during pregnancy, her breasts increase in size. When some women start taking birth control pills their breasts become bigger because the pill contains oestrogen.

Breasts are supported by connective tissue and a suspensory ligament that prevents sagging and maintains shape and firmness. Breasts are made up of fatty tissue and millions of tiny glands that are connected to the nipples by a system of ducts. These glands produce milk (in a process called lactation) to feed a baby after delivery and, regardless of the size or shape of their breasts, most women are able to breastfeed if they want to.

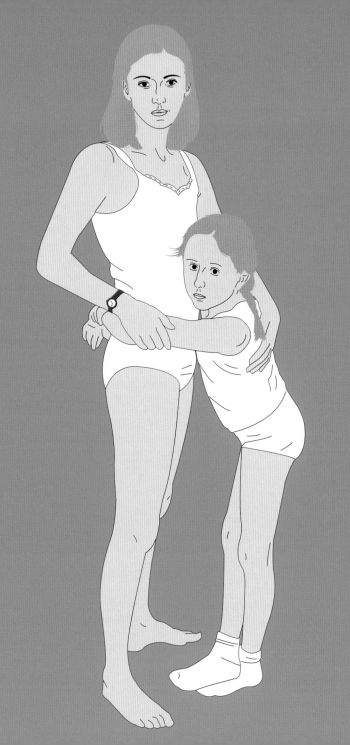

Nipples: The nipples are the most sensitive part of the breasts. They become erect in the cold and during sexual arousal as a result of the contraction of an internal network of muscle fibres. Many men also get erect nipples when they are sexually aroused. Nipples are normally a deep raspberry colour, but the areolae are browner and may have small bumps on them. These are oil-producing glands that secrete lubricant to protect the nipple during breastfeeding. It is thought that the darker colour of the areolae helps a newborn infant to locate the nipple.

Menstruation: From puberty onwards, an egg is released from alternate ovaries approximately every 28 days. This process is known as ovulation. If the egg is not fertilised, the lining of the womb is shed from the vagina in a process known as menstruation, or 'having a period'. In the UK, the average age at which a girl starts to menstruate is twelve-and-a-half, but it can be as early as nine or as late as fifteen, depending on the individual's genetic make-up. It can take as long as two years, and in some cases up to seven years, for periods to become regular, hormonal controls to settle down and the reproductive system to mature fully. As the menstrual cycle becomes regular, a vaginal discharge starts to appear that helps keeps the vagina healthy. At least 20 per cent of women have irregular cycles, and women who are ill or who have eating disorders may find that their periods temporarily disappear.

Day 1 (of a 28 day cycle): The first day of your period is day one of your cycle. Periods usually last four or five days, depending on the individual.

Days 1 to 14: Hormones promote the growth of an egg within the ovary. The uterine lining thickens in preparation for 'potential' pregnancy.

Ovulation (approximately day 14 of a 28 day cycle): When the egg is mature, hormonal reactions make it burst out of its sac and travel away from the ovaries, down the Fallopian tube and into the uterus. The egg is usually released in the middle of the cycle, and the three days prior to that and 24 hours afterwards are when a women is most likely to get pregnant if she has unprotected penetrative sex. It is common to feel energetic and more sexy around the time of ovulation, because in evolutionary terms it is important to mate when conception is more likely. Several studies on women verify that a peak in sexual desire occurs around day 14 of a regular cycle, though other studies indicate that a second peak in desire occurs just before or after menstruation.

Post-ovulation (days 14 to 28): If fertilisation of the egg does not occur, approximately eight days after ovulation the lining of the uterus breaks down and is shed with blood as a period. A dip in hormone levels at this point can adversely affect your mood. Your breasts may feel tender and swollen and, to cap it all, spots may also break out on your face. The decrease in hormone levels then triggers increased hormone production and the cycle begins all over again.

Premenstrual syndrome (PMS): The shift in the balance of the levels of progesterone and oestrogen can alter emotional and behavioural patterns and cause premenstrual syndrome (PMS) – particularly the sudden falls experienced just before a period. The list of symptoms includes crying, depression, fatigue, irritability, sensitivity, forgetfulness, apathy, feeling bloated, spots, breast tenderness, headache, food cravings, fluid retention and swelling. In serious cases doctors may prescribe the combined pill, mild diuretics, hormone therapy or antidepressant drugs.

Tips to combat PMS cramping: Though dietary advice is difficult to back up scientifically, it is thought that PMS can be affected by diet and lifestyle. Whether the effect is real or placebo doesn't really matter if you get relief from a miserable monthly cycle. A lot of the advice is common sense and makes for a healthy diet anyway, so there is probably no harm in trying it.

Many women swear by a daily dose of evening primrose oil to alleviate cramps, though some women report that it is so effective that they then have no warning that their periods are due (women are never happy). Starflower oil is also considered to be very effective and it is also good for the skin (supposedly). Cutting out caffeine may help decrease cramps and breast tenderness, and celery seed is a natural and mild diuretic that can stop you feeling bloated. Eliminating salt will reduce fluid retention, too. Saturated fat may increase oestrogen levels, making PMS worse. It certainly piles on the pounds, so stick to foods that are rich in omega-3 fatty acids, such as mackerel and tunafish. Magnesium and calcium in carrots, brown rice, oatmeal and leafy green vegetables may reduce cramping, and chicken, prunes, bananas and baked potatoes contain vitamin B6, which boosts and balances dopamine and serotonin levels, helping to control mood swings. Chocolate contains traces of magnesium but it also contains biogenic amines, which are thought to counter depression and PMS (justification at last). Opt for high-quality 70+ per cent cacao, which has less sugar and more flavour.

Every month without fail there is a period of about a week when I turn into 'psycho chick'. I cry, bitch and get furious over the silliest things – it's so stupid because when it happens I never connect it to my period, but afterwards, when it starts, I think, 'oh yeah!'
Susan, 29, UK

When I get my period I feel so bloated. I can weigh about six pounds more overnight. My jeans don't fit and my stomach feels tender. It seems to be worse since I had a coil fitted.
Marie, 41, Ireland

During a period is the time when I feel the most up for sex but I hate the mess.
Charlene, 24, UK

Before it comes on, everything seems to make me sad or upset and if anyone says 'boo' to me I take it very personally and then once my periods come I start to feel better. Alcohol also seems to have a much worse effect on me, too. I get drunk very quickly and have a terrible hangover.
Nat, 27, UK

What you see (women)

 The vulva: This is the term used to describe the whole of the external female genitals.

 The pubic mound (mons pubis): This is the pad of fatty tissue that covers the pubic bone. It provides cushioning and protection for the pubic bone during sex and after puberty is usually covered in pubic hair.

 The outer and inner lips (labia majora and labia minora): These are the outer folds that wrap around the vaginal entrance. They are made up of erectile tissue that swells and becomes engorged with blood when sexually aroused. The surface of the outer lips is usually covered with pubic hair, but the inner surfaces are smooth, shiny, rich in nerve endings and contain numerous oil and sweat glands that help to keep the vulva clean and healthy. The inner lips meet at the top in the middle to form a protective hood over the clitoris. Their appearance varies widely from one woman to another. In some women they are tiny and can hardly be seen; in other women they are large and protrude below the labia majora.

 The clitoris: The only part of the highly sensitive clitoris that can be seen directly beneath the clitoral hood is the head, called the glans. Clitorises vary in shape and size, though neither has any effect on sensitivity.

 The urethral opening: Many women go through life believing that urine comes out of their vagina, but in fact it comes out through the tiny urethral opening just below the clitoris.

 The vaginal opening and the hymen: The entrance to the vagina is partially covered by a thin, flexible membrane called the hymen, which has no known biological function. Though it only ever covers the vagina partially (to allow menstrual fluid out), a hymen that tears and bleeds after the first penetration was, and in some countries still is, the traditional sign of virginity. In fact, only 50 per cent of women have a hymen small enough to tear, and exercise or tampons often destroy it long before sex takes place.

 The perineum: This is the flat stretch of skin that starts at the bottom of the vulva and extends back towards the anus. It contains numerous nerve endings and is very sensitive to touch.

 The anus: This is the opening to the rectum. It is usually closed and has a puckered appearance.

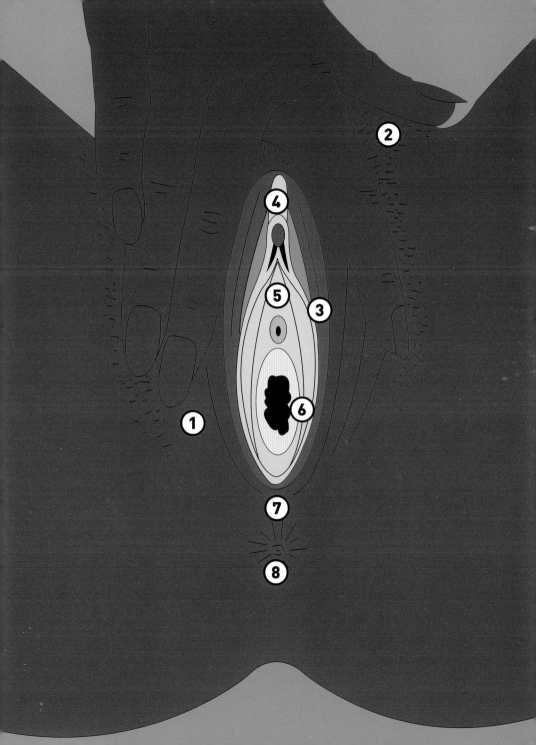

What you don't see (women)

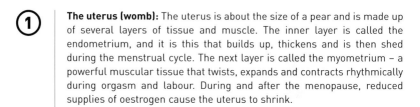

① The uterus (womb): The uterus is about the size of a pear and is made up of several layers of tissue and muscle. The inner layer is called the endometrium, and it is this that builds up, thickens and is then shed during the menstrual cycle. The next layer is called the myometrium – a powerful muscular tissue that twists, expands and contracts rhythmically during orgasm and labour. During and after the menopause, reduced supplies of oestrogen cause the uterus to shrink.

② The cervix: Cylindrical in shape, this connects the uterus to the vagina. It has a narrow opening that widens slightly during menstruation and is sometimes plugged with cervical mucus to protect the cervix from infection. During ovulation this mucus becomes a thin fluid to permit the passage of sperm. After penetration and during orgasm the cervix dips down into the vagina to enable sperm to enter the womb more easily.

③ Fallopian tubes: There are two Fallopian tubes, one at each side of the uterus, and each is connected to an ovary. When an ovary releases an egg, it travels down the Fallopian tube towards the uterus. If it meets sperm during its journey, fertilisation may occur.

④ The ovaries: These produce oestrogen and progesterone and help the ova, or eggs, to mature. When a girl is born, she has about two million eggs in her ovaries. By puberty a woman has about 300,000 eggs but only a few hundred remain at the menopause, when hormone production decreases.

⑤ The crura: These are the sexually sensitive internal wing tips of the clitoris, which run down internally on either side of the vagina under the labia.

⑥ The vagina: A 7.5cm- (3in-) canal that leads to the cervix and the uterus, though in its resting state the walls of the vagina close in on each other.

⑦ The G-spot: Possibly spongy tissue around the urethra; possibly the Skene's gland; possibly a sexual hotspot; possibly just hype and wishful thinking.

⑧ The pubococcygeus (PC) muscle: A powerful muscle that helps support the pelvic floor and contracts during orgasm.

⑨ The anal sphincters and the rectum: Two powerful muscles that control the entrance to the anus. The rectum is a passage through which faeces are excreted, having being stored in the colon, higher in the intestine.

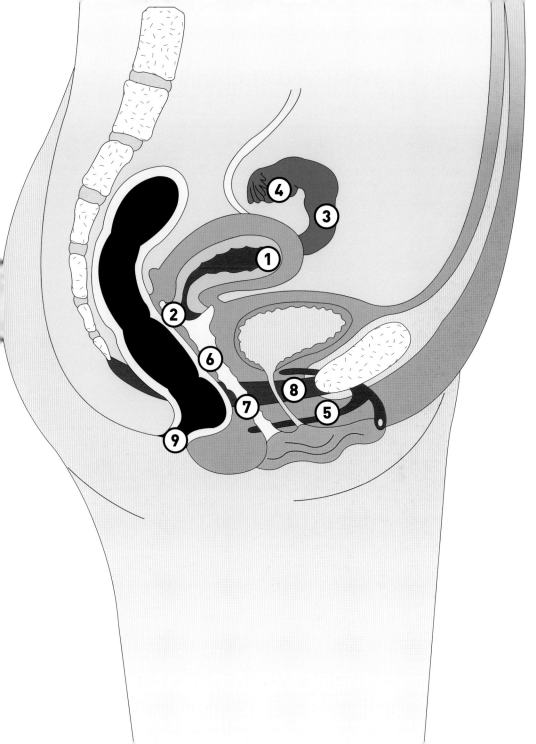

What you should know

The Clitoris

Welcome to the pleasure zone: The clitoris is the most important part of the female anatomy when it comes to sexual pleasure. In fact, it is the only part of the body whose only known function is pleasure. The head of the clitoris contains approximately 8,000 sensory nerve endings, the greatest concentration in the entire human body and twice the number in the penis. The shaft of the clitoris is supported by a ligament and anchored to the pelvic bones by two wing tips of tissue called crura. The crura run internally down either side of the opening of the vagina. During arousal the erectile tissue in the clitoris swells and increases in size. Eighty per cent of women require clitoral stimulation to achieve full arousal and orgasm, and despite the prevalence of the view that 'sex' is 'penetration', only 20 per cent of women can actually orgasm through intravaginal sex. Hardly surprising, really.

Size doesn't matter: The only part of the clitoris that can be seen directly beneath the clitoral hood is the head. It is covered with a mucous membrane that is kept moist and shiny by tiny oil-producing glands. These glands also allow the clitoral hood to glide across the head. There is no standard size or shape for either the clitoral head or its hood, which sometimes does not cover it completely. There does not seem to be any relationship between clitoral size and function – basically all clitorises are extremely sensitive. At birth, a girl's clitoris is larger in proportion to the rest of her body than it is likely to be during the remainder of her life.

Thanks, Helen: The full importance of the clitoris has only been realised relatively recently. In August 1998, Helen O'Connell, a urological surgeon in Melbourne, Australia, published a paper in the *The Journal of Urology* announcing her discovery that the clitoral nerve system actually extended much further than the visible head of the clitoris. She found that beneath the clitoral head there is an upside-down V-shaped mass of erectile tissue full of nerves and blood vessels that extends away from the clitoris into the body. In the past, anatomists (usually male) had been reluctant to dissect female sexual organs on grounds of taste, morality, or even lack of interest. Many people, particularly women, wonder how such an important piece of information could have remained undiscovered through most of the 20th century. The probable reason is that most corpses available for dissection (rather than autopsy) tend to be elderly, so their erectile tissue has shrunk, so that the full extent of this organ cannot be seen.

The Vagina

Flexible: The vagina is not a continually open space, or 'hole' as is often thought by both women and men. In fact it is a 'potential' space. In its resting state the vagina is shaped like a flattened tube, the sides of which are collapsed against each other. If you put a finger inside your vagina you can feel the walls wrap around it. The muscular tissue in the vagina allows it to expand and contract, like a balloon, and it adjusts to fit anything from a finger to a penis, or a baby during childbirth. The average vaginal canal is only about 7.5cm (3ins) long – or possibly 9cm (4ins) in women who have given birth – but once a woman becomes sexually aroused it expands, and the rear part of the vagina balloons and extends to fit a penis or dildo.

Sensitive: The outer third of the vagina contains nearly 90 per cent of the vaginal nerve endings, with an especially high concentration around the vaginal opening. As a result, the inner two-thirds are less sensitive, but the inner vaginal canal responds to firmer stimulation, such as the pressure generated by thrusting during penetration.

Self-cleaning: The vagina is lined with mucous membranes similar to those of the mouth, but they are wrinkled and folded rather than smooth. Oestrogen keeps the vaginal walls strong, healthy and lubricated, and when there is less oestrogen – before puberty and after the menopause – they are thinner and less well lubricated. In adult women, lubricating fluid is acidic, but in adolescents it tends to be alkaline. Because sperm are more mobile in alkaline environments, this means that sexually active teenagers can be more at risk of getting pregnant. The tissue in the vaginal canal is self-cleaning and very sensitive. Internal washing with soapy water or perfumed douches can irritate the lining, causing it to become red and sore, so use plain water for washing and avoid anything containing chemicals or detergents

And strong: A muscle called pubococcygeus (PC) runs between the pubic bone and the tailbone on either side of the vagina. It helps support the pelvic floor, and because it is involved in the contractions felt at orgasm, exercising this muscle can magnify the sensations experienced during intercourse and climax. It takes about three weeks of regular PC exercise to increase your muscle tone. Shooting ping-pong balls from your vagina may take a little longer.

It doesn't occur to me that a man would be sizing mine up – they are always pretty thrilled just to be there. Women might be more discerning I guess.
Daisy, 34, US

I don't take much notice of my vagina. I never put anything in it when I masturbate, but sometimes when I have a period I want to fill it with a vibrator.
Lou, 22, US

The vagina looks better when a penis is parked in it.
Tara, 26, US

242	78
STIs	**Lubrication**

I have never been able to study my vagina as much as I study my face. Frankly, it doesn't need as much attention and hardly anyone ever sees it – and if they do they're extremely nice to it!
Jeb, 25, UK

56

Sexercise

32

Bodily Fluids

The G-spot (or Grafenberg spot)

The biological UFO: Ernest Grafenberg first discovered the G-spot in 1950. He noted that during sexual stimulation the female urethra begins to enlarge, and that a swollen spot on the top wall of the vagina is involved in an expulsion of fluid that 'occurs always at the acme of orgasm and simultaneous with it'. His ideas were largely ignored until Whipple and Perry's book *The G-spot* appeared in 1981. The idea of a vaginal sex button that allowed women to ejaculate in the same way as men naturally captured the public imagination, though subsequent research has failed to support their theories. The G-spot and female ejaculation have been in and out of fashion ever since the '50s and the jury is still out.

Where it's at: What is generally accepted is that if, or when, the G-spot exists, it is located about 3cm (1.2ins) into the vagina, within the front wall, directly behind the pubic bone, along the course of the urethra. There is no doubt that many women are more sensitive in this area, but there are several arguments as to why that might be. Some theorists claim that the phenomenon is related to a bundle of nerves that are part of the recently discovered deeper clitoral complex. Others believe it could be a series of glands – called the paraurethral glands, or Skene's glands – that can be felt 'through' rather than 'on' the front wall. What is more likely is that the G-spot is actually erectile tissue wrapped around the urethra. In any event, if it exists, the size and exact location of the G-spot vary, as does its level of sensitivity.

Wet, wet, wet: Post-mortem studies of tissue from Skene's glands have revealed a similarity to prostatic tissue. This may indicate that the G-spot could be the female equivalent to the prostate and explain the phenomenon of female ejaculation, as described by Grafenberg. The content of the fluid is as controversial as its source. Some argue that it is mainly urine and that ejaculation is merely orgasm-induced incontinence. Others contend that it is the female equivalent of prostatic fluid, since some studies have shown that it contains PSA (prostate-specific antigen). The one thing sex researchers agree on is that it doesn't occur in very many women. Whipple and Perry estimated that approximately 10 per cent of women ejaculate. Further research by Bullough in 1984 suggested that 14 per cent do, and Kratochvil, in 1994, reduced this figure to a mere 6 per cent. Until scientists figure out how to turn a woman on and see for themselves, the G-spot and female ejaculation remain something of a mystery.

The Anus

History: Historically, anal sex has been used as a way of preserving vaginal virginity and as a means of avoiding pregnancy, though the technique is pretty unreliable, because semen can easily drip from the anus to the vagina.

Biology: The entrance to the anus is controlled by two powerful muscles called sphincters. The external sphincter is controlled by the central nervous system and can be tensed and relaxed at will, in the same way as the muscles of the hand. The internal sphincter is quite different. This muscle is controlled by the involuntary, unconscious part of the nervous system, which governs functions such as heart rate and stress. It responds to fear and anxiety by contracting, which is why you can't pretend that you want anal penetration if you don't – though like any muscle, the sphincters eventually become tired and relax.

Engineering: The anal canal is about 3cm (1.2ins) long, and it opens into the rectum. This contains a series of rectal valves that help to separate gas from faeces to stop you from defecating when you break wind. Faeces are not stored in the rectum, though residual traces may be found there if you have not had a recent bowel movement. Though *rectum* is the Latin word for 'straight', the tube actually has several bends. The first points towards the navel and is created by a set of supporting muscles called the pubo-rectal sling. These muscles play a major role in preventing anal incontinence. The second bend curves towards the spine.

Sensation: The anus is rich in nerve endings and surrounded by fine hairs, making it extremely sensitive to touch and stimulation. Its folds of soft, pink tissue give it a puckered appearance and, like vaginal tissue, it swells during arousal. For some women the anus plays an important part in sex, because the rectum shares a wall with the vagina and pressure in the rectum can indirectly stimulate the vagina. Many women say this gives them a different and sometimes stronger sexual sensation.

Suction: Although it is very sensitive, anal and rectal tissue is delicate and is not designed to expand in the same way as vaginal tissue. Care needs to be taken during anal play and lots of lubrication is essential. Never put anything up your anus that doesn't have a flared base as the powerful sphincter muscles may suck it up into your rectum.

I can't indulge in anal sex any more because of ulcers at the base of my colon. In the past, though, I had anal sex and I think I enjoyed it so much because it just seemed so wrong.
Margaret, 54, Ireland

I give in to anal sex with my husband every couple of months. The thing is I always fight and protest in the beginning, until I get really wet, then it feels great! I would do it more, but the pain is too intense at first.
Lisa, 28, US
CakeNYC

Every guy I have ever slept with has tried to shove his dick up my ass eventually.
Donfuckwime, 38, US

When we make love Bobby presses his finger against my anus. I am on top of him rocking and rubbing my clit. This is the only way I can come with his dick inside me.
Betsey, 27, US

242

STIs

Warning

Biological arousal and orgasm in women

Anticipation: In the early stages of sexual excitement, the veins in the pelvis, vulva and clitoris begin to dilate and fill with blood, making the whole area increase in size and feel fuller and firmer. The glans of the clitoris can double in diameter as it lengthens, thickens and emerges from its protective hood. The hood is there to protect the clitoris but if it is stimulated in a rough or painful way it automatically contracts to cover the clitoris. The breasts also swell in size, sometimes by up to 20 per cent, and your nipples may become more erect.

Arousal: It can take up to 20 minutes of physical touch and stimulation for a woman to become fully aroused (make your partner read that bit twice). Once she is aroused natural lubrication usually occurs within 10 to 30 seconds, but the amount of vaginal fluid is really not an accurate measure of a woman's state of arousal. A woman may be wet one minute and dry the next, because natural juices tend to dry up quickly.

Stimulation: As sexual tension increases, the muscles throughout the body begin to tense up or contract, breathing quickens and the skin becomes flushed. As erotic stimulation continues and orgasm approaches, the clitoris becomes less visible as it is covered by the swelling of the clitoral hood. This swelling is designed to protect the clitoris from direct contact, which, for some women, can be more irritating than pleasurable. Prior to orgasm you may feel more wet than usual, and some women report feeling the muscles in their vaginas lift or 'pull up'.

The point of no return: At the point of orgasm your breathing usually becomes even quicker and more shallow, your pulse speeds up, and your pupils dilate. Some women hold their breath at this point. You may feel your vagina tighten or lift, and you may feel your clitoris swell. The entire vulva swells. This is the area from where the sensations and contractions of orgasm will rhythmically pulse at intervals of 0.8 seconds.

Orgasm: A woman may experience anywhere between 3 and 15 spasms, which gradually become less intense and less frequent. These contractions release the engorged blood from the pelvic tissue. It is common to feel contractions in the vagina, uterus and rectum. Blood pressure and pulse rate reach a peak. Once you begin to orgasm you may feel waves of pleasure around your clitoris, vagina, anus or all three. You may not be able to identify where the sensations are coming from and frankly, you probably won't care.

I'll just get the kettle on: Within five or ten seconds of the last vaginal contraction the clitoris returns to its usual state and the dark colours of the blood-engorged labia fade. It takes about five or ten minutes for the vagina to return to normal and longer for the swelling of the labia majora and the glans of the clitoris to subside. Sexual tension takes longer to dissipate if orgasm is not achieved and it may cause the genitals and uterus to ache slightly. Muscle tension prior to and during orgasm can leave your whole body feeling as if you have been to the gym.

The biology of penetration for pregnancy

Penis friendly: During arousal the uterus moves upwards and forwards so that the cervix protrudes less into the vault of the vagina and becomes larger. The expansion and lifting of the uterus occurs because of blood flow into its walls. This movement lengths the vagina, allowing it to receive the fully erect penis. Vaginal fluid serves as a lubricant for intercourse and enables sperm to travel up the vaginal passage more easily. Without this natural lubricant, a woman would find penetration against dry vaginal tissue painful, but during intercourse vaginal lubrication decreases in order to produce greater friction between the vaginal walls and the penis.

Responsive: The walls of the vagina respond and change each time it is entered. With each stroke, thousands of nerve endings are pulled back and forth. The most sensitive part of the vagina is usually around the opening; this also becomes the snuggest part of the aroused vagina. The upper end of the vagina, with far fewer nerve endings, is more responsive to stretching and pressure. The inner lips that surround the vagina are stretched back and forth during intercourse by the penis, so they tug on the clitoral hood providing stimulation that can lead to orgasm.

Designed to aid fertilisation: It has been shown that during orgasm the muscles of the uterus produce involuntary contractions that dip the cervix down into the fornix (a small niche surrounding the cervix). The cervix sucks up the semen from the fornix, which in its relaxed state is bowl-shaped – perfect for the pooling of semen and so aiding the process of fertilisation. Obviously this is only relevant if the man has already ejaculated inside the vagina. In men, the sensation of orgasm lasts between 10 and 13 seconds. Women's orgasms last as long as 107 seconds, though presumably this is compensation for the fact that they have to give birth.

My partner, a 42-year-old male, can achieve orgasm in five to ten minutes. I usually take about two to three times as long as he does – about 15–30 minutes.
Ealine, 41, US
Lovenet

If you're having trouble coming, concentrate on your clit and how it feels when you're just about to come. Transport yourself to that place in your head, and before you know it you'll be there. This takes quite a lot of concentration, and some patience on the part of your partner, but it works.
Abbie, 27, UK
Rainbow Network

I achieve sexual arousal by penetration, definitely, but also in lots of other ways. And the orgasm part is a little trickier. Through sex I can only have an orgasm if I'm on top, and then only sometimes, although it helps if I have to pee. But since I first started having sex I have discovered the wonderful clitoris and orgasms have never been so easy. No penetration needed.
Anon, 20, US
Lovenet

Bodily Fluids

Vaginal secretions

I'm ovulating: All women have a vaginal discharge. It is made by the cervical glands that secrete mucus to plug the opening of the uterus. It can be clear, cloudy white, and/or yellowish, especially when it dries on clothing. During the menstrual cycle (around day 14 when ovulation occurs), women may notice increased wetness, and their secretions may become thin and stringy with white flecks in a clearer fluid (a little like egg white). Although vaginal fluid is acidic in adult females, it tends to be alkaline in adolescents and teenagers, meaning that sexually active teenagers are more at risk of getting pregnant or catching sexually transmitted infections. Emotional pressure, diet, the menstrual cycle, pregnancy, breastfeeding, medication, alcohol, contraception and sexual arousal can all influence the texture and smell of vaginal secretions. Noticeable changes in the colour, smell or amount of discharge may be a sign of a vaginal infection. In fact a foul smell is the most common indication of bacterial vaginosis (inflammation of the vagina).

Vaginal lubrication

I'm aroused: Vaginal lubrication increases during sexual arousal when the small blood vessels in the vaginal walls become engorged with blood. The pressure from this congestion causes small droplets of the straw-coloured, fluid portion of the blood (plasma) to ooze through the vaginal walls. These droplets appear as beads and coalesce into a layer of shiny lubricant that coats the walls. If you don't have sex this lubrication will combine with, and increase, your natural vaginal secretions. The amount of lubrication is affected by hormonal changes during the menstrual cycle and menopause. Commercial lubricants and saliva are useful substitutes when the vagina doesn't feel wet enough for enjoyable sex or masturbation, but they are no substitute for desire or arousal.

Female ejaculate

I'm not sure: Female ejaculate is a clear fluid usually associated with stimulation of the urethral sponge, or G-spot. The fact that the fluid comes from the urethra has caused an ongoing controversy about whether it is urine or something similar to prostatic fluid. In the 1980s, researchers examined samples of both ejaculate and urine from the same group of women. Although their ejaculate contained traces of urea and creatine (from urine), otherwise it was significantly different in composition to their urine. If female ejaculate exists, it is believed to originate in the Skene's or paraurethral glands that surround the urethra, and the urea and creatine may just be trace elements that join the mixture as it passes through the urethra.

Semen

Eat me: Semen is a milky, white, sticky combination of glandular secretions made up of sperm, fluid from the seminal vesicles and the prostate gland. The secretions provide liquid transport that protects the sperm and facilitates their movement, and fructose, which provides an energy source for sperm. Semen is alkaline, which enhances sperm mobility, and also contains an antibiotic that destroys certain bacteria, as well as enzymes that digest cervical mucus. The make-up of semen changes throughout the day. Daytime ejaculations can contain more sperm and seminal fluid, while night-time ejaculations may contain more prostatic fluid. During ejaculation most men only expel between 2 and 5ml (about a level teaspoon) of semen but there are between 50 and 150 million sperm per millilitre. Often the components of semen are not well-mixed, and there may be glutinous threads among the white emissions of the prostate.

Semen is an irritant to the eyes, and produces a burning sensation if it gets near them but it can be an effective moisturiser for the skin. Basic semen has a slight metallic taste because it contains zinc. Semen contains about seven calories per teaspoonful, and its flavour is affected by diet.

Foods that make semen taste bad: Asparagus, chicken, garlic, onions, dairy products, red meat, broccoli, cauliflower, Brussels sprouts, greasy food, spices, coffee and chocolate are all thought to make semen taste unpleasant.

Foods that make semen taste good: Plums, mangoes, pineapples, nectarines, oranges, lemons, limes, parsley, coriander, spearmint, peppermint, grapefruit and green tea, sweeties and apple juice are thought to make semen taste sweet. Diabetics' semen tends to have a honey or cantaloupe flavour, because of the excess sugars in their bodies.

Smegma

Clean me: Smegma is formed in minute microscopic protrusions that cover the whole inner surface of the foreskin cavity. It has the colour and texture of cream cheese and it moisturises the glans to keep it smooth, soft and supple. It lubricates the cavity between the foreskin of the penis and the glans, allowing smooth movement between them. It also has antibacterial and antiviral properties that help keep the penis clean and healthy. Smegma production begins in earnest during adolescence when the penis grows rapidly, while older men produce less smegma. If smegma is allowed to accumulate in the foreskin cavity it begins to smell and can cause infection. A healthy foreskin can be pulled back and the pocket between the foreskin and the glans can be kept clean and healthy by regular washing.

Breastmilk

The white stuff: The breasts are exocrine glands. This means that instead of secreting substances directly into the blood as hormones do, they secrete substances into body cavities or onto body surfaces. Examples include the sweat glands, which secrete sweat, the gall bladder, which secretes digestive juices and, of course, the breasts, which secrete milk. Human breastmilk contains fats, iron, amino acids, immunoglobulins and a host of other beneficial chemicals that are easily absorbed by babies. Breastmilk adapts its nutritional properties to the changing needs of a baby as it grows. It contains antibodies that boost a baby's immune system and has mild anti-bacterial and healing properties. Breastfeeding uses up about 1,000 calories a day, so it is a good way of getting back in shape too. Breastfeeding mums need to drink eight to twelve cups of fluid daily to keep their fluid intake up. Onions, garlic and strong spices can alter the flavour of breast milk, while alcohol or medication can find their way into breastmilk. Vanilla is considered to be the closest flavour there is to breastmilk, which has a naturally sweet taste.

Blood/menstrual blood

First stop – the kidneys: Our blood accounts for approximately 8 per cent of our body weight and is the body's transport medium, carrying nutrients, wastes, gases and hormones. Blood is sticky and has a distinct and slightly salty flavour. Menstrual blood is apparently slightly sweeter, more like saliva, with a slight metallic taste – though I can't vouch for that. Menstrual blood is a mixture of blood, the detached tissue from the wall of the womb, mucus and nutrients. During her period a woman will bleed for up to five days. This does not affect her ability to have intercourse, though she might be more in the mood for a hot cup of cocoa and her slippers. The average blood loss during a period is only about 40–60ml (8–12 teaspoonfuls). Sometimes periods arrive unexpectedly and stain the sheets. If this happens don't use hot water to remove the blood stains because heat cooks the protein in the blood, making the stains more difficult to remove. Soak and agitate the sheets in cold water to remove the blood before machine washing.

Sweat

It's a good thing: There are 2.5 million sweat glands distributed over the skin's surface. In fact, the only areas that are not covered are the nipples and parts of the genitalia. Sweat is 99 per cent water, but the exact composition is determined by diet and health. It helps regulate body temperature, prevents overheating, and has a nice, acidic salty flavour when fresh but smells rancid when stale.

Saliva

Powerful stuff: Saliva helps keep the mouth moist, clean and free of infection. It also dissolves food chemicals so that they can be tasted and starts the process of breaking down starchy food as part of digestion. Normally, the glands produce just enough saliva to keep the mouth moist, but when food enters the mouth, the glands become activated and create more saliva. The salivary glands can output more than a pint per day. Kissing also increases saliva production.

Urine

It's mainly water: Fresh urine is normally a pale to deep-yellow colour. Certain foods, such as beetroot, rhubarb and cranberries, can affect the colour, and some drugs and vitamin supplements make it become cloudy. Vegetables such as asparagus make your urine smell differently and some illnesses, such as diabetes, make it smell fruity. If left on the skin for a prolonged period, urine can be an irritant and cause the equivalent of nappy rash in adults. Urine is 95 per cent water, but in certain diseases its composition changes to include glucose, red blood cells, white blood cells and bile. The presence of abnormal substances in urine helps doctors diagnose both illness and pregnancy.

Tears

Not crying but cleaning: Tears are saline, which means they are sterile, and they also contain an enzyme that destroys bacteria. They are released continually from the lacrimal gland above the eye and flow down over the eyeball. Then they drain away into the tear ducts and down into the nose. Their function is to clean, lubricate and protect the surface of the eye. If the eyes are irritated, tears spill out over the eyelids, soothing and cleaning the surface of the eyeball. Humans are the only species who shed tears when emotionally upset. Research into the subject is pretty non-existent, and science books simply propose that the relationship between tears and emotions are something to do with stress reduction. The majority of the population have probably worked this theory out all by themselves. When the chips are down, a good blub really helps.

STI and HIV transmission from body fluids

Remember: Semen and blood are the most efficient transmission fluids for infections. Vaginal secretions transmit infection less effectively but are still a risk. The HIV virus has been found in tests on saliva and breastmilk, but no definite cases of 'sexual' transmission involving only these fluids have yet been discovered. Breastfeeding has been established as an important route of transmission of HIV from mother to baby.

Periods are something I feel afraid of. I don't understand how it doesn't hurt. It looks so violent. When my girlfriend is bleeding I don't want to go in there.
John, 25, Ireland

I hate it when I kiss a guy and he has lots of spit in his mouth. It really makes me want to gag.
Bea, 26, Australia

He pisses on me and and I piss on him and there is this sense of apprehension before it happens – and then it is warm and wet and heaven sent.
Karl, 33, UK

The security guard in our building had really bad BO. It was so gross, but it turned out that he could not smell. He died last year when he was frying food in his apartment and he could not smell the fact that the kitchen was on fire. I wonder if lots of people with BO have the same problem.
Lou, 38, US

Every time I cry my boyfriend and I end up having sex.
Leah, 19, UK

What you see (men)

① The shaft of the penis: This is the body of the penis, which runs between the head and the pubis. Within it are three spongy erectile caverns, which fill up with blood during sexual arousal causing erection.

② The head of the penis: Also known as the glans, the head of the penis has a much higher concentration of nerve endings than the shaft and is extremely sensitive. In circumcised men the head of the penis is permanently exposed. In uncircumcised men it can be seen when the penis is erect and when the foreskin is rolled back.

③ The coronal ridge: Also known as the crown of the penis, this is the sensitive 'projecting' ridge at the base of the penis head.

④ The frenulum: A highly sensitive, V-shaped, or triangular, fold of tissue that runs up the coronal ridge from the shaft to the head.

⑤ The foreskin: The roll of skin that covers the head of the penis in uncircumcised men. Normally it can be easily pulled back to reveal (and clean beneath) the head of the penis. However in some men the foreskin is very tight and pulling it back can be uncomfortable or even painful. Men or boys with very tight foreskins are more prone to infection and in some of these cases doctors may recommend circumcision.

⑥ The urethral opening: This is the hole at the tip of the penis, which is the opening to the urethra through which urine and semen are released.

⑦ The scrotum: This is the thin-walled, soft, elastic sac, containing the testicles which hangs below the penis. The scrotum's primary function is to keep the testicles at their optimum temperature, which is lower than that of the body.

⑧ The perineum: This is the area that runs between the scrotum and the anus. The perineum is rich in nerve endings and contains a central ridge – the median raphe – which is a continuation of the scrotum. Pressure on the perineum can also put pressure on the prostate gland internally.

⑨ The anus: This is the opening to the rectum. It is rich in nerve endings and surrounded by fine hairs, making it extremely sensitive to touch and stimulation. Its folds of soft, pink tissue give it a puckered appearance and, like vaginal tissue, it swells during arousal.

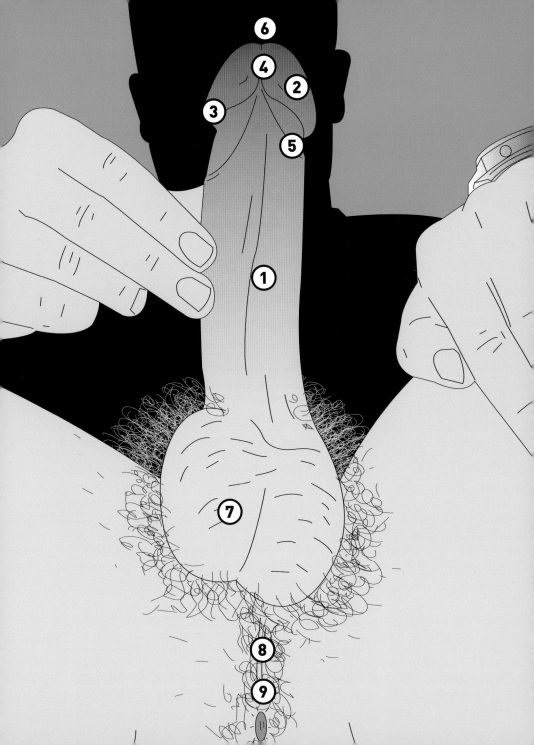

What you don't see (men)

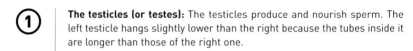

(1) **The testicles (or testes):** The testicles produce and nourish sperm. The left testicle hangs slightly lower than the right because the tubes inside it are longer than those of the right one.

(2) **The epididymis:** This is a canal that leads from each testicle into the vas deferens. Sperm produced in the testes develop the ability to swim in the epididymis. Contractions and the wafting effect of tiny, hair-like cilia then move them through to the vas deferens at ejaculation.

(3) **The vas deferens:** These ducts lead from the epididymis to the seminal vesicles, where they form the two ejaculatory ducts. It is these ducts that are cut in a vasectomy.

(4) **The seminal vesicles:** These secrete the seminal fluid that makes up the bulk of semen. The fluid contains fructose, which gives the sperm energy for movement, and prostaglandins, which break down the mucous lining of the woman's cervix. The seminal vesicles contract to empty the fluid into the ejaculatory ducts.

(5) **Corpora cavernosa:** Cylinders containing spongy erectile tissue and blood vessels that fill with blood, causing erection.

(6) **The urethra and urethral sphincter muscles:** Urine and sperm both travel through the urethra. The urethral sphincter muscles contract to allow either urine or sperm to travel down the urethra for expulsion via the penis.

(7) **The bulbourethral glands (or Cowper's glands):** These secrete most of the preseminal fluid that seeps from the penis prior to orgasm.

(8) **The prostate gland:** This gland secretes about a quarter of the fluid that forms the ejaculate and squeezes it into the urethra as the sperm move through it during orgasm.

(9) **The pubococcygeus muscle (PC):** This muscle helps support the pelvic floor and is involved in the contractions that occur during orgasm.

(10) **The anal sphincters and the rectum:** Two powerful muscles that control the entrance to the anus. The rectum is a passage through which faeces are excreted, though they are stored further up in the colon.

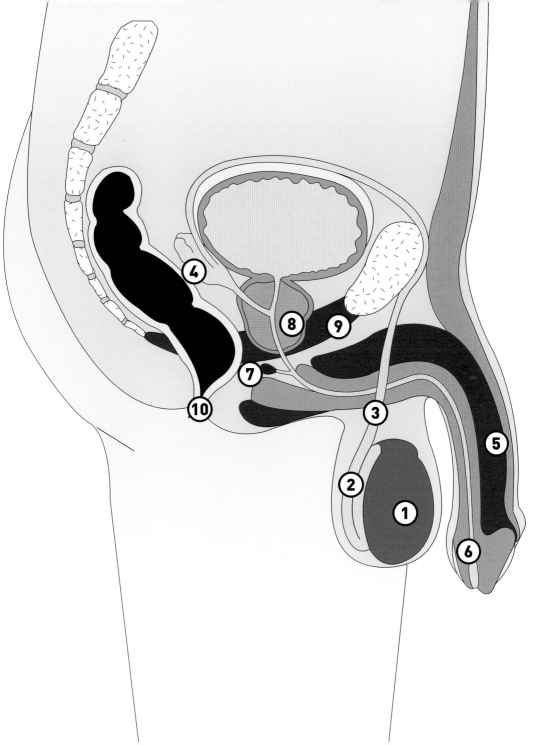

What you should know

The penis and the scrotum

Hydraulics: Anatomically speaking, the penis has a number of different parts that are made up of erectile tissue containing thousands of sensory nerve endings. The body of the penis, which runs between its head and the pubis, is called its shaft. Within it are three spongy erectile masses: two corpora cavernosa, one on either side; and a single corpus spongiosum on the underside. They run down inside the body beneath the prostate gland and towards the anus, forming the root of the penis, and are anchored in place by ligaments. During sexual arousal, the spaces that they contain become filled with blood, making the penis erect.

Construction: The head of the penis can usually be seen when the penis is erect and is permanently exposed in circumcised men. Formed from an extension of the corpus spongiosum, it has an extremely high concentration of nerve endings and is surrounded at the base by the highly sensitive coronal ridge (also known as the crown of the penis). The frenulum, which runs up from the foreskin to the head of the penis on the underside, is the most sensitive area of the penis. It contains an artery that can sometimes become damaged during sex, resulting in a considerable amount of bleeding. On either side of the frenulum, a collection of glands secrete a creamy substance called smegma, which spreads all over the glans, moisturising it and keeping it smooth, soft and supple.

Circumcision: The roll of skin that covers the head of the penis in uncircumcised men is called the foreskin. Male circumcision is the surgical removal of the foreskin that normally covers and protects the head of the penis. In some countries and cultures, this skin is routinely removed soon after birth for reasons of health, hygiene or religion. In some cultures, boys are circumcised at puberty. About half the men in the world are circumcised, but, unlike female circumcision, male circumcision does not affect a man's ability to experience sexual pleasure.

Balls: The scrotum is the thin-walled, soft, elastic sac that hangs behind and below the penis. Externally, a ridge, called the median raphe, divides the scrotum in two; internally, a central division, called a septum, divides it to form a separate compartment for each testicle. The scrotum's primary function is to keep the testes at an optimum temperature that is lower than that of the body – if the testes are at a higher temperature than that of the body for a long period, sperm production suffers and infertility

My penis is my prize. I stroke it every night and I expect my woman to treat it with the same respect.
Ben, 35, UK

I know that most men think about their penis when they think about sexuality, but I consider my whole body to be a potential temple of pleasure.
Jonathan, 32, UK

Self-delusion plays a very big part in a man's relationship with his body. My father-in-law thinks he still has the body of a hot rod – he seems blissfully unaware of the reality. I envy him.
Nigel, 46, UK

As a circumcised male, I wonder what it would have been like to remain uncut. What did I miss out on? Also, I sometimes wonder if it matters to women.
Louis, 52, UK

I can't imagine how a circumcised penis could reach the same length or be nearly as comfortable during sex as an uncircumcised one, because of the lack of skin. I love my skin!
Bob, 22, Australia

can be the result. When it is warm, the scrotum relaxes and becomes looser in order to ventilate the testes. When it is cold, the scrotum contracts so that the testes are closer to the warmth of the body wall. The testes produce both sperm and testosterone. Within each testicle is a system of around 630m (690yds) of ducts called the seminiferous tubules. These are the organs in which sperm are produced, nourished and matured for about 45 days in 'nurse' cells (the cells of Sertoli) attached to each tubule's lining. Each testicle produces nearly 150 million sperm every 24 hours, but if ejaculation occurs twice or more in a day, it can take between five and seven days to replenish their stores.

Penis size

All men are equal, but some are more equal than others: According to the respected sex therapist Dr Bernie Zilbergeld, the male penis comes in only three sizes: large, extra large and so big you can't get it through the door. This myth seems to be confirmed by the monstrous members displayed in porn mags and movies, but the reality is that porn stars are selected for size and photographed from below with closely shaved pubes to make their appendages look bigger. Unfortunately, men don't often have the opportunity to see 'average' erections. Comparing themselves to porn stars who are hung like donkeys only adds to a collective sense of male penile insecurity.

What size are your genes?: The size, shape and weight of the penis, scrotum and testicles in an adult male are determined by embryonic testos-terone levels. If your mother was a shot putter you may have a natural genital advantage, but according to the Kinsey Institute for Sex Research in the US, the 'average' size of most men's erections is 15.25cm (6ins). Ninety per cent of all penises are between 13 and 18cm (5.1 and 7.1ins). When a penis is soft, it usually hangs loosely away from the body and averages about 7.9–10cm (3.5–4.5ins) in length and 2.25cm (1in) in diameter. The shortest functioning penis to have been recorded was 1.5cm (0.67in) long and the longest was 30cm (13.3ins). The average circumference is between 10 and 12.25cm (4.5 and 5.5ins).

Extra large, please: Surveys suggest that almost all men – regardless of sexual orientation – wish they had a larger penis. However, Masters, Johnson and Kolodny, in their book *Sex and Human Loving* (1986) state that erection can be thought of as 'the great equaliser', because men with

I have slept with a couple of circumcised men and one who was not. He did seem a bit less responsive to a couple of techniques that worked on the others, but I don't know whether it was because of his foreskin or not.
Marie, 35, US

My humour and charm is what works for me. On close examination my body is overweight, flabby and rather shameful, but saying that, I don't care – my wife loves me and life is too short to worry about these things.
John, 46, UK

Women think that they have it bad – yeah, right. Try being an average guy at your local gym – it's a mixture of humiliation and fantasy. Men constantly look at each other's bodies – no, not in a sexual way, but with envy and sometimes with pity.
Keith, 29, UK

My penis is the only one I've got, so I can only do my best with it and accept it!
Jim, 47, UK

a smaller non-erect penis usually have a larger percentage volume increase during erection than men who have a larger one. Unfortunately for the less well endowed, it is (usually) the flaccid penis that gets noted in the communal showers after sports.

Small but perfectly formed: The male obsession with size is not actually something that bothers females. Contrary to popular opinion, the length of the penis is relatively unimportant for vaginal penetration, because the inner part of the vagina has fewer sensory nerve endings. A very large penis can actually be very uncomfortable, and for oral and anal sex the smaller penis is often a blessing.

Which way is up?: One-quarter of all penises bend in some direction and some bend downwards even when erect. Unless the bend is severe or causes pain, nothing is wrong or abnormal, and sexual intercourse should not be affected. Although both men and women become smaller with age, the length of penis does not change.

Cheating: Size is always measured when the penis is erect, because its dimensions vary more when it is flaccid. Size can also be affected by the time of day, mood and temperature. Looking in the mirror is the best way to visualise your penis – this is the way others see it. You have an aerial view that makes it seem shorter, because you don't see the full length of the shaft and the balls underneath. If you want to look well-hung, make sure that the room you are in is warm. If you are cold and unrelaxed, your balls will shrivel close to your body and there will be less blood flow to the penis, making your whole package appear smaller. After a bath, or in a warm room, your scrotum and testicles will hang down further away from your body, blood flow to the penis will increase and you will look better endowed.

How to measure your penis (if you must): According to Harold Reed, MD, Director of the Reed Centre for Ambulatory Urological Surgery, Florida, USA, this is the correct way to measure the length of the penis:

- While standing, make your penis erect.
- Angle your penis down until it is parallel to the floor.
- Set a ruler against against your pubic bone just above the base of your penis, and measure to the tip.
- Now wash the ruler.

The anus

Tight ass: The anus plays an important part in men's sex because it allows access to the sensitive prostate gland. That said, anal tissue is not designed for penetration and it does not expand in the same way as vaginal tissue, so care needs to be taken and lubrication is essential. The entrance to the anus is controlled by two powerful muscles called sphincters. The external sphincter can be controlled at will but the internal sphincter is controlled by the involuntary part of the nervous system, which governs functions such as heart rate and stress. It responds to fear and anxiety by contracting, which is why you can't pretend to want anal penetration if you don't want it, but, as with any muscle, the spasm of contraction can only be held for so long before the muscle gets tired and relaxes its grip. The anal canal opens into the rectum and although faeces are not actually stored there, residual traces may be lurking around, particularly if there has not been a recent bowel movement.

Where did that cucumber disappear to?: Never put anything that does not have a flared base into your rectum. Your sphincter muscles may suck it up inside you. Doctors in A & E have to remove things such as shampoo bottles, lightbulbs and even hamsters from people's anuses on a daily basis, and, frankly, they have more important things to do.

The prostate gland

I know it's here somewhere: The prostate gland is located about 4cm (1.6ins) from the anus in front of the wall of the rectum and just below the bladder. The walnut-sized gland secretes prostatic fluid, which combines with seminal fluid and sperm to create semen. Prostatic fluid contains similar chemicals to the fluid produced by the seminal vesicles. It acts as a lubricant, prevents infection in the urethra, protects and energises sperm and makes the vaginal canal less acidic. Production of prostatic fluid increases significantly during sexual arousal. Prior to orgasm, seminal fluid floods into the prostate and, on orgasm, the prostate contracts and empties during ejaculation. Some men mistakenly believe that having their prostate stimulated makes them more vulnerable to prostate cancer or prostatitis (inflammation of the prostate gland). In fact neither of these ideas are true, though doctors do examine the prostate in their search for bacterial infections or cancer. In a process known as 'milking the prostate', they pump the gland until its fluid is ejected into a cup (without orgasm).

242

STIs

Biological arousal and orgasm in men

Anticipation: When a man is not sexually aroused, the arteries supplying the erectile tissue in his penis are constricted and his penis is flaccid. Arousal is caused by sexual thoughts, images, anticipation of sexual contact and direct stimulation as well as the sex hormones. The spinal cord relays these messages to the brain, which then initiates the process of erection.

Game on: The parasympathetic nerves in the penis release nitric oxid, which causes the expansion of the spongy caverns in the corpora cavernosa. This compresses tiny exit veins, trapping blood from the arteries in the penis. Once the vascular spaces are engorged with blood, the penis becomes enlarged and rigid. As arousal grows, increased blood flow makes the skin of the scrotum thicker and darker in colour and the testes become firmer. The state of erection can vary with age. Younger men may experience more rigid and frequent erections. Older men still get hard, but the process can take longer and the penis may not be as stiff or stand as upright as before.

Stimulation: In the '50s, Kinsey asked men how quickly they ejaculated after stimulation. His results showed that three-quarters of all his subjects reached orgasm within two minutes of starting sexual intercourse. This figure was recently supported by a study on a group of 20-year-old Japanese males who were blindfolded and masturbated to orgasm. Their average time was also two minutes. Mind you, what young man wouldn't come quickly if he was blindfolded and given a hand job by an attractive young woman (with a blindfold, all women are attractive).

Orgasm: If stimulation continues, about two to four seconds before emission a man reaches a point called 'ejaculatory inevitability' when orgasm is imminent and he is past the point of no return. The testes tighten and are drawn closer to the body in preparation for orgasm. Initially there is a feeling of deep warmth or pressure, which indicates that orgasm is inevitable. Then sharp, intensely pleasurable contractions involving the PC muscles are felt in the genitals, perineum, anal sphincter and rectum. These rhythmic muscle contractions are accompanied by intense pleasure and many systemic changes, such as generalised muscle contraction, rapid heartbeat and elevated blood pressure. The first few contractions are intense and close together, occurring at about 0.8-second intervals. As orgasm continues, the contractions diminish in intensity and duration and occur at less frequent intervals. Semen does not actually appear until a few seconds after the point of ejaculatory inevitability because of the distance the seminal fluid has to travel through the urethra. Men experience a sensation of pumping and, finally, a warm rush of fluid and a shooting sensation as the semen travels through the urethra and ejaculates. If ejaculation does not take place for a period of about two weeks, sperm are passed out in urine.

Zzzzz: After ejaculation there is a latent or refractory period, ranging in time from minutes to hours, during which a man is unable to achieve another erection or orgasm and the penis returns to its flaccid state. The length of the refractory period varies with age and, of course, levels of sexual interest. It can be a matter of minutes in a young man, but men over 60 may have to wait a couple of days. The more frequently you ejaculate, the less volume and force your ejaculation will have. Basically, you start running out of semen. The average distance a man ejaculates is 18–25cm (7–10ins), but sexual abstinence can help you to shoot longer distances. If you don't ejaculate for more than three days, you may find you can shoot up to 90cm (3ft) or more.

Erection for vaginal penetration

Mission almost impossible: Erection allows the penis to serve as a penetrative organ that enables semen to be delivered into the vagina close to the cervix, giving the sperm a better chance of survival. After being produced in the testes, the sperm are delivered to the body's exterior through a system of ducts including the epididymis – this part of the journey takes a tortuous 20 days, during which time the sperm develop the ability to swim. It takes four or five days for this to happen, until eventually they can manage a relaxed 2.5–5cm (1–2ins) an hour. The sperm then join up with the seminal fluid in the ejaculatory duct to form semen and only then do they enter the urethra. When sexual stimulation reaches a certain critical level, a spinal reflex initiates a massive discharge of nerve impulses. The sphincter muscle of the bladder constricts, preventing expulsion of urine or reflux of semen into the bladder, and the muscles of the penis undergo a rapid series of contractions that propel the semen out of the urethral opening at the tip of the penis. Tightening of the vaginal muscles puts pressure on the penis and assists in male orgasm. Once sperm have entered the female reproductive tract, they only have a limited amount of time to travel up the Fallopian tubes in search of an egg to fertilise. If they fail in their mission, they die within three days.

My penis doesn't go soft straight after sex and sometimes I can stay nearly hard and keep moving in and out of my girlfriend – or she lies on top of me and pushes in to me. Then she makes herself orgasm like that and when I watch her come it makes me so horny that I get really hard really quick and then I can come again in just a few minutes. This happens most times we have sex, so I get two orgasms – but she doesn't mind that she only has one, because she said that with her last boyfriend she didn't have orgasms with him inside her.
Leonard, 27, UK

I can still have three orgasms in a row, which I think isn't bad for my age. I blame my girlfriend, because she never wants to stop.
Roy, 47, UK

We have been trying to have a baby for about six months now. At first we just had sex like normal, but for the past two months we have been avoiding sex for the week before she ovulates and once we know she is fertile we have a lot of sex.
Tony, 37, UK

SOLO SEX

I have touched myself and made myself reach a great orgasm while driving my stick-shift Ford Explorer down a suburban road in broad daylight. It was so wild to think that the people in the cars around me had no idea what was going on. **Janice, 24, US** *CakeNYC*

Solo sex

Though it probably doesn't need explaining, masturbation describes the act of stimulating your own genitals for sexual pleasure. Young children manipulate their genitals because 'it feels nice', but masturbation for sexual purposes usually begins at the onset of puberty, between the ages of 11 and 15. Sometimes masturbation begins much later in life and some people never masturbate at all. Reasons range from cultural and religious beliefs to lack of desire, but guilt, modesty and inhibition can also make people resist the very natural urge to stimulate themselves.

Because it is about personal pleasure rather than procreation, masturbation has been much maligned. Frowned on for boys, it was unthinkable for girls, and only ten years ago dictionaries still defined the word 'masturbation' as 'self-abuse'. Swiss physician SA Tissot (1728–97) is largely responsible. He developed a theory that sex (and especially masturbation) could starve the brain and the nervous system, eventually leading to madness and blindness. Backed by the church, the idea caught on, to the extent that in Victorian Britain, masturbation was considered to be a pathological perversion guaranteed to cause insanity. With such strong medical, religious and social disapproval, it has taken centuries for masturbation to be acknowledged as harmless. However, although the medical theories have been disproved, masturbation remains very controversial in some cultures and religions and is still not readily discussed. We might share our sex lives with our friends, but we certainly don't swap masturbatory techniques.

Despite its chequered history, masturbation is (and probably always has been) the most common way to enjoy relaxing safe sex. It doesn't require a relationship, cuts out the stress of pleasing anyone else and is completely safe. You can enjoy it throughout your life and tailor it to your physical needs and abilities. Young people tend to masturbate a lot, while people who are in a relationship, or much older, may do it less (though like riding a bike, you never forget how to do it). Lots of people in relationships continue to masturbate privately. It doesn't constitute being unfaithful and offers sexual relief if a partner can't provide it for whatever reason. Some adolescents feel that frequent masturbation is a sign that they are not getting enough of the real thing (sex with a partner). In fact, adolescents rarely 'get enough' and masturbation is the one sexual act that offers them – and everyone else – the freedom to learn how to satisfy themselves sexually, with no ties and no pressure to perform. As Woody Allen said, 'Don't knock it, it's sex with someone you love'.

Getting to know you

My way: Many people find a masturbation technique that works for them when they are young and then stick to it for life – it could be pulling clothes or fabric between their legs or rubbing their genitals into a mattress. When people get stuck with set masturbatory habits, orgasm becomes their sole goal and how they reach it is secondary. In fact, to get the most out of solo sex you need to reverse this way of thinking and make the process more important than the end result. Real arousal is about more than genital stimulation and good solo sex is about much more than a rapid orgasm. Although ultimately you probably want to (and will) have an orgasm, if you diminish the build-up by rushing things, you reduce the potential pleasure to be had.

Relax: Oddly, shyness, modesty and guilt seem to be just as inhibiting for men and women in private as they are in public. Anything that interferes with your ability to let yourself go completely will stop you relaxing – so switch off, choose a time when you know you will be alone and make yourself comfortable. Adolescents often have a more difficult time obtaining privacy. As a result, young men frequently masturbate very quickly for fear of being caught by parents or siblings. This can set a pattern of early ejaculation that may be difficult to break later on. Young girls may find that even if they know they are alone, fear of intrusion means that they can never relax enough to achieve orgasm.

Behind closed doors: In most homes you can be pretty sure that there will be a lock on the bathroom door. This guarantees you privacy and usually a big mirror too. The first step to exploring yourself is opening your eyes. After a relaxing sensuous bath, take a look at your body in the mirror (a full-length one is best). Appreciate yourself, warts and all. Don't rush. Linger on your breasts, nipples, thighs, stomach and bottom. Squeeze your spots, trace your scars, wrinkle your cellulite, cup your balls. Rub moisturiser or talc all over your body and note what parts feel good when you touch them. Rest a mirror against the wall, sit in front of it on the floor and take a look at your genitals. Touch them and note any changes in their size or colour and the sensations that you feel. Do you feel aroused? Are you getting an erection?

Imagine: Sexual pleasure is derived from much more than physical stimulation. Arousal may be either visible (erection or engorgement of the vulva) or just sensed in the genitals, but the whole body, including your brain, is part of the experience. In fact the brain is your body's most

My female cousin and I were 11 years old. We were playing 'Mommy and Mommy' in my room. We had a pillow between us and we were humping it. All of a sudden I felt so funny that I felt wet in my panties. I never knew I was having an orgasm.
Terry Luv, 24, US
Kuma2

I never masturbated until I was 40 years old because I am a person who lives out her fantasies daily and I've done most of the things that people masturbate over.
Eva Norvind, US
alias Ava Taurel

God only put men on earth because vibrators can't mow the lawn.
Suzanne, 37, UK

Tightening my arsehole and concentrating on having an orgasm helps bring it on. Sometimes I stick my finger in my vagina as this seems to stabilise the clitoris and is a bit exciting. My legs are apart and I don't move very much.
Flora, 22, UK

It's much better than having sex with a man I don't care about.
Louise, 23, UK

I have this fantasy about two women together shopping and trying on clothes in the changing room and being able to glance at their nakedness when I walk past. I like the idea of the surprise. Works every time. Maybe it'll change when I get a girlfriend.
Jake, 19, US

The role of fantasy can perform a number of functions, from making sex more tolerable with an undesirable partner to spicing things up a bit (I have fantasised the person I was with was a celebrity). When masturbating, I can 'wish' it was a particular person, or role-play something that would normally be taboo, such as using fruit or vegetables.
Melissa, 42, Australia

Watching porn always gives me a quick fix, but for more intense situations vibrators are the bomb. And when I'm feeling real kinky, I like adjustable nipple clamps. Don't knock it till you've tried it.
Blu, 38, US
Kuma2

powerful sex organ and your imagination is the best masturbatory tool of all – so crank it up. Exploring sexual fantasy may feel dangerous at first, but it is a natural, effective and private way of exploring your sexual identity. Fantasies can involve wildly erotic or dangerous situations in which you would never actually allow yourself to become involved, but most therapists, as Freud and Jung did, view fantasy as a healthy and harmless way of tapping into subconscious sexual energy.

I get by with a little help from my . . . : Erotic material is often an essential part of masturbation, though most fantasies never get further than the imagination and the scenarios people fantasise about during solo sex don't necessarily reflect what they would do in reality. For those who need a little visual help, porn is widely available on video, the Internet or in print, but there are alternatives to commercial material. Get creative and make some DIY erotica. If you have a home video or a digital or a polaroid camera (you don't have to have any film processed), make images of yourself during masturbation and sex. Draw or write down your sexual fantasies. Record your stories onto tape and listen to them while you masturbate. The act of illustrating and recording your fantasies in this way is often a huge turn-on in itself.

Do you know where you're going?: Varying how you masturbate helps you build up a more intimate knowledge of your own physical responses. It provides an opportunity to understand and explore your own body – in fact, it's one of the main tools doctors use to help people who have problems achieving orgasm or controlling their sexual responses. You learn how to orgasm through masturbation and the more confident you are about your own sexual geography, the better you can guide a sexual partner. After all, you can hardly expect someone to press the right buttons for you if you can't tell them where they are in the first place.

Things your mother should have told you

Lies, damn lies: Almost everything negative that people say about masturbation is untrue – but let's spell it out anyway. It is not true that masturbating means you've lost your virginity, are perverted, dirty, oversexed or sex-starved. Masturbation doesn't cause madness, blindness, hairy palms, genital or kidney damage. And it doesn't 'waste sperm' either, though older men may find that ejaculating more often means ejaculating less semen.

Masturbation for women

It's different for girls: The experience of arousal is different for individual women and may change at different stages of life, or times of the month. You may need to be in a sexy frame of mind before you become physically aroused, and if you are tense or distracted, your brain may not respond to sexual signals. Usually though, once your brain gets turned on, it sends your body into action and your juices start to flow. Sometimes, women become aroused from accidental or indirect stimulation – riding a bicycle or a horse, for example, or wearing tight jeans with a seam that rubs the clitoris. In this case things happen in reverse. It's your body that alerts your brain to stimulation and your brain then decides whether to quell or magnify the sensation. Generally, clitoral stimulation is the most effective way to achieve sexual arousal and orgasm, but everyone enjoys different things and there's no right way of going about it.

Forget the laundry: Orgasm has been described as a triumph of stimulation over inhibition. If you have very little privacy it can be difficult to relax enough to follow through on feelings of arousal. Women, in particular, find that it takes time and concentration to stay in the moment and allow their arousal to build and eventually take them over the top into orgasm. Even small distractions can disturb your focus. Irritating music or a phone ringing may be all it takes to stop you losing yourself in your sensations. Don't try and muddle through. Turn off the music, take the phone off the hook and go back to where you were. Some women who have never had an orgasm may find that they need to stimulate themselves for far longer than seems reasonable. This is often a result of their inhibition and anxiety about never actually achieving orgasm. It takes many women up to 20 or 30 minutes to become fully aroused (enough time to do the vacuuming and get a wash on), so it is worth persevering. If you want to speed things up, the best thing to do is to use a vibrator and just keep going until you have an orgasm. Once you have experienced what climax feels like, you'll find that orgasm comes more easily – and laundry waits.

Clean shirts – 0, orgasms – 3: Some women can achieve a number of orgasms during solo sex. Other women feel inadequate because they can only achieve orgasm through masturbation and they don't know how to achieve it with a partner. Changing this requires confidence and communication. If you can orgasm by yourself, you can teach your partner how to masturbate you. This will also increase your chances of experiencing orgasm through penetrative sex. That said, open communication often proves to be far more difficult than the most elaborate of sexual techniques.

AKA
Playing with yourself
Fingering
Wanking
Muff ruffling
Petting the bunny
Exploring the deep south

Learn how to make yourself come. You're responsible for your own orgasm. Not any man.
Jean, 35, UK

Try not to make orgasm your goal. Because if you're constantly thinking about it and worried about it and anxious, whether it's with a partner or solo, I'm not going to say it'll never happen, but it's more difficult.
Shaz, 27, US

My first experience with masturbation was when I was about 16. I enjoyed it so immensely that I wanted to experience it over and over. I tried different things till I found something that suited me.
Cassie, 23, US
Kuma2

I have about one orgasm for every ten my partner has during sex, but I can always make myself come when I masturbate. I have given up trying to show him how.
Jean, 35, UK

I use a lot of water-based lubricant as I never really produce enough naturally when masturbating.
Violet, 27, US
Moonlite Bunny Ranch

Once I had my first orgasm I realised that I had to learn to masturbate if I wanted to control my ability to orgasm during sex. I read up about it and the best books I found were Female Sexuality, *by Lonnie Barbach, and* Liberating Masturbation, *by Betty Dunston.*
Lara, 21, UK

I started to enjoy dildos after having babies. When I was younger, I preferred pure clitoral stimulation without anything penetrating me, but as I grew older, things inside me started to feel better.
Blaze, 45, US
Moonlite Bunny Ranch

I have one vibrator that I rarely use. I call it 'Mini Me'. I'm still pretty old-fashioned and I like my hand.
Luv2BSpanked, 32, US
Kuma2

Techniques

Everything but the girly bits: There are many different ways of touching yourself and it's worth experimenting with the pace, pressure and strength of your strokes. Try touching yourself everywhere but your genitals at first. Stimulate yourself through your clothes or your knickers and try massaging different parts of your body, such as your breasts, nipples and inner thighs, using massage oils or artificial lubricant.

Legs together: Rubbing your thighs together puts indirect pressure on your clitoris and is a great way of stimulating yourself secretly – try it when sitting on a bus or at your desk. Alternatively, lie on your back or your side with your legs pressed together. Without using your hands, clench and release your pelvic floor muscles and squeeze your vagina.

Using fabric: Lie face down on a bed with a mound of material – a blanket or the corner of a duvet – between your thighs, rubbing against your clitoris. Don't rub too hard, though, because friction can be abrasive.

Moving against an object while standing: Tilt your pelvis and move it against a bathroom sink, say, or the edge of a bed – or alleviate wash-day boredom and try the washing machine during a spin cycle. Press in and rub against the object in an up-and-down and circular motion.

With water: In a shallow bath or shower, adjust the water temperature (make sure it's not too hot) and use the shower head to aim a gentle jet of warm water down onto the vulval area and the clitoris. Keep your legs slightly apart and rotate your hips. Start with the water pressure low and build it up slowly. Don't aim the jet directly into your vagina as there is a risk of getting an air bubble in your bloodstream.

Lying on your stomach: Tuck your hands underneath your stomach and reach for your genital area – a pillow can help raise your hips up to give you better access. Move your index and middle fingers between the valley of the inner and outer lips of your vulva and up, down and over the clitoral areas, occasionally brushing the head of the clitoris.

Stimulating the clitoris: The shaft of the clitoris runs from the visible tip and extends internally down either side of the inner labia. Rubbing the labia indirectly stimulates your clitoris, and pulling on the inner lips moves the clitoral hood back and forth, which can be very arousing. Stroke the clitoral hood, then pull it back and use a fingertip to brush the clitoral head lightly. Moisten your index finger and use it to rub the clitoral head in a circular motion. Some women find that their clitoral head is so sensitive that only the lightest touch is pleasurable.

Simultaneous clitoral massage and vaginal penetration: Massage the palm of your hand against the whole clitoral area and use your other hand to slide your fingers in and out of your vagina.

Simultaneous clitoral stimulation and anal penetration: Stroke the clitoral area with your fingers and massage the rim of your anus with your other hand. Once your sphincter muscles have relaxed, gently slide a lubricated finger in and out. Don't put a finger that has been in your anus into your vagina as doing so can lead to infection.

Stimulating the G-spot: There's only one way to make your mind up about the G-spot and that is to have a look for it yourself. Masturbate normally until you feel orgasm approaching. Then squat, or lie on your stomach, and place one or two fingers into your vagina, keeping your thumb on your pelvic bone (just above your pubic hair). Press your fingers into the the front wall as if you are trying to press up towards your thumb on the outside. You are looking for an area that feels different and more sensitive than the other vaginal tissue. It might feel as if someone is pressing on your bladder and you need to pee, possibly slightly tingly and maybe even a little uncomfortable. If you find a sensitive spot, stroke, press or pulsate the area and see if you can bring yourself to orgasm. The process can take quite a long time, but it can lead to a very strong and deep orgasm, so it's worth a try. DIY G-spot orgasms are actually quite awkward because it's difficult for your hand to maintain the pressure. Instead of using your fingers, you might want to try a G-spot vibrator. This is similar to a regular vibrator, but has a slight curve at the end that is designed to vibrate against the G-spot. If you can't find your G-spot, don't worry (you are not alone). Concentrate on the different feelings inside your vagina and combine what you're doing with stimulating your nipples or clitoris to see whether this enhances them.

Delaying tactics: If you want to masturbate for longer, when you feel you are close to orgasm, stop for a few minutes and then start again. When you eventually orgasm you may find the experience is more intense.

Use different things – feathers, fur, chiffon, leather. Touch yourself through your clothes and not through your clothes, in different areas and different positions.
Renee, 22, UK

My favourite fantasy to masturbate to is this scenario. A girl ties me up with a silk scarf to an elaborate Victorian iron bed. She then goes down on me, while a man, in full uniform, watches from the corner of the room, moving around so he can change views, seeing my face as I get more out of control.
Angela, 37, UK

I only discovered my G-spot when I was 43, which is a shame really, but I suppose it is nice to know that you can still discover your sexual self when you are going grey.
Beth, 45, UK

I used to think I was a freak of nature because I never seemed to orgasm with pure penetration using my dildo. I seem to be one of many women who commonly come with sustained clitoral tickle.
Jilly, 33, UK

Using sex toys

Battery operated turn-on: Vibrators are a great help during masturbation because they offer intense and sustainable stimulation, but women are generally reluctant to advertise the fact that they use them. Things are changing, however, and the day when vibrators can come out of the closet or the knicker drawer is fast approaching. Manufacturers are at last thinking in terms of what women want, as opposed to what men think women want, and sex toy aesthetics are slowly shifting away from buzzing, prosthetic, veins-and-all pork swords.

Petting the bunny: If you buy your vibrator online, you can usually read product reviews (and products are generally delivered in discreet, unbranded packaging). Some models have independently controlled devices for clitoral stimulation and vaginal penetration that allow you to get used to the individual sensations. The rabbit, for example, has little bunny ears that work the clitoris and a shaft for the vagina. Shaft sleeves are a low-tech alternative. They come in a variety of textures and slip over individual fingers. Some expand to go over vibrators and dildos as well.

Look, no hands: Strap-on or long-handled designs can help women with limited manual dexterity or a physical disability to enjoy masturbation. Vibrating pouches can be strapped around the waist and rest against the vulva, transmitting vibrations to the whole area. Long-handled wand vibrators can be clutched between the thighs and dildos with suction cups can be attached to hard surfaces.

Things your mother should have told you

The wetter the better: Lubrication makes masturbation feel nicer. If you are fully aroused but don't feel very wet, try dragging some of your natural lubrication out to the vulva from inside the vagina using your finger. Alternatively, add saliva or use a commercial lubricant. Water-based lubes dry out quickly but can be reactivated with water. Lots of people use bathroom products for masturbation, but perfumed moisturisers can irritate your vagina and cause bacterial vaginosis (BV). Sex toys should be covered in lube before use.

PMT: Masturbation may help relieve premenstrual syndrome, though some women say that orgasm makes their cramps worse.

Sexercise

AKA
Kegels
Pelvic floor exercises

I put a pillow between my legs, lie on my stomach and squeeze my inner thighs together – therefore I orgasm. I also squeeze my inner thighs, vagina and bum to fall asleep at night. I have a a lot of built-up tension – it's how I release it.
Fiona, 24, UK
Lovenet

Stories abound about women whose pelvic control is so advanced that they can squeeze a penis in their vagina, or shoot ping-pong balls from their vaginas.
Lucy, 36, UK

After reading the G-spot book, I experimented with Kegel exercises and started breathing properly during masturbation. Then one lovely night it happened: a delicious clench from the inside against my G-spot and I was squirting everywhere.
Anon, 26, US
Lovenet

Kegel clenches changed my genital confidence. I am in control of my muscles.
Maryam, 34, UK

Super muscle: In 1952, Dr Arnold Kegel accidentally put his finger on a simple method for increasing genital strength: exercising the pubococcygeus (PC) muscle. During his research into ways of helping incontinent people develop better bladder control, he discovered that his tests on stopping and starting the flow of urine were very beneficial for women with 'waterworks' problems or weak, post-pregnancy, pelvic floor muscles. What Dr. Kegel didn't antici-pate was the number of his patients who found that his exercises had made their vaginal muscles stronger and that, as a result, they were experiencing increased sensations during intercourse. Now the standard antenatal advice is that women do regular pelvic floor exercises (Kegels) before and after childbirth to tone their PC muscle and keep everything honeymoon-fresh. Unfortunately, men don't tend to be given sex tips by their doctors, so many of them don't realise that they have a PC muscle, too, and that by giving it a workout they can increase their penile strength and make sex more enjoyable.

Super strength: If any muscle doesn't get used it loses its strength, and the muscles around the genitals are no different. Regular PC exercises not only help prevent the consequences of poor pelvic muscle tone, such as urinary incontinence and weak erections, but they can also help women and men who have sexual difficulties as a result of surgery in the pelvic region, neurological damage, obesity, constipation or who are unfit. As well as increasing vaginal and penile strength, Kegels increase sensitivity and vaginal lubrication, assist in delaying ejaculation and intensify the sensation of orgasm. And, though it is not proven, many men report that stronger PC contractions increase stimu-lation of the prostate gland, which passes through the muscle.

PC workout for women: The PC muscle is located about 2cm (0.8in) inside the vagina (it feels slightly ribbed) and runs from the tailbone at the back to the pubic bone in the front. To locate it, sit on the toilet, spread your legs and start to pee. Now stop urinating, mid-flow – the muscular sensation that you feel is your PC muscle working. (If you hear someone in the next cubicle having a very erratic pee, you'll know they've read this book as well.) Use this method to find the muscle, but don't use it as a way of exercising it, as doing so can lead to a bladder infection.

And squeeeeeze: Once you have isolated the muscle, insert a finger into your vagina, squeeze and you should be able to feel the contractions pressing around your finger. It can help to use a vibrator for practice, squeezing and contracting against it while it's in the vagina. Try to keep everything else relaxed and don't press down or squeeze your thighs, back, abdominal muscles or stomach. Breathe slowly and deeply to concentrate on isolating the sensation. When you are confident that you are using the correct muscles you can practise the exercises anywhere and at any time.

PC workout for men: The prostate gland and the urethra pass through the PC muscle, which runs from the tailbone up to where the penis attaches to the pubic bone (in animals the PC muscle is the one that wags the tail). Because it connects the front, the back and all the important bits inside, it stands to reason that if you strengthen the PC muscle, you can increase control and sensation in the entire genital area. The best way to locate your PC muscle is to stop your flow of urine in the middle of a pee. This can take some practice and the restart can be messy, but the PC muscle is the only one that allows you to do this. Repeatedly stopping the flow of your urine could eventually cause a bladder infection, so once you have identified the correct sensation you should do some 'dry' practice.

Aaand lift: Try lying comfortably and relaxing the muscles of your thighs, bottom and abdomen. Now tighten and draw in your anus (as if you were trying to hold in a fart) and your urethra (as if trying to hold in a pee) at the same time. It should feel as if you are lifting them up and squeezing from inside. Try to hold the contraction for three seconds and then slowly release it. Repeat the process as many times as you can, making sure that each contraction is strong, slow and controlled.

Exercises for women and men

Short Kegel: Contract the PC muscle as forcefully as possible for one second and release quickly. (Men may be able to feel the penis move up and down slightly with the contraction.) Repeat about 20 times, pausing and relaxing the muscle briefly between each one. The longer you hold the contraction, the stronger the muscles will become. It should feel as if you are lifting your genitals up and squeezing from inside. Try breathing in time with the clenches. Gradually build up to two sessions of 20 a day and gradually increase to six sessions a day over the course of a few weeks.

Long Kegel: Add the long Kegel squeeze exercise to the routine when you are confident with the short Kegel. Instead of holding the squeeze for one second, hold for four and release. Be careful, though, because, like any muscle, the PC can be strained by over-exercise.

To test vaginal strength: Put a slim vibrator in your vagina and see if you can move it in and out using your muscles.

To test penile strength: Put a piece of kitchen roll over your erect penis and see if you can raise and lower it at will. When you have succeeded with kitchen towel, graduate to a face cloth. Don't get too ambitious, though. Anything as heavy as a bath towel might hurt your penis.

I am familiar with Kegels, but have never set out on a routine of daily Kegels. I do believe the exercises can improve sexual experience, however. I know that during intercourse, if I concentrate on tightening my muscles and then releasing, my partner's enjoyment definitely increases.
Tracey, 28, US

I used Kegel exercises after my son was born. I do them now because it has helped keep my sexual energy high. It is also something to do while I am sitting at my desk and no one knows!
Macie, 35, US
Lovenet

I worry about my energy as I fade to grey. Kegel does give me a bit of a lift – every little helps.
Eric, 34, UK

Why don't men get information about this kind of stuff? I am in my mid-50s and suffer from bladder problems and leaks, so what do I do?
Jon, 53, UK

Doing Kegels makes me feel horny.
Lola, 25, Australia

Masturbation for men

AKA
Wanking
Jerk off
Beat off
Polish the bishop
Slap the salami
Pocket billiards
Play the organ

A lot of people consider masturbation a substitute for real sex, or something that you do out of desperation. At JackinWorld we're trying to change that perception. Masturbation is, on its own, an excellent way to learn about your sexuality and enjoy your body's built-in capacity to experience pleasure. It's for this reason that an awful lot of married people and those in long-term relationships masturbate, often in secret or guilt. It doesn't have to be that way. You should never feel guilty, sad or inadequate after you have masturbated. You're only answering the call of nature.
MJ Ecker, US
JackinWorld

The boy can't help it: Sexual arousal in men can occur both consciously and unconsciously. For most men, the ability to become erect is an automatic function, similar to breathing or blinking. But though erection is an involuntary reflex action, it's one that you can influence consciously. You can't choose to make your genitals fill with blood, but you can put yourself in the right frame of mind or situation to encourage an erection.

The boy can't always control it either: Men have an average of three to five unconscious erections during rapid eye movement (REM) sleep each night. Without conscious arousal and physical stimulation these erections won't lead to orgasm, though during puberty, nocturnal erections sometimes lead to the spontaneous emission of semen. This is because one of the functions of ejaculation is to dispose of old sperm so that fresh new sperm can be made, and in the absence of sexual activity this occurs as a 'wet dream'. These emissions gradually become less frequent when adolescents begin to masturbate or have sex. Even so, young men sometimes find themselves with unconscious erections at awkward times and places (the combination of vibrations, eye candy and boredom on public transport is apparently very difficult). In situations such as this, staying put and thinking of something off-putting may be the only option until your erection subsides.

Porn again: Many adolescent boys start masturbating before their bodies are ready to produce semen, so although they experience the sensation of orgasm, they do not actually ejaculate. Boys often use pornography when they masturbate and passing porn around between friends is a fairly common group activity. A blind eye is often turned if teenage boys are found with porn, though the same is not true for girls. Research indicates that men are around four times more likely to have looked at sexually explicit material than women, and generally speaking most – but not all – men are relaxed about using pornography. There's no harm in using it for added stimulation during masturbation, as long as you realise that it won't teach you anything about real sex. The images are contrived for visual effect and are at best fantastically unrealistic and at worst misinformative or offensive. As with anything, you have to maintain a balance and a sense of perspective. Most women just don't, won't or can't do that stuff.

Done in 60 seconds: Though there is nothing wrong with any technique that brings you to orgasm, how you masturbate can sometimes inhibit or limit the pleasure that you experience with a partner. For many men, masturbation is a form of rapid sexual relief, and some men use very rough techniques to make themselves orgasm. Sex with a partner often fails to provide such vigorous stimulation, either through masturbation or penetration, and this can make it harder for a man to maintain his erection and achieve orgasm. Masturbation offers a way of learning about different types and paces of stimulation. Taking the time to experiment with new techniques will help you discover new ways to enjoy yourself and ultimately help you to sustain your erection, delay your ejaculation and enjoy a more intense orgasm.

Techniques

Exploration and variation: When you feel aroused and are reaching for your erection, you can choose to either come quickly or take time out and pay some attention to the rest of your body. Sometimes a quickie is all that is required and it is difficult to ignore your genital hydraulics, but avoiding the obvious will add enormously to the intensity of the experience. Try stroking your inner and upper arms, your armpits, the back of your neck and your nipples. Use the back and front of your fingers, stroke your inner thighs, starting just above your knees and moving up to your scrotum, perineum and anus. Then, finally, when you can't stand it anymore, move to your penis. Experiment with your grip, making it tight or relaxed; use alternate hands, or both hands together or reverse your grip. You will really feel a difference in the sensations if you vary the tempo of your stroke, too: speed it up or slow it down.

Forehand grip: Wrap your fingers around the shaft of your penis with your thumb at the head. As your fist strokes your penis up and down, your thumb will stimulate its coronal ridge. Alternatively, try holding your penis as if you are holding a pen with your fingers stroking up and down the frenulum.

Backhand grip: This is the reverse of the forehand grip. Twist your wrist to the opposite of a forehand grip – your thumb will now be underneath your penis and your fingers will be on its head. If you always masturbate with your right hand, try using a backhand grip with your left hand for a change to experience a different sensation.

Dummy hand: Sit on your hand until it feels completely numb or alternatively, chill it in cold water to get the same effect. When you masturbate, it will feel as if someone else (with a very cold hand) is doing it to you.

Luckily my older brother showed me the way. I had no idea what was going on for quite a few years, my techniques were fairly basic, then I discovered lubricant and nirvana!
Simon, 27, UK

When I had to provide a tube of sperm for my IVF treatment, I masturbated with a magazine full of hot images. Fantasy always helps me when I am alone, it's a necessary tool and there is nothing to be ashamed of – it's not a question of being politically correct.
David, 36, UK

I use ice cream in a condom or chopped liver. I love the feeling it gives me – very sexy.
Justin, 32, UK

I am a young man with thalidomide fins. I masturbate with my feet but I tell you one thing, hands are better!
Bob, 29, UK

I use a long fake pearl necklace around my shaft. I manually stimulate my penis over the pearls and massage up and down.
Jasper, 46, UK

Twist: Lubricate your hand well and make a fist around your penis. Move slowly up the shaft until you reach its head. Now turn your hand over to form a backhand grip, keeping in contact with the head the whole time, and begin back down the shaft, using varying speeds for the best results. Alternatively, hold the head of your penis with your fingers and twist it gently, first to the left and then to the right – as if you are opening and closing the lid of a jar.

Fist: Anchor your penis with one hand and form a fist above it with the other. Push your penis into your static fist by using pelvic thrusts, penetrating it as far as you can to simulate the experience of vaginal penetration. Using plenty of lubrication enhances the sensations.

Leg thrust: Lie on your side, spread your legs and push your knees up close to your body. Leave one knee down and raise your other knee up, keeping your foot flat on the ground. Grip the head of your penis and hold it against the leg that is on the ground. Now move your upright leg down towards your stationery leg and back up again. Your penis should slide slowly and gently in and out of your hand. The faster you move your leg the more quickly you will come to orgasm.

Rubbing: Lie on your stomach in bed and rub your penis against the mattress. Variations on this technique include putting a pillow between your stomach and your erection and rubbing your penis against the sheet (under the pillow). Placing your penis in a fur-lined glove or even a sock also feels good. Alternatively, put some material – silk, cotton, satin or leather, for example – over the tip of your erection. Hold your penis with one hand and put your other hand on top of the material. Then rub the tip of your penis through the fabric against the palm of your hand. But take care – rubbing against fabric can cause abrasions.

Water: Slowly trickle warm – not hot – water onto your penis while masturbating using the fist method. The contrast in temperature between the water and your penis can be very stimulating.

Simultaneous stimulation of the balls, perineum and anus: The scrotum and perineum can be massaged, rubbed and fondled while you masturbate at the same time. Cup your balls gently in your hand and tug them. You will feel them become harder as you come close to orgasm. Try stroking or rubbing the area between your scrotum and your anus while

you masturbate. The opening of the anus has a high concentration of nerve endings and stimulating them can also increase sexual arousal. Lie on your side for comfortable access, lubricate your finger well and massage the area gently. If you want to stimulate your prostate gland as well, you may find it easier to use your thumb instead.

Prostate stimulation: If you haven't yet discovered your prostate gland, it is worth trying to find it when you masturbate. Some men enjoy prostate massage so much that they can orgasm by this method alone. Put your thumb inside your anus when you are fully aroused and close to orgasm. You should be able to feel a soft, fleshy, swollen area about the size of a walnut. Pressing it can make it feel as if you are masturbating yourself internally. Before orgasm, the prostate gland fills with fluid and the sphincter muscles of your anus contract around your thumb as you climax. It's pretty awkward to keep pressure on your prostate while working your penis at the same time, but if you are keen on the sensation, you may want to invest in a prostate massage sex toy.

Catch your own come: Curious about what it feels like to be ejaculated over? Simulate the experience by doing a shoulder stand while you masturbate. Lie down with your head close to a wall and kick your legs up so that you are resting on your shoulders. Press your feet against the wall for balance so that you can use either one or two hands to stimulate your penis. When you feel close to orgasm, try to line up your mouth with your line of fire. Don't let the semen get in your eyes, because it can sting.

Auto fellatio: If you are really keen to try this, take up yoga first. It is estimated that only around three men in every thousand are capable of doing it because you need a longer than average penis and great spinal flexibility. The mouth has an even higher concentration of nerve endings than the erect penis, so the multiple sensations of feeling and tasting your own orgasm are described as amazing by men who have been successful. Even so, it can be very dangerous to try auto fellatio, because of the risk of causing serious back damage.

Techniques to prolong erection and delay orgasm

Squeeze-release: When approaching orgasm, place your penis in between your thumb and your index and middle fingers and squeeze it for 30 seconds. Then let go and continue masturbating.

Stop-go: Masturbate until you are close to climax. Stop and wait until you start to lose your erection, then start masturbating again. Keep repeating this procedure until you decide to come. It takes considerable will-power to master this technique, but it can help control premature ejaculation and may also intensify your orgasm.

Using sex toys

Vibrators are not just for girls: It can feel great to rub them over the shaft, head and ridge of your penis or around your scrotum, perineum and anal rim. Wrap your vibrator in a cloth – a piece of silk or cotton – to diffuse vibrations that are too intense. Try holding the vibrator against your penis between your clasped hands while you masturbate. For anal stimulation, either poise the vibrator at the rim or gently insert it into the anus. Make sure it has a flared base to prevent it being sucked into the rectum.

Toys are us: Anal beads are attached to a string, like a necklace. They can be inserted into the anus and then, on the point of orgasm, slowly removed, one bead at a time. (If you remove them too quickly you may lose bowel control, which could be messy.) Butt plugs fill the rectum and are gripped by the sphincter muscles of the anus. Shaft sleeves are like finger puppets that slip over individual fingers or around the base of your penis. They come in a variety of textures to add variety to masturbation. Cock rings slide over the penis and sit at its base, wrapping around the shaft and the balls. The ring stops blood draining out of the penis and creates a feeling of fullness. (Always use an adjustable cock ring that snaps open.) Rubber and plastic dolls vary in price, quality and aesthetics. The most sophisticated versions are very realistic – and expensive – and have electric motors that make the pelvic area move. Rubber vaginas and anuses are also available. Very 21st century.

Things your mother should have told you

Wear rubber gloves: Wearing a latex glove while you masturbate feels fabulous and the slightly medical aspect is quite sexy. Using a condom feels similar and it's a good way of getting used to putting them on and wearing them during sex.

Wet or dry, sir?: Artificial lubricant can enhance the experience, though some men (particularly Africans) find a dry sensation more pleasurable.

It is a challenge sometimes to get it up and keep it up, and it takes more to stimulate me from the start than it used to. I have been told that I need to practise lengthening my stimulation time – up to 30 minutes without ejaculation.
Eric, 52, US

212
Sex Toys

I did have a few attempts at recreating a female vagina using plastic gloves and condoms, though not too successfully.
Kyle, 34, UK

Self-love is a great evening in. I recently tried out a small vibrator, running it up and down my shaft with a butt plug inserted in my anus. Once I got past all the fiddling around and settled into it, I had a strong, hard orgasm.
Bill, 36, UK

78
Lubrication

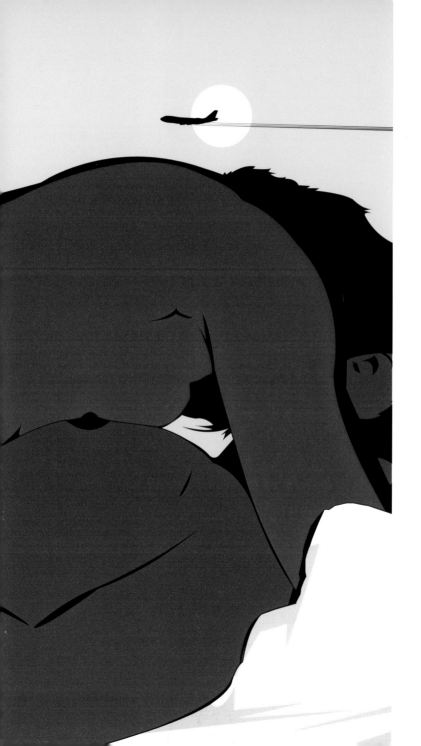

SEX

On the surface, sex is first and foremost about physical pleasure. However, sex with an emotional experience is sort of the icing on the cake. And since sex, in some ways, is an extremely awkward, strange activity, an emotional bond makes it all the less embarrassing.

Anya, 18, Canada Kuma2

Sex

Sex without love
is just a fuck.
Kimberly, 40, US
Kuma2

For great sex, it's
important to
acknowledge every
feeling and emotion
involved, so that
you're making love
with your whole
being, as opposed to
just your genitals.
Jade, US
Porn actress

I am not so conscious
of techniques. I
haven't formalised
them – I just drift in
a direction.
Lara, 42, UK

The most intimate
sex is plain vanilla
making love. Funny,
isn't it. When all the
games are aside, the
honesty and sheer
emotional tidal wave
can be daunting.
Enola, 34, US
Lovenet

Sex to me is
something you have
with somebody that
you don't love.
Kasha, 22, UK
Rainbow Network

I have had terrible
sex in the most
perfect surroundings
and great sex in
complete dumps.
It's all about who you
are with and if the
chemistry isn't there
it's not worth it.
Lucy, 28, UK

When it comes to sex, consider two things. First, there is no such thing as 'normal' and, second, sex doesn't always come 'naturally'. Practice helps. Confidence helps more.

Sex is something that (usually) happens between two people. It is a private and exclusive experience and not something you can gauge by anyone else's standards, or anyone else's experience. In other aspects of life we can judge our abilities by accepted standards – but sex is a level playing field. There is no 'ideal' model to conform to, and as we're unlikely to see how anyone else does it in real life, it's impossible to know if we are any good.

Sex is multidimensional: a mixture of chemistry, mechanics, mood and emotion. It is different for everyone and with everyone, which is why there is almost no point being expert at sex. Each time you have sex there is the potential to have a completely different experience. There are endless ways to give and receive sexual pleasure, but technical skills, positions and tricks are never as important as the people involved. The sex you have is determined by how you feel about yourself and how you feel about the person you are with. Naturally this applies to your partner, too.

Sex does not have to be meaningful, but it will always have meaning. Sex doesn't have to have anything to do with love, but you should love what you are doing. Make sure that your feelings define your actions: i.e. I will give you a blow job because I want to. Try not to let your actions define your feelings, as in: I am giving you a blow job, but I don't want to and I will probably resent it afterwards, especially if you fall asleep.

It may be helpful to think about sex in terms of mirrors. For every action there is a corresponding response. Enthusiastic loving is reciprocated enthusiastically. Apathy and disinterest? Well, who can be bothered? Inhibition or feelings of inadequacy often have parallels too, so don't be afraid to be honest. Having the confidence and the good humour to embrace the imperfections of sex will ensure that you and your partner don't take any baggage to bed with you.

The more informed you are about sex, the better your sexual choices will be. Knowing what turns you on (and how) guarantees you better sex. And understanding the risks will ensure you practise safer sex. Good sex is not just about the immediate experience, it's about feeling comfortable with what you have done and who you have done it with.

Kissing

Different strokes for different folks: Throughout history, different cultures have chosen different ways to kiss. The Eskimo kiss, which involves gently rubbing noses, originated in Iceland, while French kissing gets its name from its European roots. North American Indians press motionless lips to the cheek, and in India and Saudi Arabia some people kiss their palms and then press them to their partner's forehead. Ancient Chinese erotica links the upper lip of a woman's mouth to her clitoris, and the lower lip of a man's mouth to his penis.

Speaking in tongues: Europeans greet each other with a kiss to both cheeks. Worshippers kiss religious icons and statues. Chivalrous gentlemen kiss ladies' hands. Glamorous people air kiss and never touch. School girls blow kisses across the classroom. Ancient relatives give children sloppy kisses and 'too tight' hugs. Babies put their fingers and hands inside the mouth of anyone who kisses them. Sometimes friends kiss as a form of affection, only to discover a spark of sexual electricity that they didn't realise was there. Lovers kiss using their lips and tongues as an expression of romantic or sexual intimacy. Kissing can express as many feelings and intentions as using words. It can be soft, slow, tender, passive, aggressive, demanding or urgent.

The first time: A kiss is usually the very first sexual experience and in time it may become the bridge to further forms of sexual interaction (though kissing doesn't automatically mean you consent to them). A first kiss can feel awkward. A new partner may seem unfamiliar and strange if you are used to kissing someone else. There is no such thing as the perfect kiss (or, indeed, the perfect kisser) and it can take a little time to get to know each other orally. If a first kiss feels good, it can be a significant turning point in a relationship. But a kiss can also reveal a lack of chemistry. Poor technique and bad breath have put the brakes on many a budding sexual liaison, when confidence and a toothbrush were all that was required.

The sixth sense: We seem to know intuitively when someone is about to kiss us and the act of kissing involves all the senses simultaneously. When we feel a kiss is coming our bodies respond physically. Our lips swell, darken in colour and congest with blood, just as the genitals do. This heightens sensation in the lips' nerve endings and makes kissing and lip-touch more pleasurable. We often lick our lips before a kiss, making them wet, shiny and kissable. The tongue is soft, strong, wet and agile, and it allows us to probe and explore the soft, wet lining of our partner's mouth.

AKA
Snogging
Getting off with
Tongue sandwich
Giving a smacker
Frenchy
Tonsil hockey

My sexiest kiss happened on a wet and muddy football pitch. I had collapsed after scoring a winning goal. That girl and I went on to live together for four years. It genuinely started with a kiss.
Jayne, 30+, UK
Rainbow Network

My first kiss was pretty horrific. I was 11 and he was 13. He stared into my eyes passionately, then he said 'hang on' and spat his plate-brace into his hand. It had a bit of chewed-up food on it. I went ahead with the kiss, but I felt very sick.
Tally, 26, UK

Kissing is the most intimate part of sex for me. I don't ever allow any of my clients to go above the neck. It is always out of bounds.
Lilla, 29, US
Moonlite Bunny Ranch

The worst kiss I ever had was when this woman bit my lips.
Paul, 22, UK

Practice makes perfect: No one is born with an innate ability to deliver a mind-blowing kiss, but you can practise. Try out your technique on your arm, some soft fruit or your friends – if they will let you.

Making the first move: Avoid potential embarrassment by keeping your tongue in your own mouth until it's clear that you are invited in to someone else's. Avoid noses getting in the way by tilting your head about 25 degrees in the opposite direction to your partner (most people seem to instinctively tilt to the right). If you have a crash of noses or teeth, just laugh it off.

Eyes wide shut: Before a kiss, keep your eyes open and look into your partner's eyes. Once your lips connect, shut your eyes. This helps you to focus on the sensation – and anyway staring into space while you are engaged in such an intimate activity can be a little unsettling for your partner. Glasses can get steamed up, and sometimes they get in the way, but make sure you are guaranteed a kiss before you remove them. Taking them off in anticipation might be interpreted as a little forward.

Bad breath: Bad breath, or halitosis, is most often caused by bacteria that live on the tongue and is aggravated by drinking alcohol, eating, smoking and some medications. To find out if your breath smells, lick the back of your hand and smell it. To ensure fresh breath, brush and floss regularly. Clean your tongue with a tongue scraper or toothbrush – especially at the back – and use a commercial mouthwash. If you can't brush after eating, use a fresh breath spray or chew sugarless gum. Drinking plenty of water keeps your mouth moist and encourages saliva production.

Dental braces: These days, braces are pretty compact and shouldn't affect kissing, though they can make people feel less self-confident. Mouth hygiene is more critical with braces, particularly with 'train tracks', so clean your teeth frequently to ensure that they are food-free. There is a slight possibility of tongue grazing if you are kissing very aggressively, but there are no known cases of train tracks getting stuck together during a kiss.

False teeth: Kissing while wearing false teeth is no different from kissing with your own teeth, as long as the teeth are clean and well fitting. People with false teeth may actually enjoy kissing without having their teeth in. It makes the entire mouth into a soft, wet, smooth orifice that also makes for great oral sex.

Techniques

Butterfly kiss: Fluttering your eyelashes against your partner's face has a certain cute novelty value, though too much of it could get annoying.

Lip brushing: Brush your lips lightly and softly like a feather against your partner's lips, keeping your mouth slightly open. Trace your tongue round them and gently suck and nibble the upper and lower lips individually.

Soft little kisses: These are very affectionate, especially on the eyelids, the ears, the nape of the neck and the collar bone. They can be combined with light licking or rubbing of noses and feel nicer with dry lips.

French kissing: Gently use your tongue to part your partner's lips. If the mouth opens a little it probably means that your tongue is welcome. Find the tip of your partner's tongue and play with it. Circle it and suck its whole length like an ice lolly. Use your tongue to explore the underside of your partner's tongue as well as the gums and teeth. Your movements will probably mirror those of your partner.

Deep tongue: Purse your lips in a firm 'O' and suck your partner's tongue through your lips to the back of your throat (your whole mouth will almost be inside your partner's). Release the tongue and then suck it back in. It should be moved back and forth, as if simulating fellatio. Take turns being the passive one.

Rainbow kiss: Kissing with period blood in your mouth is probably an acquired taste (and there's a risk of contracting a blood-borne infection).

Snowball: Passing a mouthful of sperm to your partner after a blow job.

Kissing games: Traditionally thought of as reserved for the pre-teens, adults are now rediscovering games such as spin the bottle. People sit in a circle and take it in turns to spin a bottle in the centre. When the bottle settles, the spinner has to kiss the person it is pointing at.

Tasty kisses: Combine different tastes with kissing. Try salting your lips or dusting them in icing sugar or cocoa powder. Pass liquids or foods from mouth to mouth – try champagne, ice cubes, strawberries, ice cream, tinned peaches in syrup or lemon sherbet. Like the lining of the mouth,

---

Kissing should be soft and sensual. Your kiss should let the person know how much you enjoy their touch and the feel of their lips on yours.
De-Vona, 22, US

Don't kiss my face. Do suck on my lips. Don't leave your mouth as a wide gaping hole. Do pull me to you. Eyes shut nice, eyes open nicer.
Lovesponge, 26, US
Kuma2

A kiss is halfway between the mind and the body.
Ned, 32, UK

This guy just stuck his tongue right in and didn't move. Gross.
Paula, 28, Australia

It's that moment where you are both looking at each other and knowing that you are going to kiss for the first time, but not wanting to make the first move. The first kiss is such a sexy thing. You never get that back.
Tania, 34, UK

I met my future husband when I had to kiss him as a dare during a drunken game of spin the bottle aged 26.
Lisa, 28, New Zealand

oysters and caviar have a soft, wet texture and are believed to have aphro-disiac qualities. Take one end each of an asparagus spear and eat your way towards each other, meeting with a kiss. Kiss your partner's body and taste the natural salts on the skin. The easiest way to do this is to kiss under the armpits.

Love bites: Love bites are worn proudly by some adolescents as a sort of trophy. They are usually received on the neck, but you can leave love bites in less obvious places, such as the bottom or breasts. To make your mark, put your semi-open mouth against your partner's skin. Suck the flesh up forcefully through your teeth to create a vacuum. The mark of your mouth will be imprinted onto your partner's skin because the force of the suck draws blood to the surface, creating a bruise. Love bites usually last for a few days but if you want to get rid of them quickly, Vitamin E or arnica cream can be rubbed into the redness to accelerate the healing process. Alternatively, try rubbing in a squirt of toothpaste or using foundation cream to cover them.

Things your mother should have told you

Cold sores and infections: You shouldn't kiss someone who has cold sores (oral herpes) if you don't want to get one too. They are very infec-tious (over 45 per cent of people have had a cold sore by the time they are 18). Though kissing is essentially a safer sex activity, colds, hepatitis B, oral thrush and other infections can pass via the mouth. If someone who has a cold sore performs oral sex on their partner, the herpes virus can be passed on, and this can cause genital herpes.

Infectious mononucleosis: Often called 'mono', 'the kissing disease' or 'glandular fever', this is a viral infection found in saliva and it is usually transmitted by kissing. Symptoms are similar to those of a cold: fever, a sore throat, headaches, white patches on the back of the throat, swollen glands, fatigue and loss of appetite. Symptoms develop within four to seven weeks and last about seven weeks. Diagnosed by a blood test, this is a viral rather than a bacterial infection, so antibiotics won't cure it. Mono usually goes away on its own and should be treated in the same way as flu: rest, lots of fluid, paracetamol (tylenol) and gargling with salt water or sucking lozenges if you have a sore throat. Generally, people only get mono once and it usually affects 15- to 35-year-olds. If the symptoms don't clear up, see your doctor, as there are sometimes complications.

Kissing always starts the lovemaking session. I unbutton her blouse, massage, kiss and suck the breasts and nipples. I also blow on the nipples. I kiss the arms, suck the neck, trail my tongue down to the legs and kiss the secret spot – but not for long.
Fanny, 26, US

I have been told I am a great kisser, probably because I have those full, African Nubian lips.
Rebecca, 26, UK
Kuma2

I find kissing a real problem. It's more intimate than full sex, and I feel very naked face-to-face.
Dave, 33, Ireland

I think the type of kiss she gives me shows me how far she intends to go with me sexually.
Jennifer, 32, UK

I hate men who make a noise when they kiss. If they sigh or grunt it really turns me off.
Fusspot, 28, US

Touching

Aaah: Touch is a basic human need, a fundamental requirement from infancy to death. We all need to be touched with tenderness and affection from time to time. Touch is an emotive and sensual form of communication. When people are upset we put our arms around them or hold their hands, when people are ill we stroke their foreheads and when we are happy and excited we hug each other.

Ouch: Touch is the only type of stimulation that can elicit a response from the body through a spinal reflex, which does not involve the brain. This reflex action is necessary for survival. Accidentally touch a hot stove and you jerk your hand away immediately before you are badly burned. If you had to think before acting, you might be more severely hurt. Some men and women who have spinal cord injuries that prevent impulses from reaching their brains find that their bodies still show some physical manifestations of arousal (including erection and lubrication) because spinal reflexes are still present.

Goose-pimples: Physical contact is one of the sparks that triggers sexual possibility. It's the chemical frisson that sends shivers down your spine – the nipple-chilling electric tingle that activates the senses and heightens sexual anticipation. Lovers squeeze, stroke, tickle, scratch and rub as they get to know the intimate landscape of their partner's body. But while touch is so important at the beginning of a relationship, it is often neglected later on. It seems that the longer people are together, the more they forget just how good it feels to touch and be touched. Holding hands, neck rubs or running your fingers through each other's hair are simple everyday reminders of the physical bond between the two of you.

Up a bit: Rubbing, stroking, massaging or back-scratching can be a really useful way of helping a stressed-out, anxious partner to unwind. It takes away any immediate pressure to perform or respond sexually and helps men and women who have difficulty becoming aroused to relax and go at their own pace. Some skin areas are more sensitive to touch than others, and these are known as erogenous zones. There are two types:

Non-specific erogenous zones: This term describes the inner thighs, armpits, shoulders, back, feet, ears and the sides and back of the neck (generally, all skin other than genitals, anus, nipples, lips and breasts). These areas contain a normal density of nerve endings and hair follicles, but it can still be highly arousing for them to be touched.

Specific erogenous zones: These include the genital regions (the penis, clitoris, vulva and perineum), the lips, breasts and buttocks. The nerve endings here are much more numerous, and they are more sensitive to stimulation because they are closer to the skin's surface. This means they have greater potential for causing arousal. It makes sense – if you touch a man's penis and balls, he is very likely to get an erection. If you touch a woman's labia and clitoris, she is quite likely to feel sexually aroused.

Techniques

Head massage: To relax your partner, apply very gentle pressure to the area at the base of the skull on either side of the hollow spot (the occipital ridge). Keep your thumbs pressed there and use your fingers to rub back and forth through the hair and on the scalp. Then, keeping your fingers to the sides of the head, run your thumbs gently down from the base of the skull to the back of the shoulders. Pressing gently against the sides of the temple at eye level can also relieve tension.

The ears: Licking your partner's ears will make them tickle, as the sound of your breath is amplified in the auditory canal. Use fingers and lips to massage and nibble ears and ear lobes.

The feet and toes: These are often ignored, but paying them some attention with a foot massage or a pedicure can be erotic. Prepare the feet by washing them and patting them dry. With both thumbs (the best digits for foot massages) make small circular strokes from the heel to the toe. Place your thumbs at the centre of the soles of the feet and stroke firmly outwards across the balls of the feet. The big toe is very sensitive and oral stimulation on clean feet feels great.

The legs: Massaging the backs of the knees and the inner thighs can be very sexually stimulating as a precursor to genital massage.

Sexy bits: Instead of focusing on the penis and the vulva straight away, massage lubricant into the perineum, the pubis, the nipples, the root of the penis and between the buttocks. Older women who produce less natural lubrication may be more relaxed about penetration if their genitals have been massaged and lubricated. Men who have difficulty maintaining an erection will find that massage can make their erection firmer. Buttock massage can also make people more receptive to anal play.

Try using your body to rub up against him from behind. Like this, he will feel the extra sensation of you rubbing your breasts on his back, while you massage him with your hands.
Delia, UK
Porn actress

There is a relationship between the hamstring muscles and the groin, so rub the backs of his legs deeply, continuing upwards until you get into the pelvis area, and then stroke the perineum.
Syren, US
Porn actress

Give me an ear and I'll give you the world.
Jasper, 52, UK

I love to massage my husband with my DD breasts. He tells me they feel like dough balls and it sends him over the edge. I always know what to do to calm him down.
Camilla, 46, UK

When running your hands over his skin, try lifting them off his body occasionally. This can be very titillating for him, as he won't know where you're going to touch him next.
Janet, 66, UK

Breasts, nipples and pearl necklaces

AKA
Boobs
Melons
Bumpers
Knockers
Shock-absorbers
Tits
Bristols

My breasts are hot erogenous zones for me. When my partners tug on my nipples with their lips and draw their nails around the sides, stare into my eyes and kiss me deeply, I can go into orbit.
Karise, 21, US
Lovenet

I like how my nipples look when they are hard. Also, I like my lover to circle them with his mouth and hands, starting softly, then rougher as I get more stimulated. My boyfriend says I like nipple clamps and hot wax (which is not far from the truth).
Greenhoney, 27, US
Lovenet

I am not stimulated by touching in my breast area. In fact, it's a bit irritating.
DK, 42, US
Lovenet

I fantasise about having my nipples and clitoris pierced and having a chain linking the two.
Dreamer, 37, Sweden

Form and function: Human females are the only primates that have breasts that protrude even when they are not pregnant or breastfeeding. As human females evolved, big breasts came to be considered an asset for survival. Although size is in fact irrelevant in terms of how much milk a woman can make, it may have been interpreted as a sign of stored fat, which meant that if food was scarce, a female would still be able to nourish her child.

The fact that breasts provide both baby food and adult entertainment means that they send a pretty mixed-up emotional message. More recently, fashion, politics and a desire for structural support have meant that in Western cultures, naked breasts have disappeared from public view. However, this only seems to have increased their desirability. In tribes in which custom dictates that the breasts are left exposed, they have no sexual significance at all, yet here in the West, the flash of a celebrity's bra is guaranteed to grab the headlines.

The cover up: Wrapping the breasts in some form of fabric has been going on in some shape or form since about 2000BC, but the 'over-the-shoulder-boulder-holder', as we know it wasn't patented until 1914, when the Warner Brothers Corset Company introduced the alphabet cup size system that is still in operation today. Bra sizes can be a bit of a mystery for the uninitiated – for example, a 42AA bra sounds huge but actually the the '42' relates to the size of the woman's back (large) and the 'AA' relates to the size of her breasts (small).

Nipple stimulation: Men and women have varying nipple sensitivity, but both sexes have a tendency to ignore nipples during sexual play. Some people find that one nipple is more sensitive than the other, though with touch and stimulation it is possible to heighten sensation anywhere on your body. Some women and men find that stimulating their own breasts and nipples during solo sex helps heighten sensations. Like the penis and the vulva, nipples contain erectile tissue that swells when aroused or stimulated. The base of the erectile tissue is buried in the soft tissue of the breast, so to make a nipple stick out, place your fingers on either side of it, push down gently and then slide your fingers apart over the breast.

Peanut smuggling: Because nipples are often visible through clothing, their erection is often interpreted as a sign of arousal – though it could simply mean that you need to turn the heating on. Nipple responses vary

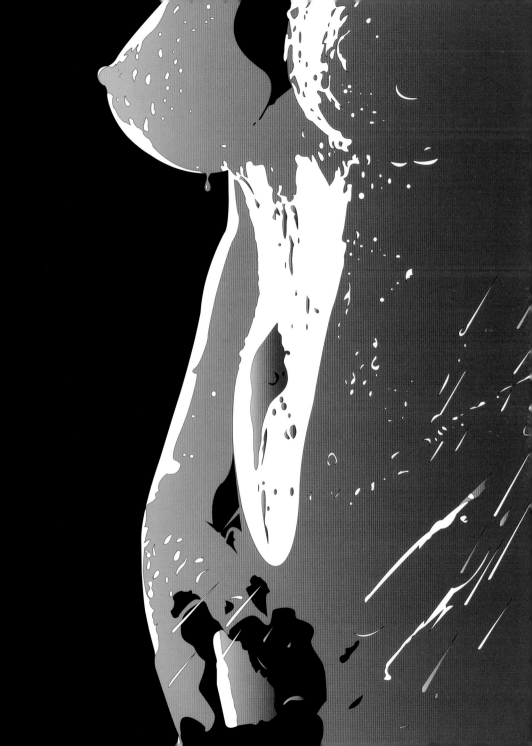

Brushing up against them with your tongue is good. Hot breath is nice too. A soft, slow tongue can twiddle at the base of the nipple, flickering there with a wet tongue until the nipple is erect and then you continue to suck and devour it like it is the most precious thing in the world.
Rebecca, 26, US
Kuma2

Start by kissing them both all over. Then circle one with your tongue, starting on the outsides of the areolae and working your way to the nipple. Once you are at the nipple, secure it between your teeth and flick it with your tongue – soft and fast. Repeat on the other breast. You can also bring both breasts together and lick them alternately.
Winnie, 32, US
Kuma2

I like my nipples being sucked and bitten quite hard during foreplay – the pain-pleasure threshold and all that.
Dennis, 30, UK

I don't like implants, I only like real women.
Aurora, 18, US

from person to person, but most men and women enjoy having their breasts and nipples fondled, tweaked, sucked and stroked during sex. With a partner, oral is often better than manual stimulation. Saliva or any lubrication makes the sensation smoother and more sensual. Though nipples may not respond at first, during full sexual arousal they become much more physically alert. In fact, stimulating your partner's nipples near orgasm will often boost arousal, making climax feel more intense.

The areola: The area around the nipple, which can be any shade of chocolate or pink (though it becomes darker during pregnancy), is packed with nerve endings and covered in tiny hair follicles that are particularly sensitive – sometimes more so than the nipple. During pregnancy, the nipples and areolae shouldn't be washed with soap in case it affects the small bumpy glands (Montgomery's tubercles) that appear at that time; they secrete a lubricant that moisturises and protects against infection.

Beards: Because the skin on the nipples is relatively delicate and thin, it's a good idea for men with rough facial hair to shave before oral stimulation. Stubble can be quite abrasive, though longer beards tend to be softer.

Techniques

Nipple tweak: Slide your hand over the breast so that your thumb and index finger encircle the nipple. Use the nipple as the axis and slowly twist the breast in a gentle clockwise and anticlockwise direction, being careful not to put too much tension on it. The nipples are so sensitive that any form of touch or movement will heighten arousal.

Tease and squeeze: Apply saliva or artificial lubricant to the breasts and tease the nipples by rubbing and squeezing them gently between the fingers. Push them softly into the breast and pull them out gently. Burrow your face between her breasts. Alternate between massaging them into your face and using your mouth to lick and suck the breasts and nipples.

Tongue: Take the breast into your mouth, wet the nipples with saliva and softly suck, lick and blow on them. Cup the breasts from underneath to support them. Gently hold the nipple between your teeth and flick your tongue back and forth quite fast over the tip, pausing and then building up speed again.

Thermals: Rub an ice cube over your nipples to make them stand up. When the nipples feel cold, put your warm mouth over them and suck and lick them until they are warm.

Pearl necklace: Place the breasts either side of the penis, squeeze them together and simultaneously massage the breasts, the shaft and head of the penis. When a man ejaculates between a woman's breasts and the semen spurts out, the white splashes around her neck and collar bone are known as a 'pearl necklace'.

Camping supplies: Snakebite kits are available from sex shops or over the Internet. They include a suction cup that can be used to pull the nipple and enhance nipple sensitivity.

Toys: Clamps with tweezers or screws can be tightened to enhance pleasure or pain. They allow 'hands-free' sustained sensation. Women with breast implants or cysts in their breasts should consult with their surgeon before using clamps.

Things your mother should have told you

Booby traps: Breast and nipple sensitivity can change if breast size has been increased or reduced through surgery. Even though breast surgery is now a relatively straightforward procedure, there are risks and uncertainties with any surgery. Occasionally, the result is temporary numbness or full loss of sensation, particularly if there is any accidental nerve damage. While most breast reductions are carried out because breast size is negatively affecting a woman's quality of life, breast enlargements are often performed for purely cosmetic purposes. For many women, breast augmentation brings new-found confidence, and with it heightened sexuality and increased breast sensitivity. Whether women who have breast enlargements are doing it for themselves or because of a desire to conform to some female ideal is anyone's guess. The image of perfect, large breasts is pervasive, despite the fact that most women don't have a 'chestal area' that fits the template. The media don't seem to differentiate between real or fake, as long as they are big. It's not surprising that 16-year-old girls beg their parents for big breasts if you think of the images that surround them. Big breasts make you rich (Anna Nicole Smith), famous (Jordan), get you into parliament (La Ciccolina) and into the papers (Britney Spears). For a young, girl DD cups can seem as important as A-grades.

Nibble and suck from the outside in, but leave the nipple for later. Move on to another area, then return to the breast. When you eventually stimulate the nipple she'll love it.
Julian, 27, UK

I like my lover to ejaculate over my chest and massage his sperm into my breasts and nipples.
Olga, 36, Holland

/ 212 \
Sex Toys

I am definitely a breast man and when my partner's breasts expanded two cup sizes during pregnancy I thought I had died and gone to heaven.
Larry, 40, UK

There is something about having a man at your breasts. He reverts to being a child. It is so sexy to have that power momentarily.
Mercedes, 41, UK

I know everyone talks about men's fixation with mammaries, which is supposed to be from breast-feeding. Well, actually it's true for me.
Dan, 22, UK

Lubrication (lubes)

Natural lubrication: There is a prevailing notion (another myth derived from porn movies) that women who are horny are wet, ready and dripping with vaginal juices. In fact, even if a woman produces plenty of vaginal secretions, they may not descend through the vaginal canal and reach the vulva, so additional lubrication may still be required for easy penetration. Lubrication makes intercourse more pleasurable and comfortable for both women and men, though in women it shouldn't be a substitute for lack of arousal. A lack of lubrication might mean that a woman may benefit from more clitoral stimulation, but it doesn't necessarily mean that she is not aroused. Lubrication dries out quickly, so a woman who is wet one minute may be dry the next, especially after orgasm. If penetration goes on for a long time, and lubrication begins to dry, it can cause irritation and soreness. Too much friction is not just uncomfortable – it can lead to bladder or vaginal infections and it can tear condoms too.

The amount of lubrication a woman produces can vary throughout the menstrual cycle and stages of life. Lower levels of oestrogen during the menopause, after giving birth or while breastfeeding can cause a decrease in natural lubrication. Alcohol, stress, tiredness, some medications, such as antihistamines, and drugs, such as cannabis, using sex toys and using condoms may also be factors.

Saliva is a natural lubricant, but it dries out quickly when exposed to air, so keep a non-alcoholic drink handy to wet your mouth. Preseminal fluid from the penis is the only natural lubrication produced by men. The anus doesn't make any lubrication at all, so for anal play you need to use artificial lubricant.

Artificial lubrication: There are water-based lubes for anal and vaginal play and penetration, flavoured lubes for oral sex, lubes for underwater and special lubes for people with ingredient allergies. The ingredients in all of them differ, and they all have their own merits. Knowing how to read the label is probably the most important part of making your choice. Some people also use household items, such as moisturiser, butter, olive oil and vaseline, but you need to remember that anything that is oil based (including some commercial lubricants) can damage a condom and make it unsafe. Test any new products for allergy by applying a small amount to your arm before putting them on your genitals. A little lube in the tip of a condom adds extra slip and slide that can increase some mens' pleasure (though too much can make the condom slip off). Use water- or silicone-based lubes, unless you are using plastic condoms (femidoms). Lubes can feel cold when they touch your skin, but you can warm them up by rubbing them between your hands, or running the tube under a hot tap.

Water-based lubricants: Typically the main ingredients are de-ionised water and glycerine. These are great for any kind of penetrative sex and foreplay and are the only lubes that are safe to use with condoms. Plain water-based lubes taste slightly sweet and so are suitable for oral sex. These are more easily absorbed, are less irritating to the delicate tissues in and around the genitals and rinse away easily with plain water. They dry up quickly and have a tendency to get a bit sticky, but adding water reactivates them.

Silicone-based lubricants: These are very similar to water-based lubes but are completely waterproof, which means they are more difficult to wash off. They last longer than water-based lubes and don't need to be replenished as often. They are safe to use with condoms, diaphragms and other latex barriers, but they will erode silicone sex toys.

Petroleum-based lubricants: These are easily available and good for male masturbation and anal play. They last longer, but they should never be used with any latex products such as condoms, diaphragms and cervical caps, because they are oil-based and may erode latex. They may also damage sex toys, leave stains and are difficult to wash off.

Oil-based lubricants: Usually made from natural products such as butter, vegetable and nut oils, oil-based lubes are good for use with dildos and for anal penetration, but they must not be used with latex products such as condoms, diaphragms and cervical caps, because oil erodes latex. They stain easily and are difficult to wash off the skin.

Flavoured lubes: Flavoured lubes that contain sucrose are not suitable for penetration because sucrose can cause yeast infections. Newer versions that use artificial sweeteners may be more acceptable.

Benzocaine: Some lubes contain benzocaine, which has a numbing effect. They are mainly used for anal sex, but pain is your body's way of telling you that you might be damaging yourself, so benzocaine increases the risk of injury. Also, numbing sensations can reduce pleasure.

Glycerine: This is the most common ingredient in lubricant and is chemically very similar to sugar. If you are prone to yeast infections, you should try lubes that are glycerine (and sucrose) free.

Spermicides: Some lubricants contain spermicides, which destroy sperm, and so provide additional protection when used with barrier contraception.

Nonoxynol-9: This detergent-based ingredient is added to many lubes as a contraceptive, and it has also been thought to provide some added protection against STIs and HIV. Recent research shows that it doesn't work as effectively as previously thought, and it can cause strong allergic reactions (anal or vaginal inflammation) in some people, which increase the risk of HIV infection.

I find it quite embarrassing to introduce the idea of using artificial lubricant into sex with a new partner, as he may imagine I am such an old hand – which just isn't the case.
Saskia, 20, UK

Saliva always does the trick, but I make sure I don't have a milk drink, like hot chocolate, before bed. That tends to dry my mouth out. Cigarettes and booze do, too.
Jim, 32, UK

I like it like Niagra Falls – wet and plenty of it.
Kerry, 19, UK

For any kind of anal play, fisting or Olympic sex that lasts for hours, I need lubrication, otherwise I dry out and the whole thing becomes painful and boring.
Amanda, 39, UK

Stupidly, I always forget to buy myself some proper lube and end up using whatever is in the fridge, with mixed post-sex results. Sometimes I get cystitis, other times just heavier vaginal discharge. I must buy the right gear, it can't be good for me.
Jean, 25, UK

Hands on (female)

Use plenty of lubrication and don't be afraid to try new movements. Be gentle and work your way up slowly – don't just jump in and start fingering.
Evianca, 26, US
Lovenet

Every woman is different. Use lube if she is dry, or attempt to get her more aroused. Cut your damn first finger nail! Ask how hard she likes to be rubbed. Like penises, clits have varying amounts of use and can be as sensitive as a feather or as tough as leather. In general, though, the hand should be followed by the tongue.
Anon, 26, US
Lovenet

You can use everything: lips, tongue and gentle blowing in certain areas. Taking your time with it means you want to find out what works. I think women appreciate you trying, even if you don't always get there!
Jim, 53, UK

History: In the late 1800s, wedding manuals emphasised the importance of the clitoris and even recommended that the groom give his bride her first orgasm by manually stimulating her clitoris before deflowering her. Sounds reasonable. Then, in the early 1900s, Sigmund Freud decided that playing with the clitoris was immature and that women who were really grown-up needed to 'abandon clitoral pleasures and effect a transfer to achieving orgasm vaginally'. Whether this idea caught on because new psychoanalytical theories were so popular, or because it was simply more convenient for men, the subsequent and still prevailing notion that penis-in-vagina thrusting is the acme of sexual pleasure has caused endless confusion for women.

Communication: The reality is that for most women manual clitoral stimulation is one of the quickest and easiest ways to achieve climax or enable penetrative orgasm. As with any sexual activity, there is no way of knowing what someone likes unless you ask, or they tell. Though initially they may be shy about guiding you, most women love direct or indirect clitoral stimulation – it's a crucial part of female sexual arousal. Letting her know that you are willing to learn will help her to relax. If a woman feels she is under time pressure or unsure that you are committing yourself fully to what you are doing, she won't be able to relax enough to really let go. Once she is at ease, get her to show you what strokes she prefers by encouraging her to masturbate in front of you. Alternatively, she can guide your hand and fingers until you know what you are doing. Manual stimulation is something you do 'with' someone, rather than 'to' them.

Variation: A basic knowledge will help you to feel more confident before doing any hands on. Like women, labias and clitorises come in all shapes and sizes – thick, curling inward, flaring out, hanging down or barely there. Textures vary, too: from silky smooth to deep and crinkly. What colour? Pink, red, mauve and chocolate, with the post-childbirth versions coming in slightly darker shades.

Navigation: Any position that allows you to touch her genital area is suitable for manual stimulation, and she can tell you which one feels best. She can be lying down with her legs open and you can be between her legs or beside her. You can sit cross-legged behind her and reach around to the front, or she can lie down with her bottom raised and you can put your fingers inside her and press down on her G-spot. Leaning your wrist on her pubic bone with your fingers pointing down gives you leverage and will prevent hand cramps. It also mimics how a women touches herself and leaves your other hand free to explore.

Don't go directly to the head of the clitoris. Although it is your ultimate destination, going around the houses builds up the anticipation. Work the sides of the labia – the clitoris extends beneath them – and the vaginal opening before you touch the clitoris, using the soft pads on the tips of your finger. Stroking down from the clitoris towards the vagina may feel more natural than working in the opposite direction. Arthritis and repetitive strain injuries (RSI) can limit your ability to use your hands for extended periods of time. Varying positions and using vibrators may help, though vibrators can actually make RSI worse.

Lubrication: Most natural lubrication is found near the vaginal opening, as secretions come from the inside walls of the vagina. Try dragging some towards the clitoris, or add saliva to your fingers. (Hormonal fluctuations during each month can leave her drier at certain times.) Stimulation always feels better when the clitoris is wet and saliva is both natural and readily available. If you are using a commercial lubricant – available in pharmacists and supermarkets – choose one that is water-based (though you should test anything you buy against your skin for allergies first). Try wearing a surgical glove with lube on. This gives a really smooth touch and prevents the possibility of infection from dirty fingernails.

Menstruation: The idea of vulval stimulation during a period may be unappealing to some. Fluctuating hormone levels, direct contact with menstrual blood and a reluctance to make a mess can be off-putting for both parties. However, many women feel very sexual at this time of the month, so don't dismiss the idea. Avoid mess by putting a towel underneath her and place a pillow under her bottom to raise her hips. Blood flow tends to be much lighter at the beginning and end of a period.

Things your mother should have told you

Take one thing at a time: Never penetrate both the vagina and anus with the same fingers without washing them inbetween times. The vagina is very sensitive to infection – especially germs from dirty fingernails or bacteria crossing over from the anus. Keep your fingernails short with smooth edges. Calluses will also feel rough against the skin.

A sure-fire way for a woman to come quickly: have a finger, a penis or a vibrator in your vagina and a finger in the rectum, then pinch your perineal muscle while the pussy is being stimulated.
Ruby, US
Moonlite Bunny Ranch

78
Lubrication

One person lies down with her left leg up, bent at the knee, and the other person kneels over her chest with her legs spread – forming an X-shape. Both can reach their partner's vagina – the one on top supports herself with just one hand. Also you can see each other, and watch what you're both doing.
Hannah, 17, UK
Gingerbeer

Too often men grope, searching for what, I don't know! Get down there, look inside, play and explore her. Very important: do not go straight for the clitoris. Go slow, tease a bit, lightly run your fingers along her labia – get her worked-up first. Take your time. To really add a punch to finger-play, lick your fingers after touching her, and make sure she sees you do this. Always a winner.
Tracey, 28, UK
Lovenet

I don't think I am very good at foreplay – my girlfriend always insists we go straight to penetrative sex. I suspect its because I do nothing for her with my fingers. I am too embarrassed to ask her, as it will be humiliating to know.
Josh, 19, UK

Instead of a man relying solely on his fingers to stimulate your clitoris, he could try Rigatoni. These are finger covers that give many pleasur-able sensations when used with water-based lubricants. They are available from most good sex shops.
Lou Paget, US
Sex educator

Techniques

General arousal: Initially, it can be very arousing for a woman to be touched everywhere *but* her genitals. Try rubbing her neck, back, arms, stomach, inner thighs and pubic bone and eventually massaging her vulva through her clothes. Get her to keep her knickers on and slowly slide a finger underneath to feel the real thing.

Genital massage: Lightly run your fingers up and down her inner thighs and lower tummy, skimming over the pubic hair and the vulval area. Use saliva or water-based lubrication, as it can be uncomfortable if genitals are massaged when they are dry. Trace your fingers over every crevice, the inner and outer lips and the clitoral hood, massaging and stroking up and down, gently kneading the soft flesh. Try placing the fleshy palm of your hand just above the pubic hair at her bikini line and applying a little pressure as you move it back and forth. Use your other hand to stroke the vulva and clitoris.

Perineal massage: Cup the entire opening of the vagina in the palm of your hand with your wrist resting on her bikini line. With the tips of your fingers, massage the perineum (the skin that runs between the vagina and the anus). Rub backwards and forwards with your wet fingers, which should be pointing towards the anus, and occasionally move them to touch the vaginal opening and clitoral area.

Indirect clitoral stimulation: Always start with indirect touching before progressing to the clitoris, because some women need to be fully aroused before direct clitoral contact, otherwise it can be uncomfortable or even painful. Rest your wrist on her bikini line and place two well-lubricated fingers over her vulva on either side of her clitoris, with the tips pointing towards the anus. Move your fingers in small circles, feeling the pubic bone below the flesh. Keep them wet and vary the pressure and speed. Rubbing the outer and inner lips by holding them between your thumb and index finger will drag on the hood and gently stimulate the clitoral head.

Direct clitoral stimulation: As arousal increases, extra blood floods the genital area and the clitoris plumps up, as if it is having a little erection. Direct contact with the clitoral head before she is fully aroused can hurt because it is extremely sensitive, and if you are rough, the hood contracts to protect itself. The clitoris generally responds to gentle movement. To stimulate it directly, pull back the hood and touch it very gently with a well-lubricated finger. Rub in a circular motion around the head and along the sides. Use your other hand to pull back the labia, placing gentle tension on the clitoral area. Experiment with different pressures, speeds and strokes. Your partner might not like to be rubbed and may prefer a constant light pressure on or around the clitoral artery, which runs slightly to the side of the head itself.

Heavier stimulation: Very gently pinch the clitoris between your thumb and forefinger and massage in a circular motion. Try spreading the lips wide open with one hand (using two fingers), then use the other fingers to massage, vibrate (flick back and forth) and tease the clitoris.

Toys

Get the buzz: These days, any sensible girl who doesn't want to wear herself out uses a vibrator. They provide intense and sustained stimulation for the whole clitoral area, and vaginal stimulation too. Vibrators can be very useful for a woman who finds it difficult to achieve orgasm. They speed up the process considerably.

Embarrassment: One of the main reasons sex toys aren't used in sex play is that some couples are embarrassed about discussing their desire for them. They can also find shopping for them a bit daunting, though this is less of an issue now that they can be bought online so easily. Some women feel that vibrators are fine for solo sex, but they feel odd about their partners using one on them. In fact, most partners will probably find the idea very exciting and as pleasure is the destination, no one really minds how you get there.

Keep it simple to begin with: If your partner is shy about using sex toys but you feel they would be a positive addition to your sex life, you could introduce the idea gently by starting with a simple shaft sleeve. These are not battery-powered, and they look a bit like textured finger puppets. They come in a variety of textures and finishes and can make the sensation of manual stimulation feel different. Alternatively, you could introduce her to a very small and discreet finger vibrator: a tiny device that slips over your finger and takes one battery. They're either shaped like a small bullet with a separate cover or they wrap around the finger like a ring. If she's enthusiastic about the extra sensation, graduate to a bigger and bolder vibrator.

My thumb is my best vaginal tool. I use my thumb to push in deep and wiggle around. But it's great to put a thumb in my arse and have a vibrator up my fanny.
Madeline, 20, UK

I like to lick my finger and circle her clitoris. The bigger it gets, the nearer I get to its head.
Roger, 52, US

212
Sex Toys

I have recently discovered sex toys. It may sound odd, but although I find it hard to orgasm vaginally with a guy, when I have my huge vibrator inside me I can come in a few minutes. I don't know why it works. Maybe it's because it is so big and it's stationary instead of thrusting and I can press on my clitoris, too. I don't care as long as it works, but my boyfriend doesn't want me to use it because he doesn't want me to get used to the size – in case I start to think he is too small.
Lu, 30, UK

The Grafenberg spot

It exists: The Grafenberg spot has been responsible for over 50 years of late-night duvet rustling and a lot of disappointment. In a controversial report in 1950, with 'research' provided by his wife and some of his patients, German gynaecologist Ernest Grafenberg documented an area inside the vagina that could theoretically induce both orgasm and female ejaculation. It became known as the G-spot, and Grafenberg's name found immortality as a vaginal pleasure zone.

It doesn't exist: Within ten years, Grafenberg's research had been overshadowed by a surge of academic and public interest in another area of particular female sensitivity: the clitoris. This tiny organ represented sexual liberation to a generation of feminists who were trying to tell men that there was more to 'free love' than vaginal sex (if you didn't play at the door, you didn't get in). Some women felt they had been tolerating vaginal penetration for too long, and Grafenberg's discovery of an organ inside the vagina didn't help the 80 per cent of women who couldn't orgasm without clitoral stimulation.

Confused?: In 1981, the publication of Whipple and Perry's *The G-spot* revived and expanded Grafenberg's research. The G-spot became the 'must have' item on the sexual shopping list, and women's magazines sacrificed rain forests to tell us. All that men and women had to do was find it . . . but that didn't prove to be very easy. In fact, the search continued for 20 years, and has only recently been called off. In August 2001, Dr Terence Hines, Professor of Psychology at New York's Pace University, reported that the evidence for the G-spot's existence had been based on just a dozen females, and that only four out of the twelve showed signs of G-spot sensitivity. According to Hines, 'Women have been misled for about 20 years about an important part of their sexuality, and some women might feel very bad about themselves and their sexuality if they can't find the G-spot – but there is nothing there to find'.

Best keep looking, pet: Whether the existence of the G-spot is scientifi- cally proven or not is largely irrelevant, if stimulating the area creates a pleasant sensation - and for many women it does. That said, as G-spot stimulation is usually manual, the hand that stimulates internally undoubtedly rubs against the clitoris in the process. The fact that women in an aroused state can orgasm when their genitals are being rubbed externally and pumped internally is not exactly news, but no doubt Mrs Grafenberg had worked that out too.

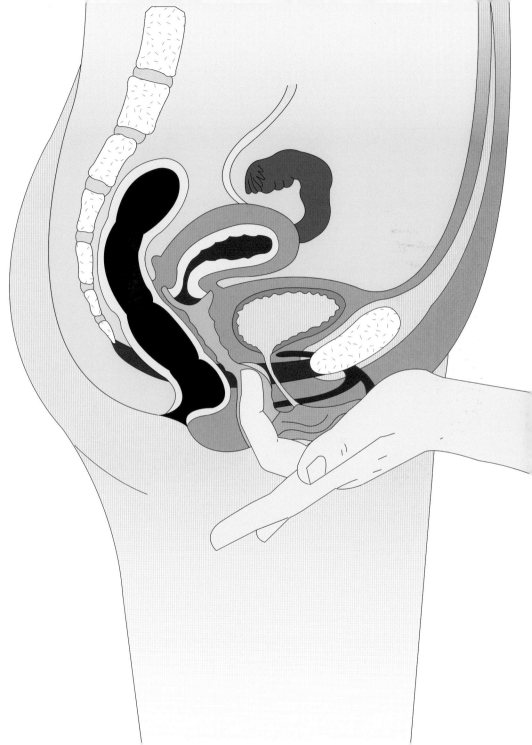

Insert the fingers just a little way into the vagina and curl them up and stretch them out – sort of like a 'come here' motion. One or two fingers is best.
Nick, 25, UK

I recommend vaginal rear-entry, pointing and thrusting slightly downwards. You need to practise Kegels to really get the effect. I use Ben-Wa balls, which come in graduated sizes and ring when you clench (you can hear it inside, but no one else can). They are usually sold as finger-massage balls.
Anon, 26, Australia
Lovenet

About one or two inches in, on the upper surface of the vagina, there are some ridges that get hard when she is very aroused, so stimulate at an angle upwards towards her pubic region.
Anon, 18, UK
Lovenet

212

Sex Toys

Techniques

Up a bit, left a bit: Whether you ever find anything approximating it or not, playing hunt the G-spot can be good fun. Once your partner is aroused, curl your fingers up behind her pubic bone, about 5cm (2ins) inside her vagina, and press behind her tummy button as if you are making a 'come here' motion. Pressing into the front vaginal wall, explore from the pubic bone up towards the cervix. The G-spot may feel slightly swollen and ridged, but it varies from woman to woman. Try using your other hand to press down on her stomach just above the bikini line or press your fingers against the urethral opening. Finding the correct location can be a subtle process and she really needs to guide you. If your partner experiences a sensation of needing to pee, it is often a sign that you are in the right place, but pressing hard in the wrong spot may feel as if you are knocking on her bladder. There is not much room to manoeuvre, but experiment with rocking, massaging and circling movements. Try rotating your fingers right around the vagina and coming to rest on the G-spot. Try moving your fingers in small, slow circles, or point your fingers more sharply upwards and then rock them forwards and back. If she doesn't feel anything special you could try some different positions. She can lie on her stomach with her legs apart and her hips raised on a pillow. You may be able to put more pressure on the spot when you are pressing down like this. You can lie beneath her (facing her bottom) while she kneels on all fours, though keeping your hand in the air may be tiring. If so, try it with her straddled across you while you reach up inside her. In this position she can manoeuvre herself against your fingers. The G-spot responds more to pressure than touch, so if she tells you that you have hit a more sensitive area, you should press it firmly. When she feels orgasm approaching, a firm rapid pumping motion is most effective (but this bit can be tiring).

Toys

Help is at hand: There are several dildos and vibrators on the market that are specifically designed for G-spot stimulation. They can reach further than fingers, and are curved at the top to reach in over the pubic bone. They allow for firmer pressure and using them is less tiring than using your hands. The key is getting the angle and position just right, and as you won't have the benefit of feeling with your fingers, you will need even more guidance to ensure that you are in the right spot. You can increase sensation by pressing on the stomach when you are using a dildo or vibrator.

Female ejaculation

The mysterious female anatomy: If the G-spot is something of a mystery, female ejaculation – the emission of fluid from the urethra at the point of orgasm – is a riddle wrapped inside an enigma. According to the ubiquitous Whittle and Perry, the phenomenon is usually associated with G-spot stimulation, and some doctors have speculated that that the release of fluid might mean that the G-spot (if there is one) could be the female equivalent of the male prostate gland. Other doctors argue that because G-spot sensitivity is located along the lines of the urethra, stimulation in this area causes a relaxation of the muscles at the neck of the bladder, which leads to an 'ejaculation' of urine. The ejaculation camp contends that can't be so, because the fluid ejaculated has a different chemical make-up to urine. Whoever is right, not many women experience ejaculation and those who do produce varying quantities of fluid. Some gush, others don't even realise that it has happened. It's said that ejaculation is more likely to occur in women who have strong pelvic floor muscles. Experienced ejaculaters describe their technique as an ability to push out, using the PC muscles when orgasm is approaching. And because we spend most of our lives controlling the sensation of pushing out body fluid, wind, waste and so on, this takes a bit of practice.

Fisting the vagina

Puppeteering: The vagina is designed to expand during childbirth, though dilation is a slow process. This capacity for expansion makes it possible to get a whole hand inside a vagina, but it needs to be done carefully and very, very slowly. Naturally, everything depends on the size of the hand relative to the size of the vagina. Putting a small female hand in a big vagina is easier than a putting a big male hand in a smaller one. Fisting is a sex act that should only be entered into by consenting, sober and patient partners who have lots of time and lots of lubricant. Latex gloves make the process safer and smoother. Start with a couple of fingers and gradually build up to a whole hand. If it hurts, you should stop immediately, and if you achieve full hand penetration, withdrawal should also be very slow. Sometimes after orgasm, muscle spasm or vacuum lock can make withdrawal difficult, so really take your time and ease out gently. Vaginal fisting should not be tried if you are pregnant, have just given birth or have had a hysterectomy. Menopausal women should also be careful if they are fisted, as their natural vaginal lubrication and elasticity is decreasing.

I only ejaculate when there's been a lot of foreplay first. I think what it is is that I get really wet, and when I come my muscles contract and all the wetness gushes out. I don't mind and my partner is mad for it – he wants me to come on his face.
Anna, 28, UK

I have ejaculated recently for the first time. I was taught how to do it by a woman friend of mine who manually stimulated me for a long time and when I felt orgasm approaching she told me to 'let go'. I don't really know what happened but all this liquid came out.
Belle, 35, UK

I have never had a more intimate experience with a woman, it was quite unlike anything I had ever experienced. I felt that I was reaching up into her soul.
Julian, 32, UK

114

Safer Sex

Warning

Going down (female)

AKA
Oral sex
Muff diving
Facing the nation
Giving face
Eating pussy
Going south
Blood sports

Personally, I would not waste my time with a partner who was not interested in pleasing me orally and bringing me to orgasm.
Tracey, 28, US

Make sure your neck is at a comfortable angle. Otherwise you'll pay in the morning.
De-Vona, 22, US

I had never had an orgasm with a man, but I had been able to get one masturbating on my own. When I met my current partner he gave me oral sex and I was able to climax from it – I had my first climax with a man!
Elizabeth, 52,UK

My girlfriend always pushes me off after about a minute, so I never have a chance to really explore. I think she can't let go, or thinks I get bored easily. She couldn't be further from the truth. I just want to turn her on, whatever it's gonna take.
Charlie, 19, US

Cunniwhat? The correct term for going down is 'cunnilingus'. Doesn't exactly roll off the tongue does it? Derived from the Latin *cunnus*, meaning 'external genitals', and *lingere*, meaning 'to lick', it describes the act of using the mouth to lick, kiss or gently suck the labia, clitoris and vaginal area.

We love it: According to the UK's National Survey of Sexual Attitudes and Lifestyles of 2001, three-quarters of all women experienced cunnilingus last year and for many of them it was by far their favourite sexual act. Shere Hite, the American sex researcher, comes to similar conclusions, reporting that 42 per cent of women regularly orgasm through cunnilingus.

Always have: Cunnilingus has been recorded in many classical texts, though its most fervent advocate must surely have been the Empress Wu Hu, who ruled China between 683 and 705AD. She decreed that all government officials and visiting dignitaries should pay homage by performing cunnilingus on her – smart woman. As American sex commentator Dr Susan Block points out, it gives the phrase 'sucking up to royalty' a whole new meaning.

But we're not telling: A lot of people wish that they could give themselves oral sex because they know exactly what they like and how they like it. The trouble with cunnilingus is that although it feels great, it is a very intimate act and many women are simply too shy to ask for it. Someone who loves giving oral sex will never be short of sexual partners, but good cunnilingus needs to be collaborative. Just nuzzling away may not be enough for either of you. To find out what works for her, she needs to give you a bit of honest guidance and you need to respond. A request is not a rejection, it is an opportunity for improvement. Women prefer partners who will give them oral sex without setting a time limit and they would prefer to believe that it's not being done on the basis of an exchange, though no one's kidding themselves. Top tip? Don't mimic 'porn tongue'. Thirty seconds of quick flicking, with your face miles away from her vagina is a technique enjoyed only by the camera.

Positions: Whether she is lying on a table or doing a shoulder stand, the only positional requirement for cunnilingus is that your tongue can reach her vagina. Performing oral sex on your knees can be playfully submissive, licking her from beneath the table while she reads a book, smokes a fag or pretends to ignore you can feel naughty and exciting. You can try more athletic poses, but if you are in for the long haul, go for comfort and change position or use pillows if you feel that you are putting pressure on your neck.

I've got a monkey in my mouth: If you want to avoid stray pubic hairs in your mouth, confine yourself to the moist inner labia and clitoris. If you find hair a distraction, use one hand to brush it aside and simultaneously hold her lips open for better access. She may find gentle tugging on her pubic hair pleasurable, or you can try stroking your hand through it. Some people find it erotic if the pubic hair is trimmed or shaved off completely. If a man has light stubble (from a beard) it can be a turn-on for some, but it is abrasive and can leave a rash.

Cactus tongue: The tongue goes dry quickly outside the mouth, so have a drink handy to keep your mouth moist. Foods such as whipped cream, ice cream, chocolate sauce and fruit purée can vary and disguise genital odours, but avoid using anything containing oil with latex barriers. Try strong mints, popping candy and ice cubes for different sensations. Edible lubricants come in a range of flavours. Some contain ingredients that stimulate the genitals, though they may just make your clitoris feel numb.

Green light: Some women want you to stop as soon as they've finished climaxing; others like the licking and sucking to continue well beyond orgasm. Continuing stimulation throughout climax increases the chance of a multiple orgasm and the chance of her loving you forever, though you may never be able to speak again.

Techniques

Tongueing: The tongue is soft, strong and agile. Its texture, wetness and warmth give it the edge over manual stimulation when it comes to probing and exploring, because it feels so similar to the moist genital tissue. Use the tip of your tongue and the flat of your tongue, as well as the underside, which is softer than the top. Some women will want rapid continuous licking, others prefer a long, slow caress. Your tongue can provide different textures by altering its natural flex. When it hangs limp and flat, it provides a soft caress. If it is soft and sloppy, it can lick and lap in a circular motion. When flexed and rigid it provides more direct and firm stimulation. Stay in the same place and try lots of different strokes, movements and variations.

Oral sex feels nice but I worry what he thinks about the smell and the taste. I can't really tell if I am all that clean, but he never complains and he says he likes doing it. I think it looks a bit odd seeing him between my legs.
Jayne, 43, UK

I get a sore tongue from licking my girlfriend. She can never get enough and I don't know whether she holds on to her orgasm or it takes her ages to come but she looks like she is on the brink for about ten minutes before the main event. You want to try licking someone non-stop for ten or fifteen minutes. It's hard work.
VV, 28, UK

I do it occasionally now, but I have such a bad physical reaction. It irritates my skin. Actually I think I have developed an allergy to oral sex.
Mary, 46, UK

I just wish that he would do it for longer. He goes down to wet me and then he pushes his penis in. I could do with less dick and more tongue.
Frances, 36, US

Using your mouth: The mouth offers a whole range of textures and sensations. Use every part of your mouth – lips, tongue, teeth and even your breath – using each technique in isolation or combining it with others. Covering the entire vulva with your full, warm mouth gives a pleasant feeling of being enveloped. Pretend you are kissing her in the way you kiss her mouth, and try lightly sucking different parts of the vulva into your mouth. The gentle, wet pressure can be combined with very gentle scraping of the teeth if she enjoys this. Any kind of nibbling can be painful, so ask first and be very light with the movement.

The build-up: The clitoris is central to sexual arousal in women, because it contains most of the sexually charged tissues in the body. Some find immediate direct stimulation overwhelming (a few women don't even enjoy direct stimulation when they are fully aroused). It's a good idea to build up to clitoral stimulation and create a sense of anticipation. Try to increase pressure and speed gradually by licking around the clitoral head, which contains the clitoral nerve. Once you know she's aroused, move on to the clitoris itself.

Stimulation of the clitoris: To get to the clitoral head you need to have good access. Using the index and middle fingers of both hands, put pressure on the inside of the outer lips and lift the entire area upwards to create a taut, open area for the mouth. Try gentle tongue movements over the shaft and tip of the clitoris, flicking the tip of the tongue from side to side directly underneath it. During high levels of arousal, some women enjoy having their clitoris bitten softly – but check first. Suck on the head of the clitoris as if you are sucking on a straw, and use the tip of your tongue to flick back and forth very lightly – almost touching – while creating suction pressure with your pursed lips.

Vaginal stimulation: Rotate your tongue around the vaginal opening, kissing the edges. Vary the speed and the pressure, and when the whole genital area is moist, open and ready, gently probe the vagina with the tip and the shaft of your tongue. Many women like to have fingers in their vagina while their clitoris is stimulated with your mouth.

Fast, rhythmic, continuous stimulation: Once she is on the brink of orgasm, continuous rapid stimulation is usually the most effective way of bringing on climax, but don't stop stimulating her during her orgasm. This extends the sensation.

Blowing: Lightly blowing warm breath from about 15cm (6ins) gives a cool, tingling sensation, but you shouldn't blow air directly into the vagina as there is the risk that it could cause an air bubble to enter her bloodstream.

Humming: If you hum while you lick, it produces vibrations in the throat that can heighten her stimulation. In fact, in the US, blow jobs are sometimes known as 'hummers'.

Thermals: Rub an ice cube around the clitoris or vulva and follow it with your warm mouth. Try inserting foods such as strawberries, ice cream, bananas or tinned peaches in syrup and suck them out. Don't put them in too far, though, and make sure that what goes in comes out.

Using sex toys: Try holding a vibrator against the underside of your tongue while you are quivering it against her clitoris. The vibrations will transmit through your tongue giving her a gentle, soft, wet buzz. Use a vibrator or a dildo for vaginal penetration while exploring the clitoris, labia and perineum with your mouth and tongue. Run a vibrator across her labia while sucking gently on her clitoris.

The big tease: Some women love it, others hate it, but teasing can have positive effects on the intensity of an orgasm. Just as she's going crazy for something, move on to another area or technique. Keep doing this until she's begging you to make her come, but sustain the stimulation to keep her in a heightened state of sexual anticipation.

Things your mother should have told you

Taste and smell: Normal genital odour and secretions are natural, healthy, moist and warm. Some people find them highly erotic, but for others they can be a bit inhibiting. Some women are self-conscious about their vaginal secretions and the possibility of smelling. Incorporating a bath into foreplay can ease this anxiety, while simultaneously guaranteeing that your partner is clean as well (just in case you want to return the compliment).

Cleaning: Like the eyeballs, the vaginal passage is self-cleaning, though you can clean between the folds of the vulva very gently with warm water. Avoid using soap in the vagina as it dries it out and can wash away natural protection causing bacterial vaginosis (BV).

I had one experience of cunnilingus and I never want it to be repeated. She was impatient and inexperienced and the whole thing was a complete turn-off.
Dissatisfied, 27, UK

I've spoken to lots of my lesbian friends and they seem to agree that for them, in their first relationship, oral sex was a little uncomfortable at first. Just because it's not really discussed in schools and is somehow 'less straight' than other sexual activities, and some are paranoid about their girly bits.
Hannah, 17, UK
Gingerbeer

If I just pause my index finger at the opening to her vagina and then nibble her clitoris ever so gently, I find that she comes extremely quickly. It takes three minutes.
Bez, 31, UK

Sometimes I taste a distinct sugary flavour. She tells me it's to do with ovulation.
Kevin, 23, UK

I over-clean for sure. Sometimes it makes me itchy.
Paranoid, 17, US

242

STIs

Natural changes: The smell and consistency of vaginal secretions change with the monthly cycle and are also affected by changes in diet – especially by spicy or highly seasoned food. Alcohol, drugs, tobacco and even vitamin supplements can also change the taste and texture. Vaginal deodorants that disguise your natural smell should be avoided. To ensure personal freshness, wear clean cotton underwear that allows your body to breathe. Synthetic fabrics harbour moisture and odours.

Keep your legs together: The commonest cause of a nasty smell from your vagina is bacterial vaginosis (BV). Avoid cunnilingus until you get treatment (though it is unlikely that people will be queueing up to go down on you). Sometimes women discover that the reason they have a smell coming from inside their vagina is that they have forgotten to take a tampon out.

Safety and protection: In June 2000, the UK Department of Health published *A Review of the Evidence on Risk of HIV Transmission Associated with Oral Sex* and found only two cases of HIV transmission that could be traced directly to cunnilingus. Though this risk seems small, you can catch other infections, such as hepatitis B, gonorrhoea, syphilis, chancroid and thrush. Oral herpes can be transmitted to the genitals and genital herpes can be transmitted to the mouth, even when there is no active outbreak. Don't combine analingus with cunnilingus, and use different protection for anal and genital oral sex to prevent bacteria from the anus entering the vagina. Female condoms, dental dams or non-microwaveable cling film can be used to prevent transmission of infection. If you are using a barrier, put water-based lubricant on the side that is pressed against the genitals to enhance the sensations received through the latex or plastic.

Menstruation: Though there is no reason to avoid oral sex during periods, if there is any possibility that the woman may have an STI or HIV, the risk of her transmitting it is higher, because menstrual blood is a more effective transmission fluid than saliva. Fluctuating hormone levels, a reluctance to make a mess and menstrual blood can make the idea less appealing anyway, but anyone with a barrier (and a washing machine) has no cause for concern. Some women do not bleed straight after having a bath, but the effect is temporary and not guaranteed. Less blood is likely to leak out when you are lying down. Alternatively, raise your bottom by propping a pillow underneath – this helps the blood to pool in the vagina.

Hands on (male)

AKA
Wank
Hand job
Jacking off
Slapping the salami

The men who take longer are those who masturbate a lot. They will be used to the more intense sensation of their hands. Use your tongue in combination with your mouth and hand, and build sensations with your free hand in another area.
Ruby, US
Sex worker

Once a guy has come, stop.
Jamie, 31, UK

Try foot sex: put your feet sole-to-sole with a little lubricant in the arch, then slide the penis between your feet, massaging it up and down gently.
Violet, US
Sex worker

Always have plenty of lubricant! Start out slow and soft, don't go for bust right away. Train yourself to peak and come back down several times before you orgasm, concentrating on the various sensations – the orgasm will then be very powerful.
Alan, 33, US
Lovenet

Look and learn: The quickest way to establish a man's preferred stimulation technique is to watch him masturbate. Most men have solo sex down to a fine art and have developed quite personal preferences about what type of stimulation they like. There's no point in blindly trying to gauge things such as pace and pressure when a brief demonstration from the expert himself would make all the difference. Many people use hand jobs as a way of relieving male sexual tension without having to 'put out' too much. Men sometimes complain that their partners become bored halfway through or ask them to 'show me how' and then leave them to finish things off on their own. A slack attitude to giving hand jobs means that men who suspect their partner is going to give up find it difficult to relax. All it takes to transform your common or garden hand job into a mind-blowing sex act is a little elbow grease, enthusiasm and imagination.

Polishing the bishop: Giving a good hand job is more difficult than you might imagine, and if your man is used to a certain type of stimulation, he may take time to adjust to your particular brand of hand. He may use very rough techniques or masturbate very quickly, and it can be fairly difficult for you to mimic what he does to himself. That said, being masturbated by a partner is usually so much more exciting that it more than makes up for any shortfall there may be in physical stimulation. Generally, movements should be smooth rather than jerky, and when changing hands or positions keep some contact with his penis. Uncircumcised men often enjoy having their foreskin pulled over the glans so that it forms a type of sleeve through which the penis can glide. Try not to be rough with his erection and don't stop until he wants you to (unless of course you've been at it for days).

Positions: You can give a man a hand job in any position and virtually any location. If he is lying down you can sit over his stomach facing away from him, or kneel between his legs facing towards him. Lying on your side can be harder on your wrist. Doing it while he stands is traditionally known as a 'French polish' (maid or butler's outfit not compulsory). If you both sit upright on the bed facing each other you can watch his responses. If you sit behind him and put your arms around his waist, it will be closer to the position he uses. If you lie down, your partner can position himself on all fours over you so that his balls are above your mouth.

I'm coming: You can tell how near your partner is to climax by gently feeling his balls. If they feel tight and are close to the shaft, it means he is close. To delay orgasm, try reversing the position of your hand so that you work his penis in the opposite direction. The change of emphasis will alter sensations and delay climax. Some men like to see themselves ejaculate, and you may want to experiment with different positions. If a man has a long foreskin, he can pull it up over the head of his penis and catch the sperm in the foreskin.

Techniques

Basic up and down: Glide your hand from the base of the penis to the tip. When you reach the head, swivel your hand round so that your whole palm goes over the top, encircling the head. Then bring your hand back to the base and repeat. Imagine your hands are following the red twist on a barber's pole.

Head pop: Use your thumb and index finger to make a ring around his penis, taking a fairly firm grip. The sensation of the coronal ridge popping through your tightly squeezed (and lubricated) fingers is impressive. Try positioning your tongue over the head so you can gently nibble and suck as the hands are moving.

Interactive thrust: Lubricate your hands, grasp the penis and hold it firmly. Don't move your hands, but let your partner thrust into them. This lets him control the pace.

Head rub: If you only lubricate the head of the penis and massage it using the whole hand, it feels like trying to turn a slippery doorknob – hold the base for firm grip. Gently rub the the frenulum and coronal ridge at the back of the head of the penis with the palm of your hand – these are probably the most sensitive parts of the penis. A wet hand cupped over the top of a penis can feel a lot like a mouth or vagina.

Using two hands: Interweave your fingers and wrap them around his penis with your thumbs pointing towards the head and work up and down. Then work up and down and over the top of the head, in a continuous motion. Try pressing your hand flat on his pubic hair with your thumb under his penis (it should form a kind of L-shape), placing a constant, firm pressure against the perineum. The pressure on the base heightens sensation and keeps the penis stiff while you use your other hand to stimulate the shaft.

The smaller your hands, the better!
Rod, 44, UK

Firm grip, tease them and don't forget the other parts of the genitalia, like the balls.
Fluffer, 30 ,US
Lovenet

Listen to his breath . . . watch his body as it tenses when you touch certain spots . . . don't neglect his balls . . . it's a package deal! My boyfriend wants me to write a book or make an instructional video. More women should be properly trained, I suppose . . . loving to do it is a major part of the technique.
Greenhoney, 27, US
Lovenet

In a man's penis there's a vein that runs down the side. Follow that all the way down and apply a little pressure to bring the blood to the head and then work back down again.
Vicky, 24, US
Sex worker

Don't be afraid to squeeze! The hand provides friction and the mouth provides wetness and heat.
Raj, 22, UK

212

Sex Toys

Ball handling: Place your hand palm-up under his balls. Use your thumb and index finger to make a loose ring at the top of them – they will rest in your hand. A slight downward tug will make his penis stand up and his balls feel smooth, so that you can stroke and massage them. Massaging the root of the penis under the balls and the perineum also feels great.

Slapping and beating: This involves a steady slapping of the penis back and forth between your hands, against his stomach or any other object. It feels particularly good with a semi-erect penis that is heavily lubricated.

Smurfing: He slaps his semi-erect penis back and forth across your face.

French fuck: Masturbating the erect penis between the breasts.

Using water: Using the shower head from a hand-held shower, direct the spray from the back of his penis onto his glans. Then spray water over the top of his erect penis. Put your finger over the nozzle to intensify the strength of the spray (needle-fine spray may be uncomfortable or numbing over prolonged periods).

Simultaneous prostate stimulation: For a really spectacular hand job, combine masturbation with prostate stimulation. Though the prostate can be stimulated internally (inside the anus), you can also stimulate it indirectly from the outside by putting pressure on the perineal muscles that run from the anus to the scrotum. The muscle feels quite solid, almost like the root of the penis, and using your knuckles or fingertips to knead and rub it firmly while you masturbate him can really add to the intensity of the sensation.

Using sex toys: Adjustable cock rings fit around the base of the penis and under the balls. They help to keep erection firm. A dildo with a flared base or a butt plug can be inserted into a man's anus to simultaneously stimulate his anus and prostate gland. Anal beads, which are like a solid necklace of beads in graduating sizes, can be inserted into the anus and pulled out slowly one by one as he approaches orgasm. Vibrators can be rubbed up and down the shaft of the penis, around the head or pressed against the perineum between the base of the balls and the anus. Some men enjoy having smaller vibrators inserted in their anus while their penis is masturbated for them. Make sure you use plenty of lubrication when using sex toys, and particularly on anything that will be inserted in the anus.

Going down (male)

*Oh, and shave your
testicles. It feels
better for her, it
smells less sweaty,
and it makes your
penis look bigger.*
PJ, 36, UK

*I like starting with it
flaccid and feeling it
getting hard, then
back to soft after he
has come. A true
sign of being able to
arouse him.*
Stavros, 45, Australia

*Licking the shaft
with the back of your
tongue is very
different using the
top of your tongue.*
Felice, 31, US
Sex worker

*As a male with a
disability and
erectile issues,
vaginal penetration
does not lead me to
orgasm. Performing
oral sex with my
partner. . . that
can lead to the most
brilliant brain-
orientated orgasm
I could ever
experience. Wow.*
Red, 36, US

Myth: The importance of enthusiasm cannot be over-estimated, and some partners are simply more obliging than others. Cleopatra was apparently very keen, and legend has it that at a single dinner party she managed to service 100 men. According to Rufus Camhausen writing in *The Encyclopedia of Sacred Sexuality*, her Egyptian nickname was 'she of the wide mouth', and among the Greeks she was known as the 'great swallower'. Perhaps that wasn't asses' milk in her bath after all.

Reality: Most men and women don't have 'wide' mouths. In fact, the average penis is 15cm (6ins) long, and the average distance from mouth to throat is about 9cm (3.5ins). So, do the maths. Real blow jobs usually concentrate on stimulating the top 8–10cm (3–4ins) of the penis, and fortunately these areas contain far greater concentrations of nerve endings than the shaft of the penis.

Fantasy: For many men, just the thought of someone going down on their genitals is incredibly arousing. Because it offers such a range of tantalising sensations, oral sex is a favoured (and much requested) way of experiencing penile stimulation. The mouth is a warm, wet, soft, sucking orifice, while the agile tongue provides a range of extra-special effects. Lick the head, flick your tongue gently around the ridge and up and down the frenulum. Use lubricated hands to masturbate the shaft and massage the scrotum and perineum.

To make him hard: Put it in your mouth and gently suck until it gets harder. Make a ring around the base of the penis with your fingers. This will make him hard, and it also allows you to control how far his penis goes in to your mouth. Breathe through your nose and cover your teeth with your lips. Keeping your mouth taut creates suction as you glide the head of the hardening penis in and out.

Positions: Some people straddle their partner, facing his penis to give fellatio. Frankly, unless the thought of some guy staring at your ass while you give him a blow job appeals to you, it's much more efficient to kneel between your partner's legs. It gives you access to his whole package, and keeps your hands free for manual stimulation. You can simultaneously stimulate the whole penis, scrotum and perineum, and, if you want to, you can throw in a little rimming or prostate stimulation. It's all there in front of you. If he kneels over you while you are lying down, his penis can hang into your mouth and you can stroke and pull his balls while you suck.

Mmm, strawberry: Though oral sex is not guaranteed to be 100 per cent safe, the reality is that not many people give blow jobs with a mouthful of latex. Flavoured condoms (strawberry, chocolate, banana and vanilla) can make the process sweeter, but have a drink handy in case the lubrication tastes weird. If you don't want to use a condom, you can lower the risks substantially by not allowing him to ejaculate in your mouth.

What goes around comes around: Like cunnilingus, fellatio is often more popular with the receiver than the giver. If you're not in the mood to give a guy a blow job, be honest and don't feel pressurised. But if you do it, make an effort to do it properly and with enthusiasm. Some men complain about poor-quality blow jobs, but this usually indicates that their partner is either bored, lazy or simply didn't want to do it in the first place. Statistically, fellatio is a more frequent practice than cunnilingus, so heterosexual men should consider whether the trip down south is always a one-way ticket. If this is the case, you shouldn't be surprised if your partner doesn't want to make return journeys.

Techniques

Lip service: Find the frenulum, the V-shaped ridge at the back of the penis head, and follow it, sucking and nudging it with your lips and tongue. Quiver your tongue around the coronal ridge. Cover your teeth with your lips as you glide down the shaft. Suck a whole testicle into your mouth and fondle it with your tongue.

Using the hand simultaneously: Wrap your hand around the penis with your thumb pointing towards the coronal ridge. Your hand follows your mouth as you move up and down the penis.

Humming: Humming while you suck creates vibrations in your throat and on his penis. Try altering the pitch to vary the sensation.

For an uncircumcised penis: First pull the skin right up over the head and poke your tongue through the opening of the foreskin. Circling the tip of your tongue around the head, gently bite and suck on the gathered skin. Hold the shaft and use your mouth to gently pull the foreskin back. Keep going down until you have most of the penis in your mouth. Now pull back up and use your hand to hold the foreskin down just under the frenulum (the ridge) so you can lick all around the exposed head.

78	114
Lubrication	**Safer Sex**

I like a girl to do it for her own pleasure. You can really tell the difference.
James, 28, UK

I insist that I spend some time on her before she comes anywhere near me. I lavish hours on getting to know her, building up trust that I want to give as well as receive, show her the range of sensations by performing them on her first, so when it comes to my turn . . .
Charles, 46 , UK

I like it when he gags. It might sound a bit dodgy, but it makes me feel like I have a massive cock.
Tom, 23, UK

I kneel on the floor with my back against the wall and he balances by putting his hands against the wall. Then he thrusts in and out and I have to just trust that he won't push too far. I am not allowed to touch him.
Leo, 19, Australia

Temperature and texture: Putting an ice cube in your mouth can give a cold, numbing sensation. Alternate with a hot drink. After sucking with a warm mouth, blow cool breath over the head. Sucking a strong mint before giving a blow job creates a cool, tingling sensation. Try it with a mouthful of liquid – water is best, because alcohol can sting. A mouthful of milkshake feels great for him, though it could make you feel pretty sick.

Using sex toys: Try running a vibrator over his penis while you suck or, alternatively, put the tip of a vibrator under your own tongue or chin. This will transmit extra vibrations through your mouth. An adjustable cock ring around the base of his penis can increase the pressure.

Things your mother should have told you

How to put a condom on with your mouth: Some men find putting a condom on distracts them and they lose their erection. This trick will keep him interested. Hold the condom by its edge, unroll it a little and squeeze the air from the tip. Shape your lips into an 'O' and place the condom in your mouth with the teat facing the back of your throat. Hold the penis, place your mouth over the head, tighten your lips and push firmly down, unrolling the condom as you go – be careful your teeth don't tear it.

Pork à la mode: Though many people are turned on by the taste, smell and wetness of their partner's genitals, for others they can be intimidating and off-putting. Oral sex is a very intimate act, and the idea of sucking and licking parts of the body that are more usually concerned with urination can be too great a leap for some. Incorporating a bath or shower into foreplay ensures that you are both clean. Saliva changes the taste of the penis very quickly but drinks such as beer, cola or mint tea are probably better because they clean your mouth and also disguise the flavour. The taste of sperm can be affected by what a man eats. If he's had a lot of curry or asparagus lately, you might notice a change in flavour. Vanilla ice cream makes it sweeter. If he hasn't had an orgasm for a while, his semen is likely to have a stronger flavour and a thicker consistency.

Pork scratchings: Like the vagina, the penis produces its own secretions, called smegma. In its fresh state it doesn't have a strong taste or smell. However if it is allowed to accumulate (coupled with old urine, dirt and semen) it starts to fester and give off an unpleasant odour. Actually, most men wash regularly, though not many wipe themselves after urinating.

Tips to stop you gagging

Stop holding my ears, I know what I am doing: If he starts thrusting or pressing your head into his penis, he is almost guaranteed to make you gag (though, frankly, any guy who does this deserves whatever comes up). With blow jobs you need to feel that you are doing it to him, not that he is doing it to you.

Hold the base of his penis: Holding the base of the penis or pressing the palm of your hand against his groin will give you more control over the depth of his penetration. Relax the muscles in your neck, jaw and throat, and guide the penis as far into your mouth as is pleasurable.

Remember to breathe: Half of the sickly feeling that can accompany a blow job is because you are running short of breath. Try to control your breathing – breathe through your nose and stop if you need to.

Cheat: If you can't take having his penis deep inside your mouth, you can cheat by using your hand on the shaft to simulate an extended mouth. Alternatively, try angling his penis towards the side of your mouth into your cheek, or combine the two techniques. If your hands are well-lubricated and nice and warm, the difference between your mouth and hands will be less perceptible.

To swallow or not to swallow?

No way: Lots of men and women don't like the taste or the consistency, but they feel a bit embarrassed about saying anything. The thing is, most guys absolutely love watching themselves ejaculate, so you shouldn't presume that he wants you to swallow anyway.

Yes way: Some people think that swallowing is the best bit: hey, after all that effort you deserve a snack – and it's pure protein, right?

'I'm coming, I'm coming': It isn't always easy to identify that ejaculation is imminent (though cries of 'I'm coming' are a big hint). Physical indications are muscle tension, tighter testes and an increased breathing rate. Keep up a steady rhythm and don't change anything. When you feel him coming, get ready for a mouthful. To swallow without tasting, try to get the tip of the penis as far back in the throat as possible and swallow hard immediately.

If you don't want to swallow: Ask him to tell you when he is going to come, then either let him shoot into your mouth and hold it there until you can dispose of it discreetly (spit into a tissue or try the old pillow-cough) or give him a lovely snowball kiss. Alternatively just move your mouth away, watch him pump his load and sigh with admiration.

Beauty treatments: Freshly ejaculated sperm is thought to be a good moisturiser – a good argument for having it on your skin rather than in your mouth, but watch your eyes – sperm really stings.

Deep throat

Don't talk with your mouth full: This technique had its 'fifteen minutes' as a blow job technique when Linda Lovelace took it 'all in one' in the 1972 hardcore porn film of the same name. In reality, deep throat is an acquired taste. It's difficult to do without gagging and it's harder to give the shaft any stimulation because the mouth is so full. Though most guys want to try it, the reality is often less enjoyable than a regular blow job. To overcome the natural gagging reflex that is triggered automatically when the penis hits the back of the throat (your body tries to swallow the penis), you need to learn to resist or ignore the reflex by getting used to swallowing with your mouth wide open.

No one said it was easy: Certain positions are better for deep throat. If you kneel over your partner's penis facing his feet, it opens up the mouth and throat, which helps prevent gagging. Open your jaw wide and extend your throat as if you are yawning. Put your lips around the tip of the penis, creating a vacuum with your mouth, but keeping your throat wide open. Now take the penis in to the back of your throat and try to swallow around it. He will be able to feel your throat closing around its top. A more intimidating position entails lying back with your head leaning over the edge of a bed or table while he thrusts from a standing position. This aligns your neck and throat, but it leaves you more vulnerable should he get carried away. Keep your hands against the base of his penis or his stomach so that you can push him away if you want to stop.

Breathing: Proper breathing can help make gagging less likely, but it won't stop it. To be effective, you need to exhale while going down to the base of the penis and inhale while going up. The orally gifted can manage to massage the base of the penis with their lips. Gulp.

I think using sex toys while you're giving a blow job is weird. I can understand why you'd put one in his ass to stimulate that G-spot thing that's up there, but why would you try and jam a vibe in your mouth while you're sucking him off? I can hardly get him in my mouth as it is.
Stacey, 27, US

My top tip on the head job front has to be go deep. My favourite is when she's been sucking a mint so it stings a bit and it's sort of a cold feeling, and then she literally lets me fuck her mouth. She loves it, and offers to do it all the time. We put her head on the pillows and go for it. I love looking into her eyes while I thrust in and out, and when I come I hold her head and go in deep. I guess you could say I'm a lucky guy.
Darren, 42, UK

I don't know what all the fuss is over fellatio. I tell you, if I have a choice between sex and that, I'd go for sex every time. In fact, faced with a choice between getting it or pleasing her with my tongue, I'd pleasure her.
Matthew, 20, US

69

AKA
88, 68

I'm not the biggest fan of 69, simply because I'm selfish when it comes to oral sex. I want to enjoy my partner going down on me without having to concentrate on getting him off. Likewise, I want to give him my full attention when I am going down on him.
Trish, 28, US

I prefer to call a female 69 position an '88' because they are two of the same and, like the 69, it's the same position, any way you flip it. I love it by any name though. It gives me pleasure while simultaneously giving my girl pleasure. The really erotic thing about it is if we match tempo and timing it's kinda like I'm giving head to myself.
Leh, 19, US
Kuma2

Trouble is I can't breathe when my face is in my partner's vagina, with her legs squeezing me into them. I have her full sex on me and I am supposed to concentrate on what she's doing to me? No way.
Antonia, 22, UK

A waste of a good blow job? Often thought of as the most egalitarian sexual position, 69 has its good and bad points. The combination of the visual and physical sensations can be extremely erotic during simult-aneous oral sex, but, to be honest, many people find it difficult to concen-trate on their own and their partner's pleasure at the same time. It's a bit like trying to rub your head and pat your stomach at once. Sixty-nine may simply be one of those positions that sounds and looks good, but can't always deliver the mother lode.

Which way is up?: Approaching your partner's genitals from the wrong direction can make the position less satisfying. For women, it is harder to reach the vaginal entrance and the clitoris is being rubbed against its grain, so to speak. For men, tongues go up and down the less sensitive side of the penis – without the frenulum. And some people are put off by the fact that their nose tends to get lodged in their partner's bottom. If there is a big height difference between partners, the taller person has to curl up a bit so that each partner's mouth is lined up with the other's genitals and vice versa.

Easy now: That said, 69 can be an effective form of mutual stimulation. The traditional image of 69 – a couple lying down facing each other, head to toe – is quite a relaxing position. It puts less pressure on the limbs, which makes it good for lengthy stimulation. Legs can be straight, open or wrapped around the head, waist or shoulders. A more interesting altern-ative involves one person lying on their back while the other kneels over, facing each other's genitals. If the person on top is a woman, she is more in control of how deep she takes his penis and her breasts and nipples can be stimulated as they hang down. The person lying down will need a pillow to raise the head and prevent neck strain. In some ways, the lack of body contact in this position adds to the sensation, because focus is solely on the genitals. The really adventurous can do this upside down: one partner sits on a bed with their back against the wall. The gymnastic friend goes into a headstand using the wall and their partner's shoulders for support. This is hard on the neck – don't try it if you have a neck problem – and can't be sustained long, but the rush of being upside down could heighten the sensation. Only try this on a soft surface, in case you fall over.

Wait for meeee: If you are some way from climax and you feel that your partner is on the brink, stop giving (but continue receiving) stimulation until you catch up. This increases the chances of simultaneous orgasm.

Hands on (anal)

Uranus: Despite the fact that everyone has an anus, lots of people have mixed feelings about anal play. Many women and men say that they don't like anal stimulation even though they have never tried it. Those who have, tend to look on it as simply another sensory option. There are different levels of anal play. If you enjoy having the rim of your anus massaged, it doesn't mean you have to go on to full-scale penetration. Anal penetration should only hurt if it is done incorrectly. Painful anal sex usually indicates that you are not relaxed, not using enough lubricant and trying to do too much too quickly.

It's sex Jim, but not as we know it: Though not technically a sexual organ, the proximity of the anus to the genitals means they share a lot of the same tissue and nerve endings. In women, the rectum shares a wall with the vagina, and pressing on it indirectly stimulates the sensitive first-third of the vaginal canal. The female PC muscle that contracts during orgasm is connected to both the anal and vaginal canals. In men, the prostate gland is exceptionally sensitive to touch and can really only be stimulated through anal contact. The anus is contracted by the PC muscle, which is connected to the prostate gland and the root of the penis. For men, internal anal stimulation can feel like internal masturbation, because the bulb of the penis is very close to the anus. Straight men sometimes think that wanting anal stimulation means they are gay, but it doesn't. Men happen to have a powerful sex tool lodged in their anus and the fact that they want to use it doesn't categorise them as anything other than sexually curious.

Techniques

Exploring yourself: Exploring your anus by yourself can help you to decide if anal play is for you. To warm up, try massaging the nerve endings in the perineal muscles with the flat pads of your fingers. Using light circular strokes, push gently on the anal ring (some people prefer a firmer massage). After a while you should feel your anal muscles relax and your anus will open up slightly. Because the fingers are small and flexible, they are ideal for anal penetration. If you insert a (lubricated) finger about 1.5cm (0.5ins) inside and press your fingertip against the side, you will feel two sphincter muscles contract around your finger. You may feel a slight burning sensation. As with any muscle, the spasm cannot be held indefinitely. The muscle eventually relaxes and the discomfort should pass within about 30 seconds. Even so, rough, rapid or dry anal sex hurts.

Exploring a partner: Use your fingers to relax and massage your partner's anus first, then slowly insert a well-lubricated finger. If it feels comfortable, insert your finger slightly further. Once past the sphincters, you will feel more space inside the rectum. Keep your finger there for a moment, and if it feels good for your partner, gently rub it either side of the anal walls. When accustomed to the sensation, your partner can try contracting the PC muscle around your finger while it is inside.

Nimble fingers: For women, adding anal stimulation at the right moment during clitoral stimulation or penetration may provide the extra sensation that sends her into orgasm. For men, the switch from stimulating the penis to the anus can sometimes cause temporary loss of erection, but when a man is relaxed it can lead to more rapid orgasm. Older men who can take longer to reach climax often enjoy the fact that anal stimulation speeds things up.

Things your mother should have told you

Lube: Lubricants are absolutely essential for any form of anal exploration because the anus does not produce any lubrication of its own. You need to be more than generous – too much won't be enough. Use lots of silicon, or water-based lube on your hand, wrist, anus and condom and re-apply it regularly. Lubrication assists anal play and penetration and reduces the possibility of internal damage, grazing and bleeding. Lube also reduces the chance of a condom or other barriers tearing.

Hygiene: Don't put anything that has been in the anus into a vagina without washing it first. If you have been wearing a latex glove or a condom, put on a new one before touching the vagina.

Whoops: Don't put anything that doesn't have a flared base into your anus. Those sphincter muscles are surprisingly strong, and they will suck anything they can up into the rectum. Doctors in A & E spend a disproportionate amount of time removing shampoo bottles, apples and hairbrushes from people's rectums. In an article from *Surgery Magazine* in 1986, called 'Rectal Foreign Bodies', Drs David B. Busch and James R. Starling, of Madison, Wisconsin, USA, collated a list of recently recovered objects: bottles or jars x 32; bottle with attached rope x 1; glasses or cups x 12; light bulbs x 7; tubes x 6; apple x 1; bananas x 2; carrots x 4; cucumbers x 3; plantain (with condom) x 1; vibrators x 23; dildos x 15. Get the picture?

I once caught warts from rimming on a one night stand – I was a little drunk and didn't think, just wanted to have some sexual excitement. They were treatable, but it did ruin me for a while.
Barney, 23, UK

I think hygiene seems to be more integrated into the gay than the heterosexual scene – straight guys seem not to be as considerate. So I don't blame you girls if you play at home.
Nathan, 36, UK

78 | Lubrication | Warning

Lube, lube and more lube! I find it's best to re-apply the lube every half-inch or so as he slides in a little bit deeper. Get him to pull out slightly and re-apply, otherwise your canal just doesn't get as oiled as it needs to be to prevent pain.
Charlie, 36, UK

I am so frightened of residual poo – just the idea of it on my lover's fingers makes me cringe. Thankfully, I have other holes to preoccupy her.
Jane, 24, UK

Fisting the anus

A camel through the eye of a needle?: Fisting is also known as 'hand-balling', and describes the insertion of a whole hand and wrist into the rectum and lower colon. The anus is not designed to expand in the same way as the vagina, so fisting is a risky process. That said, people do fist, so the following guidelines attempt to ensure that you do it safely. Fisting can take hours and should only be attempted by sober, patient people who know what they are doing and are armed with bucket loads of lube and latex gloves. Before you try fisting, you should spend time expanding your partner's capacity for anal penetration by inserting a series of lubricated dildos with flared bases in graduating sizes. Start with small dildos and build up to bigger and bigger ones. Never, ever, agree to be fisted by a novice, particularly if alcohol or drugs have been taken. The rectum is not a straight tube – it curves several times and has a sharp twist about 20cm (8ins) in, which rough skin or an over-eager fist could perforate very easily. Internal bleeding isn't obvious from the outside and blood poisoning or septicaemia can follow without treatment. There are no pain receptors in the intestines, so once the internal sphincters have been passed, there is no way of telling what internal damage has been done until illness (cramps, chills, fever) sets in. If you feel any sharp pain, fever or bleeding after fisting, you should see a doctor. Fisting can eventually take its toll on muscle tone. Some people who fist regularly can loosen the muscles so much that eventually they have difficulty controlling when they defecate. But after all the bad news, it has to be said that people who practise safe fisting describe it as extremely sexually arousing, and some consider the relaxation and concentration required to be an almost spiritual experience. Others believe that fisting is about power and control. Whichever, considerable trust is needed – and very short fingernails.

Things your mother should have told you

I need a wee: When fisting it is very common to experience the need to urinate, because the hand puts pressure on the bladder from the inside, so it is advisable to urinate beforehand if possible.

Now wash your hands: Fingernails can harbour bacteria, so infections are easily passed on. Use a latex glove for protection – long obstetric gloves are best, because they go some way up the arm. When taking off your glove, grab the open end so it doesn't slip off and end up getting lost inside.

I always warm up my partner with a little anal massage, as he always holds so much tension in those tender muscles. It's a great way to relax your body and mind.
John, 46, UK

I really enjoy anal, but my boyfriend, sadly, is one of the rare men who doesn't. I'm always like 'please can we do it up the bum', but he only wants to now and again. I don't think it's a turn-off for him, I think he just prefers my puss.
Amanda, 33, UK

I once had this guy's fist in my arse when I had this uncontrollable urge to cough. I had a bit of a coughing fit, which must have made my muscles crunch down on his hand. I think it really hurt him because he yelled and he didn't want to carry on after that.
David, 40, UK

Stimulating the prostate

Can you touch my what? The word prostate conjures up images of incontinent elderly gents, but this small gland is actually a hidden sexual weapon. It is difficult to extract the truth from people about prostate pleasure – the anal taboo means it remains a well-kept secret. Many men never experience the pleasures of the prostate, simply because they don't know it exists. Others worry that anything anal is 'dirty', or think that only gay men enjoy anal play. Not true. The prostate can be thought of as a sexual tool that men can use if they want.

The prostate gland is located about 4cm (1.6ins) inside the anus on the front wall of the rectum. It creates prostatic fluid, which combines with sperm and fluid from the seminal vesicles to create semen. A small soft organ (like a chestnut), it contains numerous nerve endings that are very sensitive to touch, but it does not feel distinct from the rest of the anus before real arousal occurs.

Is it safe? Some men mistakenly believe that having their prostate stimulated will make them more vulnerable to prostate cancer or prostatitis (inflammation of the prostate gland). This is not true, though doctors do examine a patient's prostate in their search for inflammation, infection and cancer. This involves massaging the prostate until prostatic fluid oozes out (without orgasm) into a container.

Apprehensions: Men who have negative associations about the idea of prostate stimulation may not be very enthusiastic about exploring its sexual possibilities. However, the sensations experienced during a medical prostate examination are a million miles away from the sensation of prostate stimulation during full sexual arousal – in the same way that there should not be any sexual sensations when a doctor performs an internal vaginal examination on a woman.

Self-love? Although it is physically possible for a man to stimulate his own prostate gland, it is very awkward and, frankly, the anus is not the first place a man's hand goes when he is trying to relieve his 'visible' sexual tension. Prostate stimulation is usually performed while simultaneously masturbating the penis, and any man who can manage both activities at once deserves a gold star for co-ordination. Some men (particularly straight men) are embarrassed about asking a partner to give them prostate stimulation, but getting someone else to do it is much better and more relaxing than DIY.

We keep a vibrator in the freezer so it's really cold when I use it to stimulate his prostate. Sometimes the cold makes his anus 'freeze up', so it takes plenty of KY to work it in. Then I put jelly all over my fingers and masturbate him with one hand while I'm working the vibrator on his prostate. It takes a bit of locating, because you're not using your fingers to guide you, but once I have, he goes off like a rocket.
Wendy, 41, UK

Remember to breathe. I get really drowsy after coming through prostate wanking unless I control my breath the whole way through. It's probably because it's so horny that if you don't take care you pant like a dog the whole way through and hyperventilate from it!
Andrew 49, UK

I have had one terrible experience with someone who really had no clue as to what they were doing. It hurt like hell and I doubt I'll ever try again with anyone else. As a Bottom you have to know if your Top knows his stuff.
Gerald, 30, UK

Techniques

Sex: Though any man who has had his prostate gland stimulated properly never forgets it, some men just don't enjoy having their anus penetrated, so make sure you ask him if he wants it first.

Five: You need to get organised. You'll need lots of lubricant, because anal tissue is delicate, and you should really wear surgical gloves to prevent bacteria transferring from dirty fingernails or residue faeces. You can buy surgical gloves in any pharmacy – they are routinely used for applying fake tan or hair dye, so the assistant won't automatically be thinking 'aha, rectal examination'. Buy a big pack. For many people, latex gloves are such a turn-on that the sight of them alone is enough to get them aroused.

Four: Once you have your props, you are ready to begin. He should lie on his back with you kneeling between his legs. This allows both of you to stimulate his penis throughout the proceedings. Once he's aroused, warm up his anus by massaging the nerve endings in the perineum (the ridge between his scrotum and anus) with the flat pads of your fingers. Pressing gently but firmly in a circular motion will stimulate the prostate inside.

Three: When he is visibly excited, the muscles around his anal rim (sphincters) will twitch, and if you rub over the opening with your gloved and lubricated finger you can judge whether he is ready for your finger. As you insert your finger, the sphincter muscles will contract. This may feel uncomfortable for him at first, but like any muscle it can only stay in spasm for so long, so within about 30 seconds it should have released.

Two: Carry on masturbating him as you insert your finger further in. Press towards the front of his body, fingernail facing his back, and make a 'come here' motion. Pressing the gland may give him the sensation of wanting to urinate, but it won't actually make him pee.

One: The prostate gland will only increase in sensitivity when it is directly stimulated, so rub your finger all over the gland or pulse your finger – ask him what feels good (though if you're getting it right, he may not be able to speak at this point). As he comes closer to orgasm, his anal sphincter muscles will contract around your finger and the gland will swell as the blood vessels expand. On orgasm, the prostate contracts, empties and semen shoots out of his penis. Amazing.

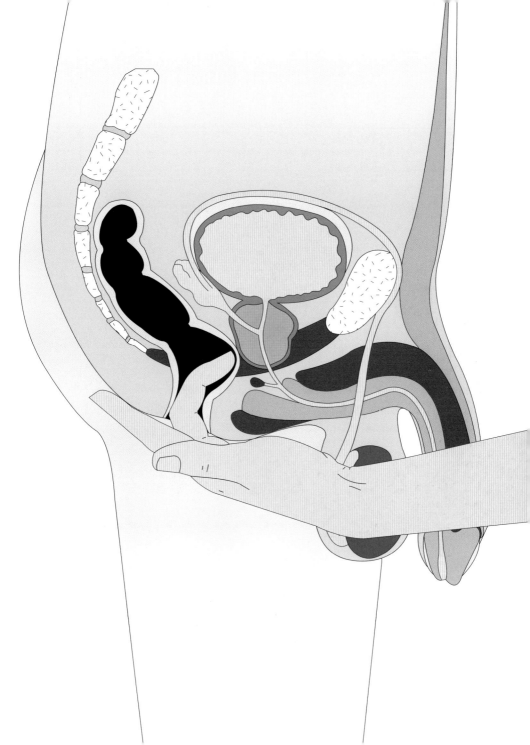

Going down (anal)

AKA
Rimming
Butt sucking
Chocolate kiss

He only lets me do it occasionally, but I know he likes it. He gets really wrangled if I mention it afterwards, though.
Reon, 57, UK

114

Safer Sex

I had no clue what he was going to do. We were fooling around, and he just said to me 'are you ready', and for some reason I said 'yes'. He flipped me over, pushed my bottom apart and kissed me there! It was really nice. I said to my girlfriend how wild it was and she said 'oh that? We do that all the time!'
New convert, 27, UK

As a heterosexual man I cannot possibly see why that would in any way appeal. There are plenty more attractive parts of her body, which have the added benefit of not being what she uses to go to the toilet.
Anon, 33, Australia

Rimming: Licking and probing the anal rim with the tongue is usually known as rimming. It is a gentle way to receive anal stimulation, because the tongue is agile and flexible and saliva keeps the whole experience smooth and lubricated. It can be exciting and sensual for those who enjoy it; some people do it to relax the anus in preparation for anal penetration, and others as a sexual act in itself. The anus is surrounded by more social taboos than any other part of the body, which means that while some people feel that there is a naughty thrill to be had by rimming, others feel that it is the last thing on earth they would be willing to try – even if they are quite happy to engage in anal stimulation with a hand or a penis. Rimming may put your mouth in contact with faeces, which carries health risks, such as contracting mouth infections, hepatitis A and parasitic infections.

Arousal: Rimming feels a lot nicer if you're aroused in the first place. Run your hands and lips over your partner's body, and then start to massage the buttocks. Lick, nibble and kiss them, working your way down the crack to the anus. Play with your partner's genitals while you probe the anus with your tongue.

Cactus tongue: Keep a drink handy in case your mouth gets dry. Edible lubricant will keep everything wet, and if you're worried, flavoured lubes disguise the tastes and smells of your partner's body.

Techniques

Anal kiss: Licking, kissing, nibbling, flickering, swirling and deep thrusting with a wet tongue along, around and into the opening of the anus provide a wealth of different sensations. Plug your tongue against the entrance to the anus and leave it there, pressing gently at first and building up to firmer pressure.

Circle kiss: Lick in and circle around the anus, making smaller and smaller circles while feeling the different textures of the anus opening and its muscles.

Around the world: Lick from the balls down to the anus and back again.

Positions: Your partner can sit on your face, or hold their legs behind the elbows while you kneel beside the bed.

Things your mother should have told you

You are what you eat: One of the concerns that people have when it comes to anal play is the prospect of coming into contact with faeces in someone else's back passage, or, indeed, exposing someone to their own. This is a particular worry when it comes to rimming. Though the anus and the rectum act as a passageway rather than a storage area, some residue may remain, so if you engage in anal play, you should be prepared to get dirty. Eating a healthy, high-fibre diet with plenty of fruits, vegetables and grains ensures better-formed stools (healthy ones should be bulky, slightly moist and well-formed, like a small banana). These exit more cleanly than soft ones and are also less messy and smelly. Don't overdo the fruit and vegetables, because the more fibre, the softer your stools.

Cleanliness is next to godliness: You can clean the outside of the anus like any other part of your body: gently and with a wet flannel. Soap can leave the skin quite dry, and too much cleaning can damage the delicate skin, so go easy and try to use milder soaps. Some people clean internally using enemas or douches, but, if used in the wrong way or too frequently, these can destroy the natural oils in the anal passage and can irritate the lining, leading to constipation, haemorrhoids and other health problems. There are several different types of internal cleaning:

Bulb syringe enema: These can be bought over the counter at a pharmacy and are made up of a rubber bulb attached to a slender plastic tube. You fill the bulb with water and squirt the water into your anus until it feels full (try doing this part in the bath). Then you sit on the toilet and wait for the water to pump out. Because the water may not evacuate fully and you may pass a little liquid for a while, it is best to carry out the procedure well in advance of anal sex play.

Shower attachment enemas: These can be bought by mail order, on the Internet or in sex shops. These work on the same principle as the bulb syringe enema. They are attached to your shower head and have adjustable flow and speed settings. Take care that the spray isn't too powerful, or you may damage the delicate lining of the rectum.

Colonic irrigation: Some people opt for professional colonic irrigation (an expensive form of water enema) as a form of whole-body detox. Frankly, a bowl of bran cereal and a bath is cheaper and probably just as effective.

You have to have a healthy body to have a healthy mind and a healthy sex life. I go for colonic irrigation when I know my system is junked up and I need a detox. I feel cleaner – health-wise and spiritually.
Megan, 30, UK

All that enema stuff is a waste of time. I often think it's just homophobic people's way of telling us we're dirty. You can wash your arse the same way you wash your cock. What's the big deal?
Rob, 36, UK

I like to have a shower with my boyfriend before we do anything much, so neither of us have any inhibitions about being clean before we get into a long night of steamy sex. I very much recommend it!
Lisa, 29, UK

I like doing it to my girlfriend, but I don't think I would enjoy her doing it to me. It's not that I think there's anything wrong with it – obviously, or I wouldn't do it to her – it's just not my bag. But I really like what it does to her, and, actually, watching her get into it turns me on.
Kayla, 20, New Zealand

Safer sex

Safer sex is nothing new: The exchange of bodily fluids, however pleasant, has always been a dangerous occupation. The ancient Egyptians and Romans used condoms, and in the 17th century a physician named Dr Conton manufactured one from fish bladders and lambskin to protect King Charles II of England from syphilis. Things haven't changed much. Barrier methods such as condoms are still the most simple and effective way of preventing the spread of infection and having safer sex.

What does 'safer' mean?: When it comes to discussing the risks attached to sex, it is easy to sound alarmist. The point most people forget is that safer sex presumes that there is an infection to be prevented in the first place. In reality, we know that there are lots of long-term monogamous couples out there who are sure that they are free of infection. These couples probably don't use any protection and they probably don't need to. The problem is that illnesses such as HIV can lie dormant for decades, so sexual history has to be taken into account. You may be able to trace your own sexual history, but to be sure you are free from HIV or other STIs, you also need to be able to account for your partner, and all your partner's partners, and all your partner's partners' partners – and, frankly, that is just impossible. This means that safer sex precautions should be an integral part of sex for everyone who changes partners or is unsure of their, or their partners' sexual health and history. Anyone who is worried should have a test at their local Genito-urinary (GU) clinic. It can take three months from your last unsafe behaviour to get the all-clear with some STIs, but it is the only way of really being sure that you are free of infection.

Misconceptions: Teenagers sometimes believe that 'safe sex' simply means their parents won't catch them. Youth and naïvety have proved to be lousy at protecting anyone from things like pregnancy and STIs, and recent figures on STIs and HIV published by the UK's Public Health Laboratory Service reveal that teenagers are still naïve about the risks. UK studies show that one in ten young women may have the STI chlamydia (the biggest cause of tubal infertility in the UK) and of the cases diagnosed last year, 34 per cent were in females aged between 16 and 19. Cases of gonorrhoea rose by 27 per cent last year (double the figure for 1995), and 40 per cent of them were in women under 20. Despite the fact that HIV has already killed 3 million people worldwide, a huge number of newly diagnosed HIV cases are teenagers who just don't seem to get the message. The myth that HIV is a gay disease seems to have contributed to the general complacency. There were 3,551 new cases of HIV diagnosed in the UK in 2001, compared to approximately 370 in Australia. In the UK, 50 per cent of new cases were through heterosexual sex, and only 39 per cent resulted from sex between men. Last year's 18 per cent rise is the highest ever recorded. The optimistic view is that these figures include people who were previously infected but only came forward for testing in 2001. The pessimistic belief is that another 11,000 people in the UK have the HIV virus but don't know it yet.

Can we talk (before we have sex)?: Taking precautions or bringing up the subject of safer sex often seems to be more difficult and embarrassing than just hopping into bed, particularly with a new partner. Feelings of passion, shyness, insecurity or fear (of losing a partner) can make negotiating protection more difficult. It seems it requires greater emotional intimacy to discuss safer sex precautions than it does to engage in sexual intimacy – but if this is the case, you ought to seriously question why you are having sex with someone with whom you don't feel comfortable enough to talk. The heat of the moment will seem like a terrible excuse later on. Remember, it can take less than five minutes to ejaculate, but it can take a lifetime to deal with the consequences.

She sounded so posh: How a person looks and sounds doesn't reflect their health status: many STIs have no visible symptoms, so your partner may not even be aware of being a carrier. Seventy per cent of women don't show any symptoms when they have an STI such as chlamydia or gonorrhoea. Many remain undiagnosed – and don't forget, for every infected woman, there is an infected partner, too. In many countries, HIV and AIDS was big news in the early '80s and massive government spending on advertising meant that most people were aware of the dangers. There is a suspicion that young people who missed these early campaigns haven't grown up with the information they need on STIs, contraception and HIV. There is also increasing concern about the fact that STIs are on the increase in people aged 35–45+. The increasing frequency of separation and divorce has meant that many older people suddenly find themselves single after long-term monogamous relationships and they just aren't aware of the risks of STIs and HIV. Information about sexual health has tended to be directed at teenagers and men and women in their 20s, because this is where the rate of infection is highest, but obviously the message needs to be spread wider.

The term STI (sexually transmitted infection): This is not specific to one infection. It includes a variety of infectious bacterial and viral organisms: amongst them are gonorrhoea, genital warts, chlamydia, herpes, hepatitis A and B and HIV. If these infections are diagnosed promptly, most of them can be managed. If they are left untreated, they can lead to serious health problems, such as infertility, cervical cancer and AIDS.

Different sexual activities carry different levels of risk: Many people think that transmission only occurs with ejaculation. In fact, it can happen via preseminal fluid, blood or any genital contact. Kissing is relatively low-risk, but although there are no proven cases of HIV being transmitted by kissing, infections such as mononucleosis, oral thrush, cold sores and hepatitis B can be passed, especially if oral hygiene is poor. Sharing sex toys also involves a small risk, because body fluids or bacteria can be harboured in absorbant materials or cracks and be passed from one partner to another. Make sure any shared sex toys are clean or cover them with a condom.

I didn't know that you could get hep A from rimming until recently, and as it is one of my all-time favourites, that naturally got me pretty worried. I didn't think I was at that much risk because I never go with anyone who could do with a wash, but, all the same, I started using cling film with lube on both sides. Now I hear you can have a vaccination against hep A. Cool. I'm off to the docs.
Bobby, 22, UK

Now I know anal isn't everyone's cup of tea, and I don't want to make anyone drink tea they don't want to, but if you are curious, always use a condom. A lot of nasty bugs are lurking in your arse, and If you don't use a condom, you are risking infecting yourself with all kinds of them.
Olivia, 20, UK

I gave a guy a head job when we were drunk and we used flavoured condoms. The banana one tasted really bad – like really cheap milkshake. I reckon the mint one was the best, but you could still taste the condom.
Eric, 26, UK

Risk

Oral sex: This has been shown to be a less risky activity than anal sex, but not if either you or your partner has HIV, an untreated STI, such as herpes, gonorrhoea or warts, or you have open cuts or ulcers in your mouth. Oral sex with a woman carries a higher risk for HIV transmission if she is menstruating. Allowing someone to ejaculate in your mouth increases the risk.

Rimming: Because faeces can carry parasites, bacteria, hepatitis A and B and anal warts (these may show no outside symptoms), licking the anus can allow infections to be passed on. Hepatitis A is on the increase, but a vaccination for it is available from GU clinics.

Fisting: Inserting the hand into the vagina or rectum carries a risk if there are cuts or open sores on the hand. Fisting can cause cuts or tears in the lining of the vagina or rectum. These tears can become infected and they can also make subsequent sexual activities more risky. Latex gloves reduce the risk.

Penetrative sex: Infections that can be transmitted through penetrative sex include herpes, genital warts, chlamydia, gonorrhoea, HIV, trichomoniasis, syphilis, chancroid and pubic lice. If you have unprotected penetrative sex when either you or your partner has an STI, you can spread the infection. The levels of HIV in vaginal fluid vary. They are likely to be highest around the time of your period, when HIV-bearing cells are shed from the cervix along with blood. A woman's chance of being infected by a man with HIV is twice as great as a man's chance of being infected by a woman.

Anal sex: Without a condom, this carries a particularly high risk for HIV transmission. This is because the rectal wall is just one layer of cells thick and can tear quite easily. Also, because of their role in the body's immune system, there are more T4 cells in the blood around the anal area and it is these cells that HIV infects. Minor cuts and scratches may be invisible to the naked eye, but still may allow infected body fluids into the bloodstream.

If you have sex with someone who has an STI or HIV: If you or your partner has an STI, abstain from sex until it has been treated. Most STIs can be cleared up or managed, but sometimes partners don't disclose the illness out of embarrassment and go on to infect their partner and re-infect themselves. Certain STIs, such as herpes, recur and someone can be infectious without showing any symptoms. If you have had unprotected sex with someone who you know is HIV positive, don't panic. Rule one is not to abandon safer sex practices while you wait for tests and results. Contact your doctor or GU Clinic as soon as possible (within 24 hours) and have a test – everything will be kept confidential. If you and your doctor believe there is a high chance of being infected, post-exposure prophylaxis (PEP), a course of anti-HIV drugs, may be prescribed. There can be severe side-effects and their effectiveness is still unclear, so this will only be recommended if you are at high risk.

Prevention: Safer sex is about lowering the risks of catching a sexually transmitted infection. Using barrier protection to prevent exposure to body fluids such as blood, seminal fluid, semen, vaginal fluids and the discharge from sores is the most obvious way to protect yourself and your partner, but there are lots of other things that you should be aware of, too.

• Be informed so that you can assess how risky a sexual activity might be.

• Be confident enough to discuss risks and protection with your partner.

• Wear condoms and use lubricant for penetrative vaginal and anal sex and put a fresh condom over sex toys each time you share them with a partner.

• Good personal hygiene will help to prevent you developing infections such as thrush that can be passed on sexually. Dirty nails harbour bacteria, so keep them clean. Keeping your nails short and filed will help to prevent them causing scratches or abrasions.

• Drinking or taking drugs can impair your ability to think clearly and make appropriate decisions about protection. A couple of glasses of wine can make us feel more relaxed and less shy, but alcohol or drugs can encourage us to take risks. The Durex *Sexual Behaviour World Survey 2001 Report* reveals that more than a fifth of British teenagers were too drunk to think of using a condom when they first had sex.

• If you are having oral sex, not allowing your partner to ejaculate in your mouth and avoiding swallowing semen lessen the risk. Don't perform oral sex without using a condom or barrier if you have cuts in your mouth, feel a cold sore coming or if a woman is having her period and you are not sure if she is free of infection.

• Have a hepatitis A vaccination if you want to rim, or use a barrier such as non-microwaveable cling film, a cut-up condom or a dental dam.

• When stimulating the G-spot, prostate gland or when fisting, wear a latex glove and use lots of lubricant.

• Don't put anything that has been in the anus into the vagina without cleaning it first, to avoid transferring bacterial infections.

• Don't kiss a partner who has mononucleosis, cold sores or oral thrush.

• Don't have sex if you have sores or other symptoms of infection or during an outbreak of herpes. Get checked for infections at least once a year and get the correct treatment if you become infected.

First rule of HIV/AIDS: don't freak out until you have a reason. You may have done something risky, but all you can do is get tested and be safer next time.
Les, 55, UK

I was married for 26 years, then alone for another six years. I have been seeing this guy for about three months, and recently I found a cluster of genital warts. It made me feel dirty and contagious and we nearly broke up because I was so upset. I was so ashamed to go to the clinic, but the doctor was a really amazing woman. She was really reassuring and she didn't have issues about me being in a relationship with another man. She said that it was quite common, and she treated me for it. I guess I've just been sheltered, but dealing with it definitely takes a weight off your mind.
Jim, 47, UK

A lot of women don't realise how at risk we are. Actually we have a much bigger chance of picking something up than guys. I think women should be more aware.
Rachel, 20, UK

Protection (condoms)

Keep it simple: We are lucky enough to have a very simple method of preventing STIs, HIV and pregnancy available. The ingenious device is tiny, inexpensive, widely available and often given away free in both nightclubs and GU clinics. Designed several thousand years ago, it has become increasingly sophisticated as a product. Though we know them as 'rubbers', it wasn't until 1843, when Goodyear vulcanised rubber, that the latex condom was born. It may be the 21st century, but condoms, archaic as they may be, are still what the doctor orders when it comes to safer sex.

What exactly are they?: The majority of modern condoms are still made from latex. These cannot be used with any oil-based lubricants as oil erodes latex, and some people are allergic to the material. The main alternative is polyurethane (plastic) condoms, and these are becoming increasingly popular, as they are thinner and stronger than latex, they provide a less constricting fit and they don't deteriorate with oil-based lubricant. The reason that plastic condoms have not superceded latex ones is that they are more expensive and can be a bit noisy during sex. Different sexual techniques may require a specific type of condom. For example, a straight-tip condom should be used on vibrators or dildos and a tougher or 'extra strong' condom should be used for anal penetration.

Condoms help to prevent the transmission of STIs: Condoms create a barrier against penile, vaginal or anal discharges, and any genital lesions or sores. Condoms also help to prevent pregnancy by blocking the passage of semen and they are generally very reliable as long as they are used correctly and put on before any genital contact occurs and removed as soon as it is over.

Effectiveness: In terms of protecting against pregnancy, condoms have about a 14 per cent failure rate, but a lot of this is down to misuse. Doctors estimate that if condoms were consistently used in the right way, the failure rate would be just 1 per cent. Generally, you can feel confident using any condom that is in date, and is stamped with a quality approved standard mark (the British Standard Kitemark or the European CEN mark). Novelty condoms may not be as effective. Check the expiry date and don't use old, damaged or sticky ones. Using two condoms together reduces effectiveness as they rub together and may both break. Choosing a condom that fits you well can increase sensitivity, and if a condom is too large, it may slip off. A tight condom could strain the material, but realistically, a regular-sized condom can fit over a hand and go right up to the elbow, so should be fine for nearly every penis.

Lubricants: Condoms are pre-lubricated but feel better with additional water-based lube. Big-brand water-based lubricants and condoms can be found in the toiletries section of supermarkets and pharmacies.

How to use a male condom

Step 1, open the packet: The penis has to be erect before you can put a condom on properly, and to be safe you need to apply the condom before the penis comes in contact with the mouth, anus or vagina. Open the condom package carefully to avoid tearing it with fingernails, teeth or rings. Gently squeeze the air out of the tip of the condom using your thumb and forefinger. If it does not have a reservoir tip, pinch it to leave a small space above the glans in which semen can collect after ejaculation.

Step 2, unroll: Unroll the condom a short distance to make sure it is being unrolled in the right direction – the rolled ring should be on the outside. Then hold the tip of the condom and unroll it down to the base of the erect penis. For an uncircumcised penis, pull the foreskin back before putting it on. If the condom does not unroll easily, it may be on upside down. If you discover you have put the condom on the wrong way, use a new one in case any seminal fluid has leaked onto it.

Step 3, apply lube: Condoms usually come pre-lubricated, but it is standard practice to use additional lubricant (particularly for anal penetration). As long as the condom and lubricant are compatible, adding water-based lubricant to the outside of the condom (or even a few drops in the tip of the condom) can increase sensation and make the experience more enjoyable for both partners.

Step 4, keep checking: During prolonged intercourse, check that the condom hasn't slipped off. Be careful when changing positions, as rotation can cause the condom to twist and then tear.

Step 5, remove: Take off the condom immediately after ejaculation. While the penis is still inserted, grasp the rim of the condom between the forefinger and middle finger and slowly withdraw the penis with the condom on, so that no semen spills. Check the condom for visible damage, such as a hole, then wrap it in tissue and discard. Don't flush condoms down the toilet as they are not biodegradable.

Step 6, (optional): For repeated oral, anal or vaginal intercourse, always use a new condom before there is any new genital contact, through to ejaculation.

Uh oh: If a condom breaks or slips off during sexual intercourse, withdraw the penis and apply a new condom before resuming. If you discover that a condom has split after ejaculation, talk to your partner before panicking and assess the risk of pregnancy or an STI. If you have any worries, visit your doctor or local GU clinic so you can be tested for either. Emergency contraception may be used to prevent pregnancy if started within 72 hours. It can be bought at a pharmacy, but is expensive. In the UK it is free from GPs and GU clinics.

Only abstinence is safe.
Josh, 18, UK

Men have nightmares about losing their erection when it comes to putting on condoms. If the woman is in charge of putting it on and she's doing it with her mouth, it won't happen.
Mistress May, UK

I hate that bit where you have to stop and put a condom on – it's so deliberate and obvious. It's like you're saying, 'okay, now I'd like to be screwed please, when you're ready'. I don't know anything else that safe though, so it's a necessary evil.
Fran, 38, UK

Some condoms are easier to get on than others. Plastic condoms might be noisy, but at least you know that you're not going to spend so long getting them on that you lose your stiffy.
Merv, 43, UK

I've never minded condoms, they're a hell of a lot better than not doing it at all, and that, for me, is the only other option.
Dom, 25, UK

Protection (female condoms)

I like the femidom because it means that I can put it in and know that I have done it properly. I love my boyfriend to death, but I just know that if we used male condoms and he ripped one or something, he would probably be too caught up in the sex or whatever to tell me. This way, I know what's going on and I am in control.
Harriet, 28, UK

You have to be joking! No, no, no. We tried them as a kind of experiment, and they look awful, because they hang out the front of your vagina, which is so unsexy. Plus it sounds like you've got a crisp packet stuffed up there. The most uncomfortable shag I have ever had in my life, without a doubt.
Natalie, 26, UK

I used femidoms with my first boyfriend because I discovered that I am allergic to normal condoms – they give me a rash. Now, with my new bloke, we use male condoms because Durex have brought one out that is made out of plastic.
Davina, 28, UK

Femidom: The most commonly used female condom is the femidom. Femidoms are bigger than a condom and look like a polyurethane (plastic) bag, with an inner ring that fits inside the vagina and around the cervix and an outer ring that covers the labia on the outside of the vagina. The femidom is hypo-allergenic, so it is an excellent alternative if you have a latex (rubber) allergy. Some people claim it has a more natural feel compared to male condoms. Femidoms have many advantages: proper use can provide both contraception and protection from sexually transmitted infections. For many women, relying on a male partner to use condoms is not a realistic option, so femidoms are a better choice because they don't require much partner involvement. However, because they are made from plastic, they can be quite noisy and some women complain that it is like having sex with a plastic bag inside them. Femidoms are quite expensive, but they are available free at some family planning clinics in the UK. Femidoms and male condoms should not be used together as they can stick to each other, with the risk that they may slip off or break.

How to use: Femidoms can be a bit tricky to insert into the vagina as they are very slippery. Hold the pouch with the open end hanging down and use your thumb and middle finger to squeeze the inner ring into a narrow oval for insertion, then spread the lips of the vagina. With your other hand, insert the inner ring and the pouch of the femidom into the vaginal opening, and with your index finger push the inner ring with the pouch the rest of the way up into the vagina. The outside ring lies against the outer lips when the femidom is correctly in place. A few centimetres (1in) of the open end will stay outside your body. Some women enjoy the fact that the outer ring indirectly stimulates their clitoris, though others can find this uncomfortable. Once sufficiently aroused, a vagina will expand and any slack in the condom will be taken up.

Penetration: When inserting a penis or sex toy, be careful that it goes directly into the femidom and doesn't slip in between the skin and the plastic instead. Without adequate lubrication, the femidom may twist, cling and be uncomfortable. If you change sexual positions, the outer ring needs to be held in place so it doesn't insert completely into the vagina or anus. After intercourse, remove the femidom before you stand up. Twist the outer ring slightly to keep the semen inside, then pull gently. Don't throw it down the toilet and don't try to reuse it – they are for one-time use only

Anal: Some people use femidoms for anal penetration because they are stronger than latex and less likely to tear or break. The easiest and probably the safest way to use them is to wear the femidom like a condom over the penis or sex toy. Apply lubrication to the outside and then penetrate the anus as normal. It is advisable to keep one hand on the base of the femidom at all times so it doesn't slip off inside the body. Polyurethane does not deteriorate with exposure to oil-based products and withstands storage better than latex.

Oral and manual sex

Latex gloves: Though oral and manual play and the use of toys are less risky than other forms of sex, it is still wise to use latex gloves, condoms or customised barrier protection to ensure complete safety. Latex surgical gloves (not washing-up gloves) are skin-tight and are worn over the hand for anal and vaginal insertion. (If you are allergic to latex, you may need to use cling film instead.) Don't use the same glove on more than one person's genitals (including your own). If you are switching between anal and vaginal activity, try wearing two gloves on the same hand and stripping one glove off when changing area. To make a tongue guard, cut the four fingers off a latex glove but keep the thumb intact – stick your tongue in the thumb hole for protected oral or anal stimulation.

Cling film and condoms: These cheap alternatives can be cut into any size and either wrapped around your partner like a loincloth or cut into smaller patches, which can be very comfortable for analingus or cunnilingus. Using lubrication on the inside of the barrier will increase sensation and pleasure. It is important to make sure that you don't buy the cling film used for microwaving, as it has micro-holes in it. Condoms (non-lubricated) can also be cut open to make a thin latex sheet to cover the vagina or anus during oral or finger play, but they only cover a small area. Plain latex and polyurethane have no taste of their own, although some condoms and gloves may have powder that can be washed off. Try flavoured barriers, or flavoured water-based lubrication, on the side of the barrier that you will be licking.

Barriers of the future

EZ-ON: A roomy condom that pulls on like a sock. It is very easy to put on and, unlike other condoms, it can be worn either way out. It is said to offer greater vaginal stimulation and it has a less restrictive feel. It looks a bit odd as it has a frill around the base and it is a bit noisy. EZ-ON is already available in The Netherlands.

Janesway: This product is a pair of women's cotton panties that can be worn during sex. The gusset, which is made of latex, not only covers the whole exposed area, but includes a type of female condom that goes inside the vaginal canal. Future styles will allow the latex gusset to be replaced, so that the panties effectively become reusable. Its advantages may include the fact that the panties can be worn before sex so that the fun is not interrupted. Trials are currently being arranged.

Bisexual bikini: A Japanese company has developed a pair of latex pants that have a type of condom attached to them. They can be used by either men or women – the condom either goes over the penis or up the vagina. They can be used for vaginal or anal penetration, but for anal sex, the pants must be worn by the person penetrating.

I had an allergic reaction to nonoxynol -9, a spermicidal gel that I used to use in addition to the condom. I broke out into a rash so severe.
Jlanekah, 36, US
Kuma2

As a disease-free straight man, I have never been concerned about the safety issues regarding giving or receiving oral sex. Of more concern to me, has been that my partner is hygienic. Nothing worse than a smelly vagina.
Frocho, 32, UK
Gingerbeer

I don't really tell the ones that I have one-night stands with but, if I see a meaningful relationship coming on I will let him or her know I have HPV (genital warts). The guy who gave me the disease didn't tell me and I found out later when I went to the clinic, so when I have one-night stands I use a condom. I am not worried right now because I am only 20, so I have all the time in the world to look for a new partner.
Nikki, 20, US

Going in (vaginal)

Fucking
Shagging
Screwing
Rogering
Bonking

I love good old-fashioned screwing, but only if I am really aroused, as having something put up me when I am dry totally stops me feeling like doing it.
Bessy, 44, Australia

I did my sexual experimenting in the late '60s, when a young man was made to feel guilty about the perfectly natural desire to have penetrative sex with a woman. There was so much encouragement to spend hours on foreplay, but if you were allowed to have sex at all, it had to be slow and gentle. I'm glad women today have calmed down about politics in the bedroom.
William, 58, UK

Men have learned that the majority of orgasms occur through clitoral stimulation. It's not that penetration doesn't feel good – it just means that the vagina doesn't produce the same number of orgasms as the clitoris.
Candace, 37, UK

Sex: To most heterosexual couples (and the dictionary), sex means vaginal penetration with a penis. It is the most prevalent sexual practice throughout the world (95 per cent of men and 97 per cent of women in the US have shagged at some point). But despite its popularity, intercourse is a rather imperfect form of sexual connection because the male and female arousal clocks operate at different speeds.

Sex: Men become aroused more quickly than women, and once a man is sexually excited and his penis is erect, he is ready for intercourse. Women, however, take longer to become aroused, and less than a quarter of women who orgasm do so through penetration alone. The rest require clitoral and vulval stimulation, and plenty of it to reach the point at which orgasm becomes inevitable. Obviously this depends on how hot a woman is for her partner – George Clooney may get the juices flowing quicker than George Bush – but the time difference is often a cause of sexual frustration. Unless both parties are prepared to wait, or sex carries on afterwards, penetration is actually the quickest way to end a sexual encounter. Worldwide, every night, women reach for the tissues, questioning themselves and their inability to have a vaginal orgasm. It's easy to blame men, but the fact that male and female sexual timings are out of sync is simply an evolutionary oversight that we can only hope will eventually be corrected. In the meantime, we need to find some sort of orgasmic equilibrium between the sexes. Seventy-five per cent of men in partnerships always have an orgasm with their partner. Only 28.6 per cent of women do.

And more sex: There is still a misguided view that sex is about male performance and female pleasure. Making men responsible for female pleasure means that some women simply wait for sexual feelings to happen to them, but this doesn't really work. Good sex requires communication and confidence. It's no surprise that the women who are confident enough to murmur 'up a bit, left a bit, mmm, just there', are the ones who have no problem having orgasms in the first place. When it comes to vaginal penetration, there's no doubt that God put the clitoris in the wrong place, but any woman who can achieve orgasm through masturbation can experience vaginal orgasm, too. It is easier for women to have orgasms with their partners when they are stimulated manually and orally – so that's the best way to start. Once you achieve this, you can considerably increase the odds of experiencing vaginal orgasm with your partner by incorporating manual stimulation into foreplay and opting for penetrative positions that continue to provide additional clitoral stimulation.

Going in (anal)

AKA
Buy the ring
Get some brown
sugar
Go Greek
Arsefucking
Buttfuck

*There is nothing
like coming when
your ass is being
stimulated at the
same time: with a
tongue, a butt plug,
arse beads or your
lover's hot cock. It
feels good. There are
so many nerve
endings in the arse,
why shouldn't it? The
psychological barrier
was tougher to get
through than
anything else.*
Erica, 24, US
CakeNYC

*I can only do anal if
I am completely
pissed. It hurts so
much that unless I
am relaxed – i.e.
semi-conscious – I
can't let him in there.*
Angela, 34, Ireland

*He did the dirty
Sanchez – fucked
my arse, wiped
his cock in his hand
and drew a
moustache of shit
across my upper lip.
It was demeaning,
humiliating and
I loved it.*
Karl, 20, US
CakeNYC

Incentives: Depending on the era and the culture, anal sex has either been accepted or condemned. Though 12 per cent of heterosexual men and 11 per cent of heterosexual women in the UK reported having anal sex in 2001, the act remains a crime that merits imprisonment in many parts of the world and in many American states. Despite this, the Lauman report puts the proportion of men and women who had 'heterosexual anal sex in the last year' in the US at 9 per cent. Since around 1981, HIV has been used as an argument by those who are morally opposed to anal sex. Often associated with gay men, in many cultures anal sex has been practised as a means of preserving virginity, a form of contraception and an alternative to vaginal intercourse during menstruation. But plenty of people do it, simply because they like it. Because men have the prostate gland, arguably there is more reason for them to experiment in receptive anal penetration. For women, the fact that the rectum shares a wall with the vagina is an incentive. Anal penetration offers a feeling of fullness in the rectum and women can be simultaneously stimulated clitorally. Of course part of the attraction may well be the fact that anal sex is seen as 'taboo'. The thrill of the forbidden can be a powerful stimulant.

Care: If anal penetration is performed correctly it should not hurt at all, but the process needs to be slow because the anal sphincter muscles are more used to pushing out waste than taking in a penis or a dildo. Anal sex is something that you have to want. If you don't, your sphincter muscles will clench up and any penetration will hurt. The membranes of the anus and penis need to be fully lubricated – silicone-based lubricant is best – and the muscles should be completely relaxed with massage before anything is inserted. Once the internal sphincter finally relaxes, you can penetrate. The pressure of penetration may cause further contraction, but this should subside after about 30–60 seconds. Once the penis or toy passes the sphincter and the contraction occurs, stay in the same position until your partner says it is OK to go deeper. If entry has been difficult, it may not be advisable to thrust in, but avoid coming out too far in case the sphincters clench up again. Because rectal sizes and shapes differ considerably, it is important to get the angle correct so that entry is smooth and comfortable.

Trust: Because anal penetration is a slow and collaborative process, it requires both commitment and communication. The increased risk of STI and HIV transmission also means that appropriate protection is more necessary than in other forms of sex play.

Going in (with a strap-on dildo)

Dildos: When most people think of sex, they think of vaginal or anal penetration with a penis, but many couples use dildos or vibrators instead. Anyone who hasn't got a penis, or has a penis that doesn't get erect or stay erect, can participate in vaginal and anal penetration by using sex toys. Women can enjoy the sensation of being the penetrator by strapping on a dildo for vaginal or anal intercourse. They may not get a lot of physical sexual sensation, but the psychological role reversal can be erotic.

Dildo harnesses: These fit around the hips and hold a dildo in place against the pubic bone to simulate a penis and allow penetration of a partner. There are two basic types of strap-on dildo:

Single strap: A single strap radiates out from an upside-down triangular central flap that has a central hole through which the dildo is inserted. The dildo has a flared base so that it does not slip through the hole. The straps rest on the hips and form a G-string at the back that comes between your legs and attaches to the base of the triangle.

Hip and thigh straps: The second type of harness is designed for men. It has hip and thigh straps but the flap of material that holds the dildo is shorter to accommodate the scrotum and has smaller straps that run back between the legs and attach at the back. A male wearing a strap-on should place the dildo above his genitals. In this position he has the option of penetrating both the vagina and the anus simultaneously, either from the front or the rear.

Materials: The best dildo harnesses are made of leather or nylon and have ring pulls, buckles or velcro to ensure a snug fit. It's easier to control a firm dildo than a floppy one. If you are using a dildo for vaginal penetration, choose one that has a slight curve, which will follow your partner's natural shape. Choose a longer dildo as the harness will take up to half an inch away from the length.

Control: Dildos are quite difficult to control. Because you can't feel what is happening inside your partner's body, using one is sometimes a disappointing experience. You need to have good co-ordination and a good imagination. If you get into a stroking rhythm, try to make sure that you avoid coming out completely (you may not even be aware that you have come out) – re-insertion can interrupt the flow. Try inserting the dildo all the way and rocking your pelvises together, rather than thrusting in and out.

AKA
Prodding
Tooled up

A dildo doesn't have to be something you buy in a sex shop. I like to boil and peel a couple of eggs and insert them into my partner's anus. I like watching his face as I gently massage and persuade his anus to take another.
Hub, 33, UK

212
Sex Toys

I had a boyfriend who loved having me stick a dildo in him. That was a really empowering feeling, I must say. But as for me and going in the back door, I would have to be really, really relaxed and really into it. It may never happen.
Monica, 25, US
CakeNYC

I've never done it, but I'd really like to wear a strap-on and do my girlfriend from behind. I don't think she would let me and I would never get around to going out and buying a strap-on. It's the sort of thing you think about when you're feeling turned on.
Helen, 40, Australia

Positions

Options: Basically there are only five or six sexual positions, and everything else is a variation on each theme. Positions for vaginal, anal and strap-on penetration are pretty interchangeable, and the best thing to do is try a variety and find what works best for you.

The missionary position: This is the most frequently used sexual position in the world and it has a multitude of variations. It derives its names from missionaries who tried to persuade other societies around the world that this was the 'approved' method of lovemaking. The locals were apparently too imaginative in their choice of positions.

Receptive 'missionary': The missionary position is a relatively passive one, but it is comfortable, allows deep penetration, eye contact, kissing and closeness. It is suitable for anal and dildo penetration, too, though you might want to prop your bottom up on a cushion. For women, missionary positions don't often place the penis at the correct angle for G-spot or clitoral stimulation. You may feel pinned underneath the weight of your partner and you won't be able to contribute much in the way of pelvic movement. If you hold on to each other's buttocks, you can create an easy rocking motion that will probably give additional clitoral arousal. If your partner is very heavy or you are pregnant, missionary positions are not an option. Besides being squashed, you have very little control over penetrative depth.

Penetrative 'missionary': You control the depth of penetration as well as the speed of the thrust. Arching your back allows for deeper penetration, while lying on top of your partner allows full body contact, shallower penetration and better clitoral stimulation for women. Placing a pillow under your partner's lower back will increase the contact between her clitoris and your pubic bone or raise the anus to make it more accessible. It can be tiring to support your weight and holding yourself up can affect your ability to control ejaculation.

Receptive 'on top': If you have good thigh muscles, you can squat on your haunches and bounce up and down. If you are strong enough to be able to control this movement, you can pause at the top for a few seconds before sliding down the penis again. This will give your partner an incredible sense of anticipation – but be warned, it can lead to a very rapid climax. This position is very tiring, so unless you have buns of steel you may not be able to sustain it for very long. You can either sit upright or lie on top of your partner, which distributes the weight more evenly. Women on top can try rocking backwards and forwards to stimulate different parts of their vagina and clitoris. On top is good for pregnant women with a big bump because it doesn't get in the way and they can control the depth of penetration to some extent, as long as they have strong thigh muscles.

Penetrative 'on top': In most 'on-top' positions, you lie flat and your partner straddles you face-to-face as if riding you like a horse (that's probably where the expression comes from). Good for vaginal, anal and dildo penetration, on-top positions work well where the person lying down is heavier or less athletic. Unless you are sporting a dildo, the inactivity of being under your partner can sometimes cause loss of erection or make ejaculation difficult, though this depends on how energetic your partner is. If you have a tendency to ejaculate quickly, it may help to slow things down.

Receptive 'from behind': Rear-entry positions allow for deeper penetration. They are suitable for vaginal and dildo penetration, and are probably the most popular positions for anal intercourse. Rear entry doesn't give much stimulation to the clitoris so it may help to incorporate some manual stimulation into foreplay. Some women feel that with rear-entry positions they don't have much control and that it is something being done 'to' them rather than 'with' them. For women who are self-conscious or unsure of their partner, it can feel as if their partner doesn't want to see them or look at them. That said, when a couple feel relaxed and communicative, the sense of anonymity can be a real turn-on. If a woman lies on her stomach with pillows under her pubic bone to raise her bottom in the air, she can also slip a little vibrator or her hand in under her clitoris while she is being penetrated. Rear entry is sometimes painful for a woman, because the penis can go in so deep that it hits her cervix. This depends on the level of a woman's arousal, the size of her vagina, the length of the penis and the depth of thrusting. It is a good position for a pregnant woman, because there is no pressure on her stomach, and also if one partner is very bony, because there is more padding on the buttocks.

Penetrative 'from behind': Some say that rear-entry sex is the most satisfying 'deep sex' and is best for thrusting sensations. You can hold on to your partner's hips and move together, or you can hold your partner still while you thrust in and out. Rear-entry vaginal positions are better if a man has a smaller penis because the vagina shortens, causing a greater sensation of fullness for her. The natural curve of the vagina fits with the curve of the penis, so deep thrusting is usually more comfortable than in other positions.

As a Bottom, in the end I just really dig a hard shaft. Rear entry isn't just one position, you can do it standing up, bent over the kitchen table, on your side, curled up in a ball or sitting on his lap. I like it on my knees in front of a mirror, so he can see my facial expressions and I can see his. That's really hot.
Brad, 32, Australia

For me, cervix pumping is pretty damn important, so for that it just has to be from behind.
Lorena, 40, US

We have this role-play thing going where we are a gay couple – I wear a strap-on dildo and screw him like I'm a big man with a big penis. I don't suppose that many guys would go for it because so many of them are worried about thinking they might be gay, but my man is pretty enlightened. Lucky for me, because that means I can fulfil all my fantasies!
Steph, 26, UK

She bent me over to do me up the butt, but it hurt. I thought it was the position, but looking back I just don't think we had enough lube.
Sharon, 19, UK

When I am penetrating him, I like him to be on all fours (in front of a mirror if possible!) and I like to thrust all slow and gentle. When he's penetrating me, I like to sit on his lap and bounce around like I'm in a car going down a bumpy track.
Alli, 34, US

Late at night we were walking on the beach and it started to rain really hard so we ran into the public toilets to take cover. Because we'd gone to the beach to have sex, we ended up doing it standing up in the toilet cubicle. From that experience I would say to anyone who is taller than their boyfriend, 'don't bother', because you spend the whole time bending your knees and trying to make yourself short enough for his penis to reach. That combined with the smell of public toilets wasn't exactly erotic.
Debbie, 35, UK

I like to be taken from behind up against a wall. It is like role-play. In my mind I am being taken against my will and I can't escape. I like rough dominant sex like that
Sasha, 37, UK

Low-impact positions: Many couples enjoy sex side-on, either face-to-face, or rear entry. These positions are especially good for partners of different weights, pregnant women, people who do not enjoy deep thrusting and older people who may have arthritis or who are less mobile, because they put less pressure on joints and muscles. They are also the best positions for people who are trying out anal sex for the first time. Sideways positions are the most equal in terms of weight distribution, because neither partner is on top. And they are among the most intimate and relaxed positions for intercourse, too. Because movement is more limited, the experience tends to be softer, more leisurely and relaxed. For some, this can mean it feels less passionate and exciting, but for others it can mean closeness, warmth and full body contact. As neither partner is taking the weight, it allows for longer penetration and even a comfy snooze afterwards. Trial and error is the only way to find out what is comfortable and what isn't, but bear in mind that some of the more elaborate arrangements may not be sustainable for long. If your partner wraps their legs around your waist, make sure that they are underneath the fleshy area between your lowest rib and your hip bone. Many of the variations on sideways positions can be made more comfortable with pillows or supports with a little bit of experimentation. But if you begin to feel stiff or experience cramp, change to a different position for a while.

Sitting: Most sitting positions do not work for heavy thrusting, but they can maintain blood in the pelvic region and this can assist in maintaining an erection. A woman on top in a sitting position can rock back and forth, increasing her clitoral stimulation. Sitting positions are good for couples of different sizes if the lighter one is on top. They are also good if a women is pregnant, as long as she is well-supported.

Standing: In standing positions, one partner usually uses a wall as support and penetrates either from the front or from behind. These positions are excellent for quickies in confined spaces, such as aircraft toilets and broom cupboards. They work better if you are fairly equally matched in height. Standing, well-balanced with legs apart, one partner leans forward using the door, hand basin, mirror or wall for support and the other penetrates them from behind. If there is room, one partner leans over and holds the toilet seat for support while they are entered from behind. Alternatively, a flexible female partner may be able to keep one foot on the floor and raise the other to rest it on the toilet seat. You can then have face-to-face vaginal sex.

Body contact

Body talk: Communicating physically is similar to speaking and listening. You need to understand the conversation to be able to respond appropriately, sensitively or creatively. It's like dancing: you need to be able to lead or follow, to anticipate what will work next or to instigate change without upsetting the rhythm.

Shallow thrusting: Opting for shallow thrusting rather than deep penetration can heighten sexual tension. As you inch your way in and out of the vagina or the anus it builds anticipation for the inevitable deep thrust. The opening and the first-third of the vagina is in fact much more sensitive than the interior canal, so slow, shallower thrusting in the early stages of penetration will probably be more stimulating for a woman. The head of the penis is generally larger than the shaft, so it rubs snugly against the nerve-filled tissue and stimulates the clitoris, too. Because the head, the frenulum and the coronal ridge are the most sensitive parts of the penis, small thrusts will rub the ridge of the penis in over her pubic bones and back out again, which feels sensational.

Anal and dildo penetration: Shallow thrusting will mean a tighter grip around the head as the sphincter muscles clasp the shaft. This can be uncomfortable if your partner is not used to it, but gentle, shallow movements may help the sphincters to relax. If you are shallow thrusting with a strap-on dildo, it is easy to fall out, especially if your movements are too dramatic or jerky. You may need to hold the dildo in one hand if you want to use this technique.

Slow, deep thrusting: Slower, deeper thrusting can be languid, fluid and involve close body contact. Your partner may wrap their legs around you while lying on the side and rock gently against you while you thrust deeply without really withdrawing. You can cover your partner with your body and only raise your hips to thrust, or your partner can sprawl across you and push the pubic bones against you, again without really withdrawing. In positions like these, thrusting doesn't have to be in and out. Circling, rocking or even keeping very still can vary the sensations and heighten arousal for both of you. Deep thrusting in certain positions with a woman can help to position your pubic bone to make direct contact with her clitoris (try getting your partner to lie across you with legs straddling one of your legs). The in-and-out movements will pull on the labia, which also indirectly stimulates the clitoris. Using a pillow to raise her pelvis up makes it easier for deep in-and-out thrusting.

It's best when he is on top and I am on my back with my legs over his shoulders. There's loads of variations on this theme – sometimes he holds my ankles together in front of his face, lifting my bum off the bed and making it all very tight. It can be very deep like this, but we go slowly, staring into each other's eyes so that he knows when it's getting to be too much for me.
Simone, 30, Australia

Anal penetration is something you build up to, not something you suddenly decide to do. I have to be with someone who I really trust and can relax with, and it takes quite a lot of finger play before he goes in. I like it slow enough for me to say stop if it starts to hurt. It sounds like a lot to ask, but believe me, my boyfriend says it's worth it.
Jade, 24, UK

In the end, it's all about what mood you are in. Sometimes you want a quick bang, and sometimes you want to make slow and beautiful love. You don't want to eat the same food everyday, so why would you always have the same sex?
Mohammed, 44, US

Slow anal and dildo: Slow thrusting is gentle, allows close body contact and may also help to delay orgasm. With strap-on dildos, slow, deep thrusting makes things easier to control and avoids the possibility of slipping out.

Rapid, deep thrusting: In men, rapid thrusting tends to be an indication of approaching orgasm. It is quite tiring and can't be sustained for very long, so it should either be interspersed with less energetic movement or saved until orgasm is inevitable. Rapid, deep thrusting may be uncomfortable for some people, particularly if they have a small build.

Squeezing: If your partner has strong vaginal or anal PC muscles they can be squeezed around your penis while you rest inside (it feels a bit like squeezing a lemon). This focuses you both on the micro sensations in your genitals, and if you are both very aroused and nearing orgasm, squeezing can help encourage pre-orgasmic spasms.

Body contact: Full body contact, in which your whole body rubs against your partner's, can be very sensuous. You can hug, clasp, rub, scratch, stroke, kiss, grab, caress, lick, suck, pull in, pull out and on and on. Alternatively, penetration can involve exclusively genital contact. In this case, there is no physical contact except between the genitals.

Angles for G-spot and prostate penetration: Certain positions, such as rear-entry or on-top, mean that the penis or dildo thrusts into the front wall (G-spot) of the vagina, which can be more sensitive than other parts. The deeper part of the vagina is often sensitive to pressure, especially as women approach orgasm. For some women, this is the key to orgasm, though for others it can be uncomfortable or even painful. For anal penetration, getting the angle right for entry can be tricky, because the rectum has many different bends. The penis or the dildo should be angled towards the prostate gland during male anal penetration.

Pelvic rocking: During this motion, you and your partner don't lose genital and pelvic contact. Your pelvises are jammed up together (it doesn't really matter who is on top) and you create friction by pulling your pelvis in the opposite direction to your partner's and then coming back together. For women, this is great for additional clitoral stimulation and it can also stimulate the G-spot. The penetration can be deep and the thrusting can be either gentle or very forceful. It is a good motion for women who are approaching orgasm.

Passivity: If one partner is passive, then the other partner will be responsible for the type of motion. A woman on top may gently raise and lower herself over the head of her partner's penis or dildo, a man on top may thrust rapidly and deeply. However, if one partner remains passive throughout, it can either indicate a lack of interest or give the active partner licence to control the pace entirely. Needless to say, this isn't conducive to great sex – unless you are consciously acting out a fantasy and you find that it's a turn-on for you both. Penetration is collaborative. No one wants to have sex with a sack of potatoes, nor to have no say in the pace or position.

The coital alignment technique (CAT): This was devised by American psychotherapist Edward Eichel in the 1990s. The coital alignment technique is essentially a revised missionary position that involves rocking rather than thrusting to put rhythmic pressure on the clitoris during penetration. CAT is suitable for heterosexual couples, but two women with a strap-on dildo may also find it effective. You position yourself on top of your partner so that your pelvis is further up her body. The head of your penis or dildo penetrates her vagina but your shaft is outside, pressing against her pubic bone. You rest your full weight on your partner, which makes you slide towards her shoulders and head. She wraps her legs around yours and rests her ankles on your calves. She pushes up and forward to force your pelvis backward. You allow your pelvis to move back, but continue to press against hers. During the upward stroke, your penis or dildo disappears into her vagina. During the downward stroke, you force her pelvis back and down, which presses her clitoris against the base of your penis. During the downward stroke, the shaft of your penis or dildo will reappear. Rock backwards and forwards like this, keeping a slow and steady pace . . . and bingo.

Farts: Penetrative thrusting occasionally causes air to get pushed back and trapped in the vagina or anus. Once the penis or dildo is withdrawn, it tries to escape, and when the damp walls of the vagina or anus close back in on themselves, the air creates fart-like noises on the way out. Of course, these are not real farts, but plenty of people feel mortified because they assume that their partner thinks they have broken wind. Because the problem usually only happens when the penis or dildo is being withdrawn, one trick that can be used to save potential embarrassment is to discreetly insert a finger to open up a passage that allows the air to escape silently.

Sometimes, when I am really tired, I can be really passive. I always thought that, as a woman, you can get away with it if you're doing missionary and you just make lots of noise and keep touching their shoulders. But then one day my husband said that I should just say if I am too tired and he can have a wank. I guess I wasn't getting away with it after all.
Petra, 44, UK

I wish I had been told about fanny farts before. I went with a girl and she did it twice. I thought she was farting for real and tried to make a joke about it, but she got all huffy and blushed. Now I feel a real prick.
Keith, 18, UK

When we have been really going for it and I am really moist, then sometimes I make fanny farts. It's awful if you are with someone you don't know very well – it makes you want to say, 'It wasn't a real fart', but that would make you feel stupid, too. I've been with the same guy for quite a while now, and I think he actually quite likes it – it's kind of 'down and dirty'.
Jodie, 29, Australia

Missionary

THE MISSIONARY POSITION

Good for vaginal, and strap-on. A very popular position that is good for whole-body contact. It allows weight to be partially rested on the partner beneath. Can be sustained for reasonable lengths of time. Great position for partners who want to kiss during sex.

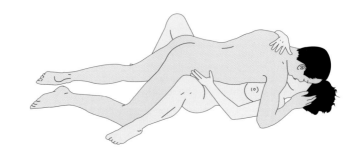

THE PELVIC TILT

Good for vaginal, anal and strap-on. Also good for G-spot and prostate stimulation as it tilts the pelvis upwards, so the penis or dildo hits the spot as it thrusts. In women, the vulva is pressed flat against the pelvic bone, causing friction on the clitoris, urethra and labia. Try different angles to change the internal position of the penis or dildo.

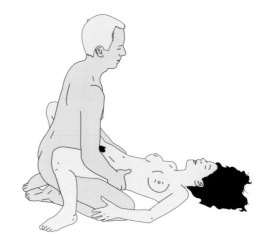

THE SPLIT

Good for deep vaginal, anal and strap-on. This position allows the angle of penetration to be varied, which allows a range of different sensations. It allows partners to watch each other's faces, and in certain variations, a woman can stimulate her clitoris with her hand.

KNEES TO CHEST

Good for deep vaginal, anal and strap-on. Requires a degree of flexibility, but allows for deep penetration. The further back the legs, the deeper the penetration. Women can press a hand to the stomach to feel the shape of the penis or dildo as it pumps in and out. This maximises (G-spot) stimulation. Try legs to one side so the side walls are massaged.

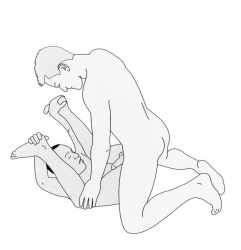

On top

THE SQUAT

Good for deep vaginal, anal and strap-on. Strong thigh muscles are required, so you may not be able to sustain it for very long. Pausing at the top for a few seconds heightens the anticipation. Works well if the person lying down is very heavy. Good for pregnant women, but penetration can be too deep in later pregnancy – unless you want to trigger labour.

PELVIC SLIDE

Good for vaginal, and strap-on. She slides her body up and down, rubbing her clitoris against your pubic bone. One of the best positions for giving a woman a penetrative orgasm. Also good if she lies at an angle with her legs between yours.

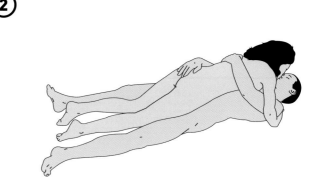

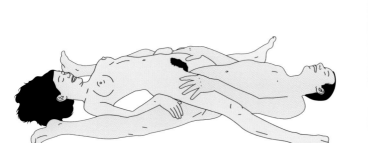

(3)

THE 70

Good for vaginal, anal and strap-on. This position doesn't allow for much movement, but the physical sensations are entirely concentrated on genitals and the partner on top can be manually stimulated, too.

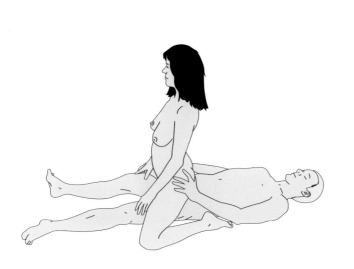

(4)

FACING AWAY

Good for vaginal, anal and strap-on. Person on top can lean forward to change the angle of the penis or lie right back so that weight is more evenly distributed (while having sweet nothings whispered in the ear). Both can stimulate their own genitals and have access to their partner's. This position bends the penis backwards away from the body, so be careful – it can cause discomfort and, occasionally, a penile fracture.

From behind

DOGGY STYLE

Good for vaginal, anal and strap-on. Low-impact. Good for overweight people as it puts minimal strain on the muscles. Make sure you are kneeling on something soft. Hold the hips for balance. Good for the smaller penis, too, as this position shortens the vaginal barrel and makes penetration feel deeper. Partner can lean down and forward, so that the bottom is sticking up in the air for even deeper penetration. Good for G-spot and prostate stimulation too.

WHEELBARROW

Good for vaginal and anal, but probably too wobbly for strap-on. Very athletic. Even with strong arms and a light partner, it is difficult to sustain for prolonged intercourse. Allows for very vigorous thrusting.

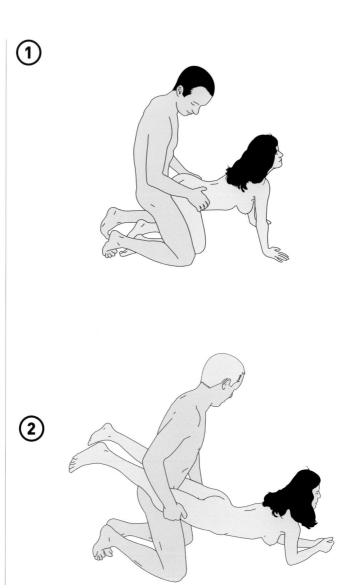

① ②

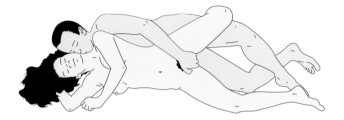

SPOONS

Good for vaginal, anal and strap-on. A comfortable position, probably the easiest for newcomers to anal sex. Allows close body contact, holding and mutual genital stimulation. Lean forward or curl the upper body away to increase the depth of penetration. Good for later in pregnancy, too.

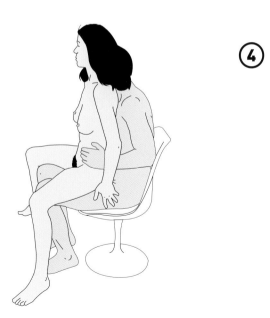

REAR-ENTRY SEATED

Good for vaginal, anal and strap-on. This position is good if the partner below is heavier. It does not allow a huge amount of movement but the person on top can enjoy additional genital stimulation.

Low impact

THE WRAP

Good for vaginal
and strap-on. The
legs underneath
you should be
positioned in the
gap of soft flesh
between the hips
and the bottom of
the ribs. Very close,
good for kissing and
eye contact. Easy on
the joints and very
relaxing. The
pressure is on the
contact points of
your shoulders and
hips, but if you are
lying on a soft bed,
this should be
very comfortable.
Bolster pillows
behind your backs
can help to prop
you up.

THE L-PLATE

Good for vaginal,
anal and strap-on.
Allows penetration
with minimal
pressure on the
joints. Hands are
free to explore and
stimulate genitals.
Some people find
that they feel too far
away from one
another.

KNEELING

Good for vaginal, anal and strap-on. One partner kneels on the floor next to the bed and leans on the mattress, resting on the elbows with the upper body is diagonal to the mattress. The other partner enters from behind. A good position to experiment with different types of thrusting, from shallow to deep. Good for prostate and G-spot stimulation.

④ **ROCKING CHAIR**

Good for vaginal, anal and strap-on. Rocking back and forth and making circular motions while sitting astride your partner gives good clitoral stimulation. The decrease in penis stimulation can delay ejaculation. Gives good penetration. Useful if the partner lying down is less mobile.

Sitting

KNEELING

Good for vaginal, and strap-on if your chair is at the right height. The partner beneath can use the edge of the chair to add leverage. The arms can come around to the front to stimulate the clitoris or play with breasts. The kneeling partner is in charge of the motion.

SITTING

Good for vaginal, anal and strap-on. The person on top uses the toes to lift up or bounce, though the seated partner can thrust upwards, too. Good for circular motions, grinding and clitoral stimulation. Penetration is not that deep, though you can experiment with the angles. Good for hugging, kissing and full body contact.

Standing

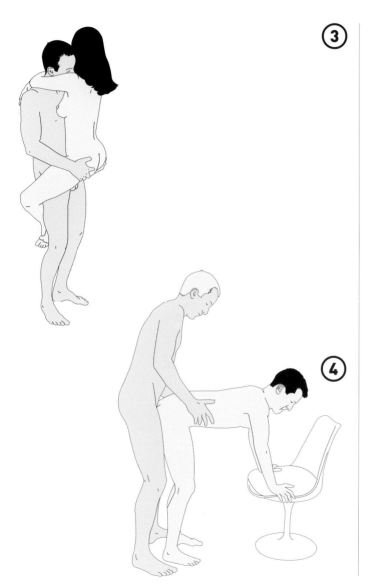

③ THE LIFT

Good for vaginal. This is only possible if the person being penetrated is very light. It can be made easier by resting the feet flat against a wall behind the person standing, so that the weight can be pushed away. If the standing partner is very strong, the other partner's buttocks can be held and swung back and forth. Not so good for vigorous thrusting and is difficult to maintain for any length of time.

④ REAR-ENTRY STANDING

Good for vaginal, anal and strap-on. The perfect position for small spaces. Makes for intense, deep penetration and vigorous thrusting and is, in fact, also very low impact. Good for G-spot and prostate stimulation.

Sexual practices (UK)

These statistics are taken from Natsal 1990 *(The National Survey of Sexual Attitudes and Lifestyles)*, by Kaye Wellings, Julia Field, Anne M. Johnson and Jane Wadsworth, and its 2000 update. The data is based on a random sample of nearly 20,000 British people aged 16–59.

Women

- 76.2% of heterosexual women had vaginal sex last month (2000)
- 60.2% of heterosexual women had non-vaginal sex last year (1990)
- 41.6% of lesbian women had non-penetrative sex last year (1990)
- 76.9% of heterosexual women had oral sex last year (2000)
- 41.0% of lesbian women had receptive oral sex last year (1990)
- 44.3% of lesbian women gave oral sex last year (1990)
- 11.3% of heterosexual women had anal sex last year (2000)
- No figures available on lesbian women having anal sex with dildos

Men

- 72.5% of heterosexual men had vaginal intercourse last month (2000)
- 65.5% of heterosexual men had non-penetrative sex last year (1990)
- 54.3% of gay men had non-penetrative sex last year (1991)
- 78.1% of heterosexual men had oral sex last year (2000)
- 56.0% of gay men had receptive oral sex last year (1990)
- 61.4% of gay men gave oral sex last year (1990)
- 12.3% of heterosexual men had anal sex last year (2000)
- 33.8% of gay men had receptive anal sex last year (1990)
- 40.3% of gay men had penetrative anal sex last year (1990)

Figures for gay and lesbian activity are based on men and women who had at least one same-sex partner in the past five years. The percentage of gay men having penetrative anal sex is substantially lower than the number of men and women having vaginal intercourse. This suggests that efforts to stem the spread of HIV should place greater emphasis on transmission via vaginal sex.

On the importance of orgasm

- 48.7% of men agree that orgasm is necessary to male sexual satisfaction
- 43.3% of women agree that orgasm is necessary to male sexual satisfaction
- 37.4% of men agree sex cannot be really satisfying for women without orgasm
- 28% of women agree that sex without orgasm is not really satisfying for them

Frequency of orgasm in females and males (US)

These statistics have been taken from *The Social Organisation of Sexuality*, 1994, by Edward O. Laumann, John H. Gagnon, Robert T. Michael and Stuart Michaels. Their data is considered to be the most comprehensive and representative survey of adult sexual practices in the US.

Masturbation and orgasm

- 58.3% of women don't masturbate at all
- 7.6% of women masturbate once a week
- 61.2% of women always or usually have an orgasm during masturbation
- 36% of men don't masturbate at all
- 26.7% of men masturbate once a week
- 81.5% of men always or usually have an orgasm during masturbation

These statistics indicate that the more often men and women masturbate, the more likely they are to experience orgasm.

Education is a significant factor when it comes to achieving orgasm. The report also indicated that 95 per cent of men and 87 per cent of women with at least some college education were very likely to achieve orgasm when they masturbated.

Orgasm between regular sexual partners

These figures are based on heterosexual couples who have had a primary sex partner for the past year.

- 75% of men in partnerships always have an orgasm with their partner
- Women's estimates of how often their partners orgasm during sex – 78% – are very close to the figures given by their partners
- 28.6% of women always have an orgasm with their partner
- Men's estimates of how often their partners orgasm during sex are on average 15% higher (at 44%) than the real figures

These statistics indicate that sex doesn't always end in orgasm for both men and women. The discrepancy in the male estimate of female orgasms indicates that men either cannot tell when their partner has had an orgasm or their partners have faked orgasm. The difference between the numbers of women and men achieving orgasm indicates that couples have a lot of work to do to make sex and orgasm more democratic.

The first time I orgasmed I was 15, when someone went down on me. I didn't have an orgasm again for a couple of years. I really believed all that stuff about girls not masturbating, so it never occurred to me until I read a dirty book when I was 18. That gave me the idea of masturbating, and I soon got into the swing of things. Now I can orgasm whenever I want.
Jackie, 30, UK

I kind of feel sorry for women, because so many of them don't come. At least a guy can do that whenever he wants!
Luke, 21, Australia

I've never met anyone else to have experienced this, but I can't come from sex. I can come from a hand job, but only if I do it myself. I can't if it is with someone else.
Adam, 24, Australia

It is always easier to get your rocks off with a guy who knows your body and knows what works for you. That's the only justification for monogamy!
Beth, 36, US

How was it for you?

There's no surprise that the French call an orgasm a 'little death' – for me it feels as though my spirit leaves my body and the only thing I can feel is this warm flood of energy pumping through me. If that's what death really feels like, I'm not scared!
Janette, 60, Canada

Girls think they are the only ones to have different kinds of orgasms. Ours, too, can range from a smallish kind of involuntary spasm to a little collection of whole-body rushes.
Mark, 27, UK

If I can't sleep or if I have a lot of different anxieties, then I'll jerk off. The feeling of release that goes with orgasm makes you relax, and it also makes you sleepy.
Dave, 54, US

I have to admit, if you spunk too quickly, you feel pretty dumb. In my experience, though, most girls are sweet about it, especially if you are willing to go for round two!
Nick, 22, UK

Orgasm: Although orgasm is perceived in the genitals, it is essentially a cerebral event. It has been described as 'a state where the body takes over and the brain is out of touch with reality'. Initially, the sensations are similar for both sexes: a feeling of deep warmth or pressure that indicates that orgasm is inevitable. Then sharp, intensely pleasurable contractions involving the pubococcygeus (PC) muscles are felt in the genitals, perineum, anal sphincter and rectum. In fact, having an orgasm can feel as if your whole body is sneezing, except it's a lot bigger and an awful lot nicer. Orgasms vary in length, depending on the person, their mood, their levels of arousal and so on. On average, men's orgasms don't last very long (10–13 seconds), though what they lack in length, they make up for in frequency. Women may not orgasm as often as men, but the sensation lasts considerably longer when they do (12–107 seconds) and women can have multiple orgasms, too.

Goals: Anyone who has ever read anything on sex will have seen the lines, 'sex should not be goal-orientated'. Granted, sex shouldn't be all about orgasms, but to avoid or delay a climax, you need to feel sure of your ability to have them in the first place, and the statistics on the previous pages indicate that for many people this simply isn't the case. For every book that advocates losing the 'goal', there are a million couples for whom orgasm could and should be a realistic and achievable goal . . . if only they could increase their sexual confidence. Orgasm is something that most healthy women and men can experience if they are sexually aroused and receive appropriate stimulation. That said, anxiety or over-emphasis on orgasm *can* undermine the pleasure of intimacy, closeness and simply getting to know each other (and it's guaranteed to keep orgasm at bay). Many studies have come to the conclusion that, for most people, close physical contact and affection is at least as important as climax.

Own goals: Most research on heterosexual intercourse indicates that when it comes to sex, men need to slow down so that women can catch up. Same-sex couples may have an advantage when it comes to mutual orgasm, simply because their arousal clocks are ticking in sync. Though studies in the past had indicated that orgasm was not particularly important to women, a study by CK Waterman and Emil J. Chiauzzi in 1982 found that, contrary to previous research, women who achieve orgasm with a partner rate their sexual satisfaction more highly than women who don't. After testing 42 couples on the relationship between orgasm and enjoyment, they concluded that both sexes enjoy having orgasms. Never!

Orgasm (female)

History: The female orgasm has had a rather mixed history. The ancient Greek mathematician Hippocrates (470–410BC) had a theory that conception occurred as a result of mixing male and female semen and that women required sexual pleasure to ensure theirs was plentiful. Unfortunately, Aristotle then suggested that only male semen was fertile, so female pleasure went out the window. Through the Middle Ages, the male-dominated Church and the medical profession took the view that female sexuality was associated with the devil. Abstinence and chastity were advocated, if not always practised. In the 17th century, female arousal was diagnosed as an illness. The symptoms included chronic arousal, persistent erotic fantasy, vaginal lubrication and general melancholy or irrational behaviour. By the 18th century, female clitoral orgasm had been acknowledged, but in the 1920s Freud proposed that 'adult' women should concentrate on experiencing orgasm vaginally. In the 1960s, research by Kinsey in the US turned attention back to the clitoris again. In fact, there was a backlash against penetrative sex altogether until 1981, when the arrival of the G-spot put the vagina back on the sexual map. Women were understandably confused. The debate about what makes women have orgasms has gone on forever, but it hasn't made having them any easier.

Difficulties: Achieving orgasm is more difficult for most women than it is for men, but it is still hyped as the ultimate objective when it comes to sex. This makes it hard for women to be honest about the fact that it doesn't happen as often, or as easily, as they might wish. Some women find that they come very close to the point of orgasm, but then they stop. This may be because of inhibition, fear of losing control, the wrong kind of stimulation or even just distractions. Most sexual therapists suggest that women who have difficulty achieving orgasm with a partner go back to basics and concentrate on masturbation, either in private or with a partner, to increase sexual confidence.

Types: Many of the debates around female arousal have focused on the different types of orgasm that women can experience: clitoral, vaginal, G-spot and uterine. More enlightened sexologists believe that suggesting orgasm is located in a specific area reduces sexual pleasure to an endless quest for specific body-part stimulation. However, scientists seem particularly keen to construct classifications of the female orgasm, including vulval, uterine and blended (a combination of the two). Frankly, most women don't care. They would settle for any of them.

Clitoral orgasm

Eighty per cent of women who can achieve orgasm report that they cannot do so without clitoral stimulation. The statistics on the numbers of women experiencing orgasm with regular sexual partners (28.6 per cent) indicates that this is clearly not being taken on board. Women who masturbate are well aware of how important the clitoris is to female sexual stimulation, but often underestimate what a revelation it is to male partners. For men, feeling the gradual swelling and erection of her clitoris is incentive enough for most of them to incorporate clitoral play into future sexual encounters.

Vaginal orgasm

The skin of the inner vagina is not in fact very sensitive. Fewer women achieve orgasm through vaginal penetration and most who do still require clitoral or vulval stimulation beforehand. Vaginal orgasm usually occurs when women are highly aroused, and the pressure of penile thrusting sends the woman into orgasm. In its nature, it feels less centred on the genitals, more internalised and, for some, stronger. A good way to begin experiencing vaginal orgasm is to use a large (larger than your partner's penis) vibrator combined with masturbation. This can get you used to the feeling of your PC muscles contracting around a shaft.

G-spot orgasm

Orgasms from G-spot stimulation can feel different from clitoral orgasms – less concentrated in the vaginal area and more 'rolling' or diffused. Sensations are experienced as less electric and 'deeper' than clitoral orgasms, probably because they are transported along the pelvic parasympathetic nervous system, which serves the womb, instead of the more superficial pudendal nerve, which serves the clitoris. As orgasm or ejaculation approach, there's a temporary feeling of wanting to pee.

The orgasmatron orgasm

Dr Stuart Melroy, a surgeon from North Carolina, USA, has invented a titanium generator that can be implanted under the skin of the buttocks. Electrodes stimulate the third sacral nerve and produce instant orgasm. It has been developed to help women who cannot orgasm 'naturally'.

There is nothing like making a woman climax. Apart from being able to watch your own personal porn movie (her face and body) with you as the star actor, you feel proud, too – like you're a sex god because you turned her on so much. Sometimes I'd rather get her off than get off myself, but usually there's time for both.
Dale, 28, UK

I like to come while the penis is inside me, because I've been told that I have very strong internal muscles that clamp down when I come. Men find that sexy, and I find it sexy too, but I always have to have him touch me at the front as well. I hear a vibrator is good for that.
Marie, 29, UK

One way for me to orgasm, and one way only: a bloke is fucking me with two or three of his fingers (four when it's going very well), and he is gently sucking my clit at the same time. I hold on to his head and sigh a lot while he does the business. I find most men are happy to help a girl out, so long as she's clean and promises sex after.
Lou, 24, UK

Faking it

Putting on the brakes: Many people, women in particular, find that they can reach a certain level of arousal, but that inhibition or anxiety prevents them going over the top into orgasm. People who have no problem climaxing on their own during masturbation can find themselves unable to repeat the experience with a partner. This makes things difficult, because anyone who is inhibited is unlikely to feel comfortable about making sexual demands or asserting their needs.

A vicious circle: With such a heavy emphasis on orgasm during sex, many people believe that if they or their partner don't achieve it, then the sex wasn't any good. The *Journal of the American Medical Association* published a report from the University of Chicago that estimates 43 per cent of women as having some form of sexual dysfunction. They may never have experienced orgasm but it is quite likely that plenty of them have faked it. Women (and men) fake orgasm as a way of making their partner feel better, yet this actually compounds any problems that were there in the first place. If your partner believes – and partners generally want to believe – that you can have a rip-roaring orgasm after five minutes of vaginal intercourse, it is difficult to admit later that you (and most women) actually need 20 minutes of manual stimulation just to become aroused. Men don't fake orgasm as often. For them, it is more often to do with losing interest in the sexual activity and wanting to have it over with, rather than an inability to have an orgasm. A few men whose penises remain reasonably hard after they've come can find themselves ending up in a vicious circle of their own. Because they feel that they come too quickly, they try to conceal their climax from their partner and carry on. This can make it quite difficult to come a second time, which can mean they end up faking it later on during sex.

Breaking the habit: The problem with faking it is that your partner is unlikely ever to find out how to please you, because it seems that you are being pleased already, and you will never be able to express your delight should you experience a real orgasm. The irony of faking it is that you do it with the best will in the world. You want your partner to feel good and you don't feel able to be honest or to make demands. You fear failure, or being viewed as a sexual failure because you can't orgasm, yet faking ensures that sex is all about orgasm rather than intimacy and locks you into a predictable pattern. Failure becomes a self-fulfilling prophecy. However well-intentioned, faking orgasm can undermine a relationship, and it's difficult to come clean. If you don't orgasm and your partner does, the situation needs to be discussed – you can do lots of things to change it.

Fixing it

A virtuous circle: If you can't orgasm (or have stopped being able to) and you feel that your problems with orgasm are linked to ill health or psychological issues, you can ask your doctor to refer you to a specialist. In the majority of cases, lack of orgasm is down to inhibition and the problem can be overcome with practice. Masturbation is the easiest way to find out what will bring you to orgasm and what the sensation feels like. Statistics suggest that the more women and men masturbate, the more likely they are to achieve orgasm. Once you are confident with your own techniques, you should introduce them into sexual activities with your partner. But this means you have to be willing to guide your partner. Negotiating for what you want sexually can be difficult for both parties, but honesty really is the best policy. If you say what you need, your partner will also feel more relaxed about making sexual requests. This ultimately leads to a more intimate, experimental and creative sexual relationship.

Fantasy and toys: Using fantasy (either privately or together) can sometimes provide the necessary trigger for orgasm. Some people think they are averse to sharing a fantasy, though that doesn't mean they don't experience increased arousal as a result of it. Several studies have shown that women are not always aware that they get turned on by porn or fantasy. In tests in which women were asked to watch porn movies, most of the women denied being aroused, yet physical tests showed signs of vaginal lubrication and engorgement. Introducing sex toys can also be a very effective way of heightening stimulation to encourage orgasm. Older men who find it more difficult to stay erect may find that cock rings or butt plugs help them stay erect, give arousal a boost and hasten orgasm. Obviously two people have to be sensitive to each other's tastes. If your partner doesn't enjoy engaging in fantasy or using sex toys, it may actually be a turn-off instead of a turn-on.

A fair compromise: For men who feel they come too quickly, the squeeze-release and stop-go techniques described in the masturbation chapter can be used during sex to delay ejaculation. Another option is to orgasm quickly the first time and tell your partner. Then concentrate on stimulating your partner for the next 20 minutes or so, while your own arousal levels heighten. By the time your partner is reaching orgasm you may, if you're young, be ready to orgasm again (the recovery period is longer for older people). Ultimately, two people in a sexual relationship ought to try to find some orgasmic equilibrium. You may not always both want to orgasm during sex, but it's always nice to have the option.

When I was depressed, I only used to climax occasionally. My wife knew about it, though I did pretend once or twice because I knew it was making her anxious. In the end she persuaded me to go to the doctor, who diagnosed depression and said that not climaxing was a symptom. I'm just glad my wife encouraged me to get help.
Jed, 66, US

212

Sex Toys

If I thought she'd faked it, I'd be really insulted.
Helen, 40, Australia

For years I just couldn't get my 'orgasm ship to sail'. The only sexual pleasure I got was knowing that I was pleasuring him. I had never masturbated, but when I discovered porn online, it gave me a buzz. I can't say it happened the first time, or even the tenth, but in the end, the big one happened. I was so proud! I'm trying to teach my man how to do it to me. He hasn't quite got the hang of it yet.
Liz, 23, US

Orgasm (male)

For all you lads wanting to last a bit longer or in search of multiples, you might want to look into tantric sex. This claims that orgasm and ejaculation are different things and you can have one without the other, and if you stop the ejaculation a few times and just have an orgasm (or is it vice versa?) then you have a more powerful one at the end. But to make your orgasm more powerful you have to keep delaying it and not letting yourself, and then it'll be more intense.
Seb, 19, UK

I'd love to know what orgasm feels like for a woman – from what I've heard, it's better than it is for us. A male orgasm is very concentrated in your balls and cock, and it's like a short burst of intense feeling, not these waves and ripples that women talk about.
Pete, 50, US

I choose when to come. It's really simple. If you feel like you're getting too close too soon, change positions, slow down, go down on her, do anything to stop the build-up.
Lochie, 38, Australia

History: In ancient Rome, ejaculation was believed to deplete man's 'vital juices'. A process known as infibulation, in which the foreskin was pierced on both sides and closed over the head of the penis was sometimes used as a way of preventing erection and ejaculation. Some Eastern traditions hold that semen is a man's most precious possession and should not be wasted. The Taoist and Tantric movements suggest that 'visualisation of sex energy' and 'retention of breath' can assist a man who is trying to control ejaculation. Elsewhere, men opt for 'visualisation of bank balance' and 'retention of beer gut'.

Getting technical: Technically speaking, male orgasm is a nervous system response, while ejaculation is a reproductive one and it is possible to have one without the other. Boys as young as seven can experience orgasms through masturbation without actually ejaculating. The first wet dream is a sign that the reproductive system has kicked in and the testes are now making sperm.

It's not just men who can't wait: All male animals have a biological urge to mate quickly. Once erect, waiting or lingering with a partner increased male vulnerability in hostile environments. Coming quickly may be in a man's nature, but nurture also plays its part. Adolescents often learn to masturbate very quickly because they are afraid of getting caught. Once the pattern of coming quickly is established, it becomes increasingly difficult to lose it, though many men find it easier to slow down once they get into a regular relationship with someone and their confidence starts to increase.

Delaying tactics: If you want to delay your orgasm with a partner (particularly someone new) try masturbating beforehand to relieve some of the sexual tension. This will stop you coming so quickly when you have sex, and will allow you to concentrate on pleasuring your partner.

What it feels like: The sensation of orgasm in men can feel localised in the penis and testicles, but some men can experience 'whole-body orgasm', particularly if ejaculation has been delayed. Men describe a sensation of pumping and, finally, a warm rush of fluid and a shooting sensation as the semen travels through the urethra and ejaculates.

After ejaculation: Men enter a recovery phase called the refractory period, which usually means a little snooze. During the refractory period, a partial erection may be maintained, though most men lose their erection, but ejaculation is physiologically impossible (particularly if he is asleep). The length of the refractory period varies with age and, of course, levels of sexual interest. It can be a matter of minutes in a young man, but men over 60 may have to wait a couple of days.

Force and volume: The more frequently you ejaculate, the less volume and force your ejaculation will have. Basically you start running out of semen. The average distance a man ejaculates is 18–25cm (7–10ins), but sexual abstinence can help you to shoot longer distances. If you don't ejaculate for more than three days, you may find you can shoot up to 90cm (3ft) or more

Orgasm without ejaculation

Most men never try to explore the experience of orgasm beyond the normal male response. Although trying to orgasm without ejaculating may seem to defeat the purpose, some sexologists believe that men can learn how to do this and potentially have multiple orgasms – most doctors are very sceptical.

Orgasm and ejaculation are two distinctly different events, the theory goes. Orgasm is the feeling of sexual pleasure, while ejaculation is the physical release of semen. First you have to develop super-strong PC muscles (which can take a few weeks using Kegels). Stimulate yourself to the point of orgasm and then stop by squeezing and holding your PC muscles. Gradually relax all the muscles of the pelvis and bottom, then gradually build up your arousal until you nearly reach orgasm again. Repeat several times, then squeeze your PC muscle as hard as you can when near coming and hold while your body goes into orgasm. Theoretically, you should feel the pleasure but not ejaculate, so you can go right ahead and start all over again.

Ejaculation without orgasm

Normally, prostate gland stimulation occurs in conjunction with penile stimulation, but if stimulation of the penis is stopped before prostate massage begins, the result can be ejaculation without actually triggering the sensation of orgasm. This is probably worth knowing, but not worth doing.

My girlfriend thinks I might be infertile because I hardly produce any semen when I climax, but I know it's because I jerk off about three times a day and there's never much left. I know it would stop her worrying if I told her, but that's not the kind of thing you want to tell your girlfriend, is it?
Ed, 20, Canada

I've had a serious girlfriend for about a year now, and it's pretty much been the first time I've had a regular sex life. I enjoy it very much and I know she does as well, but when we have sex, I usually reach my peak before she does – but not that much before. She would like us to reach our climaxes at the same time, but that rarely happens, so I usually end up masturbating her.
Richard, 20, UK

56

Sexercise

I went with this guy once who could just carry on after orgasm, his prick didn't go soft or anything.
Steve, 30, US

Morgasms

Simultaneous orgasms? Definitely the exception rather than the rule.
Eddie, 50, UK

When I orgasm with my partner I usually want to go again very quickly, so I use a vibrator.
Eddie, 50, UK

I have had many orgasms. I don't remember the worst or the best ones I've had, they are all good, but I have had a few multiple ones, and in some ways they feel like a special treat. I have noticed that I need to be paying attention to have one.
Gemma, 51, UK

Advice from a woman: it usually takes girls longer to come than it does guys, especially if the clit isn't being stimulated. It's not like there's a magic number of minutes or anything. Do what feels right. If you can't last a long time, that's OK. Just make sure there's lots of foreplay and once you're done, make sure the girl comes through methods other than sex. Or make her come beforehand. As long as you don't leave her hanging on!
Samantha, 24, UK

Multiple orgasm

Men may be able to train themselves to come several times in quick succession by learning how to orgasm without ejaculation, as described on the previous page. Statistically, women don't have orgasms as often as men, but when they do, they can really make up for lost time. Women who want to experiment with multiple orgasms should try continuing to stimulate themselves after they orgasm. The clitoris may feel very sensitive to touch, but keep working on the surrounding area until the tension builds up into a peak once more. Some people find that their subsequent orgasms decrease in intensity, but other women find that in fact they become more and more intense. Women who can achieve a number of orgasms during masturbation on their own may find it harder to have multiple orgasms when a partner stimulates them. Incorporating your masturbation techniques into sex will help, and many people find it a turn-on to watch their partner masturbate. Unfortunately, the myth and the hype surrounding the multiple orgasm have made it yet another marker of supposedly good sex. Like all sex play, don't get hung up on the result, just enjoy the game.

Anal orgasm

Some men and women can respond orgasmically through exclusively anal stimulation, but most people require genital stimulation as well. Anal orgasm usually occurs in conjunction with normal sexual activities such as masturbation or penetration, and the sensation of orgasm is simply heightened by the added anal stimulation. Because the PC muscles run through the genitals and the anus, anal stimulation can lead to a fuller orgasmic sensation. The anus shares a wall with the vagina and is contracted during orgasm by the pelvic floor muscles. Women who experience anal orgasm probably respond to a combination of both being stimulated. When men experience an orgasm from anal stimulation, it may be induced by prostate stimulation.

Simultaneous orgasms

The idea of 'coming together' gained popularity in the late 1960s. Somehow it has become another sexual 'goal' for people to aim towards since then. The quest for the simultaneous orgasm has resulted in couples frantically timing themselves, trying new positions and either trying to force a climax or withhold it until their partner was ready. For many, the efforts required detracted from the emotional and spiritual union they were trying to achieve. Simultaneous orgasm is probably best thought about as something that occasionally happens by accident. It is unrealistic to expect it to happen regularly, though it is probably worth trying to achieve it from time to time because it may at least ensure that the slower person has an orgasm. Coming together isn't a sign of perfect sex, although it could be a sign of good luck and excellent timing. The truth is, many people really enjoy watching their partner come. Taking turns is also much more likely to result in both parties having an orgasm.

'Full-body' or SM orgasms

These were probably first described by Dr Wilhelm Reich, a radical psychoanalyst who was a young contemporary of Freud's. Reich believed the whole body to be an erogenous zone, though his arguments went off the intellectual rails when he later argued that the universe was full of 'orgones' – a kind of sexy life-force that would cure people of impotence and other ills (keep taking the pills, love). Many have since suggested that full-body orgasms tend to be experienced by people who are more sexually tuned in to whole-body experiences and they are often associated with SM play, in which nerve endings all over the body are stimulated, by whipping, say. It is thought that when a person is in pain, various chemicals, including opiates, are released in the brain, which in turn bring about a euphoric effect. In some SM circles, penetrative sex is frowned upon as it is seen as focusing on genital pleasure, whereas SM tends to explore a wide range of bodily sensations and sometimes the pursuit of the 'whole-body orgasm'. SM participants describe their orgasms as an 'altered state', similar to the feeling you get when you unexpectedly drive over a hill.

Orgasm from sensory amplification

This is a technique usually used by people with spinal injuries and paralysis who have no feelings in their genitals. Many of them have discovered that by mentally transferring sensitivity to functioning parts of their body, they can, with practice, achieve orgasm. The idea is to enjoy every erotic possibility available, including thoughts, visual treats, stroking, kissing and erotic affection, while stimulating skin areas just higher than the level of paralysis. Over a few months, the area can become more and more excitable, so that eventually orgasm is experienced.

The prostate, the base of your cock, and your anal sphincter get stimulated when a man is fucking you. This stimulation may help you experience an orgasm and/or ejaculation or an anal orgasm. I sometimes lose my erection while my ass is getting pounded, but I still experience an orgasm due to the inner stimulation.
Greg, 28, US

Orgasm is the most extreme sensation of pleasure and pain, because it is in the hands of my mistress. I am restrained, so I am not responsible for what happens to me. My orgasm is an unconscious response to her domination.
Sub, 40, UK

I am paraplegic and don't really have sensation below my waist. But the feeling I have and my senses of touch, taste and smell are very important elements of my sex life. I have orgasmed giving oral pleasure while nails were being dug into my back. People with disabilities have a lot more sex than a lot of other people realise.
Ray, 40, UK

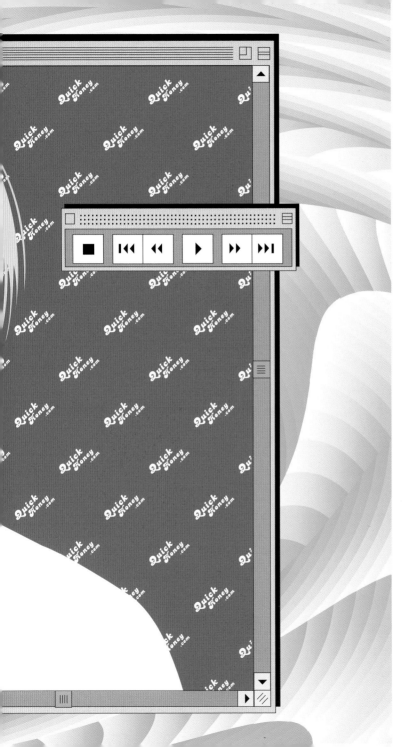

SEXPLORATION

My slave lets me use him as a footstool. He licks my feet clean, sucking between the toes and nibbling off any hard skin. Sometimes I restrain him and force my foot into his mouth, making him smell and sniff it.
Mistress Troy

Sexploration

Warning

Warning: This chapter contains strong words, violence and graphic descriptions of sometimes illegal sexual acts that you will most probably never choose to try. For many people, it will be more information than they want about things they didn't need to know. For the rest of us, it's just really interesting.

Stimulants: Though most people stop short of defecating in a partner's mouth, large numbers of law-abiding adults routinely use stimulants, both legal and illegal, to spice up their sex lives. Alcohol and drugs make people less inhibited and more adventurous. However, they can also make you take risks that you wouldn't otherwise take. People who are wasted are less likely to practise safer sex and more likely to wake up in the morning hungover and regretful. Drugs are associated with numerous health risks, and studies show that they also have conflicting impacts on libido and may cause reduced vaginal lubrication and erectile dysfunction.

Cannabis has been used as an aphrodisiac for centuries, though Indian ascetics employed it to 'destroy sexual appetite'. Many people say that having sex when stoned makes the act last longer, but the reality may be that it just feels longer because you are so off your head. Low doses of speed (amphetamine) may increase sexual desire, but higher doses can prevent orgasm, disrupt the menstrual cycle and interfere with libido. Cocaine can apparently increase sensitivity when rubbed into the vagina, anus or penis tip, though some people say it just numbs their genitals, and some research suggests that coke affects women's libidos more adversely than men's. Thirty-six per cent of regular cocaine users report impotence and lack of interest in sex (too busy talking). Poppers (nitrates) are popular for anal sex as their muscle-relaxing effect makes penetration easier – and some say that taking poppers at orgasm intensifies the sensation. Poppers cause the blood vessels to dilate, which can improve erection, but it can also result in dangerous changes to blood pressure that may affect the heart. Little recent research has been carried out into the effect of acid (LSD) on sexual response. Some users report that it is heightened, but strong hallucinations can rule sex out altogether and there is always the risk of a 'bad trip'. Ecstasy (MDMA) does not increase sexual desire, but it does enhance the sensual aspects of touch. In one study, 67 per cent of users reported that ecstasy lowered their inhibitions, but 45 per cent reported that it also inhibited orgasm. And though heroin users compare a hit of heroin to an orgasm, few drugs have a worse effect on sexual response. For addicts, heroin is more important than anything, even relationships.

Fantasy and porn

Tell it to me baby: US research conducted by Harold Leitenberg and Kris Henning, of the University of Vermont, USA, suggests that the most common erotic fantasy is sex with a past, present or imaginary lover. The second most common fantasy involves being overpowered or sexually submissive. Partners often fantasise privately during sex, though many couples enjoy voicing their thoughts. Sexual narratives or explicit language can push arousal through the roof. Men and women who have difficulty reaching orgasm often respond quickly to descriptions of sexual acts. Some people don't like speaking, but do like listening – or vice versa. There are those who make a special effort to acquire the vocabulary of a porn star, but others find that simply describing what they are doing, seeing and feeling does the job. When talking dirty for the first time with a partner, it is advisable to start off with something mild and gauge the reaction. Calling your new girlfriend a 'slut' might not go down too well.

Pornography: The word pornography means 'the writings of prostitutes' and comes from ancient Greek. Erotic material has been around nearly as long as people have been having sex, and there's enough niche markets out there to ensure that every taste is catered for: Asian babes, milk poppin' mommas or BDSM, to name a few. Visual images of sex can have a powerful and immediate impact on arousal, and remembered pictures or texts can be conjured up at a later date in the form of sexual fantasy. Most people can remember their first encounter with erotica. It may have been one of your parent's books or a porn mag passed on by a school friend. Some people use just one or two images as their arousal trigger: perhaps something they discovered when they were young and hold on to for life. Some people don't feel the need to use porn once they have a partner who offers the real thing, but many (men in particular) carry on using porn magazines and videos for sexual gratification. Adult cable TV channels and the Internet mean that porn is more widely available than ever. Too available, some argue.

The debate: One of the arguments in the ongoing debate about whether pornography is sexist is that most porn portrays women as objects whose sole purpose is to satisfy men's desire for depersonalised sex. Arguably the same could be said about the young boys featured in gay porn. But there is no doubt that 21st-century visual porn is an acquired taste, and that some of it degrades, exploits and dehumanises both women and men. That said, a lot of first-class literature (*Sons and Lovers*, *Lolita* and so on) was once considered to be pornographic. Luckily, good sense prevailed.

I have only one fantasy. I use it during penetrative sex to get myself to orgasm. I imagine that I am a teenager and I am wearing a patterned cotton nightdress. I just think about the nightdress being pulled up over my bum while I am being fucked. God knows what it means, but it does it for me.
Iris, 29, UK

I like my man to come just before I do, so when I am ready, I just give him a couple of sentences and that is enough to bring him to orgasm. I just tell him how wet my pussy is, and how rock-hard his big cock feels, and bang, he's there.
Stacey, 28, US

It's a funny subject with a new partner, if you whisper in a girl's ear 'I'm going to fuck you like the dirty bitch you are', some of them go crazy with desire – others just go crazy.
Jack, 34, Australia

If we're stressed or not in the mood, he reads to me from this collection of erotic fantasies we have. After about ten minutes, we both have a raging hard-on! Works every time.
Patrick, 41, Australia

Looking for love

DATING TIPS:

Always meet in a public place, and never at your home.

Always take a mobile phone and tell a friend where you are going.

Make the first date for a coffee – that way you can make a quick getaway if it turns out to be really awful. You're under no obligation, so leave if you're not having a good time.

Sex with a stranger is always risky. Make it clear that you're just looking for a purely sexual encounter and don't do anything you're not comfortable with.

Ultimately I know that anyone, like me, who has to find a partner online must be lacking.
Charlotte, 23, UK

I put all these stupid specifications in my personal ad, like 'must be tall and not bald'. I got a lot of replies I was interested in, but the funniest one was from a short bald man called Richard, who joked about my discriminatory ad. I married him.
Rebecca, 49, Australia

Chat-rooms: There are thousands of chat-rooms devoted to erotic conversation on the net and each day 200 new ones are added. Relationship therapists cite chat-rooms and online porn as a growing problem in the breakdown of many relationships. If you make a one-to-one connection with someone in a chat-room, be aware of the pitfalls. Because people in chat-rooms are protected by anonymity, they tend to be more sexually explicit and adventurous than they would be in real life. This means that intense sexual relationships develop at a more rapid pace than they would normally. If you want to explore chat-rooms, make sure you set up an anonymous, free, web-based account (such as Yahoo or Hotmail) so that any potential stalkers or weirdos can be ditched without drama. You will be asked if you want to have phone sex the minute you log in to a central chat-room, but don't give out any phone numbers or personal details.

Internet dating: Searching for romance, casual sex, swinging couples or a fetish partner are all made easier thanks to Internet dating. Dating sites will allow users to post a personal profile and a photo for others to view. Generally, sites will charge a monthly fee, which allows you to correspond by email with people. Some sites also offer a photo doctoring service. It's cheaper than cosmetic surgery, but if you ever get to meet anyone in the flesh, make sure the lights are dimmed. People often find that their Internet dates are a bit of a disappointment when they meet them in the flesh. No one in a chat-room ever seems to be plain, overweight or over 47, but reality is often . . . reality.

Dating agencies: Dating agencies charge a fee to match up your tastes and attributes with those of a possible partner. Dinner in a restaurant is the most common first date, and you are under no obligation to see the person again if you don't want to. Some agencies organise parties, outings or group dinners where larger groups of people can meet.

Personal ads: More people than you can imagine meet their partners through ads. You are far more likely to be successful if you place an ad than if you respond to one, and placing one also gives you the opportunity to be specific about your interests and what you definitely don't want (i.e. no marrieds). If you want a long-term relationship (LTR), say so. If you just want a fling (fun and frolics), make that clear. Never reveal your telephone number in the ad. Make sure you place your ad in a publication that represents your views and tastes. If you are looking for a zoophilia partner in a mainstream listings mag, you're barking up the wrong tree.

Paying for it

Phone sex lines: Most sex lines are just a recording (lots of groaning). Others take credit card payments and allow you to chat to a professional. In both cases, the caller is expected to masturbate to orgasm (usually ASAP because the tariff is so high). Phone sex may not seem like quite such a good idea when the phone bill arrives.

Sex clubs: Sex clubs cater for every taste. Strip joints are the most common, though they specialise too (men and women, bi, straight, gay or lesbian). Sometimes dancers and strippers are also sex workers, and can arrange a one-to-one after the show, but not always. Lap dancers perform erotic dances for a fee, hovering just above their client's lap. Clients are not allowed to touch the dancers, though their fee is usually allowed to be slipped into their bra or the top of their pants. Some clubs host live sex shows. Customers can watch anything from group sex to naked lactating women spraying the audience with milk. Nearly all sex clubs make a large amount of their profit by charging exorbitant prices for drinks.

Escort services: Escorts are men and women who will accompany a person on a date, for a fee. People who do not have a partner, but need to take someone to a social function can employ an escort through the Internet and magazine adverts. Most escorts are also sex workers, but if you don't want sex, look for 'no bedroom services' on the ad.

Sex workers: Professional sex workers cater for nearly every desire, including straight, gay, male and female sex. Niche-market sex workers specialise in particular types of sex, such as SM. Recent statistics in the UK show that one in every 23 men has paid for sex in the last five years, and the figure rises to one in 11 men in London. People go to sex workers for all kinds of reasons: to try out something that their partner is not interested in; to have sex if they can't find a partner; to experiment with their sexuality in private; or simply because the idea of a sex worker turns them on. In many parts of the world, paying for sex is illegal, though there are loopholes. In the UK, streetwalking and kerb-crawling are against the law, though, broadly speaking, contacting a sex worker through advertising is not. In Australia, it seems to be acceptable for sex workers to work from a house, but not for them to work from the street. Sex workers advertise on the Internet or in the adverts at the back of magazines and newspapers, providing a contact phone number. Clients arrange an in-call (where the client goes to the sex worker's place of work), or an out-call (where the sex worker visits the client's home). Out-calls are usually more expensive.

TIPS FOR PUNTERS FROM SEX WORKERS:

It's a business transaction. Negotiate your terms first. It is normal practice to pay in advance.

Have a shower and clean your teeth first. Sex workers are as turned off by lack of hygiene as you are.

Never bully sex workers or offer more money to get them to do what they have already said 'no' to.

It is the clients' responsibility to ensure that a sex worker is not legally a child. If the sex worker is, this may be seen as child abuse in the eyes of the law. If you are suspicious, don't do it.

It is normal for a sex worker to insist on condoms for oral, anal and vaginal sex. Many sex workers are careful about safer sex and have regular check-ups, but remember, any sex worker who is willing to have unprotected sex with you will have been willing to do so with other clients. This greatly increases the chance of contracting an STI or HIV.

Dressing up

Power games: Much sexual role-play hinges on a deliberate imbalance of erotic power, and in that sense, role-play often overlaps with submission and domination. Couples select a stereotypical relationship in which one character has authority and control over the other. Some of the most common scenarios include: doctor and patient; maid and employer; sex worker and client; teacher and student; priest or nun and sinner; and owner and dog (basically any relationship in which one party might feasibly deserve being manhandled, told off or given a good hiding).

Location: Couples often find it is easier to keep up the illusion of being someone else when the environment is appropriate to the scenario they are acting out. The anticipation involved in choosing the location can be very arousing in itself. If you have an office job, try going in at the weekend and playing at interviews, board meetings or being the cleaner and MD. Alternatively, take your human dog for a walk in costume, or have a drive in the countryside and pick up your hapless role-playing hitch-hiker.

Keeping it real: While some couples experiment with role-play for a laugh, others are more obsessive. Serious role-players act out their fantasies with intense attention to detail. Staying in character is vital, and the slightest sign of a giggle is enough to deflate sexual enthusiasm. If you are going to experiment with dressing up, make sure you won't be interrupted. If you are at home, take the phone off the hook and draw the curtains. If you are going to play in the office, make sure that none of your colleagues are likely to come in unexpectedly. If your objective is to really believe that your partner is someone else, knowledge of a foreign language or an ability to mimic accents can add to the fantasy. Some couples simply imagine themselves in role and speak a sentence or two: 'You're overdue for a check-up, I'd better examine your prostate'. Others get more involved, speaking in role for a whole afternoon.

Costumes: Whether it's a set of lacy suspenders or a doctor's outfit, changing your look can help you to feel different and more sexy. In role-play, costumes and props are used to evoke stereotypically powerful or submissive characters. Common costumes might be school uniforms, hard hats and tool belts, military or medical uniforms or gym kit. Props such as latex gloves, canes, swords or cricket bats can all be used to heighten the tension. More radical costumes, such as fetish gear, maid's outfits, religious costumes and so on can be hired through party shops, but you might want to dry-clean them before you give them back.

Hair and beauty

Short and curlies: Dyeing pubic hair has mixed results. Bleaching tends to turn pubic hair orange, and can also cause severe irritation and burning on sensitive skin. Black dye tends to look the most convincing, but use dye made for beards because it is better for stronger hair. Some beauty parlours offer pubic hairdressing. The most popular hairstyle for women is the 'Brazilian wax', in which all the pubic hair is removed. Though it probably improves a woman's chances of receiving cunnilingus, it can make adult genitalia look very childlike and it itches like hell when it grows back. More moderate styles are 'the arrow', in which pubes are trimmed into pointing downward shape, 'the heart', and 'the runway', in which just a narrow strip is left down the centre. A new craze is the 'Tiffany box'. This involves shaving everything off bar a small square, which is then died a particular shade of duck-egg blue. If you are unsure about a drastic make-over, try just trimming your pubes with a beard trimmer, or a comb and a pair of scissors (make sure that you only cut your hair).

Piercing: Though many people pierce their own ears with sterilised needles, body piercing should be carried out by a qualified and experienced professional. If sterilised needles are not used, you may be exposed to hepatitis B or C, HIV or infections of the skin that can leave scars and reduce sensitivity. Body piercings come in many guises. The most famous male genital piercing is probably the 'Prince Albert'. A ring goes in through the urethral meatus at the top of the penis head and comes out on the underside, where the head joins the shaft. An anaesthetic is required, but the piercing heals very quickly. Men who have had one report that it increases stimulation of both a woman's clitoris, during vaginal sex, and a man's prostate, during receptive anal sex. In Arab countries, *hafadas* – piercings through the scrotal sac – are popular. The 'Guiche' piercing is placed through the perineum between the anus and the scrotum, while in the 'frenulum' piercing, barbells are put through the underside of the penis head, just below the frenulum. Female genital piercings are usually performed through the base of the vaginal opening and the perineum, and clitoral piercings go through or behind the clitoral hood, either vertically or horizontally. Both sexes can have nipple piercings. Some people have them just for visual effect, but others find that twisting piercings during sexual play can be extremely arousing. Nipple rings can be attached by chains to a clitoris or penis ring, so that your partner can pull you around by your genitals. For the more squeamish, clip-on jewellery may be the answer. Clit clips hook on to the inside of the vagina wall, and cock rings slip over the penis and testicles (enhancing and prolonging erection).

An old boyfriend shaved my pussy for me, and the actual act of shaving was probably more sexy than the end result. He said it was easier to lick me out, but also it reminded him of the pussies you see in porn.
Kayleigh, 22, US

I appreciate girls sorting out a bikini line, but best of all is no hair. Blokes are caring creatures, but lacking in attention to detail. I used to cut my pubic hair to make my cock look bigger, but now it's just a tangled old mess.
Edward, 19, UK
Thesite

I put a nipple clamp on my clit and then push it against my piercing. That kind of pressure and movement can get a girl going.
Lo, 29, Australia

You can use condoms with any piercings of the penis, and it is very important to use them while the piercing is healing. So long as you're not too rough, you can have sex while it's healing, unless it hurts too much, but the condom will guard against contamination by body fluids.
Ahmed Gencer
Professional piercer

Fetishes

Sexual fascination: The word 'fetish' originates from the medieval Portuguese word *feitiço*, which refers to religious relics with magical properties. In the 19th century, the term came to mean a sexual fascination for a specific body part or object. These days, people are defined as fetishists when they become aroused by things that are not usual objects of desire – for example, obesity, excessive body hair and stiletto heels. Fetishists often need increasing exposure to the object of their desire to achieve orgasm. A shoe fetishist may initially find thinking about a stiletto exciting, but over time may need to see, touch, smell and lick a shoe and masturbate into it. While some research suggests that fetishes are more common in men, it has been pointed out that very few women have been included in fetish studies, so who knows? Fetish magazines provide a platform for specialist fetishists, and personal adverts are placed by those who want to sell specific fetish items, such as soiled underwear, hair, photographs of feet and so on. The Internet also has a broad range of fetish sites.

Underwear: Underwear is collected and admired for a number of reasons. Some steal the pants of sexual conquests as a keepsake or a trophy, others buy used knickers over the Internet to sniff while they masturbate. There's money to be made here. 'Soiled' underwear sells online for a surprising amount of money; 'super-soiled' (guess that means skidmarks) sells for even more.

Rubber, latex and leather: These fetishes are mainly to do with the feel of the materials. Rubber and latex fetishists dress for sex in skirts, suits, hoods, gasmasks and shoes that are all made, usually in black, of their favourite materials. The outfits are normally skin-tight and can be tricky to get into, because the material sticks to you unless you put a layer of talcum powder on your skin first. The feel and smell of leather gives many people a feeling of power. Some fetishists say that they feel that they are taking on the identity of an animal when they wear leather.

Footwear: Any form of footwear has the potential to turn on shoe fetishists. Some require that the shoe is worn, but others prefer masturbating into it privately. High-heeled stilettos are probably the most appealing, and those into SM find a spike-heel arousing because of its obvious potential to inflict pain. Freudian theory suggests that shoe fetishes develop because babies spend a great deal of time crawling on the ground, which puts adult footwear at their eye level.

BD, SM and Sub/Dom

Bondage and domination games (BD): Restricting a partner's movement for sexual pleasure can be good for the person who is doing the restricting (the Top), as it creates a feeling of power and a sense of control, but it can also be very sexy for the person who is restricted (the Bottom), who can relax completely and not have to think about reciprocating sexual favours. Deciding who gets to be Top can be difficult if both of you are very bossy. You might want to take turns, but Cher look-alikes automatically get to go first. For Bottoms, a sensation of powerlessness and a controlled amount of pain coupled with restraints can bring about a near-meditative state. Others find that the victim-like state of struggling against their shackles gives them a psychological thrill. Many couples find that bondage enhances their sex lives, because they are released from their normal inhibitions. Bondage is often used with SM, as is role-playing. Beginners may like to tie a partner up before they give oral sex, while old hands are more likely to use a dash of sadism. Serious bondage requires a strict code of sexual etiquette. The Top cannot use bondage as an opportunity to do things that the Bottom doesn't enjoy. For safety reasons, pick a Top who you know well and can trust.

Restraints: Ropes, ribbons, chains and handcuffs all restrict a person's movements. Some are symbolic – a loosely tied ribbon to make it feel as if the hands cannot be moved – and some are actual – handcuffs, locking your partner to the bed. Metal spreader bars can be attached to both the ankles or wrists, with leather cuffs to keep the wearer's legs and arms spread-eagled. The combination of vulnerability and physical restrictions can be particularly arousing for exhibitionists. Make sure that restraints are loose enough to allow blood circulation. Make sure, too, that you or your partner can breathe through any gags or hoods – especially through latex. Latex masks that only have holes for the nostrils can slide around and inadvertently cut off air supply. Most couples only use gags for short periods, because there is always the possibility of choking.

Sadomasochism (SM): SM is a negotiated sex game between two people. SM practitioners can be heterosexual, bisexual, homosexual, trans-gendered or intersex, but the S in the SM pair is the person who inflicts the pain or punishment and the M is the person who submits to the pain, humiliation or control. Sex partners tend to negotiate a release word before play begins, so that if someone wants something to stop they can make it clear. Like Sub/Dom, SM has to be consensual because it's so important to stay in character. In its mildest form, SM may just involve a bit of gentle spanking; heavier SM might include whipping or dripping hot wax. Extreme SM may include body mutilation, and practitioners sometimes even brand each other with hot irons to show their loyalty. Once your Bottom has climaxed, reduce the force of your punishment. In the build-up to orgasm, the body will tolerate more pain because the brain releases 'feel-good' chemicals. After climax, the body becomes very sensitive to pain.

Armband and handkerchief codes: Some SM participants use a kind of armband or handkerchief code to signal their preferences and passions to prospective partners: left arm = giver; right arm = taker; black = extreme SM; duck-egg blue = milder SM; lavender = group sex; brown = likes faeces; dark blue = likes anal; grey = bondage; light blue = oral; yellow = golden showers; maroon = vampirism; purple = piercings; red = fisting; green = financial transactions; white = new to the scene; white lace = romance (aah); orange = anything. That just about covers everything, doesn't it?

Submission and domination (Sub/Dom): This is a form of sex play in which the dominant partner exercises control over the submissive one. Sub/Dom play differs from sadomasochism, although they are closely related. Subs and Doms like exercising or renouncing control, while sadomasochists like giving and receiving pain. Sub/Dom games often incorporate restraints and humiliation, but may not include penetration. Generally, they are more about the psychological thrill of power than manual physical stimulation. A dominatrix is usually female, but is sometimes a transvestite. The stereotypical image of a professional dominatrix is a tall, attractive woman wearing black thigh-high spike-heel boots and leather or rubber clothing. The most famous dominatrix in history was Theresa Berkley, who invented the Berkley Horse (an extending ladder to which her client was tied) in 1828. She stood behind it and whipped his buttocks while another woman sat in front and played with his genitals. She had a wide range of flagellation tools, including whips that were studded with needles, holly branches and fistfuls of stinging nettles.

Sensory deprivation: Blindfolds, masks, hoods and sometimes gags are used to render the Bottom speechless or blind. Hoods may be used by the Top or Bottom to depersonalise sex, and sensory deprivation can accentuate the lack of control the Bottom experiences. More physically, some claim that not being able to see, speak or hear means that their sense of touch (or being touched) is heightened extraordinarily.

I used to always be dominant, the Top, the master, always sexually active. Over the last three or four years I've preferred to be the Bottom. I am versatile: even as a slave, I am aggressive. Passive to me is not just getting fucked. I prefer being involved. I'm an aggressive slave. I actually like playing around with the notions of the roles and what they mean.
Pedro, 30, UK

There is nothing more stimulating than being in control. I like to decide whether he's going to have a hand job, head job or full sex, and I like to decide when he comes. I think surrendering himself to me has made him feel safer and more loved.
Gloria, 36, US

We've been using ropes and handcuffs for about 18 months. It started out just tying her up – like tying her hands together – but more recently I have started tying her down, to a table or something. I think it's because ever since she decided to go away to college, I have felt like she's not really mine.
Geoff, 24, Australia

Flagellation

TOOLS O' THE TRADE:

Leather whips are medium to heavy in weight. Some have rubber lashes that deliver intense pain.

Silk or satin lashes give a very light sensation. Some have weights on the ends, making them very painful indeed.

Bats and paddles are usually wooden, but sometimes leather, and can be used to produce moderate to very intense pain.

A crop is a stiff rod with a short, biting leather strip at the end. Crops are best bought at equestrian tack shops, because the ones from sex shops usually cost more and are inferior in quality. Crops deliver moderate pain, leave wide, deep bruises and make a whooshing sound.

Rods and canes can be made of bamboo or rattan (the ones in sex shops tend to be fibreglass or plastic). They deliver intense pain and make a thwacking noise.

Birches (bunches of birch twigs) are popular as they can be used on most of the body and effects are superficial.

Spanking: Putting your lover, pants down, over your knee, and imposing some discipline can be a very erotic experience. Some people like to cross-dress or have dildos inserted while they are being spanked.

Whipping: Whipping to arouse a partner is an ancient practice, and various faiths have incorporated self-flagellation as a form of worship that brings about a trance-like state. Today, flagellation is mainly seen as an erotic art and it is practised by people who enjoy bondage, domination, sadism and masochism (BDSM). Whips are also called flails, floggers and cat-o'-nine-tails. They come in a multitude of shapes, sizes and materials. Thin whips make a lovely whooshing sound and the thinner the whip, the sharper the pain. Bats or paddles make a dull, thudding noise and the impact is more diffused. The most erotic spot for whipping is the lower or inner part of the buttocks, though gents should remember to keep their legs closed to avoid ruining their fatherhood prospects.

The act: Before administering any punishment, you should prepare the buttocks by massaging and gently pinching the skin. This stimulates the brain's neurotransmitters to release endorphins, which bring on feelings of euphoria and also have an analgesic effect. Lashes should be aimed so that the end of the whip or other instrument lands in the centre of the buttocks. You should be able to deliver clean, rhythmic, controlled and accurate strokes (practise on a pillow) – but be careful, because repeated strokes on the same spot can cause lacerations. Most people are able to endure more pain as they approach orgasm and flagellation can lead to orgasm, though it's a different experience for the Top and the Bottom. A Bottom who is being flogged will experience heightened physical sensation all over the body. At a certain point, the mere jiggle of a butt plug is often enough to trigger an orgasm, whereas a Top may need to put some time aside for more orgasm-oriented sex play after the thrashing has finished. Flagellation should stop as soon as the Bottom has orgasmed, because the brain stops producing endorphins almost immediately afterwards.

Things your mother never told you: Always negotiate a release word first, and never strike in anger. Treat cuts immediately after sex play to avoid infection and remember that blood can carry HIV. Never whip soft tissue, such as the abdomen or around the kidneys. Clean whips with saddle soap or warm soapy water, but never oil them or you will soften them and reduce the impact. Never use one person's whip on somebody else.

Group sex and swinging

I must admit that the opportunity for some extra-marital action without upsetting my wife appeals. She has been talking about swinging a lot lately, but I worry about the risk of her falling for the 'stand-ins' and maybe deciding to head for greener pastures. What if he satisfies her more than I do? She says that she wouldn't make comparisons, but you can never be really sure.
Jay, 46, UK

I would like to swap my wife – on a permanent basis.
Richie, 56, US

There's a group of us who have a party every couple of months and we play dice game. First we go around the circle and each person confesses their fantasies to the group, which gets everyone pretty horny. Then we roll the dice and the person with the highest number gets to have the person with the lowest number. Sometimes the others watch; sometimes we all get in there.
Hal, 47, UK

Team sports: Group sex breaks with the old tradition that two people who are in a relationship should have sex exclusively with each other, alone and in private. It can be an exciting way to have sexual adventures without lying to a long-term partner, or a one-off chance to live out a fantasy. Group sex provides a heightened sexual experience. Hearing, seeing, touching and smelling other people having sex is a huge turn-on for those brave enough to engage in it, but couples who are tempted by team sports ought to think carefully about the impact this may have on their relationship. Are both of you capable of having sex with other people without becoming emotionally involved? Do you both want to swing, or is one partner going along with it because they feel obliged to? Are you sure you can handle hearing your nearest and dearest shriek with delight through a partition wall? If the answer to all these questions is yes, then all you have to do is find the right people. Websites, invites and personal ads are probably the best way to find partners, but don't forget to practise safer sex.

Wife-swapping: Also known as 'swinging', this is when couples swap their partners for sex. In the 1960s, 'key parties' were very popular in the US. All the men would put their keys in a bowl and the women would randomly select a set of keys (having made sure to avoid any belonging to the ugly guy with BO, no doubt) and have sex with its owner. Swinging parties are still popular. The North American Swing Club estimates that there are five million active swingers in the US. Nowadays, swinging parties are usually held at people's homes. In general, once sexual pairings have been sorted out, sex usually happens in a private room. Swingers sometimes use euphemisms to communicate with like-minded people. For example: 'likes English culture' = likes spanking; 'likes Roman culture' = likes orgies; 'likes French culture' = likes oral sex; 'likes Swedish culture' = 'likes mutual masturbation'; 'teacher' = someone who spanks; 'soft personality' = does not want penetrative sex; 'the door is always open' = couples will be expected to have sex in the same room; 'generous personality' = is willing to pay for sex; 'versatile' = bisexual. It is considered good swinging etiquette for both partners to be sexually interested in swinging – a woman who attends swing parties simply to help a man get invited is known as a 'ticket' and is frowned upon. Swing clubs are places where couples meet up and negotiate their sexual preferences before going to a hotel room to have sex. Some swing clubs provide rooms and run special activities, such as hot-tub parties, cruise ship excursions and fetish clubs.

Ménage à trois: Gay, lesbian or straight couples who want to engage a third person to have sex with may recruit through friends, adverts or the Internet, but they may also hire a sex worker. A quick skim through the personal columns shows that most straight couples want a female third, so bisexual women looking for straight couples are a hot commodity. Three-way sex with one man and two women is less satisfactory if the women aren't bisexual, because once the man ejaculates, he may be unable to get another erection for a while, and a straight woman who feels she is engaging in group sex simply for her partner's benefit may end up feeling resentful. Sometimes fantasies don't live up to expectations. Playing the starring role in an orgy of body parts may simply turn out to be very distracting, and the reality of threesomes is that sometimes people get left out or feel intimidated by the whole thing.

Orgies: Orgies have probably been around forever, but they are usually referred to as 'group sex' these days. Often involving copious quantities of drugs and alcohol, there are gay, straight, lesbian and bisexual orgies, and they tend to be wild and raunchy events with less etiquette restrictions than swing parties. If you are in luck, a boisterous house party may go this way, but generally group-sex events are organised through invites and adverts. Organisers of straight orgies often stipulate that each woman brings a male friend, or vice versa, to ensure that there is 'plenty to go around'. At a group-sex party, sexual contact may be one-to-one in a room full of people or it may be between multiple partners, and usually the only rule is that you ask before joining in. Such parties are particularly popular with voyeurs who enjoy watching other people's sex play and exhibitionists who get a kick from knowing that someone is watching them. If you are not in a scene, try doing an Internet search with the words 'group sex' and the name of your town and see what comes up.

Gang-bang: A consensual gang-bang is a sexual event – often organised beforehand – in which a number of people stand in line and wait to have sex with one person (usually a woman) until they are sexually satisfied. Various people have claimed the world record, but recently a woman called Annabel Chong was filmed in a gang-bang in which over 251 men formed an orderly queue and took it in turns to penetrate her. Prearranged gang-bangs sometimes have special themes, such as 'Santa Claus', or 'men in diapers'. Safer sex practices are always the responsibility of the person penetrating. If a condom breaks during a gang-bang, the session ends or sexual activity moves to a different orifice.

We are both straight girls and didn't do that much to each other, but put most of our attention his way. We used his prick to show each other head job techniques. I think we were just young and up for an adventure, but he thought he was the luckiest man alive and asked us to move in with him!
Verna, 22, UK

I am a highly sexual man. I think anyone in touch with themselves has to be, because we are all animals and need to put our seed wherever we can. I have only been to three sex parties, but I felt that I could really be myself, licking a woman and then having my knob sucked by a man. Everyone is beautiful, and I want to screw the world. Sex parties are liberating.
Dan, 28, UK

We went to this sex party with some friends, and I suppose I went mostly because the guy I was seeing wanted to. I got really high, and he and his best friend fucked me at the same time. It was so obvious they had it all planned and I felt like a piece of meat.
Ruby, 19, US

Extreme sports

Toilet treats: Sex play that includes faeces, urine, breastmilk or vomit is very rarely talked about, written about or admitted. However, porn videos featuring these passions are sold in their thousands, Internet chat-rooms are full of anonymous confessions on the subject and there are even social groups that are bound by their mutual interest in the things that other people flush down the lavatory.

Number one: The terms 'golden showers' and 'watersports' refer to either peeing on other people, or being peed on. Any part of the body can be given a shower, but the most common sites are the face, the mouth, the breasts, the buttocks and the genitals. Most people who are into golden showers like the smell of urine, so bear in mind that drinking lots of water increases the volume of urine but dilutes it. Sometimes showers can be part of humiliation games, but many enthusiasts find the practice a warm, sexy, intimate and entirely equal experience. A few people incorporate watersports into masturbation, by peeing on themselves (and especially on their hands) before they masturbate. The bathroom is probably the best place for them, because tiled surfaces can easily be hosed down afterwards. If you are keen to play in the bedroom, special waterproof maternity mattresses are available in some parenting shops. There is a possibility that salmonella, gonorrhoea and chlamydia can be passed through urine, but research is needed to confirm or refute this. Aiming the shower below the neck at unbroken skin may help to minimise risks, though be careful that urine doesn't enter the mouth, vagina or anus.

Number two: Scatology, or coprophilia, is sexual arousal by either the idea of, or actual contact with, faeces. One of the most notorious coprophile practices is to lie masturbating under a glass table while another person defecates on the table-top, but in reality it is probably more common for partners to defecate on each other. As with many fetishes, scatologists are usually only interested in the excrement of people to whom they are attracted. One of the problems for many couples who are into scat is constipation. If you want to be able to pass a stool on demand, make sure that your diet is fibre-rich and try to have sex at about the time of day when you normally have a bowel movement. Some find that drinking a strong coffee or smoking cigarettes gives them the 'urge to purge', though taking laxatives may be more effective. Many infections can be passed on through scat, including salmonella, threadworms, gonorrhoea, chlamydia and hepatitis A. The risk of infection is much higher when faeces enters the mouth, vagina or another person's anus.

Infantilism: This is a fetish in which people become aroused by objects or acts relating to childhood. Infantilism usually involves dressing up, and there are numerous sites on the Internet from which you can buy adult-sized nappies, baby bottles and romper suits. Some infantilists act out their desires alone – for example, they masturbate in full regalia in front of a mirror and take photos of themselves dressed up for masturbation purposes, or wet the bed or soil diapers while masturbating. Other infantilists find co-operative partners. Some couples dress as children and play 'doctors and nurses' or 'you show me yours and I'll show you mine'; others act out adult-child scenarios, such as tea parties, bedtime stories and nappy changing. Occasionally, there are elements of SM. For example, some SM games feature the role of an angry parent, and some men may cross-dress and play the role of an innocent young girl. In extreme scenes, SM partners may act out child-abuse role-play. Many professional dominatrixes include parenting in their portfolio and will punish you for being naughty. Many infantilists explain that playing the role of a baby allows them to escape the stresses and responsibilities of adult life. It also means that they can demand affection, attention and nurturing.

I usually play the adult, mostly his mummy. On the whole he is a good toddler and spends a lot of time breastfeeding, but sometimes he messes himself. Then I have to tell him off and call him a big baby. Occasionally he has to have a smack.
Alison, 39, US

Zoophilia: There is considerable debate about the moral aspects of 'zoo'. Animal protection groups see it as cruel and in many countries it is illegal, but zoophiles argue that they are not abusing animals for sexual gratification (the practice known as 'bestiality'), but enjoying loving sexual relationships with them. That said, it still takes a jar of peanut butter or chocolate spread to get Rover licking. Zoophilia is not an exclusively male preoccupation, though in the 17th century, sex between farm animals and young men was so prevalent that the Catholic Church tried to ban male herdsmen. It's hardly believable, but the US-based Kinsey reports of the 1940s and 1950s claimed that eight per cent of males and four per cent of females interviewed had had sexual contact with an animal. It also claimed that people who lived on farms or kept pets were much more likely to have experimented with them sexually. Some zoophiles simply masturbate their pets and themselves or cover their genitals with their pets' favourite food to encourage them to perform oral sex (zoolinction). Others have full penetrative sex with animals – pigs are apparently more responsive than sheep. Numerous infections (zoonoses) can be caught from animals, some of them serious. One example is toxoplasmosis, which can lead to blindness. And doctors in GU clinics also report treating zoophiles for severe bites, scratches and bruising. But, frankly, if you're playing around with a donkey, you should expect a kick in the shins.

If something hurts, confuses, confounds, upsets or exploits an animal, it should be out of the question. If there is something wrong with performing a sexual act with or on a child, the same holds true for doing it with or to a member of another species. Animals are not sex toys. Leave them alone!
Dawn Carr
People for the Ethical Treatment of Animals, UK

Once you've accepted yourself as a Zoo, be careful: there is a lot of prejudice out there. If you meet other Zoos through the Internet, don't assume that they will let you have sex with their animals. Zoos tend to be very protective of their partners.
Anon

The A–Z of everything else

Acrotomophile: A person who is aroused by the thought of having sex with someone who has an amputation. Sometimes acrotomophiles encourage partners to bandage a limb or foot. Those who are particularly attracted to amputees are called 'devotees'; those who want to be amputees are called 'wannabees', though it is unlikely that the Spice Girls knew this when they penned their first hit single.

Altocalciphilia: A fetish for high heels.

Amaurophilia: A preference for a blind or blindfolded sex partner.

Auto-asphyxia: Self-induced partial strangulation or suffocation during masturbation. Asphyxiation creates a sense of euphoria because the body produces adrenaline (epinephrine) when oxygen is in short supply. Suffocation also causes dizziness, which some people find arousing. People who like auto-asphyxia tend to keep it to themselves or die. It is thought that couples who engage in auto-asphyxiation together stand a better chance of survival because they can keep an eye on each other.

Auto fellatio: The unusual ability of a man to put his penis in his own mouth (only 3 in every 1000 can do it).

Autopederasty: A man inserting his penis into his own anus. This requires impressive flexibility and a reasonably long penis, but those who are up to it usually lubricate the anus, push their testicles to one side and pop their semi-erect penis up their bum. It is thought that ejaculation is not possible in this position. Also known as a 'hole in one'.

Avisodomy: An ancient but cruel practice of penetrating a bird with a penis. Shortly before orgasm, the man snaps the birds neck causing the bird to spasm. As the bird dies its contractions grip and stimulate the penis – apparently heightening climax.

Baby gravy: Slang term for semen.

Ballooning: The injection of a man's scrotum with a salt-water solution to make it blow up like a balloon. When the solution has filtered through into the penis, this swells to at least double its normal size for a short time (odd but impressive). This is a risky activity and requires a substantial amount of medical knowledge.

Beaver: Female genitalia. Also known by other furry monikers, such as 'teddy' or 'pussy'.

Bell dancing: A form of ritualistic self-flagellation in which a dancer sews bells, balls or fruit onto the skin to form a necklace and then dances to music. A marginally less painful variation is to tie the ornamentation to piercings. The dancing makes the objects beat against the body and pulls at the pierced or stitched skin.

Candaulism: When two people have sex while another watches.

Castration: The surgical removal of the scrotum, testicles or penis.

Chubby chasers: People who are aroused by obesity in a partner.

Chezolagnia: Masturbating while defecating.

Coprophagy: Eating faeces for sexual arousal. *Bon appétit.*

Cottaging: When gay men go to known places (often public toilets) in search of sex with strangers.

Daisy chain: A group sex activity in which everyone forms a circle and then turns to one side, to suck, lick and/or masturbate the genitals of the person next to them.

Docking: When an uncircumcised man pulls his foreskin up over another mans penis.

Dogging: The name 'dogging' comes from taking a dog for a walk late at night in order to watch couples having sex in parked cars. In known areas, couples indicate that they are willing to be watched by turning on a light in the car. Doggers gather around while the couple inside put on a show.

Emetophilia: When a person is aroused by vomit or vomiting; also known as a 'Roman shower', Emetophiles usually drink wine or urine in order to vomit it on their partner, though sometimes they force their partners to overeat or overdrink in order to trigger a gagging reflex during fellatio.

English culture: A slang term for flagellation or sadomasochistic sex play.

Eproctophilia: Arousal from flatulence.

Erotic balls: There are several famous annual erotic balls. Probably the most famous one to be held in the UK is the Sex Maniac's Ball, in London, which raises funds for people with disabilities. This ball, and others, such as the San Francisco Exotic Erotic Ball, feature thousands of people in erotic costumes who party, take photos and, if you're lucky, have sex.

Exhibitionism: When people are aroused by knowing others are watching them. In its mildest form, someone might gain a thrill from the prospect of possibly being glimpsed by a stranger. A more extreme version might be having sex in public or masturbating in a sex club.

Facial: When a man ejaculates on someone's face.

Felching: The act of sucking semen out of a vagina or anus, often using a straw.

Fluffer: The person responsible for getting the talent aroused on a porn set. Sometimes brothels have fluffers who make a guy hard before his appointment.

Freak: A client who demands unusual or possibly dangerous services from a sex worker.

Frottage: The rubbing of genitals against someone else's body in order to become aroused without penetration. Popular at rush hour on public transport.

Formicophilia: Attracting small insects, such as ants or flies, by smearing jam over the erogenous zones.

Game room: A torture chamber for SM play, also called a 'dungeon'.

Glory hole: A hole in a barrier or wall through which sexual play takes place. Often part of cottaging, a hole in a public toilet wall allows a hand or a penis to be poked through to the other side. Some people do this because they want to remain anonymous, especially if they have anxieties about their sexual orientation. Others do this because they find sexual contact with strangers arousing.

Gluteal sex: Where a man rubs his penis between his partner's buttocks without penetrating the anus, possibly leading to orgasm.

Granny porn: Images depicting older women having sex.

Gynonudomania: A compulsion to rip other peoples clothes off.

Hermaphrodite: A person who is born with both female and male genitalia.

Humiliation: Often a part of Sub/Dom sex, verbal humiliation or insults are, for some people, very arousing. Insults are said to be even more arousing when a person is being 'forced' to do something embarrassing or menial, such as scrubbing the floor or licking someone's boots. Those in the know recommend getting permission to humiliate someone, and afterwards spending a little time reassuring them that you didn't really mean it.

Hummer: Humming makes the mouth vibrate, so when combined with a blow job, humming can produce very pleasurable sensations. It's thought that random humming with a varying pitch is likely to be less distracting than fellating to 'God Save the Queen' or 'Three Blind Mice'.

Impaling: There are several ways in which people impale their (hopefully consenting) lovers. A stainless steel needle is sometimes hammered through the webbing between the fingers, or a nail is knocked through a part of the genitals or breasts into a block of wood. It is thought that the psychological effects of impaling are more arousing than the pain it inevitably causes. This is, rather obviously, not a safe-sex practice.

Incest: The term for sex between two people who are related. Incest is illegal, and there are a number of reasons for this. The practical explanation for this is that any offspring have a higher chance of birth defects and genetic abnormalities. The main sociological explanation for the origins of the incest taboo is that early tribal communities needed to forge strong links with surrounding tribes for security. If women from one tribe move to another tribe's village for marriage, rather than marrying their brothers, then the two villages have a bond. They are more likely to trade and are less likely to war.

Incubus: A mythological spirit thought to lie on top of women and have sex with them while they slept.

Inflatable dolls: Plastic dolls that are designed for genital or oral penetration.

Jailbait: Someone who is under the legal age for sexual intercourse, but looks older.

Jemima suit: A leather or rubber suit with holes over the erogenous zones.

Jactitation: Becoming aroused by telling other people about your sex life.

Kabazza: A form of Tantric sex in which the male is passive and the female uses only the contractions of her abdominal and vaginal muscles to milk his penis.

Kama Sutra: Probably the most famous book about sex there has ever been. The original version was written in India by Vatsyayana – who lived during the third and fourth centuries BC – and translated into English in 1883 by the famous British explorer Sir Richard Burton. 'Kama' is the Hindu god of love, and 'sutra' means a collection of easy-to-remember statements. The sexual positions described in most versions are just a portion of a single chapter from the original work, which contained 35 chapters. They are written with reference to both male and female pleasure, but are written from a man's point of view.

Klismaphilia: Arousal from having enemas.

Kokigami: Derived from an 8th-century Japanese practice, this involves wrapping the penis up in a paper disguise made by origami. Cute.

One of my fantasies is to fuck someone through a hole. I never know what I am fucking, whether it is an animal, a man or a woman.
Bob, 53, US

My boss does this thing where he slides up against me when he has to go past, and you can feel his hard-on. And he puts his hands on my hips to move me out of the way but leaves them there too long. He thinks he's debonair. I think he's a twat.
Gita, 28, UK

I just didn't understand what the hell she was doing. Singing while she sucked, sucked.
Music fan, 24, US

I always thought inflatable dolls were for a joke at buck nights, but somehow mine ended up going home with me. Now I wouldn't be without her.
GM, 32, Australia

My girlfriend talks to strangers about the time I came into her office and ejaculated all over her shirt. She is always really horny when she does this.
Joe, 39, New Zealand

Lactaphilia: Arousal by lactating (milk-producing) breasts.

Lipstick lesbian: A lesbian who displays 'traditional' feminine dress and behaviour.

Love: It is not known whether this is a chemical, psychological or imagined state, but the symptoms are very real. Usually occurring between two people who think each other marvellous, side-effects include passion, obsession, generosity and happiness. In its early stages, people often show a loss of appetite and concentration. Love may lead to co-habitation and often reproduction. When practised in inappropriate circumstances it can hurt like hell.

Merkin: A pubic wig, sometimes used by transexual or transgendered people to make a vagina look more convincing. They are also used by theatre actors as a modesty device in nude scenes.

Money shot: The 'cum shot' in a porn film, in which the man ejaculates semen (by the bucket-load), usually onto his partner's body or face.

Mucophagy: Consuming nasal mucous (snot) and a part of 'nasilingus' – this refers to the practice of licking and sucking someone's nostrils. It requires complete acceptance of your partner's body fluids.

Mysophilia: When someone is aroused by sniffing used knickers, dirty underpants or soiled sanitary pads.

Necrophilia: To be erotically attracted to dead bodies. Finding a partner is probably one of the biggest challenges for a necrophile, but it is rumoured that there are two categories of active necrophile: morgue necrophiles (MNs) and cemetery necrophiles (CNs). MNs supposedly have access to a morgue, and therefore to the recently deceased. CNs supposedly lurk around secluded cemeteries looking for freshly dug graves. There are no statistics on how common this is.

Niddah: An Orthodox Jewish religious observance forbidding married couples to touch from the first moment a spot of menstrual blood appears until a week after menstruation has ceased. Many couples believe that abstinence makes the heart grow fonder and that being separated makes reunion all the more exciting.

Nymphomaniac: A woman with an uncontrollable desire for sex.

Ophidicism: Inserting of eels or snakes tail-first into the vagina and masturbating while they wriggle free. Probably wise to pick a non-poisonous variety and to keep hold of the head.

Oculolinctus: Licking a partner's eyeball for sexual arousal (can transfer oral herpes).

One-eyed trouser snake: An imaginative term for a penis.

Osmolagnia: Stimulation from odours.

Paedophilia: Sexual arousal from thinking about, touching or having sex with children. This is illegal in most parts of the world, and many people see sex with a minor as the most immoral sex crime possible. Paedophiles who don't have sex with children but are found downloading pornographic images of children from the Internet can be prosecuted by the police.

Penile ligation: Binding the penis. Occasionally, two men with foreskins will tie them together with string.

Penis enlargement: There are two types of surgery. First, to lengthen the penis, internal ligaments are cut to allow a portion of the penis inside the body to be brought forward out of the body (approximately half of the length of the penis is inside the body). Second, to increase its girth, fat is grafted onto the penis, making it wider.

Piston shot: A porn-industry term that describes a close-up of a vigorous penetration.

Pyrophilia: A sexual celebration of burning. In its mildest form, chilli powder or embrocation is rubbed into the nipples or genitals to give a burning sensation. Sexual games include the use of chemicals, 'frying' genitals in hot oil, hot wax, okyu, peau flambé, fire dancing, fire walking, cigarette burns, throwing matches onto pubic hair and flagellation (whipping) with torches.

Priapism: A medical term for an erection that won't go down; priapism can be very painful.

Queening: A woman sitting on a man's head as if it were her throne. This is not to facilitate cunnilingus, but based on domination and restricting a man's breath. People who are into queening believe that the 'breath of life' of the male (his life) is controlled by the reproductive organs of the female – he is given life, allowed to continue living and allowed to reproduce by direction of the Queen.

Renifleur: A person who is aroused by the smell of urine or by sniffing underwear.

Reverse cowgirl: Enjoying penetration sitting on a male's lap with your back to him.

Rimming: Otherwise known as analingus, this is licking and kissing a partner's anus for sexual stimulation. Some prefer the anus to be clean, others prefer the anus to be in its natural state.

Rodeo: This is the rather unkind practice of saying something shocking (usually an ex-partner's name) while penetrating your partner from behind. Your partner is likely to contract muscles and try to buck you off. Don't expect your partner to see the funny side. It won't happen.

Sacrofricosis. Cutting a hole in your trouser pocket to enable you to masturbate in secret, but in public.

Shrimping: Sucking someone's toes for mutual arousal.

Sitophilia: Using food for sexual purposes. Popular masturbation props are cucumbers, bananas, warm melons, liver and honey. Some like to stuff grapes, tomatoes or boiled eggs into their anus, while others enjoy food being rubbed onto their bodies and eaten off it. Also includes adolescent games such as 'soggy biscuit', in which groups of boys masturbate over a biscuit and the last one to come has to eat it.

Sniffer's row: The row of seats nearest the stage in a strip club.

Stunt dick: A man hired on a porn shoot strictly for dick work or the money shot.

Sybian: A vibrating dildo that sits on top of an object that resembles a saddle.

Tantra: A spiritual and cultural movement known as Tantra appeared in India in the third and fourth centuries AD, and it has persisted in various guises ever since. Tantra has recently become popular in several Western cultures. The premise of this philosophy is complex, but sexual practices are characterised by ritualised, slow, non-orgasmic sex.

Taoism: An ancient philosophy that has many similarities to Tantra, including the fact that it has recently become popular in some Western cultures. Sexual practice is said to be linked to sexual development and orgasm is discouraged. The basic premise is that rather than the individual being controlled by sexual energy, this should itself be controlled with conscious intent.

Taphephilia. The term for those who gain arousal from being buried alive. It's thought to be reasonably rare. Don't forget to take a mobile.

Tribadism: A primarily lesbian form of sex play, in which two people lie on top of each other and grind against each other to provide mutual genital stimulation.

Trichophilia: A pubic hair fetish, or sometimes a fetish just for head hair. People who are trichophilic may secretly snip their partner's hair during the night to keep it as a trophy.

Urtication: Using stinging nettles to stimulate the skin on the genitals – sometimes being gently bashed with stingers before sex, or thrashing your own penis before putting on a condom to compensate for any reduction in sensation. Urtication can cause allergic reactions. Don't forget the dock leaves.

Unicorn: Also known as the 'screwnicorn', this is when a person wears a strap-on dildo on their forehead.

Vaginal tightening: A surgical procedure that reduces the size of the vagina. It can be cosmetic, but it is usually done if the vagina has been stretched during childbirth. The stretched muscle at the back of the vagina is joined together and shortened and the redundant skin is removed. The results are permanent, unless the woman has another baby. It does not cause any problems during pregnancy.

Vampirism: Also known as blood sports, this is drinking blood for sexual arousal. The term includes cunnilingus with a woman who is menstruating, sucking cuts and using a hypodermic needle to collect blood to drink. In terms of HIV and AIDS, this is the least safe form of sex.

Vanilla: Non-kinky, 'traditional' sex, usually between men and women.

Voyeurism: Watching other people – usually undressing or having sex – in order to become sexually aroused. Voyeurs might be very 'out', in that they may go to sex parties in order to watch people having sex, or they may be more covert 'peeping toms' – people who hide near homes and watch through windows. It is thought that the erotic gratification is heightened by secrecy and risk. This can become a problem for people who become obsessed by watching, or for those who get led away by the police.

Xenophilia: Being sexually aroused by strangers. Xenophiles get turned on by meeting new people, but once they have managed to seduce them, the thrill diminishes. Xenophiles like to have sex with people of different ethnicities and nationalities. As a result they 'enjoy travel and meeting people'. A lot.

Yoni mudra:. A Tantric technique in which a person seals the anus with the left heel, presses the tongue against the palate and stares at the tip of the nose. This reportedly results in a pleasant sensation at the base of the spine, which works its way up to the skull.

Zielophilia: Becoming aroused by jealousy. Zelophiles thrive on the adrenaline (epinephrine) that is produced by the body in response to anger or fear (of losing their partner). Zelophiles purposely set up sexual situations in which their partner will solicit sexual attention from rivals.

Zipper sex: Very quick sex that doesn't even involve taking clothes off.

My girlfriend once masturbated me until I came through my clothes in the kitchen. It was sexy, because I left for work feeling naughty.
Sue, 27, US

I used to like having my toes licked, but just recently I have found that it tickles too much. I don't know why I've become more sensitive.
Helen, 62, US

Approach her with your body stiff as a pole and drive straight forward to pierce her lotus and join your limbs: experts call it Madandhvaja (The Flag of Cupid).
Vatsyayana, India
4AD

If you are not too worried about coming and want the thrill of having sex somewhere you shouldn't – well that's what zipper sex is for. Get him to flop it out, suck till it's hard and then lift up your skirt. It's all over in five minutes, but you have a naughty feeling all night.
Miranda, 21, UK

SEX LIVES

I am 72 years old and my husband is 78. He knows more about my body than I do and he says he loves it as it is. Our sex life has had it's ups and downs but we knew that it was a case of either use it or lose it, so I would say we both worked at it. **Bernadette, 72, Ireland**

Sex through your life

In most Western cultures it is assumed to some extent that children are innocent and have no sexuality. However, from birth onwards both sexes enjoy touching their genitals. And why wouldn't they. Anatomically, a child's genitals are still loaded with nerve endings, and although their touching is really nothing to do with sex and doesn't lead to orgasm, it still feels nice. This creates quite a dilemma for parents, particularly if small children like to touch themselves in public. It's difficult to explain complex social boundaries to a four-year-old, and the only viable option may be to agree that it feels nice, but ask them not to do it in front of grandma.

At puberty, boys and girls experience considerable physical and emotional changes, and it can be an intensely confusing period. Generally, adolescents don't want to be different from their peer group, which can make it difficult for teenagers struggling with sexual identity. Teens tend to be caught between a rock and a hard place: too frightened to seek advice, too dumb to believe they really need it. As parents it can be terribly frustrating to watch children you love 'learn the hard way', but there are no short cuts to wisdom and understanding. They may eventually grow up and work this out for themselves. After puberty, sex tends to be either a feast or a famine. Casual sex, one-night stands, short flings, holiday romances and the odd long relationship can make the years after 18 emotionally bruising. Your social circle will largely determine the point at which you decide to settle down. Statistically, gay men tend to keep their options open, while lesbian women are more likely to form stable partnerships. As women approach 30, the biological clock starts ticking – muffled at first, building up to a loud thud by the mid-thirties. The characteristics and requirements of a long-term partner may be significantly different to those of a partner chosen for the purposes of short-term sexual gratification.

With age comes consistency, relationships and, hopefully, regular sex. But regular sex tends to be, well, regular. Navigating through the pitfalls of monogamy and monotony takes imagination and commitment. In a long-term relationship, you can only have 'reasonable' sex if the relationship is 'reasonable'. Statistically, men and women all over the world are happier and healthier if they have a close physical and sexual relationship with someone, and this is even more important in later life. Age can bring sexual insecurity – weight gained, erections lost. Lack of confidence and set patterns of behaviour can mean that sex goes on the back burner, but ignoring sex means ignoring a fundamental human need. You may not feel the earth move, but it's reassuring to know that it is still going around.

Like a virgin

I want my money back: Traditionally, virginity was something that boys lost as quickly as they could and girls held on to for as long as possible. Before condoms and contraception, this double standard was easily justified by fear of pregnancy, but the fact that there is no male equivalent to the hymen has also been significant. For centuries the hymen has been the symbol of virginity. When a blushing bride was penetrated for the first time, her hymen would tear, leaving visible evidence that her husband had boldly gone where no man had been before. We now know that 50 per cent of women don't have hymens that bleed when they tear, but previously, if a new bride didn't stain the sheets, her parents had to pay her husband compensation for her depreciated value.

Virgins recycled: In Victorian England, venereal disease could apparently be cured by sex with a virgin. One particular English brothel turned this to its advantage by supplying so-called virgins who came complete with their own medical certificates. Before sex with a new client, the 'virgin' would insert a blood-soaked sponge into her vagina and pressure on the sponge during penetration released the required evidence. The significance of virginity held through to the 1950s, when doctors in the US regularly performed a minor surgical procedure on women known as the 'lover's knot'. This involved putting several stitches in the labia of young women who had already been deflowered.

I may be a virgin, but I give a damn fine blow job: The hymen was never a reliable indicator of virginity, but it is even more irrelevant now that young girls routinely use tampons as soon as they start their periods. And what is virginity anyway? The dictionary definition of a virgin is: A person (esp. a woman) who has never had sexual intercourse. It defines 'sexual intercourse' as the insertion of a man's erect penis into a woman's vagina, usually followed by the ejaculation of semen. Does that mean that a woman is still a virgin if she has had oral sex? Is a man still a virgin if he has had penetrative anal sex, but has never put his penis in a vagina? The singling out of vaginal penetration as some hugely significant act is outdated and, frankly, naïve. With the notable exception of Britney Spears, young people are getting involved with sex earlier. There has been a huge rise in the number of teenagers engaging in oral sex, an activity that many young people presume to be risk-free. It isn't, but what is more unsettling is the thought that ongoing myths about the significance of penetration mean that adolescents don't view sucking each others genitals as an intimate act that deserves the same consideration as intercourse.

Opinions and prejudices are like arseholes – everyone has them. **Bob, 20, US**

Words are really powerful. When I was about 14, a girl told me I 'kissed like a poof'. For years I was really nervous about kissing, always worrying about getting it wrong. I guess it's the same if you tell someone they are crap in bed. Young people can be really cruel to each other, which is stupid, because it is the same young people who get hurt so easily. **David, 24, UK**

Despite how hard you try, how much you know about sex, how many positions you know and so on, the first time will never be perfect. So just do it . . . and enjoy it. Whoever buys a new video game and reads the instructions? You just bang it in and play the damn thing! **PB, 19, Spain**

/ 114 \

Safer Sex

Warning

We need to talk

114	**194**
Safer Sex	Contraception

Generation sex: The media paints a fairly dim picture of the next generation, but becoming a teenager has never been easy and arguably it's now more difficult than ever. Learning how to handle your hormones and develop relationships with the opposite sex is bad enough, but teenagers in the 21st century are increasingly bombarded with the message that sex is everything. Sex may be omnipresent, but a recent report reveals that parents are just not brave enough to talk to their kids about the indignities and risks of early sex. Only a small percentage of teenagers discuss sex with their parents, which means they either get their information from friends, from school, from the TV or from making their own mistakes. In 2001, 2,200 girls under the age of 14 became pregnant in the UK.

Sex is inevitable: Whether you like it or not, as parents you owe it to your teenage children to make sure that they are well-informed, properly protected and choosing to have sex for the right reasons. Easier said than done. Mothers of teenagers know why some animals eat their young, and surly teenagers would often prefer to eat their eyeballs than talk to their parents about something as embarrassing as sex. You can choose not to discuss sex with your children, but that doesn't mean that your children will choose not to have sex. Young adults need to get their information from somewhere, so you might as well make sure that it is reliable. Adolescents often find it easier to discuss sex with their friends, but give them a head start by making sure they know what they are talking about. Boys tend to be given less sex education, both at school and at home. They don't go through the same obvious physical stages of development as girls, and mothers (statistically the parent who gives most advice) often know less about male development, too. Fear of pregnancy makes talking to daughters seem as if it's a more urgent issue, but in the current climate, boys need as much – if not more – help than girls.

A tricky business: Talking to your children about sex is not the same as encouraging them to be sexually active, but if you are not open, you make it difficult for them to share their anxieties about sex and relationships with you. You may need to try to evaluate your own feelings about sex before you start. You can let them know your values and what sex means to you, but try not to get your beliefs mixed with the facts. Rather than pretending it's not embarrassing, be honest with your child and admit that you feel awkward and unsure. Sex is a complicated business because it is so tangled up with emotions and self-confidence, but a sense of humour really helps. Letting your child in on the big joke helps to demystify a

subject that is usually shrouded in secrecy. Informal chats that relate to something on TV or in the news may be easier for your child to digest. It also means that the subject is 'live' – an ongoing topic which is discussed regularly. One long serious talk can be intimidating, and is often never referred to again.

Start early: In an ideal world, parents would be brave enough to be honest with their children from the start. Children ask all sorts of questions before they hit adolescence. How these are answered determines their understanding of sex to a large degree. 'Mummy, why does it feel so nice when I touch myself here?'; 'What is that string hanging down between your legs?'; 'How do babies get into your tummy?' Storks may get you off the hook in the short term, but a simple and straightforward response may be better in the long run. Keep it simple to begin with – they can always come back for more information. Every child is different and you need to gauge what is appropriate for their particular stage of development. Telling a bright seven-year-old who asks how babies are made that it happens when a penis goes into a vagina may sound shocking, but the fact that they have asked the question means that they want to know the answer. It's natural for parents to want to preserve their child's innocence and protect them from the big bad world, but if you impart the truth about sex slowly and gently over a period of years, they have some idea of what to expect by the time they reach adolescence.

Em, um aah, you see it's like this: Many parents just can't bring themselves to talk about the more graphic aspects of sex – oral sex and masturbation are the two topics that parents are least likely to discuss. If you had to piece together the sexual jigsaw by yourself, you should appreciate how helpful a straightforward conversation can be. School sex-ed concentrates on reproduction, contraception, HIV and protection, so teenagers may know the basics, but they are unlikely to understand the essential subtleties of pleasure and sexual confidence.

Self-help: Some teenagers just won't talk about sex, and if this is the case, there is no point forcing the issue. The best you can do is to help them to inform themselves: give them a good book on the subject, leave information leaflets in obvious places or recommend good websites. If you suspect that your teenager may be sexually active, leave a box of condoms in the bathroom and make sure that he or she is well-briefed about safer sex and contraception.

I'd rather eat my eyeballs

Your parents have definitely had sex: The idea of chatting about sex with adults may seem excruciatingly embarrassing, but you should bear in mind that – perish the thought – they have probably had a lot more sex than you, so they may be able to tell you a thing or two. The other thing about talking to parents or guardians is that you don't have to pretend you know it all already. In fact, they will probably be nicely reassured if you don't.

Ask: If you need to know something, ask. Your parents or guardians may be feeling just as awkward as you are about raising the subject, yet one question may be all it takes to break the ice. If you are worried that asking means that it will be presumed that you are sexually active, you are probably right to a degree. If you suddenly ask your mum about blow jobs, she may assume that you are either having sex or are about to. Explain that theory doesn't have to mean practice, though obviously it will eventually. If your parents or guardians are unhelpful, or have religious or cultural beliefs that conflict with yours, talk to an older brother, sister, friend or relative whom you trust instead. You can also use the Internet and the library to find out more about specific subjects. Nothing can ever fully prepare you for your first sexual experience and the 'real thing', but knowing what to expect and how to handle yourself will give you greater confidence.

It was about 12 inches: Both boys and girls often find it easier to talk to their friends about personal issues. The problem is that most people your own age don't have a great deal of sexual experience, so they are not exactly going to be a mine of information. Many adolescents pretend to be more sexually experienced than they really are, because they are afraid of what their friends or partners will think of them if they admit to being virgins. Discussions with friends are often a group activity, too, and peer pressure and lack of privacy can make it difficult to admit to fears, feelings or sexual inexperience.

Conditioning: Studies show that while girls tend to discuss the emotional aspects of relationships, boys are more concerned with the mechanics of sex. This is partly to do with conditioning. Boys and girls feel that they are expected to behave in a certain way and they do so, and arguably sex education in its present structure reinforces these stereotypes. Whatever the reasons, teenage boys don't admit readily that they need emotional support and teenage girls never admit that they just want to have rampant sex for its own sake, despite the fact that both sexes probably want and need a bit of both.

I always hate the first thing with a new bloke. How do you tell him you want to wait for a bit? I'm amazed how people last years without actually doing it.
Sad&pathetic, US

Sex without love is fine if all of the participants are aware that these are the conditions. Sometimes a release of sexual energy is necessary for a human being. Personally, I would not like to take part in sex without some deep feelings surrounding it, but there is little doubt that some people can be just fine having sex without love.
Anya, 18, Canada
Kuma2

I think parents feel that they don't know enough about sex themselves, which makes them frightened to talk about it with children. They just hope that school does it for them. But you don't have to be a biology teacher to know about getting it on, and anything you don't know, you can look up in books.
James, 42, UK

Sexual intelligence

Sex education: In the UK, all government-funded primary (Year 6) and secondary schools must provide some form of sex education, including information about STIs and HIV. In the US, sex education varies from state to state, though there is a general mandate to cover information about HIV and STIs. Federal government involvement has been limited, and seems to focus primarily on promoting abstinence – the policy equivalent of finger-crossing and wishful thinking. Australian and British schools have similar policy goals, but programmes are not uniformly administered and success seems to depend on the quality of the teaching. Both governments advise that, beyond the basics of reproduction, STIs and HIV, issues of sexual orientation should be dealt with sensitively.

Emphasis: School sex education tends to focus mainly on biology. Pupils are taught to recognise: external body parts; the main stages of the human life cycle; the physical and emotional changes that take place in adolescence; the human reproductive system, sexual reproduction as a source of genetic variation; and how gender is determined in humans. There is a strong suspicion that the emphasis on reproduction during sex education perpetuates the message that it is more relevant to girls, and the fact that the majority of sex education teachers are female seems to further alienate boys. Most teenagers admit that they find sex education in a classroom environment very embarrassing. Computer-based sex education may be the only way to allow adolescents to access information in private.

Disabled people have sex, too: Many people are uneasy at the thought of linking sex and disability, but disabled people have the same desires, aspirations, fantasies and fears as able-bodied people. Because they experience more specific restrictions, such as lack of independence and lack of opportunity, teachers and parents of disabled children need to find ways to talk about their disability and the effect it may have on their sexual experiences. In Britain, The Association to Aid the Sexual and Personal Relationships of People with a Disability (SPOD), advises steering clear of generalisations and avoiding medical territory. It says: 'For most people, the major impact is social and psychological, rather than a direct result of physical impairment. It is important that disabled young people know how to ask for help, in terms of needing to be guided, lifted and so on, and when it is appropriate to ask for help. Everyone with a disability has the right to informed sex education and the dignity of an acknowledged sexual identity . . . everyone with a disability should have the opportunity to form relationships of their own choice'.

The first time

An unforgettable experience: Usually, the first sexual experience is not penetrative. Most adolescents fumble about for ages before getting to the main event. Though losing your virginity is hyped to be the most exciting event of your youth, in reality it is often the biggest let-down. 'The heat of the moment' is usually carpet burn and the 'sweet nothings' are a combination of 'is it in yet?' or 'sorry I couldn't wait'. For most people, first sex is rubbish and choosing a partner who is more experienced than you doesn't seem to make it any better. Interestingly, first sex may be dismal but we never forget it. The British National Survey of Sexual Attitudes and Lifestyles found that over 99 per cent of people can recall their first time – so for anyone reading this book who hasn't lost their virginity yet, make sure your first sexual experience is a positive one because you'll remember it forever.

The age of consent: The age of consent is currently 16 for heterosexual sex in the UK, but a quarter of girls and a third of men have sex before then. The age of consent for gay men is 18 or older in the US and Australia and 16 in the UK (though most are 19 before they have their first sexual experience). Generally, there is no legal age of consent for lesbian sex. Do governments think they don't exist?

Peer pressure: Although you would imagine that peer pressure would be very influential in determining when young people lose their virginity, UK statistics indicate that only about 14 per cent of girls aged 15 and 10 per cent of boys aged 15 had intercourse because their friends had done so already. It is also interesting that 49.1 per cent of girls and 26.3 per cent of boys regret having had sex so early and would prefer to have waited.

What's wrong with you?: Pressure to have sex is much more likely to come from a partner, and many young girls find it very difficult to say, 'No'. There's no doubt that many young girls are having sex that they don't want and sex without orgasm. Classic lines to look out for are: 'I love you and the only way I can know that you love me is if you have sex with me'; 'unless you have sex with me I will leave you'; 'my last partner let me, everybody does it'; 'you're frigid' or 'you're just a tease'. These are manipulative, but unusually effective with lovestruck teenage girls. Though it's hard to see the bigger picture when you are stuck in a particularly emotional moment, always remember that you have a right to say no. Having sex won't make a bad relationship good or stop somebody from leaving you, and no one who really cares about you will make you engage in sexual activity that you don't want. Trust your instincts and if you feel unsure, wait.

Preparation: Sex isn't just about intercourse. It may help to make a list of the acts you will and won't engage in at this stage. If you are lucky enough to meet someone nice, try to stick to your list, but don't beat yourself up if you go further than you intended – we're all human.

Protection: The condom is the most commonly used method of contraception for first-time sex, though too many adolescents still opt for blind faith. Nearly 20 per cent of 15-year-old British boys admitted that they had failed to use a condom during sex because they were too drunk at the time. No surprise that the UK has the highest teenage pregnancy rates in Europe, then.

Though 76 per cent of 15- and 16-year-olds in the UK agree that it is smart to carry condoms, 52 per cent of girls and 45 per cent of boys feel embarrassed about buying them. It's ironic to think that a girl might become pregnant simply because she, or her partner, was too shy. However, teenagers who live in the country can find it more difficult than those who live in towns. They often have to rely on their parents for transport, so finding an opportunity to buy a condom in privacy can be a problem. Vending machines in public toilets are a discreet solution to the problem.

Having sex: Doing it somewhere really uncomfortable or unsuitable, or rushing the experience because you are afraid of getting caught, guarantees lousy sex. You will probably both be nervous, but if privacy is ensured, it will help you to relax. Sometimes people feel that if sex doesn't work out the first time, then the relationship is ruined. But having sex is like cooking – you can have the recipe and all the correct ingredients and still burn the cake (you probably won't next time). Don't fake how good it was or how it felt. You can laugh at the experience, but you are not allowed to laugh at each other's inexperience. If you are going to expose yourself to a person physically and emotionally, you need to be sure that the person can be trusted. You need to be able to talk honestly, to say what feels good, to suggest using condoms and to say 'no' if you change your mind.

Conclusion: The decision to have sex is only dangerous if you don't protect yourself from pregnancy and STIs. The decision to have sex is only intimidating if you feel you are being forced into it. The decision to have sex is only damaging if the act leaves you with negative feelings. That said, if you are equipped with a condom, a willing partner and a large dose of the horn, the decision to have sex is not a decision – it's just fun.

I know it's not a typical thing for a guy to say, but I am a pretty private kind of person. My first time was with this girl in the year above me, and she told everyone. And she told them it was my first time. I was pretty pissed off and we haven't spoken since. She sort of made me wish I hadn't done it.
Jonas, 17, New Zealand

Don't do it to please other people. It's much more sexy and makes the sex better the longer you leave it.
Ilene, 18, UK

I don't care what the so-called experts say. I did it when I was pretty young, with someone I wasn't going out with, and it was brilliant. I haven't really stopped since.
Anon, 18

I class losing your virginity as having full sex with someone. I don't think that sex stuff like oral counts.
Sugar & Spice ,16, UK

242

STIs

Warning

Sexuality

Though some young people seem to know automatically whether they are straight or gay from a very young age, others don't recognise their orientation until much later. A 1993 UK study of 1,000 gay people found that feelings about sexual orientation started at about 14 in boys and 16 in girls. They were not sexually active at this time, and on average it was another two years before they had a sexual encounter. The teenage years are physically and emotionally confusing, and most adolescents have to deal with some sexual ambiguity. Teenagers often develop 'crushes' on people around them (a teacher, best friend or friend's parent). If a girl is stuck in a single-sex boarding school, then the target of her affections may not be male, but that doesn't mean that she is going to be a lesbian as an adult. Sometimes curiosity can lead to a same-sex encounter. If it is enjoyable, it may be the first of many, but it can also simply be put down to experience. Sexuality takes time to develop. It emerges slowly and doesn't stabilise immediately. Eventually feelings, attractions and relationships help young people to decide where they belong. Remember that statistics only indicate what people say they are, which is not necessarily the whole story.

Heterosexual (straight): People who have sexual relationships primarily or exclusively with the opposite sex. In the US, 93.8 per cent of men and 95.6 per cent of women report exclusively heterosexual attraction and experience.

Homosexual (gay or lesbian): People who have sexual relationships primarily or exclusively with their own sex. Overall in the UK, 1 in 20 women and 1 in 19 men have had a homosexual partnership.

Bisexual: People who are attracted to both genders. They may have relationships with both men and women, but not usually at the same time.

Transgender/transexual: People who are one gender biologically but feel psychologically as if they are the other gender.

Intersex: People who are born with genitals that are not obviously male or female. Some have female genitals but are genetically male, or vice versa. One in every 2,000 people is intersex, and doctors often intervene with surgery, though this often causes identity problems later on.

Pomosexual: People who don't feel that they should be forced to have their identity defined by their sex lives.

Coming out

Coming out of the closet without tripping on the laundry: The decision to come out may be more difficult if you come from a background hostile to the idea of homosexuality. Make it easy on yourself and tell a close, trustworthy friend initially, rather than a family member. Many people find it much more difficult to tell their parents than anyone else. It may be easier to start with siblings and get them on your side first. Though it may be difficult, telling your parents is probably a good idea. It prevents them finding out through gossip and it means that you can be honest about your social life.

What will we tell the grandchildren?: You've probably taken a long time to get used to the idea yourself, so your family and friends might need some time to get their heads around it as well. They may believe that you are making life more difficult for yourself, and your parents will probably be concerned that you will miss out on the so-called normal things in life, such as marriage and children. You may not want to hear these fears, but they contain elements of truth and they should not automatically be interpreted as a negative reaction. They are simply a sign that your family cares about your welfare and happiness. In fact, a reaction that involves debate is actually positive. The alternative – being met with silence or anger – is infinitely worse. Over time, people have a capacity to adjust. What seems unresolvable now can seem a lot better once they get used to the idea.

There won't be any grandchildren: Parents can sometimes seem to be more worried about how it will affect them – 'What will the neighbours think?' – than how it affects you. They may want to keep it a secret at first. Whether you co-operate is up to you, but once you have told your parents, you will probably be more relaxed about other people finding out. Parents can sometimes blame themselves for your sexuality and perceive it to be the result of their failure as parents. Do your best to relieve them of the hair shirt. There is nothing wrong with you, so they have nothing to feel guilty about. They may try to persuade you that it cannot be true because you don't fit their stereotype of a gay person. It can take time for parents to acknowledge that being lesbian doesn't automatically mean you will shave your head and dress in boiler suits, and that it is perfectly possible to be a gay man without turning into a screaming queen. Parents may suggest that this is just a phase, or even that somebody has unduly influenced you. They may transfer this resentment to a partner, so take time before you introduce anyone to your parents

Hostility: Negative attitudes to homosexuality are sometimes based on cultural, religious and moral beliefs. If this is the case, you will have to acknowledge that your family may never completely accept your sexuality. In difficult cases, it may be easier to come out by writing a letter – this will give you time to compose your thoughts. Coming out by letter can also give your family the opportunity to react in private and consider the news before discussing it with you. Support is available from a number of organisations geared to providing support for gay men and lesbians from specific ethnic or religious backgrounds.

Get off the fence: Ironically, bisexual people often have a more difficult time working out their sexuality and coming out. Bisexuality is sometimes presumed to be a transitional stage from a straight sexual identity to a gay or lesbian one. While this might be the case for some people, other people are bi all their lives. Sometimes bisexual people feel that they don't fit anywhere, because while there is a predominantly straight culture and healthy gay and lesbian scenes, there is little that caters specifically for bisexuals. Bisexuality is gradually becoming more recognised and some support is available, but you have to look harder for it. Try lesbian and gay phonelines and ask if they can put you on to an organisation for bisexuals.

Things your mother should have told you

- Come out to people individually and avoid doing so during an argument. Don't tell people on the spur of the moment, especially after a few drinks. You may regret it in the morning!

- Make sure that you are coming out for your own reasons – often there is pressure from a partner to do so. Build up to introducing your lover – an invitation to Sunday lunch isn't likely to come straight away.

- Remember to listen to what people say to you. Give them time to react and the opportunity to think about what you have told them. It is easy to become so absorbed in the importance of what is happening to you that you forget the impact coming out will have on others. Reassure everyone that you know what you are doing and are practising safer sex.

- If you're still at school, check your school's confidentiality policy before telling teachers. They may be legally obliged to tell someone else. Don't tell classmates if you don't want your parents to know. Gossip spreads quickly.

I am bi I suppose, in that I just fancy some people and I'm not gender-specific. Sometimes I feel a bit of a fraud, because although I have had sex with other women, my long-term relationships have always been with men. So I've never had the trauma of coming out to my family etc. – I mean, if they asked, I'd tell them, but because I have boyfriends, I don't suppose it would occur to them.
Natasha, 26, UK

I generally felt happier in girls' company rather than boys'. I didn't want a boyfriend, although all my other girlfriends were pressing me to get one, because they had them.
Bryony, 39, UK

I think homosexuality frightens families unless they have put all the myths aside. I think they also worry about us because it's not easy being this way. My children once asked me if I expected them to grow up to be homosexual. I said that I hoped they wouldn't, although I would support them if they did. It's much easier being straight.
Lou, 56, Canada

Unplanned pregnancy

I really wanted my girlfriend to keep our baby and so did my mother. My sister died when I was 22, and my mother never really got over it. My girlfriend felt that she was too young at 20 to have a baby. She had a row with my mother when she said she was unsure about having it, and I was in the middle. I knew my mum would have looked after the baby so it wasn't as if my girlfriend would have had to give up going to college even. In the end she had an abortion and didn't even tell me. I felt I had lost two people I loved: my girlfriend and my baby. My mother, well she was heartbroken. Looking back, I can see that my girlfriend felt as if she would be trapped. My mother shouldn't have expected her to replace my sister. I have had a lot of therapy now and I can see all this, but I couldn't back then.
Joe, 25, US

I once saw my brother and the woman he was having an affair with walking out of an abortion clinic. It's hard to know what to say in circumstances like that.
Giles, 43, UK

Finding out: The most obvious indicator of pregnancy is a missed period, though some women who are pregnant continue to have spotting that can be mistaken for a short, light period. Some women feel physical signs and know they are pregnant straight away – nausea or vomiting, light-headedness, breast tenderness, needing to pee all the time and constipation may all be an indications. Other women don't experience any symptoms at all. If you have irregular periods, an illness or an eating disorder, your periods may be absent or erratic, but you can still become pregnant, and if you don't feel any physical symptoms, it will take you a lot longer to find out. Home tests are the quickest and most private way to confirm that you are pregnant. They can be carried out at home 19 or more days after unprotected sex. If the test is negative and you still think you may be pregnant, do another. In very rare cases, a test may appear negative when the result is, in fact, positive, but it's very unlikely to happen twice. In Britain, you can get free pregnancy tests from your doctor or a family planning or GU clinic.

Help?: If you are unsure what to do, and your partner can't or won't help, your doctor, nurse or family planning clinic may be able to offer some advice and counselling. Whatever the pressure, remember it is your decision about what to do and nobody else's.

Avoiding the issue: Many young girls are so frightened to tell their parents or guardians that they are pregnant that they put off doing anything about it. However, the earlier you start dealing with the situation the more options you have. If you can't face telling anyone, phone a support group anonymously or contact social services. A trained counsellor will be able to help you weigh up all your options. Your partner may be supportive initially, but if you decide to have the baby, you cannot force the father to remain involved against his will.

It's not just teenagers who make mistakes: Unplanned pregnancies don't just happen to teenagers. Many women in their 20s and 30s make mistakes with contraception and become pregnant. If they are in the process of building their career or are unhappy with their partner, the decision to keep or abort a baby can be just as traumatic. With the biological clock ticking rather louder, there is also the underlying fear that this may be the only opportunity to have a child. But having a child is a serious and lifelong commitment, and there are no easy answers. For many women, abortion is the sensible option. That said, though many women regret having had abortions, few women regret having had a child.

Guys can't win: You may feel that whatever you do seems to be wrong. If you tell your pregnant girlfriend that what she does is her decision, you may be seen as passive and uncaring. If you have an opinion on what you would like her to do, you may be seen to be taking away her right to choose. If you want the baby, you cannot force her to keep it. If you don't want the baby, you cannot force her to have an abortion and you may also have financial responsibility for it.

Keeping the baby: An unplanned pregnancy can lead to mixed feelings, particularly for very young women. If you decide to keep the baby, you will probably worry about being able to cope emotionally and financially. You will have to sacrifice a large slice of your life to become a mother, but your baby will bring you (and your family) great happiness. Give yourself time to adjust and be prepared for mixed reactions – a baby will change other people's lives as well as your own. There are numerous local organisations that help and support young women who are going to have a baby.

Adoption: In the UK you can't formally agree to adoption until six weeks after the birth, in case you change your mind. If you decide to keep the baby, once you have had it, you will not be pressured to give it up for adoption. Adoptions can be arranged through the social services or special agencies. If your baby is adopted, then the adoptive parents legally become the parents of the child. You cannot change your mind and have the baby back later.

Abortion: There are two broad categories of abortions: surgical and drug-induced. Surgical abortions can be conducted up until 24 weeks (from the date of the first day of the last period), whereas drug-induced abortions, also known as 'medical abortions', can only be given if you are nine weeks pregnant or less. It is essential that you are tested for STIs, such as chlamydia, before surgery, to ensure that no infections are spread to the womb. In Britain, an abortion can be arranged through the NHS for no charge or privately, for a fee (private abortions can usually be performed with less delay). A woman must have a referral from two doctors. Referrals can be obtained from doctors, family planning clinics and occasionally sexual health clinics. If you don't think your own doctor will be sympathetic, go to another one. If you are under 16, you can get an abortion without your parents' consent if your doctor, or the doctor to whom you are referred, thinks having one is in your best medical interests, and that you are mature enough to understand fully what an abortion involves.

I don't agree with abortion, but I do understand why people have them. I don't believe I could put a child of mine up for adoption. In my opinion, an accident didn't just happen – two people caused it and they should take responsibility.
Oswald, 19, UK

It pisses me off when I read about pregnant girls who say, 'he never had any protection'. That's no bloody excuse. Some girls think that because it's the lad's penis that's getting covered, it's the lad's responsibility, but I know if I was female my attitude would be 'well if he thinks he's sticking that thing in me, then I'm making sure it's covered.
Justin, 19, UK
Thesite

I'm not religious at all, but I'm torn over the abortion issue. It's wrong, I disagree with it. But I also agree with it.
Anon, UK
Thesite

I was always anti-abortion, but as soon as I knew I was pregnant, I knew I would have an abortion. You never know what you'll do until you're in the situation.
Chrissy, 24, Denmark

Contraception

Different needs: Different types of contraception suit different people at different points in their lives. Considerations when choosing one include effectiveness, safety (whether it protects against STIs), possible side-effects, convenience, possible reversibility, cost and the attitude of your partner. All methods of birth control have their advantages and disadvantages. A doctor, family planning clinic or health centre will help you decide what is most appropriate for you in your circumstances. While all types of contraceptive offer protection against pregnancy, the condom and femidom are the only ones that offer some protection against STIs. Most doctors suggest using the condom with one other form of contraception, so that if the condom splits or comes off, you know that you are still protected against an unwanted pregnancy. The spread of STIs and HIV has made men more aware of the need for personal protection during sex. As a result, there is now much more of a balance between men and women when it comes to who takes responsibility for contraception. In the UK, contraceptives and contraceptive advice are free from doctors and family planning clinics – private clinics may charge a fee. Clinics are listed in the telephone directory and many of them have helplines.

Safety rates: If something is 99% effective, it means that 1 woman in 100 will get pregnant in a year even if they follow the instructions. However, the main reason contraceptives fail is human error, so we have also included statistics for this.

For women: If the form of contraceptive that your doctor suggests does not suit you or is causing side-effects, ask if you can try something else. Some hormonal contraceptives may slightly reduce a woman's libido. If this is the case, try another contraceptive or another form of the same contraceptive. Some women believe that the pill makes them gain weight, though it has not been proved that it does. However, your doctor may be able to change you to one with a different dose of oestrogen if you are concerned.

For men: There are only two options for men who want to take full responsibility for contraception: the condom or sterilisation. It is in a man's best interests that he understands how these and any other form of contraception work. If you don't want to father an unplanned child you should find out about emergency contraception too, so that you can advise your partner should the necessity for this arise.

For adolescents: British law says that people under 16 can access medical treatment confidentially and also consent to it. If confidentiality is a major concern for you, discuss it with your doctor before you disclose any information. Remember that the doctor is expected to assess whether you understand the implications of what you are doing. Alternatively, go to a family planning clinic – staff at these have a strict code of confidentiality.

Emergency contraception options (UK)

Emergency pills: These used to be called morning-after pills and they can be taken within 72 hours of unprotected intercourse. The sooner they are taken, the more effective they are likely to be. Two pills are taken within 12 hours of each other. Possible side-effects include some nausea and vomiting (better than pregnancy, which may involve considerably more nausea and vomiting).
Advantages? In the UK, now available to buy from pharmacists without prescription if you are over 16, but it's better to consult your doctor first.
Disadvantages? If you are pregnant and the emergency pill fails, there is an increased chance of ectopic pregnancy.

The IUCD: A small plastic and copper device which can be put into the womb by a doctor up to five days after sex as a form of emergency contraception.
Advantages? It is almost 100% effective and can be left in to provide long-term contraception or removed following your next period.
Disadvantages?: It is uncomfortable to have the IUCD fitted and there are risks of infection, pain and bleeding

Male condom

Effective? 98% for people who follow instructions. 86% for the rest.
How does it work? Made of very thin latex or polyurethane, it is put over the erect penis and stops sperm from entering the woman's vagina.
Advantages? Very widely available. May protect both partners from STIs. Men can take responsibility for their sexual health and their partner's contraception.
Disadvantages? Putting it on can interrupt sex. May split or come off if not put on correctly. Man needs to withdraw immediately after ejaculation.
Bottom line? Use a new condom each time and put it on before genital contact. In the UK, use a condom with a BSI kitemark (BS EN 600) and CE mark on the packet. Always check the expiry date. Don't use oil-based lubricants or massage oils with latex condoms, because they erode the material.

Female condom (femidom)

Effective? 95% for people who follow instructions. 79% for the rest.
How does it work? A soft polyurethane sheath lines the vagina and the area just outside it, and stops sperm from entering the vagina.
Advantages? Can be put on well before sex has started. Offers better protection from STIs because its extra width covers the vulva and the base of the penis. Oil-based products can be used with female condoms.
Disadvantages? Need to make sure penis does not slip in between condom and vagina. Expensive to buy. May be a bit noisy during sex.
Bottom line? Use a new condom each time and follow instructions carefully. In the UK, female condoms have a CE mark.

Contraceptive injection

Effective? Over 99%. Less room for human error as you don't have to remember to take a pill.
How does it work? An injection releases progestogen into the body. This stops ovulation, and thickens cervical mucus to prevent sperm meeting egg.
Advantages? An injection lasts 8 weeks (Noristerat) or 12 weeks (Depo-Provera), during which time you don't have to think about contraception. Some protection from pelvic inflammatory disease. May protect against cancer of the womb.
Disadvantages? Periods often become irregular or stop. It may take up to seven months for regular periods and fertility to return after stopping injections. Some women gain weight. Other possible side-effects include headaches, acne, tender breasts, depression, mood swings and water retention/bloating. Before having the injection, go on a course of the progestogen-only mini pill to check that you won't have any side-effects.
Bottom line? The injection cannot be removed, so side-effects may continue as long as it lasts and possibly for some time afterwards.

Contraceptive implant

Effective? Over 99%. Less room for human error as it is put in by a doctor.
How does it work? A small, flexible tube is placed under the skin of the upper arm. It releases a steady stream of the hormone progestogen into the bloodstream to stop ovulation and prevent sperm meeting an egg.
Advantages? Works for three years, and you don't have to think about contraception during this time. When the implant is taken out, normal levels of fertility should be re-established immediately.
Disadvantages? Periods are often irregular for at least the first year, with some bleeding in between. Some women gain weight. May be temporary side-effects such as headaches, mood changes and breast tenderness.
Bottom line? Usually put in under local-anaesthetic and no stitches are needed. The area may be tender for a day or two, with bruising and swelling. Most women can feel the implant beneath the skin, but it can't be seen. Removal is occasionally difficult, but usually a simple procedure with no scar.

EVRA Contraceptive patch (US)

Effective? 99%. No error statistics available but the technique is not idiot-proof.
How does it work? The patch slowly releases the hormones – the same ones as in the combined pill – into the bloodstream.
Advantages? Easier to use than the pill, as less chance of forgetting it. Has been designed to be swim- and bath-proof.
Disadvantages? Same as the pill. Occasionally (2.6%) causes skin irritation. Some women don't like the way it looks.

Bottom line? A 7.5cm (3ins) patch that looks like a plaster, which can be worn on buttocks, upper-outer arm, lower abdomen or upper torso, excluding the breast. Women replace the patch on the same day for three consecutive weeks, then go patch-free for a week. Currently only available in the US.

Diaphragm/cap with spermicide

Effective? 92–96% for people who use them properly. 80% for the rest.
How does it work? A flexible rubber/silicone device used with spermicide is put in the vagina to cover the cervix, and must stay in for at least six hours after sex. Your doctor will fit you for the correct size.
Advantages? Can be put in any time before sex (if more than three hours, add extra spermicide). May protect against some STIs and cancer of the cervix.
Disadvantages? Extra spermicide is needed. Can cause cystitis.
Bottom line? You can't leave a cap in for more than 30 hours after sex. Fitting should be checked every 12 months and if you gain or lose more than 3kg (7lbs) or have a baby, miscarriage or abortion.

Progestogen-only pill (mini pill)

Effective? Over 99% safe for people who read instructions and follow them. 95% for the rest.
How does it work? Progestogen taken at the same time each day causes thickening of cervical mucus, which makes it difficult for sperm to enter the womb or for the womb to accept a fertilised egg. In some women it prevents ovulation.
Advantages? Useful when the combined pill is not suitable: older women who smoke, have migraines or high blood pressure or women breastfeeding.
Disadvantages? Periods may become irregular, with some bleeding in between, or be missed. May be less effective in women who weigh over 70kg (11st).
Bottom line? It is important to take this at the same time every day. Try setting an alarm to remind you, because it is not effective if taken more than three hours late. Vomiting or severe diarrhoea can also make it ineffective. Ask for advice if you are on any medication, because some drugs stop the pill working.

The combined pill

Effective? 99% safe for people who read instructions and follow them. 95% for the rest.
How does it work? It contains oestrogen and progestogen, which stop ovulation, thicken cervical mucus and alter the lining of the womb.
Advantages? It often reduces bleeding, period pains and PMS, and gives some protection against ovarian and uterine cancer and some pelvic infections. It is suitable for most healthy non-smokers up to the menopause.
Disadvantages? Not suitable for all women, depending on their medical history. Rare but serious side-effects include blood clots (thromboses), breast

I've tried other contraceptive methods, including the diaphragm but I didn't like it. I wouldn't risk the withdraw-before-ejaculation method again – I've done that in the past and ended up worrying for several weeks because I know about the pre-come risks. I'm interested in finding out more about the male contraception pill or, indeed, the three-month injection. I certainly don't want kids for the next five years.
Justin, 19, UK
Thesite

I used the pill but I smoked about 20 cigarettes a day and always felt sick when popping them every morning so I stopped – the pill that is – and changed to a coil.
Diana, 34, UK

Basically, the pill is 99 per cent effective, but human beings are not.
Sarah, 38, UK

I get PMS – I get really angry and moody or really depressed and weepy. I am on the pill, which is meant to stop it but it doesn't, so I don't really deal with it all that well!
Badgirl, 16, UK
Rainbow Network

cancer and cervical cancer. Can cause acne, weight changes, tender breasts, nausea and headaches. Not suitable for smokers over 35.

Bottom line? Not effective if taken over 12 hours late or if you are vomiting or have severe diarrhoea. Ask for advice if you are taking any medication, because some drugs can stop the combined pill working.

Intrauterine system (IUS)

Effective? Over 99%. Less room for human error as it is put in by a doctor.
How does it work? A small plastic device that releases progestogen is placed in the womb. It thickens the mucus at its neck and thins its lining, preventing sperm meeting an egg or stopping an egg settling in the womb.
Advantages? Works as soon as it is put in, lasts for five years – so you don't have to think about contraception – and can be taken out at any time. Periods are much lighter and shorter.
Disadvantages? Irregular bleeding is common for the first three months or so. May be temporary side-effects, such as breast tenderness and acne.
Bottom line? Women are taught to check an IUS is in place by feeling for the threads high in the vagina. If it is out of place, use a barrier method and see your contraceptive advisor. It can be useful for women with very heavy periods.

Intrauterine contraceptive device (IUCD Coil)

Effective? Over 98–99%, depending on the type of IUCD.
How does it work? A small plastic and copper device is put into the womb and this stops the egg from implanting.
Advantages? Works as soon as it is put in. Can stay in for three to ten years, depending on type. You don't have to think about contraception.
Disadvantages? It can be painful to put in. Periods can be heavier, longer and more painful. Unsuitable for women who already have heavy and painful periods. Not suitable for women who are at high risk of getting an STI.
Bottom line? If fitted after 40, it can stay in until after the menopause.

Natural family planning

Effective? Using several fertility indicators combined, such as a menstrual calendar and temperature and mucus observation, it can be 98% effective. Typical use is only 80%, though. Ovulation kits make it easier to predict fertile times.
How does it work? The fertile and infertile times of the menstrual cycle are identified by noting the different fertility indicators. This shows when you can have sex without risking pregnancy.
Advantages? No hormones, so no side-effects. Gives a woman greater awareness of her body. Often acceptable if religious beliefs rule out contraceptives.

Disadvantages? If you are using an ovulation kit, it's easy to know when to avoid sex. Without a kit, natural family planning methods need to be learned from a trained teacher – in Britain, the Family Planning Association can put you in touch with one.

Bottom line? Withdrawal is not recommended as a natural method. It is not at all reliable, partly because pre-ejaculation fluid contains sperm.

Female sterilisation

Effective? Over 99%.

How does it work? A permanent method in which the Fallopian tubes are cut or blocked so that eggs cannot travel down them to meet sperm.

Advantages? Permanent, though the operation can be reversed. You never have to think about contraception again.

Disadvantages? Permanent, though you may be fertile again if the Fallopian tubes rejoin. Contraception must be used up to the time you are sterilised and until you have had your first period afterwards.

Bottom line? If in doubt, don't choose this method. Get counselling before you make the decision. A few days rest after the operation are necessary.

Male sterilisation (vasectomy)

Effective? Over 99%.

How does it work? Permanent, but the operation can be reversed. The tubes which carry sperm are cut so that sperm is not present in the semen.

Advantages? Permanent. Minor operation takes 10–15 minutes and can be done at a doctor's surgery or clinic. You don't have to think about contraception.

Disadvantages? Permanent and difficult to have reversed. It usually takes a few months for all the sperm to disappear from the semen. Contraception must be used until there are two negative sperm tests. Very rarely, the tubes rejoin and the man is fertile again.

Bottom line? If in doubt, don't chose this method. Get counselling before you make the decision. Some discomfort is likely post op.

Contraception for the future

The male pill (about time too): So far, drugs to stop sperm production have all had a negative effect on libido. A combination of a pill, implant and an injection is now being researched to combat this problem.

EVRA transdermal patch: A contraceptive patch that is stuck to the skin and delivers a combination of oestrogen and progestogen. Already available in the US, it should be available in Europe very soon.

Vaginal Ring: A flexible monthly ring designed to fit near the cervix and deliver a combination of hormones. Should be available very soon.

Sterilisation is a big decision for some people, especially if they haven't had kids. It could be something that you live to regret in those circumstances. For us, it was much more simple because we had already got a boy and a girl, and my wife had been told that it was no longer safe for her to be taking the pill. We talked about it once or twice and then went to see the doctor. No regrets.
Michael, 57, Australia

Personally, I think my husband should have a vasectomy. We certainly don't want any more children, and sterilisation is a much bigger opera-tion for women than men. Besides, I've taken full responsi-bility for our contra-ception for the past 20 years. I think it's about time for his turn! I don't know why he avoids the subject – it's probably something daft about his masculinity.
Tessa, 38, UK

I have always known I don't want kids, and I first went to the doctor to enquire about sterilisation when I was 19. They said I was too young. They are still saying it and I am 36.
Helen, 36, UK

Sex to get pregnant

Spermmmm: In theory, you could create the present population of the earth with half an eggcup of sperm. This (admittedly useless) fact would seem to be at odds with the statistics presented in *The Penguin Atlas of Human Sexual Behaviour*, by Judith Mackay. According to her, 120 million acts of sexual intercourse take place every day, resulting in 910,000 conceptions and 400,000 live births. That's a lot of pleasure, but not much procreation. In fact, birth rates are falling globally. Contraception, economics and politics are partially responsible, but pregnancy has always been quite hit and miss. A young, fertile couple only has a one-in-four chance of becoming pregnant each cycle, and the older you get, the more difficult it becomes. The average age for a woman in the UK having her first baby is now 27 and rising. By the time a woman is 35, her chances of conceiving reduce to just ten per cent per cycle. Sperm counts are lower too. Environmental factors, overheating, alcohol, smoking, chemicals in the food we eat and stress all decrease sperm production or damage existing sperm. Foresight (The Association for the Promotion of Pre-conceptual Care), claims that correcting mineral deficiencies and an organic diet can improve fertility and libido by 86 per cent. It may just be that their no-caffeine, no-booze and no-cigarettes policy simply means that sex is the only indulgence left.

It's all in the timing: If you want to become pregnant, knowing when you are fertile will help you judge the optimum time for sex. Every woman is different, but the average menstrual cycle lasts about 28 days and ovulation (when the egg is released and ready to be fertilised) takes place roughly in the middle, around fourteen days before your next period. Regardless of whether you have regular or irregular periods, you can still learn to recognise the physical signs of ovulation. If you can predict when it will occur, you can identify the days leading up to ovulation, which is when you should have sex. Though a woman is fertile for several days before and 24 hours after the egg is released, sperm have a better chance of fertilising the egg if they are ejaculated deep inside the vagina, 24 hours before ovulation. This means they can lie in wait (for up to three days) in the Fallopian tubes and pounce on the egg once it shows up.

Hocus mucus: For most of the menstrual cycle, the vagina feels relatively dry and contains sticky or chalky mucus. When a woman is fertile, her cervical mucus becomes thinner, stringy and wet (a bit like egg white). Some women are very aware of this change (wet underwear), others have to explore deep inside with a finger. If you familiarise yourself with the consistency of your mucus, you can learn to identify the difference between fertile and non-fertile mucus. Try investigating it on the toilet when you get out of bed in the morning. Push your fingers as far up as possible into your vaginal opening and test the mucus by trying to stretch it between your fingers. If it is thick, you are not fertile. If it is thin and stretches between your fingers, hop back into bed and have sex. If you don't fancy checking your mucus, an ovulation testing kit, which detects changes in hormone levels in your urine, may be the simplest way of pinpointing ovulation. You can also chart changes in your temperature by using something called a Basal Body Temperature thermometer – your temperature rises by between 0.2 and 0.6°C when you ovulate, usually staying at the higher level until just before your next period. If you get pregnant, your temperature will remain elevated. Take your temperature as soon as you wake in the morning, before you do anything else or drink anything. Trials on a new ovulation wristwatch, the PSC Fertility Monitor, show that currently it predicts ovulation to within two days. It works by measuring the changes in the acidity of sweat. Soon, you could be able to set your ovulation alarm before you go to bed at night.

Not tonight love, I'm manufacturing 150 million sperm: Having sex to get pregnant is about working with your body's natural chemistry. Women tend to get turned on more easily during oestrogen peaks, and there is some evidence that orgasm helps things along because, during the contractions, the cervix dips down into the vagina ready to receive the sperm (provided a man has already ejaculated). It makes sense to allow time for your partner's sperm to replenish. If ejaculation takes place twice a day or more, it can take five to seven days days to restore normal sperm levels. Having sex every other day in the period up to and during ovulation may be more effective than having it several times a day for three days.

Fertilisation: Only about 0.1 per cent of the sperm ejaculated reaches an egg. If a sperm is succesful, the enzymes in its head eat away the egg's outer layer, allowing only one sperm to penetrate inside and fertilise it. Non-identical twins occur when two eggs are released simultaneously and are fertilised by two different sperm. If an egg is fertilised and splits into two identical embryos, identical twins are created. If the fertilised egg (or eggs) implant in the uterine wall and start to develop, then pregnancy has started. But this doesn't always happen. Plenty of pregnancies end before you even notice they have begun, and many pregnancies start out as twins but only one embryo survives. An unfertilised egg, or one that has failed to implant, is shed during the next menstrual period.

Without wanting to sound like a puritan, if I were trying to get pregnant I wouldn't want the kind of hard fucking we normally have. If I was trying to make a baby, I would want to be all romantic and make love, not do low-down dirty deeds.
Caroline, 33, Australia

It all comes down to your attitude about having a baby. I wouldn't say we wanted to have a baby at the time, but we knew we were taking a risk by using withdrawal, and we knew it would not be the end of the world if we did fall pregnant. Now we have Jack, we are very glad about our 'mistake'!
Lizzie, 36, UK

I was trying to get pregnant for months. I hadn't met the right person, but at 42 I knew I wanted a baby more than anything else in the world, and that I probably didn't have much time left. I had a couple of flings, and said I was on the pill, but it made me feel terrible, so I'm glad I didn't get pregnant (or an infection) that way. In the end it was with a dear friend, and we've ended up together anyway!
Tamara, 46, UK

When it doesn't work

Well, my partner is ten years younger than me and childless, so we have discussed her having a child one day – she will more than likely be the one bearing a child. We do worry about society and the assumption that two lesbian women will either raise a butch lesbian, or an effeminate male child – which is, of course, bullshit.
Kimberley, 36, US
Kuma2

IVF is a difficult process and sometimes a long one. A lot of the time you feel that the whole thing is completely out of your control. The only ammunition you have is your stamina. You have to decide whether you're going to let it destroy you emotionally. When you come out on the other side, you might not be pregnant, but you need to have your sanity and your relationships intact.
Emma, 35, UK

The problem with fertility is just not knowing. I was always very good with contraception, so I have never been pregnant, but what if I can't have a baby when I want to? That makes me quite anxious.
Molly, 38, US

When sex becomes stressful: The pressure of planning can take the 'sexy' out of sex for one or both partners. Performance anxiety can be particularly difficult if you feel under an obligation to be available when the time is right. The added pressure of each sexual act possibly being 'the one' can place considerable strain on a relationship. It may also affect the libido of both parties. Try to have sex at other times of the month, so that all your sexual enthusiasm doesn't get consumed by the need to become pregnant. If you are having trouble conceiving, it might be advisable to avoid using lubrication (even saliva) as it may be damaging the sperm. A better diet will improve your general health, and it is thought that exercise can also have a positive effect on libido. (Excessive exercise will turn you off, though.)

Pregnancy without sex: Some women choose to impregnate themselves without going through medical channels. This involves finding someone willing to donate their fresh sperm, identifying your most fertile time and then inserting the sperm into the vagina as near to the cervix as possible. (Make sure that the donor has been screened for STIs, including HIV, before you have any contact with his sperm.) A clean, needleless syringe or turkey baster is usually used to insert the semen. Insemination is easiest while the woman lies on her back with her bottom raised on a pillow. She should stay there for at least half-an-hour after insemination.

Donor insemination: This is a variation of self-insemination that is performed at a clinic using frozen donated sperm. A nurse usually places the sperm in the vagina, but in special circumstances home inseminations can sometimes be organised. Donor insemination can be a costly process.

Infertility options: If you have been trying to become pregnant for a year, your doctor is likely to refer you and your partner to a fertility clinic for testing. Depending on the results, a number of things can be done. A woman can take fertility drugs to boost the number of eggs she produces. If sperm are struggling to reach the eggs, the process can be assisted by inserting them directly into the uterus, by a process kown as intra-uterine insemination. Sometimes eggs are fertilised outside the body and then implanted. This process, known as in-vitro fertilisation (IVF) usually involves hormonal treatment that encourages several eggs to mature, and can result in two or more eggs implanting. IVF is also used when there is a high chance of passing a genetic disease to the fetus. Woman who cannot produce fertile eggs and men who have poor-quality sperm can opt to use donated sperm and eggs for any of the above procedures.

Sex during pregnancy

Oh my God – I'm pregnant: During the first three months of pregnancy, levels of oestrogen and progesterone soar and their chemical balance is critical to how well you feel. Oestrogen can cause a surge in sexual feeling, but too much of it can diminish your libido altogether.

Many men and women find that news of pregnancy makes them feel very virile and horny, but other couples worry that having sex may harm the baby or cause a miscarriage. In fact, the fetus is probably happier at this point than it will ever be again (spacious surroundings, intravenous food and drink, no nappies). The cervix (the entrance to the uterus) is positioned above the space that is filled during penetrative sex, and it only has a very small opening. This is sealed off by a mucus plug until shortly before labour begins, so there is no way a penis can poke through it.

Oh my God – I'm fat: During the second trimester, your hormone levels are high but stable. You are less likely to feel ill and your energy returns. Oestrogen increases vaginal lubrication and can also heighten your libido. How you feel will depend a lot on how you experience your changing body. During the third trimester, as your baby becomes a more tangible presence, penetration may feel more threatening. In fact, orgasm and penetration are perfectly safe at this point. In four years time, your kid will squeal and kick in a urine-filled public swimming pool. Right now it kicks and wriggles when your orgasm causes uterine contractions that swish your amniotic fluid.

Oh my God – call an ambulance: In the last couple of months, you may feel enormous, clumsy and exhausted. Some women are still very interested in sex – others are not. At this point you should switch to positions that don't put pressure on your bump. This is when sex books tell women that they are supposed to get on top, but, frankly, size, weight and the fact that penetration is deeper, make it an unattractive option for many people. Spoons is probably the most sensitive and intimate position at this stage. It makes you feel like less of a whale and your partner can embrace your bump lovingly. If you are ready to drop, sex doggy-style (with orgasm) is supposedly the best position to trigger labour. Though leaning down and forward so that your bottom is sticking up in the air isn't the most elegant position for a heavily pregnant woman, it shortens the vaginal barrel and makes penetration deeper. Nipple sucking is good, too. It stimulates the release of prolactin, which can also trigger labour. If all else fails, an orgasm, a hot curry and a tablespoon of castor oil are also worth trying.

When my girlfriend told me she was pregnant, I just felt like the most virile sex machine in the world. I just wanted to impregnate everyone. Obviously I didn't, but I was very randy for that period.
Nathan, 30, US

I was having a very sexy affair when I got pregnant. We had bucketloads of sex all the way through, too. When the midwife asked me if there was any reason for me choosing to have the baby on my knees, I said: Well that's the way it went in, it might as well be the way it comes out!
Janet, 36, UK

I was quite keen on gentle sex as a form of relaxation, except for in the last month or so. By then I just felt ugly, fat and tired. That's when you really need a kind lover to understand, reassure you and not hassle you for sex.
Laura, 60, Australia

Creation is incredibly empowering. Knowing that my sperm wasn't going to end up in the end of a condom but instead was going to shoot forth and multiply – well, that's a fantastically sexy thing!
Paul, 40, UK

Sex after pregnancy?

No thanks: You've had stitches, tears, bruising, haemorrhoids and a Caesarean section. You are still bleeding, your breasts are like inflated balloons and your stomach resembles a deflated balloon. No wonder only one woman in three has intercourse six weeks after the birth. Although the physical wounds will have healed in that time, you may still be feeling tender, sore and vulnerable.

Baby blues: As levels of your pregnancy hormones zoom back down to normal, the sudden change can have a marked effect on how you feel. Most women feel weepy or even depressed (baby blues) for a few days after the birth, but this soon passes. Occasionally women experience severe post-natal depression. This is much more serious and can make simple tasks such as getting out of bed or dressing your baby seem impossible. If your feelings of depression are serious and persist, contact your doctor.

Loved-up: After the birth, your body begins to produce the hormone prolactin to enable milk production. This can also affect your mood, making you more introspective and placid. It may even switch off your sex drive for a bit, but the hormone levels usually normalise themselves in a few weeks, even if you are still breastfeeding. Sucking also leads to the release of oxytocin, the so-called 'love hormone'. This seems to help bonding with your baby and is also the hormone released during orgasm.

Worn out: When the bleeding stops, your cervix has closed and your womb is back to normal. It is safe to have penetrative sex, but you may not feel like it. Broken nights and complete exhaustion may mean that neither of you feel up to anything more strenuous than cuddling up before you drop off.

Sex: The majority of couples are having (irregular) sex again by about three months after the baby is born. Lack of time and opportunity means that, for a while, sex might not be the spontaneous experience it once was, but pride, a sense of achievement and increased intimacy can give it a new depth and meaning. Many women find that they are less inhibited and more ready to initiate and enjoy sex. Your body will be different. Your genital area will have grown new blood vessels to accommodate increased blood flow during pregnancy, and many women find that once hormone levels return to normal, orgasm is deeper and stronger. Some find that their vagina is far more sensitive than it was before, though it may also be more relaxed. Muscles can be firmed up with regular Kegel exercises.

56

Sexercise

Breastfeeding

194

Contraception

212

Sex Toys

I love my wife dearly but she has breasts like bee-stings, but when she was pregnant they were swollen and beautiful. I loved everything about them. I was once lucky enough to watch the milk shoot out when she climaxed. Sometimes she used to let me breastfeed like a baby.
Brian, 49, UK

My nipples were actually very painful throughout nursing, and the last thing I wanted was to have someone messing about with them. At that stage, they were there to feed the baby, not for him.
Heather, 50, US

Lactation is pretty sexy – kind of pervy letting an adult male drink from the breasts. But then pervy stuff is usually nice – isn't it?
Dellen, 42, UK

Contraception: Full-time breastfeeding makes pregnancy less likely in the first few months, but most women are advised to go on the pill after having a baby as it is not a guaranteed form of contraception and the last thing most women want to do is get pregnant again. Occasionally, breast-feeding babies react to the pill and break out in a rash. Switch to condoms or a cap if this happens, until your baby moves on to bottles.

Getting back to normal: Stimulation of the nipples during the first two weeks after childbirth triggers uterine contractions. This helps the uterus return to its normal pre-birth size, but can be quite uncomfortable. Initially, stimulation of the breasts and nipples is more likely to be a way of getting back in touch with each other rather than a precursor to sex, because broken sleep and hormone shifts will mean that libido is probably lower.

Preventing sore nipples and mastitis: If you plan to breastfeed, prepare your nipples before the birth by rubbing them with witch-hazel. Breastfeeding can make nipples quite sore and chapped. Expose them to the air as much as you can and rub them with a little of your own breast-milk or camomile ointment to soothe them. In the early weeks after birth, massage can help prevent mastitis (inflammation of milk ducts). Massage gently, stroking down from the collar-bone towards the nipples or in from under the armpits towards the nipples. Always stimulate towards the nipples to encourage the milk flow; never massage away from the nipples.

Wow!: It can be difficult to make the leap from nursing a baby to sexual play. The breasts take on a new and non-sexual role, and it can be confusing for both partners to then see them and the milk they produce, in a sexual way. Some women and their partners find that lactation adds a new and amazing dimension to sex. Suddenly being able to masturbate a penis between your enlarged breasts can be a novelty for the smaller-chested woman. Sexual arousal can cause the breasts to leak a little milk, which can be a bit messy and sticky, but can also be incredibly sexy. Use towels if you are worried about the sheets and either express or feed your baby prior to sex if you are concerned about leaking too much.

Sex toys: Orgasm will normally cause a little spurt of milk that can be visually very exciting for both of you. The sensation of feeding a baby can feel quite sexual, and many women report that their nipples remain permanently more sensitive after the experience.

Sex with kids around

No time: Sometimes sexual desire disappears with the arrival of a new baby, and it may be that neither of you miss it. When you're too tired and caught up in the chaos, there never seems to be a 'right time'. Older children often play up, making life even more difficult. New babies end up sleeping in your bed with you, so unless you grab some time while they nap, the opportunity for sex just doesn't present itself.

No desire: If you are breastfeeding, your oestrogen levels may be low and this can decrease your libido. They will gradually return to normal, but many mums are given contraceptive pills when they leave hospital and these can also affect hormone levels. If you are breastfeeding then you can't share the responsibility of feeding with your partner, so the physical demands on you are even greater. And after a baby, you may be heavier than you were before the birth for a while and feel insecure about your body, which can affect your interest in sex. Some men who watch their partners give birth find the experience life-affirming; others feel quite distressed and find it affects their ability see their partner as a sexual person. This is usually, but not always, just a passing phase.

The green-eyed, evil monster: As a new mother you will receive a lot of attention from your family and friends, and sometimes it's easy to forget that without your partner, none of this would have happened in the first place. Men often report feeling jealous of the new baby (who seems to be getting all their partner's attention) and it is difficult to make love to someone if you feel vulnerable or undervalued. Division of labour, especially if you have older children, may mean that you spend less time together and if you don't keep an eye on things, your relationship can start to suffer.

What about us: With kids around, sex is never going to be as spontaneous as when you were single, and keeping your sex life going requires commitment from both of you. Once the baby can be fed by someone else, take any offers of help and spend time alone together. You may just go out to dinner and talk about the children all night, but such times form the cement that will keep your relationship together. Sex is therapeutic in more ways than one. Intimacy will remind you that your relationship with each other is the primary one in the family (regardless of what the kids think). It can also relieve the day-to-day tension that builds up in any domestic environment, while orgasm releases the 'feel-good' hormones like serotonin and endorphins that make you feel great and guarantee a peaceful sleep – at least until the baby wakes up. Just don't forget to use contraception.

The only form of foreplay after the birth of our baby would be whispering in her ear, 'are you awake?'
Happy dad & miserable husband, 33, UK

At that stage, the sex we had was infrequent and more close than raunchy. It was about a year before we got back to anything like anal.
Jack, 38, Australia

My husband seemed to go right off sex when we had our second child, and at the time I didn't really mind because I was so exhausted. But I remember thinking it was strange, because with the first child he was demanding. It wasn't until about two years later, when I found out that that was when he started his affair, that I realised why. Bastard.
Lillian, 53, UK

Desire is not our problem – privacy is! Our three-year-old still can't sleep unless she's in our bed.
Andrew, 48, UK

194

Contraception

Depression and sex

It's not just you: One in five people suffers from depression at some point in his or her life. People over 65 seem to have a slightly greater risk of depression, and this risk becomes much higher in people over 85. Relationship problems can stem from depression, though they can also cause it, too. Some people have an inherited tendency to depression, but others find that stressful situations, conflict with a partner, the menstrual cycle, the menopause or simply the ups and downs of daily life can bring on either mild or clinical depression. The symptoms can include emotional withdrawal, sadness, anger, tiredness, lethargy and an inability to concentrate or relax. One of the most common symptoms of depression is waking up two to three hours too early or waking up after just half-an-hour of sleep and spending the rest of the night worrying about trivia.

Heeelllp!: Depressed people often lose interest in sex. Tiredness can mean that you don't fancy sex at night and men can experience problems in achieving and maintaining erection. Diminished brain activity can make it difficult to reach orgasm, too, so sex hardly seems worth the effort. Not wanting sex when your partner does can cause friction. For depressed people in a relationship, this can add strain to an already tense situation. Unless both partners are able to discuss what is going on with a view to resolving the underlying problems, the situation will only get worse.

Help: More than eight in ten people with depression can be treated if they consult a doctor, but as many as three out of four cases of depression are never recognised or treated. It has been shown that cognitive behaviour therapy can be as effective as antidepressants for mild depression. Depression lowers libido, but unfortunately many antidepressants – particularly SSRIs – seem to worsen the problem. For both men and women, the most common side-effects of antidepressants are delayed orgasm or inability to orgasm. Your doctor may try to change your medication if it is interfering with your sex life, though this may not be possible if you are being treated for a specific disorder. Buproprion and nefazadone are two antidepressants that don't seem to have sexual side-effects. As the dose increases, so do many sexual problems. Some antidepressants can cause problems with erection, but doctors advise that if you suffer from severe depression and your medication seems to be working in all other ways it is more important to stay on the antidepressants and take something such as sildenafil to counter the problem. As you get better and your medication decreases, symptoms and side-effects will diminish and a renewed interest in sex is often the first sign that recovery is around the corner.

Letting it go

It's all downhill from here: When you first meet a partner, sex is (usually) electric, fantastic and addictive. You can't ever imagine a time when you will get enough of each other. However, anyone entering into a long-term commitment would do well to take off the rose-tinted spectacles. Life has it's ups and downs, and the sex you have reflects this. Stress, exhaustion, children, illness, conflict, boredom and problems at work or at home can all affect libido and intimacy.

Complacency: Routine can be reassuring but it is also a passion-killer. As your home life falls into a natural but predictable pattern, sometimes sex follows suit. A Friday-night shag on the sofa with one eye on the TV and one hand on the remote control may be comfy, but it's a far cry from the champagne-fuelled love trysts that launched your love affair. It's easy to lose interest in the 'too tired, too busy or not in the mood' domestic scenario, particularly if you feel your partner is not that bothered either. Sometimes couples lose interest in sex so gradually that they simply put it down to age or overexposure. Women, in particular, can suffer from something that sexual therapists call 'responsive desire'. What this means is that even though a woman is in a meaningful emotional relation-ship, she doesn't actually become mentally aroused, or think that she wants to have sex, until her genitals are fully stimulated. One of the difficulties with responsive desire is that it means that one partner is consistently required to initiate sexual activity, and this can eventually cause resentment. If a couple are unable to discuss their sexual feelings openly, this can become a problem. Addressing sexual issues honestly (for example, saying you are fed up about always being the one to initiate sex) may be the first step towards a closer relationship, and the simpler it becomes to discuss your sexual needs, the more likely it is that they will be met. Of course this is easier said than done. Talking is often much harder than having sex, but naming a problem is the first step to solving it – and couples who have good oral communication generally find that they have better genital communication too.

But we don't want sex: Two people who have a sex-free relationship don't have a problem if they are both honestly happy with it. Some couples find that both of them pretend to want sex, when neither of them really does. Problems only arise if you want sex and your partner doesn't or, vice versa. This imbalance increases the odds that eventually just about anyone of the opposite sex who expresses a sexual interest in you will seem more sexually interesting and exciting than the person with whom you're in a relationship.

Getting it back

It's good to talk: Sex is often a fairly accurate barometer of a relationship. The dynamic of a sexual relationship is determined by the level of emotional closeness, and several major surveys have indicated that an inability to resolve interpersonal conflict is intricately connected to inhibited sexual desire. Basically, in a long-term relationship you can only continue to have sex with a partner that you love. But, arguably, you can only love a partner with whom you want to have sex, because love without sex is just friendship. If sex has become difficult or non-existent, it is usually because there are other underlying issues. Problems rarely go away if they are ignored, and despite the fact that you may presume to know your partner's needs, no one is telepathic. Research shows that men and women exhibit very different characteristics in relationship conflicts. The term 'demand-withdrawal' describes the common pattern of females needing debate and males being reluctant to engage in it. If communication becomes very difficult, writing may be a much more effective means of raising awkward subjects. It is less confrontational and allows you both to be very clear about what you want to say. Email is more immediate, but never press the send button straight away. Waiting an hour will give you time to delete anything that may do more harm than good. If your objective is to restore harmony and intimacy, attacking or blaming your partner is the last thing you should do. Relationship counselling can seem like a giant step, but a neutral environment in which an independent person acts as a filter can help you both to listen to each other in a way that is not often possible at home. The commitment required to meet at sessions and talk openly can be a positive experience, and if you end up going for a coffee together afterwards, you may find that the openness carries on afterwards – into both your conversations and your sex life.

Sexual wish-lists: If you are both committed to making your relationship work, your investment will eventually pay dividends, and the first returns usually appear in the bedroom. Once underlying tensions have been eliminated, you should try to keep sex exciting. You may want to try doing a sex therapy course such as sensate focusing or Tantric sex to get back in touch with each other physically and spiritually. Alternatively, add a little honeymoon sparkle by drawing up a sexual wish-list in which every month one of you becomes responsible for making the other's sexual fantasy come true. Sex in the back of a limo, a romantic picnic, sex underwater, a little light flagellation, oral sex in Paris, role-play, a full-body massage, a sexy bedtime story with a new sex toy – the list is as big as your imagination. Check Sex Toys and the A–Z of Everything Else for inspiration.

My husband and I have been through it all. Affairs, depression, violence – you name it. But somehow we came through all the pain and realised that what we have together is worth more than what we get when we're apart. I know it doesn't work that way for everyone, but we put a lot of effort into saving it. Three years of therapy and counselling and three years living apart made us grow up and see that nothing is easy. You can change the players, but unless you change yourself you just end up in the same situation with a new partner.
Anon, 31, US

Sex is like healthy eating or exercise – the more you do it, the more you want to do it. Sometimes you just have to make the effort to kick-start yourself.
Matt, 49, UK

We found that the quickest way to stop it getting boring was to try something new, like porn or anal. My worry is that we get a little bit more extreme every time.
Katherine, 31, Australia

Sex toys

There's no doubt that the use of sex toys expands the range of sexual possibilities available to both men and women, and shopping for them is easier than it has ever been. There are now a large number of specialist and more upmarket sex shops, which cater exclusively for women or men only. They stock an impressive array of ingenious devices and the staff are usually both helpful and knowledgeable. It's helpful to see the products, but if you are too shy to venture into a sex shop you can buy by mail-order from catalogues or over the Internet. Most online sex shops offer their own best brand or model recommendations as well as customer reviews. Online orders are usually delivered wrapped in brown paper, so you don't have to worry if the postman has to leave your package with the neighbours.

Vibrators

Cylindrical: Some are traditionally designed to look like a giant penis; others have a smooth, tubular shape. They come in a range of materials from shiny metal to bright, fluorescent jelly. The softer the outer material, the quieter the sound.

Dual vibrators: These are designed for simultaneous vaginal penetration and clitoral stimulation. They incorporate a shaft with a second prong that serves as a clit tickler. The original Japanese Rabbit version has been universally copied, particularly since it made a guest appearance on the popular TV show *Sex and the City*. It looks more like a fluorescent, pink sweetie-dispenser than a sex toy, but it is the world's best-selling vibrator. The vibrator consists of a shaft that has a rotating mid-section (filled with tumbling coloured balls), to stimulate the sensitive first third of the vagina, and a couple of rabbit ears that flutter against the clitoris. A dual control allows you to adjust the strength of the vibration in the shaft and the ears independently.

Strap-on pouch vibrators: These are held on with a harness to leave your hands free. They have a small, spiky, bumpy surface that straps snugly over the vulva and vibrates. People who don't want to or cannot hold a vibrator find them useful. There are varying speeds and intensities, and vibrations are transmitted over the whole genital area, though the sensation may be better if the vibrator is pressed firmly in place. Some models can be used during penetrative sex; others have a dildo for simultaneous vaginal penetration.

G-spot vibrators: These look a lot like other vibrators but come in a slim banana shape. The curve is designed to stimulate the mysterious G-spot, which may be located internally against the front wall of the vagina. Men may also enjoy having this vibrator rubbed against the prostate.

Massagers: Commonly referred to as 'personal massagers', these vibrators are used for external massage and stimulation. Good ones usually allow the user to adjust the speed. They are useful for people who enjoy general all-over stimulation, because the padded head diffuses the vibrations and spreads them over the whole area to which the vibrator is applied. Some of them are in fact designed to relax muscles by delivering heat to the tissues, so be careful if you are using them near your genitals. 'Swedish massagers' are strapped to the back of your hand, so you can use your hand to make yourself come without having to do any work!

Finger vibrators: These slip easily over a finger like a finger puppet or a ring. They give focused vibrations that can be targeted by your finger. Finger sleeves are shaped and contoured but don't vibrate.

Dildos: Dildos are motorless sex toys designed mainly for penetration. Like vibrators, the variations are infinite – every shape and size, colour and texture. Some have semi-realistic veining; others are designed as miniature statues. Some designs include a clitoral teaser or anal tickler. Importantly, most models have a wide base that prevents the dildo dissapearing up the anus, and some even have a suction cup, so that they can be stuck to a wall or the floor. Dildos can be used for penetration by hand or can be strapped on to someone's body (either with a harness or elastic straps) for hands-free penetration. This type is, rather predictably, referred to as a 'strap-on'.

Strap-on dildos: Dildo harnesses are usually made out of leather, elastic or PVC and fit around the hips and hold the dildo in place against the pubic bone. Other versions attach to different parts of the body – so you can strap a dildo over your mouth, chin or thigh. Hmm. Strap-ons allow women to thrust into anyone, and are good for men who cannot achieve an erection, but want to thrust. People with larger bodies should go for a longer dildo, because the extra length will be required to allow for a full range of penetrative positions.

Vibrating strap-ons: These are popular because most vibrators stimulate from the base, so the person wearing the harness feels the vibrations as well as the person being penetrated.

Double dildos: These are about twice the length of a normal dildo, and are double-headed, which means that two people can use them simultaneously. Co-ordination can be quite complicated, and one or both of you will need to hold the dildo in the middle to move it in and out of whichever orifice. An alternative is a 'coupler' – a perforated neoprene pad that attaches two separate dildos together to make a double dildo.

Complete with balls: Some dildos have fake testicles at their base. The testicles can stimulate the entrance to the vagina or anus and can be particularly good for anal penetration, because they ensure that the toy does not slide up the anal passage and disappear.

When women shop for dildos, they usually buy one that's too small for them, because the big ones look scary. Look for a dildo that is slightly larger than what you think you need. Think of the vagina as a muscle just like any other muscle in your body – you provide it with resistance to make it stronger.
Ruby, 26, US
Moonlite Bunny Ranch

Sometimes I have a problem. When I want to be penetrated by a hand or a dildo I'm not big enough to be as deeply penetrated as I would like. This happens under certain circumstances – during my period or at stressful times. If I really want to persevere I will, and I'll get the lube flowing. Otherwise, I don't have any qualms about telling my partner to give up . . . if it's not going to go in, it's not going to go in!
Abbie, 27, UK
Rainbow Network

Silicone may cost more, but it feels better and you know you're getting quality.
Ken, 40, US

Other delights in the toy box

Cock rings: These are rings, usually made of rubber, metal or leather, that fit around the base of the penis, or, more commonly, the base of the penis and the balls. They squeeze the veins that carry blood out of the penis, and can increase both size and hardness. Some people claim that they also delay orgasm. Solid rings need very careful sizing, so it's best to start off with adjustable ones. Remove immediately if there is any swelling or pain in the genitals, because this means that you are cutting off the circulation of blood to your penis. Don't be tempted to use rubber bands, don't leave a cock ring on for more than 30 minutes, and make sure you take it off before you fall asleep.

Butt plugs: A butt plug is a shorter, stubbier version of a dildo. It's advantage is that it has a base that narrows and then flares, to hold the plug in position and stop it from dropping out or vanishing up the anal passage. As a man moves around, the butt plug will stimulate his prostate gland, and women report favourable results, too. Simply apply plenty of your favourite lubricant as you insert the plug. You might need to apply more when you remove it. Butt plugs are made from plastic, silicone, firm-but-squishy jelly, latex or cyber-skin and come in many different sizes and shapes. If you are new to anal play, you might want to try a fairly slender and smooth plug to start off with, and build up to a larger model. Vibrating butt plugs are also available, and these both stimulate you and give a feeling of fullness.

Vibrating eggs or grapes: These are hard plastic balls powered by a hand-held battery pack. The sensation they create is subtle – it's comparable to having a fly trapped inside a golf ball inside your vagina or anus.

French ticklers: These fit over the tip of a penis, dildo or vibrator – or occassionally over two or three fingers pressed together – and look a lot like a limp jellyfish. French ticklers are designed to stimulate the entrance of a woman's vagina. However, most women who have used them in their sex play report disappointing results.

Nipple clamps: These look like small bulldog clips with weights hanging off them. They can be used to pinch the nipples continuously, leaving the hands free for other activities. Vibrating nipple clamps look like two small buttons, with one being attached to each nipple. The wire that trails from them transmits the vibrations from a hand-held battery-pack.

Tongue toys: Recently a number of toys have been released that seek to simulate the movement of a licking tongue. They look like a long, flattish vibrator with a pointy end, and they wag up and down – rather noisily. Some are designed specifically for the anus or vagina, but most can be used on either. Plenty of lubrication is vital.

Anal beads: These are made of plastic, silicone, jelly or rubber and are held together by a cord or a nylon string and look like a larger plastic necklace. They come in sizes varying from that of a boiled sweet to a golf ball. If you're a beginner, it's probably better to start small.

Whips, chains, masks, cuffs and so on: A wide variety of bondage and 'torture' toys is available from regular sex shops, specialist SM shops, magazines and specialist websites.

Materials

Silicone: Non-porous, naturally smooth and very resilient, but more expensive. Warms to body temperature and conducts vibrations effectively. Can be put in the top rack of the dishwasher or boiled for three to five minutes to sterilise. Don't use silicone-based lubricant with silicone toys as this erodes the material.

Latex: Feels solid but becomes softer and more flexible as it warms up. Generally cheaper, but tends to break down after extended use. Latex and vinyl products are non-porous and should be washed with mild soap and hot water. Oil destroys latex, so don't use oil-based lubricants or massage oils.

Cyberskin/thermal plastic: A mixture of silicone and PVC. Its texture is popular, but the material should be kept powdered, otherwise it becomes sticky. Difficult to keep clean and can be quite high maintenance.

Jelly rubber: Not rubber at all, in fact, but PVC. Soft, cushioning and very comfortable. Can be a little floppy if there isn't a strong inner core, but the soft outer material makes less noise. People with sensitive skin should avoid jelly rubber as it can cause vaginal or vulval tissue reactions. Jelly toys can be cleaned with mild soap and hot water.

Things your mother should have told you

- Any toy for anal insertion should have a flared base to prevent it from being pulled up into the rectum by the sphincter muscles.

- Toys made from porous materials can easily crack and harbour germs, so keep them clean and put fresh condoms over shared sex toys. Otherwise there is a possibility that bacterial infections could be transmitted.

- If your vibrator has a cord running to a battery pack, don't pull this to remove the vibrator from your vagina or anus. Don't fall asleep with your vibrator on. Don't get water inside your sex toy. Make sure you unplug any electric toys before washing them. Don't boil vibrators or dildos that have plastic parts. Remove batteries after use and store them separately.

Our picks for vaginal penetration are the Rabbit Habit and the Nubby G. Each of these vibrators is designed to be used vaginally, and both also offer some clitoral stimulation as well. Most women do not climax from penetration alone, but will get off if penetration is paired with vibration or rubbing on the clitoris.
Claire Cavanah, US
*Co-founder,
Toys in Babeland*

I don't go with all that bullshit about penetration being male. We fool around with a harness all the time, and believe me we're both all woman.
Jackie, 46, US

Vibrators with a larger head, like the Hitachi Magic Wand, don't work for me because I have genital piercings. I also need vibrations to be focused from a small point onto my clitoral hood. I use a Pocket Rocket or the Wahl, which is a very strong but extremely quiet vibrator. It's my favourite.
Violet, 26, US
Sex worker

Fantasy and infidelity

Fidelity: The word is derived from the Latin words *fides,* meaning 'faith', and *fidere*, meaning 'to trust'. Relationships involve a lot of *fides* and a lot of *fidere*, but occasionally one or other partner strays and ends up in the dog house with Fido ('faithful dog'). Most couples would acknowledge that there is a difference between a one-night stand and longer-term infidelity. Both are damaging to the primary relationship (for both parties), but a one-night stand may well be a stupid mistake, whereas long-term infidelity involves committment and constant lying.

Fantasy: Sometimes infidelity is mental not physical. Fantasy is often encouraged by sex therapists who want to help their clients achieve arousal, and many therapists encourage their patients to visualise images from porn films or magazines in an effort to help them achieve orgasm. Private sexual fantasy is generally considered acceptable, because there is no physical contact with a third party. And there's no doubt that while many people are having intercourse with their primary partner, they are doing it with someone else in their head. However, several studies suggest that in a long-term relationship, exposure to pornography can decrease the 'perceived desirability of an available sexual partner'. In 1989, US researchers Kenrick, Gutierres and Goldberg carried out an experiment in which they asked men and women to look at nude pictures from *Playboy* and *Penthouse* and then rate the attractiveness of their marital or co-habiting partner. A second group were asked to view artworks and then rate the attractiveness of their partners. The men who had been exposed to the nude centrefolds rated their partners as significantly less attractive than the men who had been viewing art, whereas the women's ratings of their partners were not adversely affected by the stimuli at all. Presuming that the first group of men weren't married to dogs and the second group of men weren't looking at royal watercolours, the experiment suggests that exposure to erotic or pornographic media that focus on unusually attractive people can create unrealistic expectations about what an average person looks like in the nude. This, in turn, might decrease sexual desire for real-life partners, who, let's face it, are never cut from the same cloth as a Playboy bunny.

The Coolidge effect: Whether porn highlights physical inadequacies or not, there is no doubt that fantasy makes you want to have sex – even if you have to do it with your eyes closed. Sustaining long-term sexual interest in anyone is difficult, and women and men are equally susceptible to the hazards of boredom. It is often suggested that this is why prostitution still thrives as an industry. Many men who use prostitutes say that they are not paying women for sex, but paying them to go away afterwards so that they can have someone new next time. The male requirement for sexual variety was named 'the Coolidge effect', after the former United States President, Calvin Coolidge, in 1976. The story goes that one day President and Mrs Coolidge were visiting a government farm. Soon after their arrival, they were taken off on separate tours. When Mrs Coolidge passed the chicken pens she paused to ask the man in charge if the rooster copulated more than once each day. 'Dozens of times', was the reply. 'Please tell that to the President', Mrs Coolidge requested. When the President passed the same pens and was told about the rooster, he asked, 'Same hen every time?' 'Oh no, Mr President, a different one each time.' The President nodded slowly, then said, 'Tell that to Mrs. Coolidge.'

Infidelity: Affairs are the most frequent and often the most damaging violations of trust between married or co-habiting couples. However, despite the fact that infidelity is so common, we are even less tolerant of it than we were ten years ago. The UK National Survey of Sexual Attitudes and Lifestyles 2000 found that an even greater number of men and women – 92 per cent – believed that infidelity is sometimes or always wrong than in their 1990 survey.

The fallout: The 'coital rate' drops by 50 per cent within the first year of marriage and continues to slide. On average, married people between the ages of 35 and 55 have sex less than seven times a month, and after 65, you are lucky if you have sex at all. These figures don't make infidelity excusable, but they may make it easier to understand why it happens so frequently. Even assuming that you don't get caught (and hurt your family) the pressure of sustaining two relationships and keeping one secret becomes an enormous strain eventually. Covering your tracks, keeping two partners happy and accounting for your time can be a full-time job in itself. Guilt, lying, stress and anxiety can cause behavioural changes that eventually bring on depression – and both your partners may disappear before this debilitating illness does. Sex with someone new may massage the ego and reassure you that you are still sexually attractive (even if you take up more of the sofa than you used to). But when the gut-wrenching, appetite-suppressing, mind-boggling blast of primary passion has worn off (as it invariably will), you will find that greener grass needs watering too. If you decide to make a go of it with your new partner, be aware that, statistically, this relationship is twice as likely to break down as your first one.

Coming out as an adult

Realising: Most people identify their sexual identity when they are in their teens, though it may take longer for someone who is gay, lesbian or bisexual (GLB) to openly acknowledge their sexuality. Environmental, religious and cultural restrictions, together with conditioning, prejudice, homophobia and fear, can all make coming out extremely difficult. Some people simply cannot accept the fact that their orientation marks them as different, so they suppress their sexuality completely.

The closet: Occasionally people who are aware that they are not heterosexual drift through life in denial and end up having long-term heterosexual relationships, marrying and having children. The fear of losing their home, family and friends then makes the prospect of coming out even more daunting. Occasionally, someone who has successfully managed to ignore their GLB tendencies through their marriage finds that they cannot keep their true feelings under control any longer and has to act on them. Some stay in their marriages and have GLB relationships on the side, but this means that they never have a fully committed GLB relationship. Infidelity is risky at any time, but when you are cheating with a partner of the same sex, getting caught may be even more damaging, especially if you don't actually want to come out.

Telling your partner: Ending any relationship is tough. Ending a relationship because your sexual identity has changed is tougher. Your partner may have already suspected the truth, but in many cases the revelation comes as a complete shock. There's no doubt that your partner will feel upset, angry, hurt and confused, and will certainly question whether your history together has been a lie. 'Did you ever love me?'; 'How long have you felt this way?' Your revelation may well be the end of the relationship, so make sure you have really taken the full consequences of this on board beforehand. But sometimes partners find that learning the truth makes them feel better about themselves. They may have felt responsible for your unfulfilling sex life. They may also feel less threatened by same-sex infidelity because they have not been traded in for a younger, slimmer, better-looking model of themselves, and because the situation is clearly beyond their control.

Telling the kids: Young children are not born with a preconceived notion of what is normal, but they learn what is 'right' and socially acceptable by witnessing the world around them. If you have raised your children to understand that GLB people are no different to anyone else, they will be better equipped to take what you are saying on board. Their age will be an important factor. If they are very young, they probably won't understand what you are saying. Children between the ages of five and ten will have limited understanding of the situation. The danger in coming out to children in this age bracket is that they will happily relay the information to anyone, and at school this can put them in a situation in which they are teased in the playground. Teenagers are likely to have a number of, often negative, preconceptions about homosexuality, so there may be a hostile reaction initially. You are asking your children to take in a lot of information. Their parents are separating and one of their parents is GLB. They will be concerned about how their relationship with you will change, and also how their peer group will respond to the idea of them having a GLB mum or dad. You will need to reassure them that your love and relationship will not change, although they may not immediately accept this.

How to do it: Use advice lines and support groups. If possible, talk to other parents who have been through the experience. It helps to know what reactions to expect in both the short and the long term. Tell your children in private when there will be no distractions or interruptions. Try to sound as if you are 'telling' them something rather than 'confessing' to something. And tell your children yourself before somebody else does.

Telling people at work: In an ideal world being 'out' at work should not affect your future career, but some organisations respond negatively and your job security and promotion prospects could be affected. Discrimination often takes a subtle form, and there are many anecdotal accounts of gay men and lesbians being passed over for promotion in favour of their heterosexual colleagues. In recent years, changes to employment rights for lesbians and gays mean that being openly gay should not contravene any rules of employment, but homophobia is still regularly encountered in some professions.

Post coming out: Coming out later in life is complicated by the fact that you will probably have a much more established social group. Your friends will have to adjust to what they may see as a radical change, particularly if you are in a heterosexual relationship, married or have children. Once you have told the important people in your life, the reactions of others will not necessarily be as important to you. Similarly, you will become more adept at revealing your sexuality, by alluding to bars you frequent, for example, by using certain dress codes or by casually referring to your partner's gender.

Mine have been brought up knowing that both their parents are gay and were introduced at a young age (fiveish) to the ideas that it's OK for girls to kiss girls, for boys to kiss boys and that love is just love. Also, we made sure that they know that some people don't think it's OK for girls to kiss girls. I try to remember things they say about sex that make me squirm and think, 'Oh no', and bring up a conversation about whatever it is. The idea is that I don't want them to grow up thinking there are things that they can't say at home. Also, I tell them that their bodies are their own and it's up to them who touches them.
Mother, 34, UK
Rainbow Network

I always knew I was different in a way, but I only acted on it when I turned 35. I was in a heterosexual marriage and met someone that I was very much attracted to, and one thing led to another.
Shakira, 45, US
Kuma2

People should love you for who you are, not for who you have sex with.
Tom, 20, Australia

Coming out as transexual\transgender

What does it all mean?: Being transexual or transgender is about gender identity rather than sexual orientation. The term 'transexual' refers to someone who dresses, acts and looks like the opposite sex. 'Transgender' refers to someone who has started the process of a sex change by taking hormone tablets or having breast implants. Someone who is transgender may or may not want to go on to have genital surgery.

People who change gender to become women identify themselves as completely female. This means that they view their sexual relationships with men as heterosexual. It is difficult enough to put this into words, and accepting the concept can be even more difficult.

Thinking about coming out: Before you come out, make sure that you are well-informed about what it means to be trans. Joining a support group for trans people can help. You will be able to obtain advice about many matters, including details of medical interventions such as hormone therapy and gender reassignment surgery. You will also receive help with the practicalities. Transgendered people have to go through the process of changing their public personas legally as well as physically and emotionally. Documents such as driving licences and passports will all need to be re-issued. Most trans help groups also run conferences and workshops at which family members, partners and friends are welcome. There are also local support groups, and the Internet is an excellent source of information.

Telling parents: Some experts warn that if you are going to take the medical route to gender reassignment, it is unwise to tell your parents until you have reached the point at which hormone therapy has already been started. Many parents try to intervene, which can be very distressing, so it is much easier for all concerned if it is a *fait accompli*. Stress to your parents that you are not going to be a different person – you are simply going to be more yourself.

The general view is that families need three years to get completely used to the idea. Ultimately, most parents want happiness for their children. If you can convince them that you have done something positive, they may begin to come around to the idea. Some trans people find that changing their name completely can help family, friends and colleagues to adjust much more quickly, because it is an obvious way of asking them to recognise your new identity.

The workplace problem: Transgender people have little protection in the workplace, and a cross-gender lifestyle without gender reassignment can still be a reason for dismissal in the UK. You need to think carefully about your particular workplace and employers before taking such a large risk. However, UK law offers transexual people protection against discrimination. Many employers will be concerned about image and presentation, particularly if your work involves contact with the public. It is particularly important to ensure that your employer is given ample notice to make appropriate arrangements for telling other staff, customers and clients. In the UK, the Equal Opportunities Commission provides guidelines for the employers of trans people. Try to be patient with your fellow workers, but be firm. You have not changed – they are simply going to see a happier and therefore harder-working version of you.

Coming out to friends: Coming out with friends is often much easier and it is rare for trans people to lose them, but it is important to acknowledge that you may be moving between social groups – for example, from a gay community to a predominately straight one or vice versa.

To a partner: Partners often find it traumatic when their lover comes out as transgender or transsexual. You may feel that you are simply trying to find your true identity, but it is important to understand that you may be disrupting the very basis of your partner's identity at the same time. Some relationships will break down, but by no means all. A partner who stays in a relationship will have to adjust to the fact that his or her partner is now a completely different gender and adapting to the new dynamics of the relationship domestically, socially and sexually can prove difficult. Partner support groups can help, but you will need to be very understanding. The more you respect your partner's feelings, the more chance you have of maintaining the relationship.

Telling a new partner that you are trans: If you don't tell partners early on, they may feel pretty angry about the deceit. A rule of thumb is that you should not disclose on the first date. Let your new partner get to know you first, or you may be judged solely by your gender reassignment. When a point is reached where the relationship looks as though it is about to become physical, tell the truth straight away – few transsexuals can disguise their sex once they take their clothes off. Lust is a powerful force and will often enable a prospective partner to get over the shock fairly quickly.

As a 73-year-old trans man, I've been aware of an enhanced psychological and spiritual scope because of the stresses of being in a sexual and social minority. My life is full of close friends, but it exists outside the perceived social norms.
Sam, 73, US

I have always passed as a boy on the streets, but since I started hormone therapy most people think I am a young man, even in close-up social situations. My family have been very supportive about the whole thing, although sometimes I think that my younger sister is embarrassed by me, which can hurt.
Finn, 24, UK

Being trans isn't easy – even if sometimes it is really good fun. I suppose my family have been okay about it – it's amazing how quickly someone can come around when they realise they could lose their only child if they don't. My friends have been supportive, and through support groups I have made countless new friends. Don't let other people's hang-ups decide who you are.
Josie, 27, UK

Female menopause

Pre-menopause: If the menopause is the time when a woman's sex hormones hit the road, pre-menopause is when they start packing their bags. This happens about three to five years before your last period, usually in your 40s, and the phase lasts until a year after your final period. Some signs or symptoms of menopause may appear during this time. Hormone levels may decrease in an erratic manner, causing irregular menstrual cycles and heavy bleeding. Some women, for example, find that their cycles get shorter, others that they lengthen.

Early menopause: The menopause often starts earlier in smokers than non-smokers. If you have both ovaries removed (bilateral oophorectomy) or a full hysterectomy (removal of the uterus and ovaries), you will have the symptoms of menopause straight away, no matter what your age, and your periods will stop completely if your uterus has been removed.

The menopause: The menopause occurs because the ovaries stop producing the female sex hormones oestrogen and progesterone. It is the fall in the levels of these hormones in the bloodstream that gives rise to the symptoms of menopause. This is a woman's transition from the reproductive to the non-reproductive phase. Menopause can occur at any time between the ages of 45 and 65, but the average age is 51.

Oestrogen: A decline in oestrogen leads to a decline in sexual response. Like oestrogen and progesterone, testosterone (the hormone responsible for libido) is also produced in the ovaries and as they cease to function, it is quite possible that libido does decrease. But some women find that the menopause marks the beginning of a new sexual awareness. Maturity can make women more aware of their needs and better able to voice their desires. More spare time, fewer distractions and no fears about becoming pregnant can make sex a more spontaneous, enjoyable and satisfying experience.

Re-adjustment: Other women find that the menopause is a time of real struggle. Menopause is a sign of ageing, and in a culture that places value on youth and beauty, grey hair and a redundant reproductive system can make a woman feel insecure. Lack of oestrogen causes major physical changes, too, such as reduced lubrication, thinner bones and thinning and shortening of the vaginal canal, which can make intercourse painful, decrease sexual desire and make women apprehensive about sex.

Symptoms and solutions

Hot flushes: Changes in circulation increase body temperature, and the resulting hot flushes can last between three and six minutes. They may occur up to several times a day and can be disabling, physically draining and lead to profuse sweating and insomnia. They generally begin suddenly on the chest, neck and face. Other associated symptoms are headaches, nausea and difficulty with concentration. Dress in layers and choose natural fibres over synthetic ones. Make sure your bedroom is cool at night to reduce the risk of night sweats. The best-known herbal treatments are black cohosh, *Agnes castus* and *dong quai*.

Lack of natural lubrication: Lack of oestrogen decreases vaginal lubrication, and what there is takes longer to appear and this can make penetration uncomfortable, so use plenty of artificial lubricant during foreplay and sex. Massage oils such as sweet almond and peach kernel work well – though not if you are using condoms.

Bladder problems: Decreased oestrogen levels also affect the bladder. Women may need to pee frequently. Vaginal irritation or stinging can occur during sex and can make women more susceptible to infections such as thrush and cystitis. Hormone treatments can help relieve the problem and you should also pee immediately after sex.

Low sex drive: Decreased androgens (and perhaps oestrogen) may result in a decline in sex drive. Some women just don't want to have sex, and it can be difficult if their partner does. Some medications, such as drugs for high blood pressure, lower sexual arousal, and antidepressants can lower libido as well. Some women are prescribed testosterone replacement treatment to combat loss of sexual desire. Discuss your problems, symptoms and any possible sexual side-effects with your doctor.

Problems: Women may experience mood swings during the menopause that can affect desire, libido and relationships. Depression is also quite common. Counselling, cognitive behaviour therapy, antidepressants, exercise and some types of alternative medicine can all help, though medications sometimes have unwanted side-effects, one of which can be decreased sexual desire. Some women find it harder to reach orgasm or find that it takes longer than before. Others find that the sensation of orgasm is less intense and that vaginal contractions do not last as long.

56

Sexercise

Hormone replacement therapies

HRT: Doctors often prescribe hormone replacement therapy (HRT), which is a prescription drug therapy that comes in different forms: pills, vaginal creams, patches and vaginal rings – pills are the most common form. It consists of oestrogen and progesterone, two female hormones that a woman's body stops producing at menopause. Many experts believe that the benefits of HRT may be greater than its risks, but scientists don't yet fully know the risks of long-term HRT. Conventional HRT is highly effective in treating symptoms such as vaginal dryness, hot flushes and depression. Negative side-effects can include weight gain, continuing periods, heavier periods, vaginal discharge, fluid retention and breast tenderness. There is also a very, very small increase in the risk of breast cancer after five years of HRT use. Though millions of women take HRT, it's not the choice of every woman. Many questions remain unanswered about HRT, and it is important to discuss the following things with your doctor: personal and family medical histories; the side-effects, benefits and risks; and whether now is the right time or whether you should wait until you are older. Women who have a family history of cardiovascular disease will be advised to take HRT. Conversely, women with a history of cancers (breast, ovarian, uterine) will be advised not to. The oral contraceptive pill is sometimes prescribed as an alternative because it also contains oestrogen and progestogen.

Testosterone: This hormone is sometimes prescribed to women who have had their ovaries removed and consequently experienced a drop in sex drive. Testosterone is also produced in the adrenal glands, and woman who have had chemotherapy or radiotheraopy targeted at these glands may also require extra testosterone. The results of studies on its effectiveness in increasing sex drive are mixed, and calculating the correct dose is difficult. Side-effects can include agitation and facial hair growth.

Diet and exercise: Drinking adequate water, switching to a low-fat, high-fibre diet with plenty of oily fish, nuts and pulses and taking regular aerobic excercise will help reduce the impact of the menopause significantly. Some people advocate increasing the amount of soya products in your diet because they contain phyto-oestrogens (other people say this is rubbish). Sex during and after the menopause can help reduce vaginal atrophy and keep the vagina expanded, while sexual arousal increases the blood flow to the genitals and keeps it lubricated. Essentially it is a case of use it or lose it.

I don't think I've reached any midlife situation with sex. I'm only 53 and still extremely sexually active. I continue to masturbate three to four times a day.
Jack, 53, UK

You know, there are a lot of new medical products being researched right now, just for women who have the menopause. But who wants to take more pills? I take oil of primrose, echinacea, grapeseed extract, alpha lipoic acid and so on. Why not just put something on which will increase sensitivity and lubrication?
Rosa, 42, UK

HRT has really helped. I had forgotten what she's like when she is relaxed. She's back to her old self, and because it has improved her hair and skin, she is more confident. For a while there it looked like the menopause hailed the end of good sex, but now it's as good as it ever was.
Eric, 63, Australia

I'm not taking anything so new that they don't know the long-term effects of it. Whatever that means to my sex life.
Dianne, 58, UK

Male andropause

Pass the testosterone: Because the female menopause manifests itself in such a physical way – the cessation of periods – it is much more obviously identifiable than the male menopause. Though some doctors consider the theory controversial, others believe that men between the ages of about 44 (occasionally earlier) and 55 sometimes experience something called the 'andropause', or the 'viropause', which is also mixed up with a male midlife crisis. Though it is essentially emotional, there are also some physical changes that result from gradually falling hormone levels. Testosterone is the most important male hormone, responsible for libido, hair distribution and body shape among other things. As its levels plummet, so do erections, chins and sexual confidence.

Going fast: Any change from one phase of life to another is accompanied by psychological adjustment and a reassessment of one's identity. During mid-life, men may find themselves pressurised by work and assume that any lack of vitality or virility is a natural part of growing older. Symptoms such as lower libido, difficulty in achieving and maintaining an erection, hair loss, dry skin, lack of energy and enthusiasm, joint and muscle stiffness, tiredness, depression, sleeplessness, anxiety and emotional stress may all be dismissed as part of the ageing process, but if left untreated, they can lead to psychological and physical sexual problems. Loss of libido and intermittent failure to achieve an erection can lead to performance anxiety and eventually significant erectile dysfunction.

Getting it up: Many men find that their erections are less firm and don't stand up as far as before. A young man's erection points upwards. An older man's erection points out at a 90 degree angle. Orgasms may may feel less intense and ejaculation will not produce as much fluid as it did before. Though men can have erections until they're very old, it can take longer to achieve them. Obviously it depends on the partner to some extent. A busty young beauty may have a more rapid impact than a well-built fifty-something matron, but older men can require almost constant stimulation of the penis to maintain erection, so matron with her strong right hand may actually be a better bet than her pneumatic opposition. If your partner finds it difficult to maintain his erection, an adjustable cock ring or a vibrator held against his penis may help. The older a man gets, the longer his refractory period is, so it may not be possible to have sex as frequently. This is normal, and doesn't mean that sex becomes inferior or less enjoyable – just different. While the frequency of sex declines between the ages of 40 and 70, satisfaction levels generally remain constant.

254

Sildenafil

Sex in later life

Good for you: If ageing is measured by time passing, then our clocks don't seem to be running at the same speed. Some people are past it at 40, while others are still young and vigorous at 70. Why? Well, apparently it has something to do with sex. One can only speculate on how many times Cassanova got his leg over, but a recent report by the UK-based Sheffield Institute for Studies on Ageing reveals that people over 50 who have regular sex are in better physical and mental shape than their less sexually active counterparts. What the study does not reveal is whether people who are in better shape are simply more sexually attractive.

Good for them: People don't stop wanting to have sex when they start drawing a pension. In UK nursing homes, 17 per cent of people over the age of 85 reported sexual interest but no activity, because of insufficient privacy, lack of a partner, illness, the attitude of staff and feelings of unattractiveness. In fact, in a recent newspaper interview, a UK care-home worker revealed that 'residents being found entwined' was not uncommon, and that four elderly people had been asked to move out of the home after being caught in 'a midnight orgy' in the day-room. Good for them. Who wouldn't use physical contact, closeness, intimacy and sex to relieve the monotony of increasing immobility and daytime TV? In 2001, the Pennel Institute published a study of existing research into sex in later life in the UK. Predictably, it found that most surveys focused on penetrative sex and managed to ignore the fact that divorce and bereavement have lead to a huge increase in the number of older people living alone. There were no questions about masturbatory habits, so the fact that many single men and women are still sexually active didn't figure.

Looking for love: The reality is that if they had the opportunity, more single people in mid- to later-life would like to be sexually active. With each passing decade, the male to female ratio decreases, because men tend to die younger. Thirty-five per cent of 65-year-old women live alone, and the older a woman becomes, the less likely she is to find a partner. And it's not for lack of trying. In old people's bridge clubs worldwide, four women are buzzing around every man – and it's not his hand that they want to see. The Internet has provided older singles with new opportunities to make friends, though apparently even Internet daters pretend to be younger than they are. For a fee, some dating sites offer to doctor your photo to make you look younger, and the standard age for an online 'older woman' is 47; for an online 'older man' it's 49. No zimmer frames, no cocoa.

Though there are thousands of senior singles who would gladly swap places with those lucky enough to have a partner, couples who have been together for a long time often find that sexual difficulties, inhibition and plain old boredom can kill any interest they ever had in sex. Physical deterioration (which starts at 30, let's face it) can make people feel less confident about themselves and their bodies. Gay men may feel the loss of their looks and their physique more acutely. Decreasing testosterone, oestrogen and libido, wobbly erections, vaginal dryness, diabetes, surgery and mastectomy can be psychologically, as well as physically, debilitating. Stroke victims may be worried about exerting themselves during sexual activity, though guidelines suggest that if you can climb a flight of stairs without getting out of breath, you are fit to have sex with your regular sexual partner.

Good vibrations: In later life there may be less emphasis on penetrative sex, but maintaining intimacy is fundamental to well-being. Older people often have established likes and dislikes, but with a new partner or a new attitude, you may find that broadening your horizons makes for a whole new interest in sex. Vibrators can supply sustained stimulation to the clitoris and vagina, and can also be used to relax and stimulate other areas of the body. Most women will require plenty of clitoral stimulation and extra lubrication before penetration and orgasm. Engaging in oral sex or mutual masturbation can take the pressure off a man to perform, and using dildos or vibrators with a good water-based lubricant will provide more than adequate penetration.

Some penetrative sex positions are better than others because they put less pressure on joints and muscles. Trial and error is the only way to find out what is comfortable, bearing in mind that more elaborate arrangements may not be sustainable for long. Some sexual positions can be made more comfortable with pillows or supports. Vacuum pumps, penis rings, penis injections and pellets that insert into the urethra can all strengthen your erection, and if you are in good health, your doctor may recommend sildenafil. Though there is no female equivalent to sildenafil at the moment, pharmaceutical companies all over the globe are rushing to patent pills, potions and creams in a desperate bid to corner the female market. The one that seems to be getting the most attention is alprostadil, a male prostaglandin, which apparently produces a pleasant tingling feeling when rubbed into the clitoris – it it is not yet available in the UK.

You learn so much over the years and your technique is enhanced. I had a heart attack when I was 60, but recovered in a very short time and have never found that it affected my sexual performance. So I have never had to seek advice or try the famous Viagra, but would certainly consider it if I thought I was in need.
Bob, 66, UK
Vavo.com

Mike and I use more props than we used to, but we still get it together regularly and I am sure that it keeps me fit, too.
Roger, 71, UK

My wife just doesn't want to have sex with me any more. She started gaining weight in her 50s and it was as if she has just let the whole thing go since then. I miss the closeness as well as the sex.
Freddie, 68, US

The slowing down of our desire for sex as we have got older together has been an advantage. We are more in sync with each other. Intimacy means there are no questions we are ever afraid to ask.
Andrew, 55, UK

Sexual fitness

Long-term benefits: Vigorous physical activity for 30 minutes or more just three times a week is all it takes to get fit and stay fit. A brisk walk, swimming, cycling or a stint at the gym all get the blood pumping. In the long term, exercise improves physical and emotional health and reduces the likelihood of heart disease, high blood pressure, strokes, diabetes and osteoporosis, and lowers both anxiety and cholesterol levels. Staying supple ensures that you can stay sexually active for longer, and walking regularly keeps bones strong in the lower limbs.

Short-term gain: Increased cardiovascular output during exercise raises the amount of adrenaline in the body. This hormone can lead to feelings of relaxation and sexual arousal directly after physical exertion, meaning that after a work-out, you and your partner are much more likely to want sex. During exercise, the body produces endorphins, which act on the brain to block pain and create feelings of exhilaration, happiness and calmness. Increased blood flow throughout the body benefits the pelvis and the genitals. This can increase arousal, sensation, lubrication, and intensity of orgasm during sex.

And sex is actually good exercise in itself: The pulse rate of someone who is sexually aroused increases from a normal rate of about 70 beats per minute to around 150 beats per minute. This is equal to the pulse rate of an athlete during maximum effort. Multiple contractions of the buttocks, pelvis, thighs, thorax, arms and neck strengthen and exercise muscles (though obviously not if you are underneath in the missionary position). Vigorous sex, from arousal to orgasm, can burn up to 200 calories – that's the same as running 15 minutes on the treadmill, except it's much more fun.

Get the habit: It's a good idea to get into the routine of taking regular exercise before you feel that you need to. If you have any concerns about your health, check with your doctor before you do anything too ambitious. And if you don't know what to do, or would like some guidance or company, contact your local recreation centre and see what's on offer. There may be a gym, for example, offering aerobic classes or swimming. Ironically, the solution to problems of age-related immobility usually involves increased movement and physical activity. For this reason, enlightened local authorities in the UK, US and Australia are encouraging recreation centres to run classes in t'ai chi and yoga for people suffering from arthritis.

The miracle sex diet

**PMS DIETARY TIPS
FROM THE *NATURAL
HEALTH BIBLE***

*Never miss a meal.
Eat little and often in
order to maintain
blood sugar levels.*

*In your premenstrual
week, your calorie
requirements may
increase.*

*Have a daily salad.
You must eat at least
five portions of
fruit a day and
three portions of
vegetables.*

*Eat a little protein
every day.*

*A healthy woman
shouldn't be drinking
more than one-and-
a-half bottles of wine
a week, and for a
man it shouldn't be
more than two. At
the WNAS we have
found that a
programme of diet,
exercise and
nutritional
supplements helps
some 90 per cent of
women get their sex
drive back within four
to six months.*
Maryon Stewart
*Women's Nutritional
Advisory Service*

*I hear that alcohol is
bad for the sex drive,
which is a damn
shame, because
women seem much
more interested in
sleeping with me
when they are drunk.*
Garth, 48, UK

Food and sex: Food and sex have enjoyed a hedonistic relationship ever since Adam and Eve tasted the forbidden fruit. Though scientists have shown that it's a myth that aphrodisiacs work, our ancestors set great store by the sex in their snacks. The Romans guzzled grapes, Montezuma chose chocolate and the Europeans . . . well, they ate bulls' testicles. Sometimes sexual strength was assumed to come from eating foods that looked, tasted or smelled like a sex organ (oysters fit all three criteria). Though there is no specific magical ingredient, nutritionists argue that certain foods, eaten regularly over time, have a beneficial effect on libido and sexual ability. It's worth noting that oysters, for example, are extremely high in zinc, which is vital for testosterone production.

The vital ingredient: If aphrodisiacs work, it's because we want them to (in clinical trials on sildenafil, 30 per cent of the men taking placebo sugar pills reported dramatic increases in erectile function). In the right circumstances, any food can be arousing because the real vital ingredient is sexual chemistry. Sipping champagne at sunset in St Lucia sure sounds sexy, but not if you are with the wrong person. Suddenly, sharing a packet of biscuits under a candlewick bedspread in a freezing cold bedroom seems terribly romantic.

Preparation: Sharing food and wine must be the most common act of foreplay on the planet, but though first dates happen in restaurants, lovers generally prefer to dine at home. Eating together can even help restore flagging sexual intensity. It's cheaper than couple counselling, but requires rigorous preparation. The following recipe involves 30 hours of advance fasting, abstinence and chastity to heighten your senses and help you lose a few pounds so that you feel less inhibited wearing nothing but olive oil.

The menu: Arrange a date with your lover for Friday evening. From Thursday morning eat nothing but raw or steamed vegetables, sesame and pumpkin seeds and fruit. Drink lots of water, lemon and ginger or ginseng tea. Keep yourself busy and set aside time to shop for your ingredients. You will need foods to eat and foods to play with. You don't want to end up sweating over a soufflé, so keep the menu simple. Opt for finger foods rather than a main meal: sashimi, oysters, asparagus with butter, caviar, gravalax, sour cream, blinis, lobster, tinned peaches, fresh mango, mashed banana, strawberries dipped in melted 70 per cent cacao chocolate, vanilla ice cream and sugared almonds. These should be washed down with ice cold white wine or, preferably, chilled champagne.

Shaving: Prepare your body. Some argue that shaving pubic hair is a necessary evil for food sex, but the jury is out. You avoid a sticky hairy mess, but there is something oddly pre-pubescent about hairless adults and it feels really scratchy when the hair grows back. Better options might be a Brazilian wax or the new craze, the Tiffany Box. This involves shaving everything off bar a small square, which is bleached and dyed a particular shade of duck-egg blue.

The door bell rings: By Friday evening you should be ready to turn down the lights, turn up the central heating and slip out of your pinny. If you have bought ready-prepared food, maintain the illusion that you are a domestic sex god or goddess by remembering to put all the packaging in the bin before your lover arrives.

Dinner is served: As you have hardly eaten for two days, your salivary glands will be working overtime. This makes for good kissing, great oral and enhances the flavours and smells of both the food and the sex. It also means that your first sip of alcohol will rush straight to your head, making you feel less inhibited and more relaxed. The process of fingering fleshy fruits, shucking pearly oysters, smearing, smelling, dribbling and swallowing is so close to a sex act in itself that it's a wonder TV chefs get anything done at all. Dribbling peach juice down the length of a buttery asparagus, slurping champagne from mouth to mouth, licking globules of shiny black caviar off your lover's erect nipples, the taste of vanilla, tongues and wetness are all guaranteed to make even the most straight-laced individual moist with anticipation.

Dessert: Blindfold your lover and feed him or her from your mouth. If using ice cream on the genitals, keep it in your mouth and alternate between the warmth of your tongue and the chill of the ice cream. Take one end each of a spear of asparagus dripping with butter and nibble your way towards a kiss. Perch raspberries on a little whipped cream over nipples (spray cans of cream are more fun; they also come in Tia Maria and chocolate flavours). Fill belly buttons with honey and lick it out. Pour olive oil over your lover's shoulder blades and watch it trail down to the crack of the buttocks. Spread it over the fleshy cheeks and press your body up behind for full-body lubrication. Spray white ejaculate over dark chocolate breasts. Remember – use food on rather than in the body. That tinned peach will be a lot less attractive when it emerges next week.

I saw a patient who had been infertile for nine years. I put him on a diet rich in zinc and they conceived within two weeks, though results aren't usually that instantaneous.
Anthony Haynes
The Nutrition Clinic

TIPS FOR A HEALTHY LIBIDO:

Avoid caffeine, including coffee, tea and chocolate. Do not drink more than two decaffeinated drinks a day as they contain methylxanthines that can aggravate other symptoms.

Avoid salty food.

Take the herbal supplement Agnes Castus. *Tests have shown that this also has a positive effect on women with menstrual irregularities.*

Oysters are great sex food – I don't know why they work, but eating something that is that visually erotic with someone you are attracted to just has to lead to a good shag.
Matthew, 46, UK

I always eat too much on a date because I am nervous, and then I feel too lumpy and fat to take my clothes off.
Sophie, 40, US

SEXUAL HEALTH

I can't get full blown erections anymore because of my disability so I use the 'stuffing' method....sometimes it works and sometimes it doesn't, but I still enjoy it. **Jim, 46, US**

Sexual health

A vagina, much like the eyes, has natural fluids that protect and self clean. You don't wash your eyes out with soap, and in just the same way, you don't need soap to wash your vagina. Many people end up in a GU clinic because of over-washing of genitals, particularly women. Over-cleaning washes away the natural protection, making you more vulnerable to thrush and bacterial vaginosis. Vaginal or anal douching, in particular, can cause problems.
Sarah, 34, UK
GU doctor

On the whole, women seem to be better than men at going for check-ups or treatment.
John, 62, UK
Doctor

I'm from a small town where everybody knows your business. When I got pubic lice, there was no way I was going to the local doctor, because he was our family doctor. I didn't want anyone that I knew to find out, so I caught a train to the city. Thank God for GU drop-in clinics.
William, 30, UK

Many people find having a sexual health problem embarrassing. Some find it so embarrassing that they don't seek help. Remember that people involved in the medical profession have usually seen it all before, and that the faster something is treated, the quicker it goes away. In the UK, healthcare is free, but in the US it's predominantly private and prescription prices are not regulated, which means that healthcare is more expensive.

If you are worried about any aspect of your health, the best advice is to phone a local health centre and speak to a nurse. In the UK and many other countries, 24-hour helplines offer confidential healthcare advice, basic diagnoses and information on self-help, local health services and late-night pharmacies. If you have access to the Internet, you will find numerous online 'find-a-doctor' sites that will help you to locate specialists.

General doctors are not always terribly knowledgeable about sexual health problems, and remember that any diagnosis they make will go on your medical records. Your doctor may enquire about your sex life, because certain health problems, such as diabetes and depression, have known links to sexual problems – but don't wait to be asked. Try to describe your symptoms as clearly and in as much detail as you can. Many people get terms confused – for example, they say they are impotent, when they mean they ejaculate prematurely. A physical examination may be needed (you can ask to have a chaperone present), and once a diagnosis has been made, appropriate treatment will be given, or you may be referred to a specialist or a psychosexual counsellor.

Genito-urinary (GU) clinics specialise in the diagnosis and treatment of sexually transmitted infections. Fifty per cent of GU clinics in the UK also have on-site sexual dysfunction specialists. The clinics provide confidential screenings and your test results don't go on your medical records. (Positive HIV tests can make organising bank loans or mortgages more difficult). GU clinics can also provide tests and check-ups to help you monitor general sexual health. You can make an appointment, and some clinics offer a drop-in service, too. There's no charge (in Britain) and all tests are entirely confidential. You don't even have to give your real name, though you might have to leave a contact address. The doctor takes your medical history, asks why you have come and discusses recent sexual contacts. You may need a genital or anal examination or a urine or blood test. The entire process can last up to an hour, though waiting times vary. Results may be given while you wait, by phone, by post or collected on a second visit.

Other specialist services

Family planning clinics (UK): These provide free and confidential contraceptive advice, contraceptive services and contraceptives. Some can test for and treat STIs, and they also offer advice on abortion. A few family planning clinics offer psychosexual counselling, too. You can get details of your nearest clinic from phone books and health centres, or by calling NHS Direct.

Urologists: These doctors specialise in the urinary system, which includes the kidneys, bladder, prostate gland and the genitals. Some urologists also look after people with problems of sexual dysfunction.

Gynaecologists and obstetricians: Doctors who specialise in female genital health, the reproductive system and childbirth.

Endocrinologists: Doctors who diagnose and treat problems with the endocrine system, which produces the body's hormones. Sometimes hormonal imbalances or deficiencies can cause sexual problems.

Sex therapists: Therapists who specialise in psychological problems relating to sex and concentrate on educating their patients in communication skills, sexual techniques and sexual functioning. They aim to change negative feelings into positive ones. Sex therapists may gradually expose their patients to the source, or situation, that inhibits them sexually in order to reduce their level of anxiety.

Couple counselling: Various organisations offer this service, but in the UK, the best-known one is Relate. You can be referred for couple counselling by your doctor, or you can contact the organisation independently. There is a strong emphasis on 'talking therapy' and communication, though success is somewhat determined by how good your counsellor is and how much you both want the relationship to work. Though couple counselling concentrates on relationships, certain counsellors offer help with specific sexual difficulties too.

Sexual surrogates: Sexual surrogacy is rare in the UK, but in certain states in the US it is more widely available. It involves the patient having sex with a paid partner who is trained to help patients overcome sexual problems, such as fear of intimacy, performance anxiety, inability to orgasm, premature ejaculation and so on. The treatment is part of a broader programme that is monitored by a therapist.

Not only did my man cheat on me, but he got genital warts at the same time. He was in the spare room for a long time, but when we eventually did make up, we couldn't have a 'make-up shag', because he hadn't been to the doctor yet. I couldn't believe it. He said he had been too ashamed. I made him go, and it was sorted out fairly quickly and without much fuss. It's like I said to him, 'It's their job, they don't even think about it'.
Hannie, 27, UK

We went to couple counselling. He was very reluctant at first, but a friend of ours talked him into it. We went privately, because the waiting list on the NHS was very long, and it was quite expensive because we went once a week for five months. It was definitely worth the money – the counsellor helped us realise that we had just slipped into the habit of contradicting one another and bickering about things that don't warrant a fight. We worked through a lot of problems, and started having sex a lot more when we liked one another again!
Anne, 53, UK

Tests and testes

The breast test: Breast awareness is essentially about knowing how your breasts look and feel normally, so that you will be able to notice any changes. Recognising changes and taking action early means that if cancer is diagnosed, treatment is more likely to be successful. The majority of lumps found on breasts are benign (not cancerous), but it is still important to check for them and to consult your doctor immediately if you find one. Until fairly recently, quite a strict code of self-examination was recommended, but now a less formal process is advised. You should check your breasts and armpits in the middle of your menstrual cycle, because during your period, they often feel lumpier than normal. Stand in front of a mirror with your arms raised and examine the contours from different angles. Does anything look different? You may find feeling your breasts is easier with a soapy hand in the bath or shower, or you may prefer to check when lying down. Though breast awareness campaigns are usually aimed at women, hundreds of men get breast cancer each year, so men should also monitor changes in their breast tissue.

The smear test: In the UK it is recommended that all women between the ages of 20 and 65 have a smear test at least every three years. The purpose is to look out for changes in the cervical cells, which may be an early indication of cervical cancer. The test can be carried out at a doctor's surgery, family planning clinic or occasionally at a GU clinic. A speculum is inserted into the vagina to hold the vaginal walls apart so that the cervix can be seen (some women may find the sensation slightly uncomfortable, especially if they are tense). A small sample of cells is then taken from the cervix. If any abnormalities are found, a doctor may want to take a closer look at your cervix (colposcopy) or he may just want to monitor you more closely and repeat your smear test at more regular intervals. Results are posted to you a month or two later, or may be available over the phone.

The testes: The classic sign of testicular cancer is a hard lump felt on a testicle or an increase in size of a testicle. Though these signs don't automatically signal the presence of cancer, you should get in touch with your doctor as soon as possible. Testicular cancer grows very rapidly, and should be seen, diagnosed and treated within a few weeks of being first noticed. All young men should check their testicles every month to feel for lumps or enlargement: this is best done in a warm bath to allow the scrotum to relax and the testicles to 'drop'. Alternatively, this is a caring and arguably more pleasant thing for a partner to do.

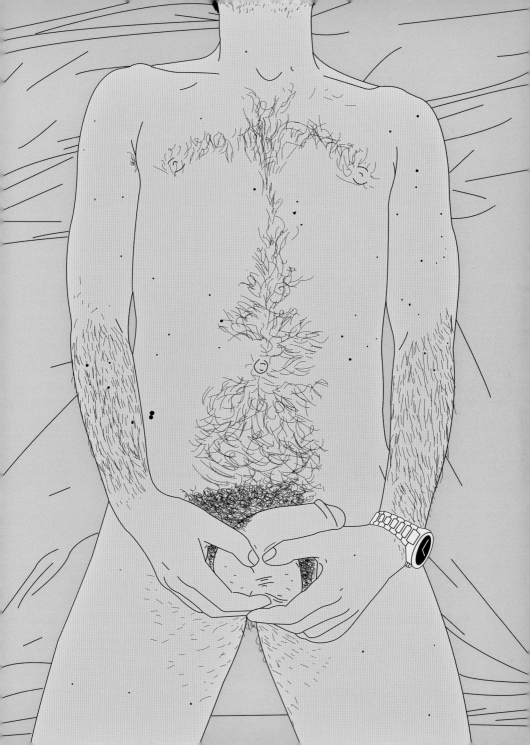

Common problems

**A NATURAL CURE
FOR CYSTITIS**

• *To treat cystitis,
drink at least 3
litres (about five
pints) of water a
day.*
• *Avoid tea and
coffee and drink
cranberry juice –
unsweetened juice
is more effective.*

*I drink cranberry
juice every day to
prevent any bladder
infections; I have
suffered all my life
and it can make life
hell. I am sick of
going on antibiotics
for treatment and I
am sure that is
depleting my natural
immunity, so
cranberry juice
seems a sensible
option. It works – I
haven't looked back.*
Estaticjill, 26, UK

*I had a burning
sensation, but I
ignored it because I
was busy. It hurt to
piss, so I didn't drink
water so I wouldn't
need to. Over two
days it got worse
until I woke up with
terrible pains all
down my sides. The
doctor said I had
cystitis that had
turned into a kidney
infection.*
Jemma, 46, UK

Urinary tract infections (UTIs): If you experience pain or irritation when you urinate and need to urinate more often, you should consult your doctor, even if initial symptoms seem mild. It is possible that you have a urinary tract infection (UTI). It is important that it is checked out, because if symptoms persist for more than 48 hours, the infection may cause kidney damage or other serious health problems. It may save time to go directly to a GU clinic, where diagnosis and treatment (with antibiotics) will be swift. Recurrent urinary tract infections, such as cystitis, are more common in women, but can also occur in men. Attacks often coincide with sexual activity (manipulation of the urethra or penetration) that is new, more frequent or vigorous than usual (hence the phrase 'honeymoon cystitis'), but they can also be triggered by an attack of thrush, by dehydration or even by wearing tight underwear in an overheated environment. Some people find that attacks are triggered by spicy food and alcohol. The decrease in lubrication and thinning of the vaginal walls at menopause may also trigger recurrent cystitis. If you have a UTI, sex will be uncomfortable. The fear of pain may put you off sex and stop you lubricating, and sex without sufficient lubrication is not only painful but is more likely to trigger inflammation, which sets off another bout. Self-help can break this cycle.

Tips to prevent cystitis

• Wear clothes that allow air to circulate (avoid synthetic underwear) and drink plenty of water – a glass every two to three hours.
• Use extra lubrication during sex and make sure that both you and your partner have clean hands.
• Urinate before and after sex to clear your urethra. Wipe yourself from front to back after going to the toilet. Never 'hold on' when you need to pee.

If you get cystitis: At the first hint of an attack, drink as much water as you can hold (even if it is in the middle of the night). Some people say that strong caffeinated drink (diuretic) can help push the fluid through too. The stream of urine you produce will be clear, and it will help flush out any bacteria. Cranberry juice contains a mystery ingredient that prevents the bugs that cause cystitis from latching on to the bladder wall and eases the symptoms. If it really hurts to urinate, try sitting in a bath of lukewarm water and peeing, or pour warm water over your genitals while you pee. If the infection hasn't cleared within 48 hours, see a doctor so that you can start on a course of antibiotics.

Thrush (candida albicans): Thrush is very common in women, and it can also affect men, especially if they are uncircumcised. It is a yeast infection that infects the vagina or penis and can also infect the mouth. The result is an extremely itchy area and creamy patches of what looks like a curdy non-smelly discharge. While thrush can be very irritating and uncomfortable, it is fairly simple to treat, by means of antifungal creams, pessaries or a single over-the-counter pill obtainable from pharmacists. Some people believe that keeping yourself clean, getting enough sleep, eating well and wearing cotton rather than nylon underwear reduce the chances of developing thrush. The problem may recur and may be triggered by taking antibiotics, which is why cystitis and thrush often follow one another in a cycle that may be hard to break.

Bacterial vaginosis (BV): This only affects women and develops when naturally occurring bowel bacteria multiply in the vagina. The most notice-able sign of BV is a strong fishy smell. This may be accompanied by a thin, watery, white-grey discharge, together with soreness and occasionally itching or swelling around the vagina. It may be contracted as a result of having sex without a condom, sharing sex toys, using IUDs, direct vagina-to-vagina contact and hand-to-vagina contact. Many women develop BV as a result of over-cleaning the vagina. Douching, vaginal deodorants and concentrated bath products or clothes-conditioners can all destroy protec-tive bacteria and change the acid-alkali balance in the vagina, allowing germs to multiply. The diagnosis is made by examining the genitals and testing the vaginal lining and a sample of the discharge. Treatment is easy and effective, by means of antibiotics and antibacterial cream or pessaries.

Haemorrhoids (piles): These are varicose veins in the anus that can bleed and be painful. Piles are common in both sexes, and are associated with constipation and straining. The extra weight of pregnancy and pushing during labour make women who have had children particularly prone to them, and postnatal piles can be very painful. Treatment is by cream or pessaries, from your doctor or a pharmacy. Generally, they shrink by themselves in two to three days, and then it helps to push them back up inside the rectum. Taking exercise and increasing the amount of fruit, vegetables and water in your diet may prevent piles. People who enjoy anal sex should discuss the problem with a sympathetic doctor. Persistent, painful piles can be injected to shrink them, or as a last resort, they can be removed by surgery, though, as with any surgery, there are risks.

I had thrush for years when I was a little girl, but I had no idea there was something wrong with me. I just knew that I got itchy and often had white stuff in my knickers. I think I thought it was normal. I don't know why my mum didn't notice from the dirty laundry. When I was 15, I was given a women's health book, and I realised that I had thrush. I went to the doctor and one pill sorted it out.
Kay, 23, UK

I had just begun to have sex and my vagina started to smell really bad. I thought it was because I wasn't washing myself after having sex, so I scrubbed myself – but it just got worse. In the end I was so sore that I cried and I told Mum, who took me to the doctor.
Joan, 18, US

I got piles when I had my first baby – they were like a bunch of grapes hanging out of my backside! It was the last straw, actually – huge boobs, sore nipples, Caesarean scar and grapes out of my bottom. I just felt absolutely disgusting. Anusol cleared them up, but a persistent one still comes back.
Emma, 37, UK

Sexually transmitted infections (STIs)

STIs don't discriminate: Though sex education campaigns often target young people, recent research has shown that as older generations become increasingly sexually active (a result of divorce, better health and increased longevity), the rate of STI infection in later years is rising. Though women are routinely screened for infection, men are not, and they are also statistically less likely to consult health professionals. As more men than women carry infections such as chlamydia, the policy of only screening and treating half the population needs to be reassessed.

In the UK: The incidence of syphilis and gonorrhoea in the over-65s rose 300 per cent during the 1990s, and syphilis is now considered to be epidemic among gay men. Anyone, of any sexual orientation, who is sexually active can contract an STI. Because some infections don't have any visible symptoms, it is best to be on the safe side and arrange to be tested if you think you may have been exposed to an STI – even though exposure to one doesn't automatically mean that you will contract it. The point is that most treatments are more effective if they are taken promptly.

Visible signs: Symptoms of an STI may include: a change in the consistency, smell or appearance of discharge; pain or a burning feeling when peeing; needing to pee more regularly; sore, swollen genitals; itching, rashes or lumps or blisters on the genitals or the anus; and a persistent dull ache or sudden, acute pain in the lower abdomen. Sexual health professionals stress that it is vital both to avoid sexual contact while waiting for test results and during treatment and to contact all recent sexual partners and encourage them to be tested as well, in order to reduce the incidence of STIs overall.

Telling your partner: Most people accept that their partners have a sexual history when entering into a relationship, but it can still be quite emotional and confusing to find out that someone with whom you have had sex has an STI. Your partner may either have become infected before your relationship started or an STI may be an indication of recent infidelity. Alternatively, you may have had the STI without knowing it and passed it on to your partner. Disclosure can be very difficult because it raises so many questions, but it is important that both partners see a doctor without delay to prevent re-infection.

If you can't face it: The most important people to tell if you find out that you have contracted an STI are the ones with whom you have had sex. They will need to be tested and treated before they spread the infection further. Because telling partners is awkward, GU clinics have come up with a clever system to limit the embarrassment. You are given a contact slip with a code written on it. You can pass this to anyone you believe you might have infected – and if you can't face doing this directly you can send the slip anonymously. The slip can be presented at any GU clinic, and the code will let the doctors know exactly which STI they are looking for.

The most common STIs

Non-specific urethritis (NSU)

What is it?: A generic name for inflammation of the male urethra. The most common cause of NSU is chlamydia.
Routes of transmission: Sex.
Sites of infection: The male urethra.
Signs and symptoms: There may be none Otherwise, symptoms may include urethral discharge, pain while peeing, general irritation in the urethra.
The test: Urine samples and swabs from the urethra are analysed – often on-the-spot, so results can be immediate. Chlamydia test results can take a week.
Post-diagnosis: Treatment with antibiotics is usually effective, but doctors advise against having penetrative sex until you have been given the all-clear.

Chlamydia

What is it?: This is the most common but treatable STI. If chlamydia is left untreated it can lead to pelvic inflammatory disease (PID) and eventually infertility. It also increases the chances of having an ectopic pregnancy.
Routes of transmission: During sex, and mother-to-child during birth.
Sites of infection: The cervix, urethra, rectum and eyes.
Signs and symptoms: There may be none, which is why regular sexual health screening is important. In women, signs and symptoms include: increased vaginal discharge; frequent or uncomfortable peeing; pain in the abdomen; irregular periods; and pain or bleeding during deep penetrative sex. Men are more likely to notice symptoms, like those of NSU above. Chlamydia of the rectum rarely causes symptoms.
The test: A doctor will take urine samples and take swabs from the sites of infection; women may need to have an internal examination. Results usually take about a week.
Post-diagnosis: Treatment with antibiotics is effective, but doctors advise against penetrative sex until you have been given the all-clear.

Genital warts

What are they?: Genital warts are caused by the human papilloma virus (HPV).
Sites of infection: On the cervix, vulva, penis, scrotum or anus.
Routes of transmission: Skin-to-skin contact, vaginal or anal intercourse. Warts can develop on your anus even if you haven't had anal sex. Not everyone who is exposed to the virus develops warts, but you should ask for an examination if you think you may have been exposed.
Signs and symptoms: Warts appear in the genital region one to three months after infection, either as small pinkish-white lumps or larger cauliflower-shaped lumps. They may itch, but are usually painless.
The test: A doctor or nurse will be able to tell just by looking, but a vaginal or anal examination may also be required.

I was in a casual relationship with a guy and he phoned out of the blue and said I had to get myself tested – he wouldn't go into details. I hadn't noticed anything wrong, but I got tested anyway. I had chlamydia. I've had the treatment now, but I still worry that I'm sterile. My friends think that I should be grateful that he told me, but I am still really furious with him for giving me anything at all in the first place.
Lisa, 22, UK

I divorced two years ago and I have been dating a bit since. I had some problems and my doctor did a urine test and told me that I had chlamydia. I didn't even know what it was. I certainly don't know who gave it to me. It's the last thing you expect as a 56-year-old divorcee.
James, 56, UK

A wart is really no big deal. I knew what it was as soon as I saw it, and I knew that it's pretty common. Treatment is painless – the only thing that can be a pain is not having sex for a couple of weeks. But, hey, I've gone longer than that before.
Dan, 30, UK

Post-diagnosis: A brown liquid (podophylotoxin) is usually prescribed. This is applied to the warts at home, but it may take from four to six weeks of repeated applications to be effective. The warts can also be removed by freezing them or by laser treatment; both procedures are uncomfortable rather than painful. Use dental dams, surgical gloves and condoms if you have sex and keep the infected area covered.

Gonorrhoea (the clap)

What is it?: Gonorrhoea is a sexually transmitted bacterial infection.
Routes of transmission: Through penetrative sex (when the penis enters the vagina, mouth or anus), rimming or touching the infected area and then your own vagina, mouth, anus or penis without washing your hands in between.
Sites of infection: The cervix, urethra, rectum, anus and throat.
Signs and symptoms: It can be symptomless. however men are more likely to notice a yellow discharge from the penis; they may also experience pain when peeing and anal irritation. Women may also have a yellow discharge. Peeing may be painful, too, and the anus can become irritated or produce a slight discharge.
The test: Genital examination, a swab taken from the end of the penis, possibly a urine sample and, for women, an internal examination.
Post-diagnosis: Treatment is by antibiotics. Doctors insist that you abstain from sex until the course has been completed and you and your partner have been given the all-clear. As with all STIs, all your recent sexual partners should be tested.

Syphilis

What is it?: A bacterial infection that has been fairly rare in the UK until recently. However, the incidence in gay men is now increasing, in what has been described as an epidemic.
Routes of transmission: Sex or skin contact, mother-to-fetus.
Sites of infection: The anus, vagina, penis and mouth, or any skin abrasion.
Signs and symptoms: Symptoms may take up to three months to show. There are three phases, and the condition is highly contagious during the first two. In the primary phase, a sore ('chancre'), which is usually painless, appears at the site of infection after two to six weeks and disappears in three to seven weeks. Without treatment, the secondary phase starts about four to ten weeks after the chancre appears. Symptoms generally include a non-itchy rash covering the body, flat warty growths on the vulva or anus, flu-like symptoms, swollen glands, loss of appetite, general tiredness, white patches on the tongue and the roof of the mouth and patchy hair loss – many other symptoms are possible, because syphilis is notorious for its ability to mimic other diseases. The symptoms usually clear up within a few months, however, without treat-ment, syphilis stays latent in the body (the latent phase) and may develop into

tertiary syphilis, anything from years to decades later. This can seriously affect the heart, the nervous system and internal organs.

The test: A blood sample, or a sample of the fluid oozing from any sores, is taken for analysis, your genital area is examined and women may be given an internal examination.

Post-diagnosis: Treatment is usually a two to three week course of penicillin injections, and this is effective during any of the phases of syphilis, though once the condition has caused heart or nervous system problems, the effects cannot easily be reversed. As syphilis is highly contagious during the primary and secondary stages, it is essential to use barrier contraceptive methods for protection and to avoid making any contact with an areas of broken skin, sores or rashes. Syphilis is not contagious during the latent phase.

Pubic lice (crabs)

What are they?: Crabs are tiny parasitic insects that live in body hair.

Routes of transmission: Crabs are usually spread through body contact during sex with an infected person's pubic hair. It has been reported that people have contracted crabs through sharing a towel or from bed linen but this is unlikely. Crabs crawl from hair to hair and cannot jump or fly, so contact must be intimate and sustained.

Sites of infection: Crabs usually live in pubic hair, but occasionally they are found in underarm, leg, abdomen and chest hair, eyelashes and beards.

Signs and symptoms: Itching in the infected area; black specks in your under-wear (from lice droppings); brown eggs in your pubic hair; flaky skin, like dandruff; and, of course, the little crawling beasts themselves. Don't scratch.

The test: The lice can be seen, so diagnosis is usually immediate.

Post-diagnosis: Warn everyone you slept with in the two weeks before noticing symptoms and avoid sexual contact for a week after treatment finishes. Pubic lice are treated easily with a medicated lotion available from pharmacists without prescription. Clothing and bedding should be washed. Treatment should be repeated a week afer the initial one.

Herpes

What is it ?: A virus (*herpes simplex*) that hides away in the body, undetected and symptomless, after the initial outbreak. Some people never have another episode; others do, especially when they are feeling run down, stressed or depressed. There are two types: type 1 (HSV1) and type 2 (HSV2), but the strains cross over.

Routes of transmission: Through skin-to-skin contact, which includes contact between the mouth, anus, vagina or penis, in any combination.

Sites of infection: (HSV1) infects the mouth or nose (cold sores); (HSV2) infects the genital and anal area.

Signs and symptoms: Genital herpes can cause flu-like symptoms, backache,

I had quite a lot of unprotected casual sex in a stage of my life in which I was drinking too much and doing too many drugs. When I finally got it together, I knew I had to go for tests. When I found out all I had was trichomoniasis and crabs, it was actually the cause of quite a celebration. Both these things are treatable, and when I think of what else I may have caught, I got off pretty lightly.
Frank, 28, UK

I didn't really know much about syphilis, except that for some odd reason most of the continental philosophers seem to have gone mad from it. When the doctor said I had it, I was like, 'I'll go mad and die'. He was very quick to explain that syphilis isn't really like that anymore – they just give you a few penicillin jabs and that's it. The worst bit was contacting people I'd had sexual contact with. At first, I just couldn't face it. I felt like, well, 'Nobody told me'. But my father said that I had a moral duty to do it, and he was right. If you like someone enough to fool around with them, you owe them that.
Simon, 25, UK

headache, swollen glands and fever. Small fluid-filled blisters develop, causing itching or tingling in the genital region, and these burst and turn into sores. These can be very painful during the first episode, especially when urine, which is acidic, passes over them, but they eventually dry out, scab over and heal over in two to four weeks. Many people don't notice these symptoms.

The test: The genitals are swabbed and the samples analysed, and a urine sample may also be taken to confirm the diagnosis – the results come in about two weeks. Women may have an internal examination so that the cervix can be checked and you can be screened for other STIs, though doctors will defer this if the vulva is painful.

Post-diagnosis: Medical treatment is required to clear up first-time bouts of genital herpes. People who suffer from severe recurrent bouts may need continual treatment. The virus stays with you for life and the blisters and sores are highly infectious during an outbreak, so any direct contact will spread the virus. After the first outbreak, symptoms are less pronounced. Avoid kissing or oral-genital contact when you have a cold sore, even if you use a condom or dental dam, because the virus can change and cause genital herpes. Between outbreaks the chances of infection are reduced, so herpes sufferers often resume their sex lives after an outbreak, but use condoms. Partners can have a blood test to establish whether they carry the virus, though the results are not always reliable.

Trichomonas vaginalis (TV)

What is it?: 'TV' is a tiny, single-celled organism that causes an infection in the vagina and sometimes in a man's urethra.

Routes of transmission: Having penetrative sex (when the penis enters the vagina, anus or mouth). Sharing moist towels, washcloths, jacuzzis and baths may spread trichomoniasis, but non-sexual transmission is rare.

Sites of infection: A man's urethra and a woman's vagina.

Signs and symptoms: There may be no symptoms. However, sometimes symptoms include: a change in the appearance and smell of any vaginal discharge (frothy and greenish); soreness around the vagina; and pain while peeing or during sex. Possible symptoms in men include a discharge from the penis and pain during peeing.

The test: A genital examination, a urine sample and, in women, an internal examination.

Post-diagnosis: TV is treated with antibiotics. You shouldn't have penetrative sex until the doctor has given you and your partner the all-clear.

Hepatitis A (HAV)

What is it ?: A viral infection that causes damage to the liver. Hepatitis A is just one of three of the more common types of hepatitis. 99.9 per cent of people recover completely and are then immune to subsequent infection. A vaccination is available (and it can sometimes be taken in combination with the hep B vaccine), though doctors often only give the vaccine to people who say they are going to travel abroad to a place where hep A is common. A GU clinic is more likely to help you if you explain that you are into rimming.

Routes of transmission: The virus is transmitted through oral and anal contact and faeces. Although hep A is not traditionally thought of as an STI, it can be passed on through anal fingering or any other activity in which you come into direct contact with faeces.

Signs and symptoms: Fever, nausea, jaundice, fatigue, weight loss and a distaste for fatty foods, alcohol and cigarettes.

The test: The virus is detected by a blood test.

Post-diagnosis: There is no treatment for hep A, though avoiding alcohol and plenty of rest are advised. Ask for advice at your GU clinic before having sex. Use dental dams or non-microwaveable cling film for rimming.

Hepatitis B (HBV)

What is it?: A viral infection that can cause ongoing damage to the liver. If you think you may be at risk, discuss having a vaccination with your doctor – it is safe and effective.

Routes of transmission: Hep B is transmitted through infected blood or bodily fluids in the same way as HIV, though hep B is more infectious than HIV.

Signs and symptoms: About a third of people infected have no symptoms at all, but when they are present they include: nausea, fever, vomiting, aching, jaundice, yellow eyes, dark urine and pale stools. In the majority of cases, flu-like symptoms pass after a few weeks, often without lasting liver damage.

The test: The virus is detected by a blood test.

Post-diagnosis: Lots of rest, no medications, no alcohol and a low-fat diet are recommended to those diagnosed with HBV. Symptoms usually begin to pass after several weeks. Chronic carriers may have injections of interferon, either daily or three times a week, or combination drug therapy. Discuss having a hep A vaccination with your doctor, because any infection with hep A can cause complications in treatment of an infection with hep B.

Hepatitis C (HCV)

What is it ?: A viral liver infection once known as 'non-A, non-B hepatitis'. About 80 per cent of people with HCV become chronic carriers.

Signs and symptoms: The same as with hep B.

Routes of transmission: Hep C can be transmitted in blood and possibly in semen. In many people the route of transmission is uncertain.

The test: The virus is detected by a blood test.

Post-diagnosis: Injections of interferon, three times a week for 6–12 months are the standard treatment for hep C. Combination drugs (ribavarin and interferon) are now becoming available. No vaccination is currently available .

Being too embarrassed to tell your girlfriend doesn't help you in the long run. I didn't tell mine that I had crabs, but of course she found out because she caught them off me. To start with I said I must have caught them off her, but in the end I confessed that I had known I had them and she was pissed off. In fact, we nearly broke up over it. She said that I should have told her so that she could protect herself. It's not that I didn't know that, but there was never the right time to bring it up. Especially if you've only been together for two weeks.
Darren, 23, UK

I am sure I got cystitis from faeces. It just seems too coincidental that I have never had it before, and then the first time I used a vibrator for both my arse and my vagina, bang: I've got a urine infection.
Liza, 27, US

If I can't be bothered to get up and have a wee after sex, I can almost guarantee I'll get cystitis.
Angie, 48, UK

HIV and AIDS

Medical advances: The idea that HIV is a gay disease is a fallacy that has made heterosexuals very complacent. In fact, 48 per cent of those who became HIV positive in the UK in 2001 acquired the disease through unprotected heterosexual sex; only 37 per cent contracted it from homosexual sex. Most of the heterosexual diagnoses are now made in Britain's Afro-Carribean communities. In 2001, Britain recorded its highest ever annual increase in HIV infections, though the 3,425 people diagnosed then probably haven't been given a death sentence. Since 1996, HART (highly active anti retroviral therapy), a life-preserving cocktail of drugs, has lowered the AIDS-related death rate by 75 per cent. However, levels of drug-resistant HIV have increased five-fold in the last four years and the rapidly mutating virus seems to be doing it's best to outsmart any available treatments. In the UK alone, one in four people carries a strain of the virus that is at least partly resistant to the currently available treatments. It's thought that 10 per cent of the estimated 16,000 people on the drugs are not responding to them at all. This therapy involves patients taking up to 30 pills a day – to suppress the virus rather than kill it. To be effective, the pills have to be taken at particular times of the day, and this often means tailoring mealtimes to the treatment timetable. If people don't take the tablets correctly HIV can become resistant to them, so they have to switch to other drugs. Many people can't handle the side-effects, which can include erectile dysfunction (low doses of Viagra are sometimes recommended), inability to orgasm, raised levels of oestrogen, which may reduce libido and cause depression, and lipodystrophy (changes in the distribution of body fat, causing weight gain and weight loss and affecting self-image).

Routes of transmission: The body fluids that contain sufficient quantities of HIV to infect another person are blood (including menstrual blood), seminal fluid, vaginal fluid and breast milk. It is thought that saliva, sweat and urine do not contain enough HIV to infect another person during sexual contact, although ingesting the urine of someone who is on combination drugs may build up your own resistance to those drugs. The virus generally passes from one person to another through the internal lining of the sex organs and rectum during penetrative sex without a condom. There is a lower risk of contracting HIV through oral sex without a condom, though transmission is possible if there are any cuts or abrasions in the mouth of the person perfoming oral sex and an infected person ejaculates into the mouth. Sharing needles to inject drugs can also lead to transmission, and a mother can pass the virus on to her child during birth or breastfeeding.

Testing: The HIV test is a simple blood test that looks for the HIV virus, which may not be detectable until up to three months after exposure. You will be asked to come back three months later for a follow-up test (if you have unprotected sex during this time, the result might be a false negative). Testing is usually done at a GU clinic and some clinics can give results on the same day.

Living with HIV

'There's something I need to tell you . . . ': These seven scary words have been uttered 47,201 times in the past 20 years by people in the UK telling a partner that they are HIV positive. Of them, 12,248 are dead already, though many had managed to leave their lovers with the gift that keeps on giving. 'Living with HIV' was once a contradiction in terms, but is now a realistic, if heavily medicated, possibility. The problem is that many people with HIV, particularly those who are feeling healthy or are in relationships, don't necessarily want to live like monks. Sexual needs don't disappear just because you have told someone that you are HIV positive, though sexual relationships obviously become more complicated and long-term couples can find that anxieties about the diagnosis can interfere with sexual pleasure. Singles may be reluctant to find new partners, and people who are upfront about their HIV status may find that they cannot do so. And living with HIV presents a conundrum. If we are to believe the advertising campaigns, using a condom and practising safer sex prevents the transmission of HIV. But if someone admitted to you that they were HIV positive but said they practised safer sex, would you have sex with them? Er, um, basically - no you wouldn't. That's why so many HIV-positive people don't tell new partners about their status. They just follow the guidelines on safer sex and keep their fingers crossed.

Real life: Closeness and touch are fundamental for human well-being, and arguably someone with a serious illness is more in need of love, affection and intimacy than ever before. Denying this aspect of themselves or their relationships does nothing to help the physical and psychological health of HIV-positive people. Abstinence rarely works for long, and suppressing sexual urges can put people with HIV in a position in which they are less, rather than more, able to make sure that sex is safer. Nothing is guaranteed, but practising methodical and consistent safer sex significantly reduces the possibility of transmission, and you and your partner should try to be realistic about the risks. Support groups acknowledge that many HIV-positive couples fall back on the 'you could be run over by a bus' analogy. Not very scientific, but it may not be far from the statistical truth.

Vigilance: The key to living with HIV is to be vigilant about safer sex. If you don't practise safer sex and a partner becomes infected, any resistance that you have developed to the HIV drugs that you take may be passed on. This leaves even fewer treatment options. Similarly, if your partner is also HIV positive and you don't practise safer sex, there is a chance that you could be re-infected with a different or more resistant strain of the virus, which will complicate your drug regime. Ultimately we are all responsible for our own sexual health. You can't assume that someone is HIV negative or rely on partners volunteering information about their HIV status. The disease can lie dormant for ten years, so it's quite possible that anyone (including you) could be infected and not know about it. HIV can be given, but only to someone who puts themself in a position to receive it.

I found out about my HIV status while I was in a long-term relationship. I had counselling and they brought up the subject of my partner. I felt utter disbelief about my situation and I had a real fear of breaking the news to anyone, but she turned out to be understanding and supportive. We didn't have sex for quite a while – mostly because of the stress – and we took advice first. Safer sex when you are HIV positive is the same as safer sex when you are not.
David, 29, US

As an HIV-positive male I actively sought a partner who had the same HIV status as me. I met Bob about a year ago, and part of the reason our relationship works is that, finally, neither of us have to worry about infecting other people and we can both support each other through drug treatments and side-effects. I know there is a possibility that we could reinfect each other, but because we practise safer sex, we feel it is a risk worth taking. If I didn't have Bob I would be on my own.
Ross, 35, US

Not tonight, darling

Female sexual health problems

Vaginal dryness: Some women just don't lubricate as much or as quickly as others. If you are not aroused, afraid of having sex or don't want to have sex, you are unlikely to lubricate, though STIs or urinary tract infections can also cause irritation and dryness. Changes in hormone levels during breastfeeding can mean that you may not lubricate as much as usual, even if you are turned on. The drop in the level of oestrogen at the menopause (and after it) means that women don't lubricate as easily or as copiously as they used to. Commercial lubricant works well if a woman is fully aroused but still feels too dry for penetrative sex.

Dyspareunia (painful sex): This can be caused by a mixture of physical and psychological factors, emotional difficulties and conflicts in relationships, though vaginal infections or STIs can also lead to the problem. Painful sex inevitably decreases arousal and excitement, and many women go off sex if it becomes associated with pain. Extra lubrication, foreplay and stimulation can help, as can reducing the time spent on robust penetrative sex. Seek help from your doctor, a GU clinic or a psychosexual counsellor if you start to feel any physical pain during sex.

Vaginismus: This is when the pelvic floor muscles in the lower third of the vagina contract involuntarily, making penetration impossible. It occurs during sex, and sometimes also during a gynaecological investigation, when inserting a tampon or finger into the vagina. Sometimes past sexual trauma or distress are the cause of vaginismus, though fear or anxiety about sex can both cause and exacerbate the problem. Vaginismus can have a very destructive effect on a relationship. Partners may feel sexually rejected, even if they know that nobody is at fault. Many women with vaginismus enjoy other aspects of sex that don't include penetration, and many of them can achieve orgasm in other ways. Psychosexual counselling often helps, though women with vaginisimus may find that sexual satisfaction does not really improve, even when penetration is possible.

Pelvic inflammatory disease (PID): PID (inflammation of the uterus and fallopian tubes) is usually caused by an infection (such as chlamydia or gonorrhoea) that has not been treated properly. It can also develop when the cervix dilates during a miscarriage, childbirth or an abortion, or when an IUCD is inserted. PID can be mild, acute (sudden and severe) or chronic (long-term). It is often symptomless, but acute PID can include severe

Sometimes, no matter how aroused I am, nothing happens. It never occurred to me to use lube until my current boyfriend suggested it. Now I'm a convert – it's better than the real thing and I even use it for masturbation.
Penny, 31, Australia

Menopause was a funny thing for me, because I actually became more interested in sex. But I didn't seem to have any natural lubrication.
Norma, 68, US

I am actually very aroused by the idea of sex, but the muscles in my vagina just won't co-operate with my mind. They say that you can practise your way out of it, so I try very gingerly with my smallest finger. My therapist is convinced that it's related to some kind of sexual trauma.
Ruth, 38, US

I know that my vaginismus was psychological because it started after I was raped.
DD, 29, UK

abdominal pain, a high temperature, heavy periods, nausea, a change in vaginal discharge, a fast pulse and pain or discomfort during sex. The long-term consequences are chronic pain in the lower abdomen and infertility and it is vital that partners get treatment too. The diagnosis is made by an internal pelvic examination or by ultrasound (the procedures may be uncomfortable). In severe cases, a gynaecologist may need to carry out a laparoscopy. This normally involves a general anaesthetic, and then a small cut is made to allow the doctor to see the internal organs through a tiny fibre-optic device incorporating a camera. Treatment is with antibiotics, bed rest and pain-killers. In severe cases, a stay in hospital is necessary so that antibiotics can be given intravenously. Vigorous activities, including sex, should be avoided until any inflammation has gone.

Endometriosis: Endometriosis is a relatively common condition that can affect women of menstruating age, in which the cells that normally line the uterine cavity appear outside the uterus. Groups of cells may implant on the ovaries, the Fallopian tubes, the surface of the uterus or anywhere on the lining of the abdominal cavity. Symptoms can include abnormal or heavy menstrual bleeding and pain, and fertility is often negatively affected. There can also be some pain with deep thrusting during intercourse. However, having sex should not make the condition worse, so try different positions to find what's most comfortable for you.

Polycystic ovary syndrome (PCOS): This is a common condition that often starts during the teenage years. Its symptoms, caused by a hormone imbalance, can be mild, moderate or severe. They include irregular periods, hair growth on the face and other parts of the body, weight gain, patches of dark skin and acne. The most common treatment is the combined contraceptive pill, which can help to keep hormone levels balanced, lower the risk of endometrial cancer and lessen hair growth and acne. Your doctor should monitor your condition in case there are any complications.

Skin irritations (on the vulva): While vulval cancer is very rare, inflammatory skin conditions, such as eczema, scabies and lichen sclerosis (which can manifest as scarred white or pigmented skin or as open wounds) are more common and can cause pain and embarrassment. Some women with inflamed vulvas mistakenly believe that their condition is to do with lack of hygiene and use DIY methods to clean (household antiseptic) or to cure (inserting garlic cloves) their problem. In fact, these remedies can severely aggravate the skin. Most vulval skin conditions are treatable.

I had a bout of PID, and then it all went quiet for about 12 months. When we started trying to have a baby, it came back. It was at that point we thought maybe it was to do with my husband not using protection. He got checked out and he had chlamydia.
Rosemary, 45, US

I have endometriosis, and I have pain with sex. My doctor has prescribed pills, and I take one about 45 minutes before sex. It doesn't take the pain away completely, but it helps. Another thing that helps is lots of foreplay. It lessens the intercourse time.
Emma, 40, US

I have polycystic ovary syndrome, which is basically due to a hormone imbalance. Having a higher testosterone level has certainly not helped my low libido, despite my being told that it would. I have gone up and down with my sex drive, but it's always been way less than my husband's. And now I have a really super-low oestrogen level, so I wonder if that's contributing to my lack of sex drive. It's so not fair, that's for sure. I want it back.
Mary, 43, NZ

Losing your mojo

Male sexual health problems

Premature ejaculation: Coming too soon is the most common male sexual problem, and it's the most difficult one to define. The majority of men can ejaculate within two minutes if they receive sufficient stimulation, though on average penetrative sex lasts five to ten minutes and many men are happy with this. So premature ejaculation can be said to occur if you come before you want to, soon after penetration. The problem can sometimes be caused by chronic prostatitis, but it usually has a psychological basis. It is often worse with new partners and is usually to do with lack of confidence or sexual technique and stress. Practise masturbation techniques (stop-start or squeeze-release) to slow yourself down a bit. Focus on non-penetrative sex for a while – you can still give your partner orgasms. However, many modern sexologists argue that this is still focusing on the penis and orgasm, and doesn't reduce stress. You may want to think about other distractions that work for you, rather than practising techniques that make you more anxious. Some people claim that thinking about something that turns them off helps. Others find that an antidepressant, prescribed by their doctor, helps to delay things.

Retrograde ejaculation: This is a condition in which a man experiences orgasm, but does not ejaculate semen through the urethra. Instead of being propelled out of the penis, it passes backwards into the bladder. Its only significance is that the man is effectively infertile. The most common cause is damage to nerves after surgery on the prostate gland or the neck of the bladder that prevents the bladder sphincter from closing off to allow the semen out; diabetes and excess alcohol intake can also have this effect. Consult your doctor if you suffer from this problem.

Prostate problems: The first signs of prostate problems are usually changes in patterns of urination: frequency (peeing in the night); urgency; incomplete emptying; and dribbling or starting a flow of urine. There may also be pain in the lower back and a burning pain when passing urine. In young men, the most likely cause is an acute bacterial prostatitis (inflammation). Prostatic enlargement tends to be a problem of later life and prostate cancer is also more likely in older men (80 per cent of men over 80 have some degree of prostate cancer). See your doctor if you are concerned, because early diagnosis and treatment are important. It is thought that looking after your general health, giving up smoking and drinking plenty of water may help protect against prostate problems.

My husband maintains that there is nothing wrong with his sexual functioning, which makes me think that I must be suffering from the, 'What? Already?' disease, because that's what I always end up saying.
Kelly, 39, UK
Lovenet

My partner has difficulty getting aroused and getting erections. He has been taking an orgasm-inhibiting medication for the past five months. I have dealt with this by giving his mental well-being a higher priority than good sex.
Julian, 54, UK

I orgasm without ejaculating, which has it's problems. The good news is that I'm very popular in the blow job department as they don't have to do the whole spit or swallow thing.
Fludey, 38, Australia

Having had surgery for prostate cancer, I don't actually ejaculate and sometimes I have trouble achieving or maintaining a hard-on, but I have been with my partner for 24 years and he is very reassuring. Our sex was never very penetration-based, and I don't need a hard penis to make him come. Making him come can be very satisfying in itself.
Ian, 62, UK

Psychological issues: Because so many sexual problems are related to anxiety or inhibition, doctors need to treat 'the person not the penis'. Sometimes the physical problems are easy to sort out, but underlying psychological problems take longer to fix. Relationship difficulties, fear of intimacy or commitment, problems at work and general depression can be contributing factors. First-night erection failure in a new relationship is not uncommon, but the ability to have an erection is closely tied to male self-esteem. Losing it, even temporarily, can create a cycle in which fear of failure makes failure more likely. The problems are common, understandable and usually correct themselves, but psychosexual counselling may be required.

Dyspareunia (painful sex): Painful sex may have either psychological or physical causes. Sex can be painful for men if the foreskin is too tight, if they have an infection of the glans, an STI or if their partner is insufficiently lubricated. Peyronie's disease (scar tippue on the penis, which causes the erect penis to bend) can also cause pain, but can sometimes be treated. And some men report pain or discomfort when using injection therapy for erectile problems. See your doctor or a psychosexual counsellor.

Sex after vasectomy (male sterilisation): The volume of ejaculate remains the same after vasectomy, because the vast majority of semen comes from the prostate gland and seminal vesicles, which are unaffected. Despite this, it has been speculated, but not proven, that vasectomy may reduce sexual performance if the concept of 'firing blanks' affects a man's self-esteem.

Erectile dysfunction (impotence): The inability to have or sustain an erection affects about five per cent of men at 40 and 18 per cent between the ages of 50 and 59 – but only a tiny proportion ask for treatment. ED can be caused by both physical and psychological problems, though invariably these contribute to each other, creating a depressing cycle in which failure breeds discontent and discontent breeds failure. ED is a medically recognised disability, but in the UK, treatment is currently restricted to men who have certain specific illnesses that cause the problem, such as diabetes, multiple sclerosis, Parkinson's disease, prostate problems, pelvic or spinal cord injuries and renal failure. Other conditions, such as heart disease and high blood pressure can cause ED, but these are so common that treatment is restricted for financial reasons. Anyone who is in 'extreme distress' about their condition may be able to use this as a way of getting free treatment, though treatment has to be started and continued in hospital. Treatments include pills, injections and vacuum pumps.

My erection is better in the morning. This is unfortunate, as partners tend to like sex better in the evening, after you have spent time together.
Okie, 69, UK
Lovenet

I hardly ever have erections, so who knows whether I'll have any problems? I find that I am so damn grateful when I get the opportunity, and it stands to attention.
Henry, 49, UK

I have never been with a man before who I couldn't turn on in a big way, so when it became clear that my partner has difficulty with erections I felt insulted and thought that he didn't think I was sexy enough. Then I realised that I often have difficulty in reaching orgasm, and that it has nothing to do with how much I desire the person I am with.
Janet, 46, UK

I was totally impotent for a year when I was put on a drug that is known to numb guys below the waist (Paxil). I got off the drug, and my woody was back in a week. Excellent.
John, 54, US
Lovenet

Sildenafil (Viagra) and other options

I'd do whatever it takes to be able to have sex in a normal relationship. I've used Viagra, and, yes, it worked. It makes your dick hard and allows you to do the deed. I don't see any negatives, other than the price.
John, 54, US
Lovenet

I think it is unfair that someone with prostate cancer can have Viagra on the NHS, but I can't because I am suffering from psychosexual problems. Do I not pay the same taxes as someone with prostate cancer? This country is run by idiots who don't take sex or psychological problems seriously.
John, 44, UK

I believe Viagra also has positive effects on female sexual function. It increases clitoral blood flow and enhances female orgasm too. I know it is not really supposed to be for women but my partner had lost interest in sex before trying out my prescription. Since then I have found a number of reports on the web that support my theories.
Haroon, 48, UK

Eureka!: Sildenafil is more commonly known by its brand name Viagra. It started life as a humble blood-pressure tablet, but initial trials on UK students run by Doctor Ian Osterloh, a physician working for a drug company, revealed that it was not very effective. He abandoned the tests, however, he became a bit suspicious when none of the students wanted to give back their tablets. When he found out why, he realised he was on to something big and Viagra was developed. The drug works (it really does) by relaxing the blood vessels in the penis, increasing blood flow and enabling erection. The blue, diamond-shaped tablets are available in three strengths: 25mg, 50mg and 100mg. Your doctor will recommend the appropriate dose, though if 50mg tablets are prescribed, it is cheaper to cut a 100mg tablet in two with a sharp knife or a pill cutter than it is to buy dedicated 50mg tablets. Sildenafil should be taken on an empty stomach and it starts working within about an hour, though it may take longer to work if you've just eaten. Once you have taken it, you have the potential to get an erection for the next eight hours. The erection comes and goes according to the levels of desire being experenced and it goes down naturally after orgasm. Viagra is effective in up to 85 per cent of men with ED.

Safety: Sildenafil is very safe (one study showed the rate of heart attacks among those taking sildenafil was slightly less than among those taking a sugar pill), but it is dangerous if used with nitrates, prescribed for angina, or poppers or if your blood pressure is very low. If it is, the result can be a serious and potentially fatal drop in blood pressure. It shouldn't be taken by men who do not have recognised erectile dysfunction and a doctor should be consulted before combining sildenafil with certain HIV drugs, because some of these can prevent the body from expelling it from your system, causing levels to build up. The most common side-effects are headaches, facial flushing and a stuffy nose, and in rare cases vision is affected by a blue tinge.

Paying for sex: When sildenafil became available on prescription it opened the floodgates. In 2001 Britain's Health Service spent £25 million on drugs to combat impotence and it isn't in a hurry to increase the amount. As a result, people who have erectile dysfunction but don't suffer from a condition on the 'approved' list cannot have free sildenafil. Generally, family doctors see them without charge and then write a private prescription (at £6 to £8 a pop, it's not exactly free love). Many men opt for the privacy of buying online, but doing this without any idea of your medical condition or the dose you require is not clever. Many websites that sell sildenafil do an online 'diagnosis' and then add a crafty consultation fee.

Placebo erections: Cures for impotence can help a man achieve an erection, but none of them in fact increase libido or make a man feel physically aroused. That said, some men find that the psychological benefit of knowing that they can 'keep wood' for six hours helps them to relax about sex in a way that was previously impossible – in the clinical trials of sildenafil, 30 per cent of the men who were given sugar pills reported improved erections, too!

Alternative treatments

Apomorphine (Uprima): Apomorphine is generally considered to be less effective than sildenafil, but its advantage is that it gives men taking nitrates for angina a treatment option. Like sildenafil it comes in tablet form (in two strengths: 2mg and 3mg) but because it dissolves under the tongue, it works faster than sildenafil. Erection occurs within 20 minutes, and it should last for up to two hours. Use of apomorphine should be monitored by a doctor. It is effective in over 50 per cent of cases, though a strict head-to-head comparison with sildenafil has not been undertaken. Apomorphine causes nausea.

MUSE (Medicated urethral system erection): This comes in the form of a tiny pellet (half the size of a grain of rice), which is inserted into the urethra (where your pee comes out). It dissolves into the erectile tissue and if the penis is massaged you should have an erection within ten minutes; it should last about one to two hours. Occasionally, the pellet can scratch the lining of the urethra and cause some bleeding, so care is needed when it is inserted. Make sure that your doctor is aware of any other medication you are taking before you start using MUSE. This works in about 43 per cent of men.

Alprostadil: This is a self-administered injection treatment that contains the same substances as MUSE and works within ten minutes. It sounds very intimidating, but to some – self-injecting diabetics, for example – the choice between injecting the shaft of the penis and never having sex again makes alprostadil seem a pretty good option. Alprostadil erections tend to be stronger and remain after orgasm, eventually fading away as the drug leaves your system. It is up to 90 per cent effective, though about one per cent of users experience priapism (a painful and prolonged erection). If this happens, go for a walk, take a cold bath and go to your local A&E department after four hours if nothing else has worked.

Hormone treatments: If a man produces too little testosterone, hormone replacement therapy that increases testosterone levels can improve things.

Alternative treatments: Yohimbine, an extract from the bark of the African yohimba tree, has been used in the past, particularly in patients whose impotence has psychological causes. It has an 33 per cent success rate, which is only marginally higher than the results for placebo testing. Yohimbine has also been used in high doses to help people who find it difficult to ejaculate, but its side-effects include raised blood pressure and anxiety.

Future treatments: Two new drugs – tadalafil and vardenafil – are currently in the trials stage, though both still conflict with nitrates. They seem to be very similar in effectiveness and side-effects to sildenafil, though tadalafil works for up to 36 hours and its absorption is not affected by food.

HERBAL ALTERNATIVES
There is no research to show that any of these work apart from Gingko biloba. This helps maintain circulation to the body's extremities, and can therefore help you achieve an erection. It also improves sexual desire in people taking antidepressants, 84 per cent of whom become excited more easily and achieve orgasm more quickly. It should be taken for at least four weeks to have the maximum effect, but can be taken for longer if necessary. It is available through the Internet, or from specialist herbal outlets. Consult with your doctor before self-prescribing.

I've had experience of herbal viagra. My friend dared me to try it, so I took the tablets and went clubbing. I'd also taken ecstasy that evening and my friends decided it would be amusing to let my female friends know what had gone on. They, in turn, kept at me all evening and I had an erection that wouldn't go down. Very embarrassing.
Justin, 19, UK
Thesite

Getting your mojo back

Other treatments for erectile dysfunction

Each treatment has its own advantages and disadvantages. Your doctor may ask whether you are able to have erections at night, because if you are, this might indicate that the problem is psychological, and if so you may be referred to a therapist.

Counselling: Men who suffer from erectile problems may well be affected psychologically, even if the cause wasn't psychological to start with. Sexual counselling, preferably with your partner, may help to reassure both of you.

Vacuum pumps: These are probably the most effective (if least aesthetic), means of giving a man a hard-on. The procedure involves pushing the limp penis into a suction cylinder and pumping to increase blood flow into the genitals. When the penis is erect, the pump is removed and a tight band is placed around the base of the penis to prevent the blood from flowing back out. Unlike natural erections, a pump erection is only hard above the band and it can also make the erect penis feel a bit cold. Because the band is tight, ejaculation can sometimes be prevented. The band should not be kept on for longer than 30 minutes, because it can damage the penis.

Penile implants: Most specialists won't consider surgical implants unless other methods have failed. The operation involves putting semi-stiff tubes within the shaft of the penis – these can be inflated to make the penis erect. It permanently alters the internal structure of the penis and damages the erectile tissue; the operation cannot be reversed.

Vascular recontructive surgery: This procedure is a form of microsurgery that involves re-routing part of the existing blood system. It is rarely used these days because the operation is tricky and the problems can recur.

For partners: People whose partners have erectile difficulties often feel frustration at their powerlessness to elicit a sexual response. Frequently, however, a man's erectile difficulties have underlying causes that no amount of sexual attractiveness can overcome. Your partner cannot make an erection happen, nor is an erection a reliable indication of his feelings for you. A man can be turned on and still fail to have an erection (indeed, over-excitement or nerves can be as much of a problem as lack of interest). Stimulation can help, but it may make your partner feel even more anxious. If he knows he can satisfy you without an erection, he will feel less anxious.

Orgasm addicts

Sexual addiction: Having sex can be a wonderful way to escape from real life. It can relieve stress and alleviate boredom, particularly in people who are dissatisfied with the way they normally spend their time. The constant reassurance and physical intimacy of sexual contact can be beneficial for everyone, but perhaps it is even more so for people with low self-esteem. But occasionally people feel that they cannot control their need for sex. There is a clear difference between having a high sex drive and sex addiction. A person with sex addiction does not see sex as a 'fix', but views it as the single most important thing in life – more important than family, friends and work. Someone is drawn to an addictive behaviour or substance because of the way it affects the emotions. It enhances some feelings and numbs others. When you satisfy your craving, emotional pain is reduced momentarily and the hope is that it will not come back. It generally does. Over time, more and more of the behaviour or substance is required to produce the desired effect. Sex addiction is thought to be related to a dependency on the chemicals in the brain that are stimulated by sexual arousal and orgasm (endorphins and encephalins). Often sex addicts cannot stop their sexual behaviour for very long and sometimes certain behaviours or fantasies become an obsession. Sex addiction is associated with drug and alcohol abuse and dysthymia (low-grade depression). Treatment with SSRI antidepressants (fluoxetine), which release the same 'good feeling' chemicals in the brain, may help.

Compulsive masturbation: Although many people masturbate, compulsive masturbation can be seen as a form of addiction. Some people just can't stop even though they have masturbated so many times in a day that they cannot orgasm or their genitals hurt. The cause may be severe anxiety, which is temporarily relieved by the release of serotonin in the brain at orgasm.

Porn addicts: Pornography often plays a large part in compulsive masturbation, and some people feel that they are so addicted to the fantasy world of porn that they are no longer aroused by sex with another person or sex that doesn't involve pornography in some way.

Cybersex addicts: Psychosexual counsellors are increasingly reporting patients who cannot stop having cybersex. Some find that the thrill of having explicit written conversations with strangers while they masturbate becomes more exciting than real-life sex, and the ease with which sex is available online can encourage the compulsion. This can both take up great deal of time and be damaging to existing sexual relationships.

Addicted to sex workers: Some people find themselves addicted to the services of sex workers and find that they only want sex that they pay for. The problem can affect the ability to have a normal relationship, and is likely to involve underlying psychological issues that should be addressed.

Love addiction (erotomania): Love addiction is a broad term for a desire for another person that becomes so obsessive that it drives out all other thoughts, including, sometimes, the need for self-care. The target of this obsession need not be a partner. The one-sided relationship can be between people who were once friends, between a parent and a child or a therapist and a client, or even with a celebrity whom the addict has never met. Recognising and treating love addiction can be very difficult, because denial and delusion are often particularly common. Depression is often experienced by people trying to give up their love addiction, because fear of abandonment is often part of the obsession, which may also be based on an underlying psychiatric illness or an immature personality. Some people don't want to lose their obsession – they like it. Others realise that it is having a negative effect on life and relationships and go into therapy or counselling. Treatment with antidepressants may also help.

Sexual desire disorder: Persistent lack of interest in any sexual activity, aversion to sex and sexual phobias may stem from medical or emotional factors, including depression and stress. They may also be the result of physical or sexual abuse or childhood trauma. In chronic cases, phobias or lack of desire will prevent a person establishing sexual relationships. In other scenarios, lack of desire may not be a problem at all. If you have no partner or your partner is unwell, lack of desire may be welcome. Even within a relationship, reduced desire won't cause problems if it is mutual. There are times in everyone's life when desire is reduced or disappears completely: if you are busy, anxious or unhappy; when the first flush of a new relationship is over; during pregnancy and early parenthood; and sometimes in the early stages of the menopause. But problems arise when lack of desire is not mutual. A partner may feel rejected and respond by withdrawing or looking for intimacy elsewhere. Sometimes temporary lack of desire becomes permanent, simply because you're used to it. Sexual counselling or therapy may help.

Prescription drugs: Some drugs have a detrimental effect on the libido and sexual function in both men and women. These include medications for blood pressure and angina, sedatives, tranquillisers and some antidepressants.

I've come to realise that I've been using unprotected sex as a form of self-abuse – I've put myself (and my family) through this cycle every six months or so as a form of punishing myself. I convince myself that I just want to be a free-living good-time girl. I get drunk and sleep with people I hardly know without protection. Then I get obsessed with the fact I might have AIDS and get really depressed and distraught. Eventually I go for a test, find out I'm clear and vow never to do it again. It has to stop. So far, the worst thing I've had is warts, but it could be much worse.
Alli, 28, UK

I'm engaged to be married soon, yet I'm having such a hard time getting in the mood. We've tried everything and I just haven't had any success. At the end of the day, I think I'm just someone who isn't very into sex. It isn't a huge problem, because I often talk dirty to him while he masturbates in bed, so I don't think he gets too frustrated. But sometimes I worry.
Charlotte, 24, US

Sex with a serious illness

212

Sex Toys

Physical problems: Serious illness can physically restrict your ability to have sex. Pain interferes with arousal, while immobility, surgery or loss of feeling can make sex almost impossible. Some illnesses, such as diabetes, directly affect a man's ability to have an erection, and many medications that relieve pain or depression interfere with sex drive and reduce libido. The stress of surgery triggers the release of hormones that lowers libido, though the effect usually lessens over time.

Psychological problems: Feeling incapacitated dampens anyone's enthusiasm for sex. You may feel insecure if your body has changed physically. Hair loss due to chemotherapy, colostomy bags, catheters, a mastectomy or steroid bloating can all make someone feel very vulnerable. Fear of hurting yourself or over-exertion can also make sex problematic.

Get used to it: Adjusting to your new self means trying to live your life as normally as possible. If sex was an important part of your life before you became ill, you should aim to restore sexual intimacy as soon as you feel able. Ask your doctor how your condition might affect your sex life, or get anonymous advice by calling a helpline or a support group.

Get in touch: As a first step, massage techniques can be used as a way of allowing your partner to become familiar with any physical changes. Touch builds trust, and as your partner accepts your condition, so will you. If your partner is overly conscious of your condition, ask your nurse or doctor to talk things through, and consider couple counselling if necessary. Many support networks also offer advice to partners.

Get comfortable: Explore positions that are comfortable for both of you and stick to foreplay and gentle masturbation until you have worked out how much you can do. Use additional lubrication, and if you find that you need more intense stimulation to become aroused, explore using sex toys. Orgasms may feel different – either less or more intense. If you are unable to orgasm, focus on the pleasurable feelings that can be experienced as a result of massage, contact, kissing and closeness.

Get a partner: People with a serious illness often find it difficult to meet new partners. If you have access to the Internet you may be able to make contact with other sufferers online. Many support groups also hold regular meetings, at which you can make friends with people who've had similar experiences or suffered the same problems as you.

I have fibromyalgia, which gives me acute pain, and it has made me stop and 'smell the roses'. Genitalia have ceased to be the primary focus for pleasure, both for giving and receiving. Most of all, my mobility issues have taught me patience.
Cherryl, 47, US

You can't see musculo-skeletal pain. I don't look as if I have a disability, so people forget. My friends tell me I should get out more, but they forget that movement hurts me so much.
Jacob, 43, Australia

When I had a stroke my doctor didn't mention sex. I just assumed it was like cigarettes and booze – one more thing I had to give up. My wife insisted that I was being old-fashioned and phoned a helpline for people who have had strokes. To think I might never have had sex again, just because I was shy about talking to a doctor!
Len, 67, UK

Musculo-skeletal problems: Although movement is more likely to aggravate arthritis and musculo-skeletal pain initially, in fact it is the best way of improving such conditions in the long term. Doctors recommend that people who are stiff, sore and immobile try to take regular gentle exercise to keep their joints and muscles flexible. Sex is a good form of exercise, and horizontal jogging is a much more exciting way of following your doctor's orders. The normal pulse rate of about 70 beats a minute increases to about 150 beats a minute during sexual arousal. Contractions of the buttocks, pelvis, thighs, thorax, arms and neck strengthen and exercise muscles, and you can tailor the level of exertion to your abilities. Taking a pain-killer about an hour before having sex may make things more comfortable, and you can use bolster cushions to prop yourself up and take any strain off your muscles. Your joints may feel more comfortable after a hot bath or shower, too. Women with arthritis may find that pain and drug treatments decrease natural lubrication, which can make penetrative sex uncomfortable, but water-based lubricating gels can often relieve the problem.

Stroke: Strokes are often associated with general ill health, high blood pressure and lifestyle factors such as smoking, obesity and lack of exercise. These conditions can also affect your sex drive. For example, cholesterol-choked arteries can inhibit erection, so reduced sexual function in men can be one of the first signs of clogged arteries. Though still in its early stages, recent research indicates that the same could be true of women: blocked arteries may reduce the swelling and engorging of the vagina during sex – a problem that has previously been blamed on the menopause. From the age of 55, the number of men experiencing strokes doubles with each decade. Seventy-one per cent of those who have a stroke cite fear as a reason not to have sex after experiencing a stroke.

Heart problems: The British Heart Foundation recommends doing the stair test after a heart attack or bypass surgery: if you can walk up and down two flights of stairs with no exhaustion, you are well enough to have sex. Less than one per cent of heart-attack fatalities occur during sex. Interestingly, though perhaps not surprisingly, the majority of these occur when someone is with a new partner or being unfaithful to an existing one. Symptoms such as breathlessness may be less likely after a good night's sleep or when you are most relaxed, though patients who tend to become short of breath may need to take a more passive role during sex. But also ask your doctor whether your medication affects your sexual ability.

Mastectomy: Mastectomy is an operation to remove part or all of one or both breasts, normally to treat cancer. Thirty-nine per cent of women report changes in their sex life following mastectomy, and these are largely attributable to problems relating to self-image, as well as post-operative stress. With a full mastectomy, sensation is lost and can't be brought back – which can be devastating. Both partners' sexual desire may be affected, though time and, perhaps, counselling can help. Breast reconstruction is fairly routine for women who have lost a breast, but it won't restore sensation and entails further surgery. Though physical sensitivity may be gone, once the skin heals, sympathetic and loving massage with appropriate creams will show how much you care and boost your partner's confidence.

Hysterectomy: One in five women in the UK has to have a hysterectomy – the removal of the uterus and sometimes the ovaries, Fallopian tubes and cervix – at some point in her life. Once the physical healing is complete, a woman is capable of enjoying sex again, although psychological healing can take longer. The majority of hysterectomies are performed when a woman is aged between 40 and 50. Following a total hysterectomy, a women will go through the menopause. Women who are left with one or both of their ovaries intact have a 50 per cent chance of going through the menopause within five years of their operation. Though some doctors believe that a hysterectomy shouldn't affect female sexual response, 33–46 per cent of women report that their libido becomes lower and that they have difficulty achieving orgasm. Some women report no change in sex drive and some women feel that hysterectomy relieves their worries and previous symptoms, such as cancer, severe infection, heavy bleeding and uterine prolapse, and therefore their anxieties. How hysterectomy affects your sexual response depends on how much tissue has been removed. The removal of the ovaries decreases the supply of the hormones (oestrogen and testosterone) responsible for vaginal lubrication and libido, unless hormone replacement therapy (HRT) is given. A complete hysterectomy may also shorten vagina, changing sensation and sometimes making penetration uncomfortable. Doctors advise that sexual relations can resume six weeks after the operation, if the woman feels like it. If sexual response has been affected and regular, HRT is not helping, testosterone replacement therapy may be useful. It is prescribed more often in the US than the UK and some women find it highly effective, though there may be side-effects. Another option, still undergoing trials, may be the Eros suction device, which fits over the clitoris. In trials it has been shown to increase lubrication, arousal and satisfaction.

I had a partial mastectomy in my early 30s, and I had recontructive surgery because I really wanted to have an attractive and 'normal' body. A few years ago I had the implant removed for medical reasons, but I won't replace it. I'm not a young woman anymore, and I don't get my self-worth from having beautiful breasts. Both my husband and I feel attracted to each other and affectionate, regardless of the fact that he is getting fatter and hairier and I only have one-and-a half boobs!
Pattie, 62, UK

The implant was a huge turning point. Until then I had been really low, but then I felt, 'This is my body and it doesn't look too bad'.
Joan, 43, Australia

We used to have sex about four times a week. A lot of women say a hysterectomy didn't affect their libido, but it knocked mine sideways. I have to really work at becoming aroused now and orgasms are rare.
Nancy, 54, UK

Diabetes: Up to 50 per cent of men with diabetes experience erectile problems or impotence. Diabetes can damage the nerves that cause the blood vessels of the penis to expand. The arteries may harden and narrow, and this affects the blood supply to the penis – which is what causes erection. The penile blood vessels become inflexible, less elastic and unable to relax, which means that blood flow and pressure may be inadequate to sustain an erection. Little is known about how diabetes changes women's sex lives, but it is thought that there may be a similar impact because the blood flow to the genitals during arousal is probably reduced. After diagnosis, a doctor or specialist will advise you to follow a rigorous medical and dietary regime, which will manage the condition to some degree. This type of self-help can often mitigate sexual dysfunction. Unfortunately, erectile problems that may have developed in the early stages, before diagnosis, can leave a man feeling inadequate and anxious, which, in turn, may provide a psychological basis for further erectile dysfunction. If your impotence appears to be rooted in psychological issues rather than physical ones, talk to your doctor about counselling and therapy. If it is the diabetes that is having a direct physical impact on your sexual function, you have a number of options. You will need to seek advice from your doctor or specialist, who may suggest vacuum pumps, injections, penile implants, sildenafil or apormorphine. These have all been designed to help men who cannot achieve or maintain an erection. Your consultant will advise about which treatment is most suitable for you.

Prostate cancer: Prostate cancer is the second most common form of male cancer (lung cancer is the most common). It normally only affects men over the age of 45, and 20,000 men in the UK are diagnosed every year. It is thought that prostate cancer is hereditary, because men whose fathers and brothers have had the condition are at increased risk. Symptoms of prostate cancer include problems with peeing, needing to pee during the night, impotence and lower back pain. If the cancer is a slow-growing one, your doctor may decide that it does not need treating. Otherwise, early prostate cancer can be treated successfully by surgery or radiotherapy. Unfortunately, while surgery and radiotherapy on their own don't really affect sex drive, there is a considerable risk of impotence. In advanced cases, hormone therapy (oestrogen, or drugs that stop the production of testosterone) is sometimes used to control the cancer, though it does not cure it. But hormone therapy is not ideal, because it affects sex drive and can also cause impotence. And while physical causes of impotence can often be treated, lack of libido is not resolved so easily.

The problem is that prostate cancers need testosterone to grow, so depriving the body of testosterone can stop the cancer spreading. But testosterone is the male sex hormone, so anything that decreases testosterone decreases libido and causes impotence. Because the treatment has to be taken indefinitely, scientists have been working on a new drug, Cassodex. This intercepts the male hormones but is less likely to cause impotence, though side-effects include breast tenderness and swelling. Discuss Cassodex with your doctor.

Post-prostatectomy sex: The nerves controlling erection pass very close to the prostate gland. In radical prostate surgery, for prostate cancer, in which the entire prostate gland is removed, damage to the nerves is common and over half of those operated on suffer erectile dysfunction as a result. Some surgeons now offer a 'nerve-sparing' procedure, but even with this, erections cannot be guaranteed. If the nerves have been spared, the sucess rate for achieving erections with sildenafil (Viagra) is significantly higher, though it may be months or even a year or two before function returns. As well as affecting erections, radical prostate surgery removes a large part of the ejaculatory system and so affects ejaculation and the sensation of orgasm. The procedure also makes men infertile.

Benign prostatic enlargement: Surgery for the more common condition of benign (non-cancerous) enlargement of the prostate gland is very different. The operation is usually performed using a fibre-optic device that is inserted through the penis, and erections are only affected in around ten per cent of men. Most men undergoing this surgery are in their 60s or 70s, a time in life when erections are becoming more rare. This type of surgery does not usually effect orgasm, but 50 per cent of men notice that they ejaculate hardly any semen (retrograde ejaculation). This may render the man infertile, although it cannot be relied on as a form of contraception or protection against STIs. Some tablet treatments for benign prostatic enlargement (alpha-blockers) can also affect ejaculation, but the problem resolves itself when the tablets are stopped.

Testicular cancer: This is the most common cancer in men aged 20–40. It is curable in 95 per cent of cases, but is seen more and more often, although it is still less common than lung and prostate cancer. The main risk factor is a history of an undescended testicle in childhood, and the risk is particularly high in adult men who still have a testicle that has not descended into the scrotum.

I've had diabetes for a long time, and as I get older I find my impotence is slowly getting worse. I can get an erection about 60 per cent of the time, by using fantasy, and if I am lucky I get oral stimulation, too. I still get pleasure when it doesn't get hard, but it isn't as fulfilling.
Ian, 66, UK

If you have had your prostate removed you can't ejaculate, but you can come. This makes me a popular lover. I'm probably the safest guy around.
Henry 49, US

I was really hysterical about the prostate cancer. The doctors kept telling me that there is a really high success rate, but I just heard the word 'cancer' and thought, 'I am going to die'. (And, believe me, that doesn't do much for your sex drive.) In reality, I am fine. I am reasonably healthy, have a new and loving boyfriend, and my sexual capabilities haven't faded.
Tom, 79, UK

I thought the surgery had taken away my erections, but it was actually stress and they came back later.
Nigel, 68, UK

Sex with reduced mobility

Desires and hang-ups: Disabled people have the same desires, aspirations, hopes, fears, dreams, fantasies, worries and hang-ups as everyone else – though the rest of society doesn't always expect or understand this. Many disabled people find that they are asked to conform to other people's moral attitudes. If you're disabled, family, friends and carers may tell you what is acceptable and what is not, but you may find quite a difference between what they actually do and what they tell you to do. Information and communication are vital to everyone's sex life, but disabled people may find it harder to access information on sex and may be discouraged from discussing their sexual needs.

Becoming disabled: People who become disabled or develop a chronic illness can find that sex becomes a problem. On the other hand, some people find that becoming disabled offers an opportunity to experiment with sex and challenge traditional sex roles to which they may have previously conformed. Very few people have such a severe disability that they are not able to engage in sex of some kind. If penetrative sex is not possible, it does not mean that your sex life is over. Oral sex and masturbation don't require as much flexibility or energy, but can be just as sensual and fulfilling as intercourse. Making the most of what you can do physically takes imagination. Try swapping roles, so that the partner who is usually on top or behind tries being beneath or in front. Remember that different things stimulate different people. For example, people with spinal cord injuries can find that areas at which paralysed and non-paralysed tissue meet are particularly sensitive. Be open with your partner about what you can and can't do, and what you like and don't like.

Body-image: Everyone has anxieties about their body and personal appearance, but people with disabilities may find their insecurities more pronounced. Other people's prejudice or ignorance may mean that disabled people are more likely to be on the receiving end of sexual or romantic rejection. There are not many disabled sexual role models, true, but think about who you are and what you can offer rather than who you are not and what you cannot do. Self-esteem can be a very sexy quality, and it is one that many able-bodied people lack. But if you are gay, bear in mind that that some male gay communities have a particularly strong culture of bodily perfection that can exclude some disabled people. The fetish scene appears not to be so prejudiced or fixated on a particular ideal body shape or type, and swingers tend not to make judgements about appearance, being usually only interested in engaging with a couple.

Finding partners: Disabled people may encounter more than their fair share of rejection. There is a UK-based self-help group called 'Outsiders', which has local equivalents in the US and Australia, for people isolated because of disability. Outsiders seeks to help with confidence building and finding partners. Staying positive, getting to know people in your area and living as independently as possible will increase your chances of doing so.

Sex workers: Some disabled people who find it difficult to go out and socialise also find it difficult to find a sex partner, and using the services of a sex worker is sometimes the only possibility if they want to have sex. Arrangements with sex workers can be made over the phone, but unless you can arrange for someone you trust (who doesn't have a problem with you accessing sex workers) to be around, don't arrange for the sex worker to come to your home. If the sex worker is not known and trusted, you may be leaving yourself vulnerable to theft or abuse. And if you are sufficiently mobile to visit a sex worker, remember to ask relevant questions about access first. If you cannot contact one yourself, be careful who you ask to help. It is illegal in the UK to solicit or procure sex for gain, and this means that if you ask someone else to arrange a visit, you may be asking them to break the law. It is rare for someone to be prosecuted in these circumstances, but you ought to be sensitive when you approach the subject. Your carer or assistant may find your request compromising or offensive. And don't automatically assume that sex workers are comfortable with disability. Before meeting up, tell them exactly what your disabilities are and be prepared to answer questions.

If your partner has a disability: Many people enjoy the company of a disabled friend, but fear letting the relationship become physically intimate. Often, able-bodied people are simply frightened of what other people will think. If the person you are attracted to is disabled, it may help to think about whether you want to allow other people's prejudices to affect your decisions. Be prepared for some sexual problems, too. Disabilities such as paralysis, spinal cord injury, multiple sclerosis, blindness and deafness can all affect sexual functioning and, therefore, orgasm. Different sexual approaches, positions or stimulation techniques can be used to reach orgasm. For some, focusing on different parts of the body with massage can also be a pleasurable part of sex. However, there are no specific positions for people with disabilities and the most important thing is to enjoy what you can do. Many mixed-ability couples experience initial difficulties, but with information, support and practice, they can find techniques that suit them.

I have found some amazing sites on the internet from which you can download audio porn to listen to, which leaves me free to concentrate on what I am doing.
Paul, 56, Australia

Because I have trouble controlling my muscles, I pass a bit of urine during sex. My doctor tells me that urine is sterile, so it's not 'dirty'.
Tammy, 29, UK

I have always got a lot out of swings and slings, as I can swing backwards and forwards without getting tired. I think that kind of relief from gravity is quite sexy, and I am looking forward to trying it in water.
Dave, 40, Australia

My disability has not affected my options for sexual partners. I think some people are curious. They want to know if you can 'do it'. And, yes, I let them know real quick that indeed I can 'do it' – but it might just take me a little longer to get my panties down!
Martha, 41, UK

Massage

Keep in touch: Massage is a great way of maintaining physical contact at any age, but older people tend to get a lot more out of it than over-excited whippersnappers who can't sit still for five minutes, let alone enjoy a slow, sensuous body rub. Though therapeutic masseurs put a lot of oomph into a massage, giving one shouldn't be physically straining. Anyone can give a relaxing sensual massage so long as they observe some basic safety principles: use a medium or gentle pressure without digging into the muscles; don't work directly on the spine; and don't press heavily on the base of the skull and the top of the spine.

Check-up: Massage provides the perfect opportunity to check your partner for lumps on the breasts or scrotum, for moles that appear to be changing colour or for any unexplainable physical changes. If you find anything suspicious, your partner should consult a doctor.

Sensate focusing: Couples who have problems with arousal, low libido or impotence, or simply don't enjoy sex, are often advised to go back to basic touching. Sensate focusing is a technique developed by Masters and Johnson to help men and women who are having sexual difficulties. Partners concentrate on using touch to learn how to give and receive pleasure, rather than worrying about sexual intercourse. The treatment is carried out under the supervision of a therapist, and consists of three different phases. The first phase involves couples learning how to stroke each other's bodies. Then the couples progress to stroking each other's genitals, and eventually they graduate to sexual intercourse.

And that's the good news: The bad news is that massage is one of those things that is great to receive, but, in all honesty, is a bit of a bore to give. Most people can't be bothered to make the effort, because subconsciously they are not sure that it will be reciprocated with the same level of attention, if at all. Life, however, is a virtuous circle. If you enjoy being stroked intimately and caressed, the chances are that your partner will as well. You may find that once you get into it, giving a massage is actually very rewarding, and, naturally, it earns you endless brownie points. Massage is about intimacy and investing quality time in each other, but the power of undivided attention shouldn't be underestimated. Thirty to forty minutes of consistent touch can build serious sexual anticipation, regardless of whether sex was on the agenda at the beginning. With a new partner, be clear about the type of massage you are planning. If a back rub is expected, it may be a bit surprising if you start on bum massage.

I find stroking and massage really good to build up to love-making, but I am a person who gets a lot out of visual stimulation, so it is important that we have the lights on, even if there's only a candle. I like to see what and who I am doing!
Ben, 21, UK

This woman insisted that I took all my clothes off, so she could give me this supposedly erotic massage. I was cold and uncomfortable, and it made me feel like a body on a slab being inspected. Not my thing at all.
Jessica, 26, Australia

Just not too hard! I love massage, but not feeling like I am being pinched and punched.
Winston, 47, US

I love to be touched on my back, tickled, scratched and stroked – it doesn't matter. I think it must be my erogenous zone or something.
Leslie, 28, UK

Oils: Use massage oil or lubricant, and rub it between the palms of your hands to warm the lotion up before you apply it. Water-based lubricants absorb quickly and tend to become sticky, but they can be reactivated with a little water. Oil-based lubricants and special massage oils work better, but if massage leads to penetrative sex, the oil will reduce the effectiveness of latex condoms or barriers. Wearing a latex glove can make the sensation feel very smooth and give it a medical feel, which can be quite sexy. Essential oils (almond, peach kernel, grapeseed) should be diluted with a carrier oil. Some massage or essential oils contain elements such as nut traces, which can trigger allergies. Apply a tiny bit to the skin first and wait to see if there is a reaction. Some people hate to be oily and may prefer to be rubbed with body lotion or even to leave their skin dry. Don't use massage oils on anyone who is in the first three months of pregnancy. If you are in doubt about a physical injury, make sure that they have checked with a doctor first. Don't massage someone who has a heart condition, any serious injury, eczema or cancer or who is taking any type of medication. Massaging someone who has just had a very heavy meal is not a good idea. You may see it again.

Comfort: Remove jewellery, watches, contact lenses, scratchy clothes (it's more sensual if both partners are naked) and keep your nails short. Sofas or very soft mattresses don't support the body uniformly, and using them can put unsafe pressure on joints. Instead, ask your partner to lie on a firm, supportive surface with a doubled-over duvet or towels on top of it for comfort – put pillows under the neck and any unsupported areas. For comfort, turn up the heating, especially if you are naked, and cover parts of the body that you're not working on with a towel; a hot bath beforehand can help to bring up body temperature. Dim the lights, light candles, burn incense, play relaxing music and use scented oils. Try placing a warm towel over your partner's eyes to cut out distractions. Maintain some form of body contact from start to finish, because the nerve endings in the skin tense up if you take your hands off your partner during a massage.

Positions: How you position yourself when giving a massage can affect the quality of the experience. Kneeling, bending down or standing for a sustained period of time and at an awkward angle will put pressure on your body, making you uncomfortable and less able to concentrate on what you are doing. Try kneeling behind your partner, resting their head in your lap with your hands coming over their shoulders. Kneeling or lying by their side or sitting astride will allow you access to their whole body.

Types of touch

Stroking: Place your hands flat on your partner's and travel lightly up the arms, around the shoulders and straight down the body (either on the front or the back) and all the way down to the feet, ending at the toes. Without removing your hands, follow the same path in the opposite direction and repeat several times, gradually increasing the pressure.

Brushing: Sometimes, you can change the sensation of a massage by using props, such as paintbrushes or fabric. Rubbing soft-bristled brushes over dry skin can feel fantastic, as can rubbing with satin or fur. Use your nails to scratch the back if your partner likes the sensation – try using a hairbrush instead, if they are too short.

Fanning: Place your palms flat on either side of the spine just above the hips, but not directly on the spine. Slide your hands slowly forward until they reach the shoulder blades. Next, move your hands in a curve that takes them over the shoulder blades to the shoulders and then back along the sides of the ribcage, then return. Repeat this several times, applying slightly more pressure each time. Your fingers should face towards your partner's head.

Kneading: Use your thumbs, fingers, knuckles and the soft areas of your palms to gently knead the muscles and fleshy areas. Squeeze rhythmically, first with one hand and then the other. This technique works well on the shoulders, upper arms, inner and outer thighs and calves. The secret is to knead into and under the skin to get to the muscles. Avoid the ribs, shoulder blades and sides, because these can be ticklish.

Scratching: Everyone likes having an itch scratched, and for some people it's a real turn-on. Start off scratching your partner's back, and then gradually move to more sensitive areas, such as under the arms and the upper thighs. Some people like their head or pubic hair scratched, too. Partners can do this to each other when lying side by side. Be careful that you don't get carried away and draw blood – unless you're asked to do so.

Frottage: Rubbing up against someone fully clothed or naked, as foreplay or to the point of climax, is called frottage. If naked and standing, lubricate your partner's front and try rubbing your body against the thighs, buttocks and chest.

It's a challenge to get it up and keep it up sometimes, and it takes more to stimulate me from the start. My wife's erotic massage really gets me in the mood, but we have to have a whole night ahead in order to do it. Wish we weren't so damn social, because maybe we'd have sex more often.
Jed, 48, UK

My wife and I used massage as a way of getting back in touch with each other. For many years, we were bored of sex, but we went to sex therapy. They taught us 'body focus', without sexual goals. It's helped me appreciate my wife and all that she is – her body, not just her obvious sex centre.
Jeremy, 44, UK

I absolutely hate anyone touching my body in a sexual way. It makes me feel very self-conscious, because I can imagine they are grabbing my flesh and thinking, 'God this woman could lose a few pounds'.
Lana, 31, UK

I like to be pinched, quite hard, but not so hard it bruises. Especially not on my bottom.
Sally, 56, UK

Sexuality and gender

Beaumont Trust (UK)
Support for transexuals and transvestites and their families and friends.
Tel: 07000 287 878
Thurs 7–11pm for transexuals
Tues 7–11pm for transvestites
http://hometown.aol.com/
bmonttrust/index.html

GALOP Helpline (UK)
For lesbian, gay or bisexual people who are experiencing homophobic violence, abuse or harrassment.
Tel: 020 7704 2040
(Mon 4–7pm; Wed 2–5pm)
email: galop@onetel.net.uk

Lesbian & Gay Switchboard Helpline (UK)
Support and information for lesbian, gay and bisexual people. Also provides numbers for all regional switchboards.
Tel: 020 7837 7324 (24hrs)
www.llgs.org.uk

Rainbow Network (UK)
Gay and lesbian website made up of 35 constantly updated sections.
www.rainbownetwork.com

Regard Helpline (UK)
Counselling, support and information for lesbian, gay and bisexual people living with disabilities. Services include a database of accessible venues.
Tel: 020 7688 4111 (office hrs)
Minicom: 020 7688 0709
www.regard.dircon.co.uk

Gay.com (UK/US)
With sites in the US, France, the UK, Latin America and Italy, gay.com connects the gay community globally.
www.uk.gay.com

Gay and Lesbian Hotline (US)
Tel: 001 212 989 0999
(Mon–Fri 4–12pm; Sat 12am–5pm)

Gay and Lesbian Helpline (US)
Tel: 001 434 982 2773
(Sun–Thurs 6.30–9.30pm)

Transgender Splendor (US)
Information, support and outreach for trans people and their loved ones.
www.prairienet.org/tsplendor

Queer Resource Directory (US)
Comprehensive resources for gay, lesbian and bisexual people.
www.qrd.org

FFLAG Friends and Family of Lesbians and Gays (UK/US/Australia)
Support for parents of gay, lesbian and bisexual people.
UK: 01454 852 418 (24hrs)
US: 202 467 8180
Australia: 03 9511 4083
www.fflag.org.uk
www.pflag.org
www.pflag.org.au

Australian Bisexual Network (Australia)
Tel: 07 3857 2500
www.optus.net.com.au/~ausbinet/

Chameleon Society (Australia)
Social group and counselling service for cross-dressers and their partners. Based in Victoria.
Tel: 03 9517 9416
http://home.vicnet.net.au/~csvl

Gay and Lesbian Switchboard (Australia)
Tel: 03 9510 5488/1800 631 493

Sexual health

NHS Direct (UK)
Help and advice on all health issues plus local family planning and STI clinics.
Tel: 0845 4647 (24hrs)
www.nhsdirect.nhs.uk

National AIDS Helpline (UK)
Confidential advice, information and referrals on sexual health, STIs and AIDS.
Tel: 0800 567 123 (24 hrs)
Ethnic language line: 0800 917 2227 (Daily 6–10pm); Mon: Bengali; Tues: Urdu; Wed: Arabic; Thur: Gujerati; Fri: Hindi; Sat: Punjabi; Sun: Cantonese.

Terrence Higgins Trust (UK)
Issues relating to HIV and AIDS.
Tel: 020 7242 1010
(Every day 12noon–10pm)
www.tht.org.uk

Jewish AIDS Trust (UK)
Provides the Jewish community with education, counselling and support in connection with HIV infection and AIDS.
Tel: 020 8446 8228 (office hrs)
www.jat.ort.org

Positively Women (UK)
Charity offering support for women living with HIV by women living with HIV.
Tel: 020 7713 0222 (Mon–Fri 10am–4pm)
www.positivelywomen.org.uk

Blackliners (UK)
Voluntary organisation providing sexual health and HIV support to people of Asian, African and Caribbean origin.
Tel: 020 7738 5274
www.blackliners.org

The Herpes Viruses Association (UK)
Information and counselling for people affected by the herpes viruses.
Tel: 020 7609 9061 (office hrs)
www.herpes.org.uk

Male Health (UK)
Provides information about the key health problems that affect men.
www.malehealth.co.uk

Net Doctor (UK)
Medical information presented in clear and understandable language. Extensive sections on sex and sexual health.
www.netdoctor.co.uk

Durex (UK)
Durex direct site: condom purchasing and safer-sex tips.
www.durex.co.uk

AIDS Hotline (US)
Run by the Centres for Disease Control and Prevention. Advises on risk, prevention, testing and treatment.
Tel: 1 800 342 2437

Body Positive Helpline (US)
Nationwide support for all HIV+ people. Includes advice, support, and referrals.
1 800 566 6599
Mon–Fri 10am–6pm

Gay Men's Health Center (US)
Tel: 001 212 367 1000
Hotline 001 212 807 6655
www.gmhc.org

Michael Callen Audre Lorde Community Health Center (US)
356 West 18th St, New York.
Tel: 001 212 271 7200/212 271 7287
www.callen-lorde.org

Women's Health Line (US)
New York Department of Health.
Open Mon–Fri 8am–6pm.
Tel: 001 212 230 1111

Center For Women's Health (US)
A natural approach to health and healing.
1500 Boston Road, Darien, Ct.
Tel: 203 656 6635

The Directory UK, US and Australia

National Herpes Helpline (US)
Support, advice and information for people with herpes.
Tel: 919 361 8488

Hepatitis C Helpline (Australia)
Tel: 03 93491111/1800 800 241

Women's Medical Centre (Australia)
Provide help in locating services and finding support groups for young women with medical conditions.
Tel: 02 9231 2366

FPA Health (Australia)
Reproductive and sexual health questions.
Healthline: 1300 658 886
(Mon–Fri 9am–5pm)

Australian National Council on AIDS, Hepatitis C and Other Related Diseases
Website with publications and updates on related issues.
www.ancahrd.org

Sexual function

Impotence Association (UK)
Helpline for people experiencing impotence and their partners, also information on female sexual dysfunction.
Tel: 020 8767 7791 (Mon–Fri 9am–5pm)
www.impotence.org.uk

Women's Health (UK)
Information on gynaecological health, heavy bleeding, fibroids, hysterectomy, menopause, HRT, pelvic inflammatory disease and ovarian problems.
Tel: 0845 125 5254
(Mon–Fri 9.30am–1.30pm)
www.womenshealthlondon.org.uk

Secrets Revealed (UK)
Tips on everything from multiple orgasms to how to stay hard for hours.
www.sexsecretsrevealed.com

Chart a New Course to Your Health (US)
Confidential advice and information line for those who need to know more about erectile dysfunction. Established by the American Foundation for Urologic Disease.
Tel: 1 800 835 9021

North American Menopause Society (US)
Website seeking to inform women going through the menopause, including information on sexual functioning.
Automated request line: 1 800 774 5342
www.menopause.org

Impotence Australia
Support, advice and information.
Tel: 02 9280 0084 (Mon–Fri 10am–6pm)
www.impotenceaustralia.com.au

Young people

Brook Advisory Centres (UK)
Advice, counselling and medical help about contraception, pregnancy, abortion and sexual health. Centres across the country.
Tel: 0800 018 5023 (Mon–Fri 9am–5pm)
www.brook.org.uk

Childline (UK)
Free helpline for children and young people in trouble or danger.
Tel: 0800 1111 (24 hrs)
www.childline.org.uk

Sexwise (UK)
Free, confidential advice line on sex, relationships and contraception (under-19).
Tel: 0800 282 930 (Daily 7am–12pm)

RUThinking (UK)
Information for under-18s on sex, relationships and contraception.
Tel: 0800 282 930
www.ruthinking.co.uk

Likeitis (UK)
Advice and information for young people on pregnancy, STIs, contraception, sexuality, periods, puberty and peer pressure; run by Marie Stopes International.
www.likeitis.org.uk

Thesite (UK)
Thesite.org aims to offer the best guide to life for young adults, aged 16–25; includes plenty of information on sex and sexual health.
www.thesite.org

Teengrowth (US)
Website advice and information on health care, alcohol, drugs, emotions, family, friends, school, sex and sports.
www.teengrowth.com

National Helpline for Gay, Lesbian, Bisexual and Transgendered Youth (US)
Tel: 800 347 TEEN
(Sun–Thurs 7–10pm; Fri–Sat 7pm–12am)

Teenwire (US)
Website produced by Planned Parenthood for young people. Info on sex, sexual health, relationships and parenting.
www.teenwire.com

Kid's Helpline (Australia)
Advice on relationships, sexual abuse, sexual activity, pregnancy and more.
Tel: 1800 551 800
www.kidshelp.com.au

Contraception

Family Planning Association (UK)
Information service on family planning and all aspects of sexual health.
Tel: 0845 310 1334 (Mon–Fri 9am–7pm, weekends 8am–6pm)
www.fpa.org.uk

Planned Parenthood (US)
Contraception and parenting information.
Tel: 1 800 230 PLAN
www.plannedparenthood.org

FPA Health (Australia)
Reproductive and sexual health.
Tel: 1300 65 88 86
www.fpahealth.org.au

Shine (Australia)
Information and advice on contraception and sexual health.
Tel: 08 8364 0444
www.shinesa.org.au

Mid- and later-life

Age Concern (UK)
Information line provides a service to older people and their relatives and friends, as well as carers.
Tel: 020 8765 7200
www.ageconcern.org.uk

Hysterectomy, Menopause and HRT (HMH) (UK)
Support group for any woman going through or having had a hysterectomy, the menopause or undergoing HRT treatment.
Tel: 01309 673 178
(after 6pm and at weekends).

Relate (UK)
Counselling, sex therapy, relationship education and training to support couples and family relationships throughout life.
Tel: 01788 573 241
www.relate.org.uk

VAVO
Vavo provides a range of online resources for predominantly over 45-year-old members. Includes a sex and relationship section with chat board.
www.vavo.com

50 Connect (UK)
Magazine-style website for seniors, includes articles and chat.
www.50connect.co.uk

Seniorsite (US)
Chat, advice and info, also pages on sex, sexual health and reduced mobility.
www.seniorsite.com

My Dr (Australia)
Health website that includes extensive content for older people, including information on sexual health, prostate health, the menopause and more.
www.mydr.com.au

Health

Arthritis Care (UK)
For people affected by arthritis.
Tel: 080 8800 4050
(Mon–Fri 12–4pm)
www.arthritiscare.org.uk

British Heart Foundation (UK)
Confidential, accurate and up-to-date information for patients and the general public from specialist nurses.
Tel: 08450 70 80 70 (Mon–Fri 9am–5pm)
www.bhf.org.uk

Breast Cancer Care
Medical information, emotional support and details of local support groups.
Tel: 0808 800 6000
www.breastcancercare.org.uk

Diabetes UK
Support and advice from nurses and dieticians.
Tel: 020 7636 6112 (Mon–Fri 9am–5pm)
www.diabetes.org.uk

Prostate Cancer Charity (UK)
Helpline staffed by urological nurses who can provide information and support regarding prostate cancer.
Tel: 0845 300 8383 (Mon–Fri 10am–4pm)
www.prostate-cancer.org.uk

American Diabetes Association
Provides information and other services to people with diabetes, their families, healthcare professionals and the public.
Tel: 0800 342 2383
www.diabetes.org

National Prostate Cancer Coalition Fund (US)
Help and advice for sufferers and families.
Tel: 888 245 9455
www.4npcc.org

National Cancer Institute (US)
Tel: 301 435 3848
www.nci.nih.gov

American Heart Association
Information on heart disease and strokes.
Tel: 1800 242 8721
www.americanheart.org

Breast Cancer Support Service (Australia)
A national service providing practical and emotional support.
Tel: 13 11 20

Diabetes Australia
Information and resources on diabetes.
Tel: 1800 640 862
www.diabetesaustralia.com.au

National Heart Foundation (Australia)
Advice on protection against heart disease and information on coping with heart disease.
Tel: 1300 362 787
www.heartfoundation.com.aus

For disabled people

SPOD (Association to Aid the Sexual and Personal Relationships of People with Disabilities) (UK)
Promotes disabled people's rights to equal choice. Advice, counselling and treatment for sexual and personal relationships and sexual function.
Tel: 020 7607 9191
(Tues and Thurs 11am–2pm)
www.spod-uk.org

Outsiders (UK)
Social organisation for people with a disability. Offers a confidential list of members, personal communications and recommendations, a free forwarding service, a library-by-post service, support by telephone, body-image workshops.
Tel: 020 8220 5949
www.outsiders.org.uk

People First Programme (Australia)
Advice on everything from sex to relationships, aimed at people with learning difficulties.
Tel: 9227 6414 (Perth); (08) 9841 4035 (Albany)
www.fpwa-health.org.au

New Mobility (US)
Website and magazine for those with a disability who are not frightened to discuss sex occasionally.
Tel: 215 675 9133
www.newmobility.com

Drugs

National Drugs Helpline (UK)
Free, confidential and anonymous service giving advice and support.
Tel: 0800 776 600
(24 hrs, Welsh-language speaker available on request); ethnic language line: 0800 917 6650 (6–10pm);
Mon: Bengali; Tues: Urdu; Fri: Hindi; Sat: Punjabi; Sun: Cantonese.
www.ndh.org.uk

Release (UK)
Voluntary organisation that gives advice to drug users, their families and friends, specialising in legal issues.
Tel: 020 7729 9904 (24 hrs)
www.release.org.uk

Alcoholics Anonymous (UK)
Support groups to overcome problem drinking.
Tel: 0845 769 7555
www.alcoholics-anonymous.org.uk

Alcoholics Anonymous (US)
Support groups to overcome problem drinking.
Tel: 001 212 870 3400
www.alcoholics-anonymous.org

Drughelp (US)
Information, treatment options and crisis support for issues around drug abuse.
Tel: 800 662 4357
www.drughelp.org

Alcoholics Anonymous (Australia)
Support groups to help people overcome problem drinking.
Tel: 02 9663 1206
www.alcoholicsanonymous.org.au

Narcotics Anonymous (Australia)
Tel: 02 9565 1453
and ask for your local helpline.
www.naoz.org.au

Family Drug Support (Australia)
For family and friends of drug users.
Tel: 1300 368 186
www.fds.org.au

Psychological health

MIND (UK)
Confidential help on a range of mental health problems and their consequences.
Tel: 08457 660 163
(Mon–Fri 9.15am–5.15pm)
www.mind.org.uk

The Samaritans (UK)
Telephone counselling service giving
confidential support.
Tel: 08457 909 090 (24 hrs)
www.samaritans.org

**National Institute of Mental Health
Information Line (US)**
Provides information and literature on
mental illness (by disorder) for
professionals and the general public.
Tel: 1 800 647 2642.

Sex Addicts Anonymous (US)
Support group to overcome sexual
addiction and dependency.
Tel: 713 869 4902
www.sexaa.org

Sexual Compulsives Anonymous (US)
Tel: 604 290 9382

SANE Australia
Helping those who face mental illness.
Also provides an online helpline.
Tel: 3 9682 5933
www.sane.org

Life Line (Australia)
Crisis support and telephone counselling
on any subject.
Tel: 13 11 14 (24 hrs)
www.wesleymission.org.au/centres/
lifeline

Law

Liberty (UK)
Support for individuals suffering injustice
and fighting libertarian causes.
Tel: 020 7403 3888 (office hrs)
www.liberty-human-rights.org.uk

Citizen's Advice Bureau (UK)
Free confidential advice on legal and
financial issues and social services.
Tel: 08707 509 000
(Mon–Fri 12–4pm; Sat 10am–1pm)
www.nacab.org.uk

American Civil Liberties Union
Works with courts and communities to
defend and preserve the rights and
liberties of all people in the US.
Tel: 001 212 549 2500
www.aclu.org

Legal Aid Office (Australia)
Tel: 02 9219 5000 (office hrs)
www.legalaid.canberra.net.au

Sexual abuse

Rape Crisis (UK)
Referral services to local centres for
women who have been sexually abused
or raped.
Tel: 0115 934 8474 (Mon–Fri 9am–5pm)
www.rapecrisis.co.uk

Survivors (UK)
Help for men who have been sexually
abused or raped.
Tel: 020 7613 0808 (Tues 7–10pm)
www.survivorsuk.co.uk

Incest and Sexual Abuse Survivors (UK)
Helpline for those who have suffered
sexual abuse from a family member.
Tel: 01636 610 313
(Tues 9.30am–4.30pm; Fri 1–4pm)

**Women's Aid Domestic Violence
Helpline (UK)**
Support and information for those who
have suffered domestic violence.
Tel: 08457 023 468 (24hrs)
www.womensaid.org.uk

**Advocate for Survivors
of Child Abuse (US)**
Tel: 1300 627 380

**Sexual Assault Counselling Referral
(Australia)**
Referral to nearest counselling service.
Tel: 9926 7580

LawStuff (Australia)
Legal issues for under-18s in Australia.
www.lawstuff.org.au

Childhelp USA
Dedicated to the treatment and prevention
of child abuse.
Tel: 800 422 4453 (24 hrs)
www.childhelpusa.org

Rape Crisis Centre (Australia)
24-hour support for sexual assault victims.
Tel: 1800 424017

**Yarrow Place Rape and Sexual
Assault Service (Australia)**
Advice and support for victims of sexual
assault.
Tel: 1 800 817 421

**Partnership Against Domestic
Violence (Australia)**
Government website including
publications and links to support groups
and other relevant organisations.
www.padv.dpmc.gov.au

Kid's Helpline (Australia)
Advice on relationships, sexual abuse,
sexual activity, pregnancy and more.
Tel: 1 800 551 800
www.kidshelp.com.au

Online shopping

Ann Summers (UK)
Lingerie and sex toys from their shops in
most major UK towns; also available
online.
www.annsummers.com

Sh! (UK)
Women's erotic emporium. Shopping
online or in their London shop. Sex toys,
clothing and books for women of all
sexual orientations.
www.sh-womenstore.com

Prowler (UK)
Britain's longest established gay sex
shop; also available online.
www.gaytimes.co.uk/prowlerdirect

Clone Zone (UK)
Sex toys, magazines and videos for men
from their stores around Britain or online.
www.clonezone.co.uk

Axfords (UK)
Tailor-made corsets for both men and
women. Styles include traditional, back-
lacing, boned, satin, leather and PVC.
Orders online or by phone.
Tel: 01273 327 944
www.axfords.com

Blowfish (US)
For people of all genders, persuasions,
orientations and relationships. Adult-only
sex toys. Will ship to UK and Australia.
Tel: 1 800 325 2569 (Mon–Fri, 10am–5pm)
www.blowfish.com

Diaper Pail Friends (US)
Infantilism site with an online store
selling adult-size romper suits, nappies
and more.
www.dpf.com

Expectations (US)
Leather goods for men; guaranteed
delivery, usually within 48 hrs.
www.expectations.co.uk

Good Vibrations (US)
Online shopping for a large selection of
toys and erotica.
Tel: 800 289 8423
www.goodvibes.com

House of Harlot (US)
Manufactures, wholesales and sells via mailorder a range of high-quality, well-tailored, well-designed garments and products aimed at the fetish enthusiast.
www.house-of-harlot.com

Purple Passion (US)
Leather, latex clothing, canes and corsets; a small collection of SM/fetish books.
Tel: 001 212 807 0486
www.purplepassion.com

Toys in Babeland (US)
Sex toys and books.
Tel: 001 212 375 1701
www.babeland.com

Achievable Concepts (Australia)
A site for disabled people that sells specially adapted sex toys; ships to UK and US.
Tel: 03 987 30182
www.achievable concepts.com.au

Aussie Playground (Australia)
Sex toys, lingerie, fetish gear and more. International deliveries available.
www.aussieplayground.com.au

Meeting people

Messy Bedroom (UK)
Sex, dating and relationships online for women.
www.mymessybedroom.com

Dateline Online (UK)
Dating agency for straight people.
www.dateline.uk.com

Love and Friends (UK)
Dating agency for straight people.
www.loveandfriends.com

MegaFriends (UK/US/Australia)
Online personal ads for dating, travelmates, pen-pals and business partners.
www.megafriends.com

Swingeradz (UK/US/Australia)
Online personal ads for swinging couples.
www.swingeradz.com

Swinging Life (US)
For swingers, including a calendar of events, online shopping and contacts.
www.theswinginglife.com

Courses

For Your Eyes Only (UK)
Pole- and table-dancing lessons from professional dancers in Mayfair, London.
Tel: 020 7499 6816 (10am–6pm)
www.fyeo.co.uk

Tantric Massage in West Cornwall (UK)
Work with individuals or in couple counselling, using Tantric massage disciplines. Courses in Tantric sex. Weekend courses available
Tel: 07754 089 797
www.tantric-massage.co.uk

Miss Vera's Finishing School (US)
For boys who want to be girls. Full-fun course in cross-dressing and gender transformation.
Tel: 001 212 242 6449
www.missvera.com

Body Electric (US)
Erotic workshops for women only.
Tel: 001 212 969 0497

Cynthia Newhart (US)
Erotic education (women only); classes in erotic spirituality.
Tel: 510 869 4383
www.bodyelectric.org

Sacred Harlots (US)
Erotic sexuality (women only).
Tel: 718 768 9503

Tantra (US)
Tantric sex and alternative philosophies.
www.tantra.org

Touching Body and Spirit (US)
Workshops in erotic and sacred sex.
Tel: 1 800 248 3413

OZ Tantra (Australia)
Workshops to explore sacred sexuality, intimacy, and relationships.
Tel: 1800 623 262
www.oztantra.com

Balls and fairs

Sex Maniac's Ball (UK)
Annual ball hosted by Tuppy Owens as a fundraiser for people with disabilities. Has included a kiss'n'enter zone, a fantasy fayre, dungeon, lesbian lounge, male maze, lap-dancing for couples, and group massage, silhouette frottage, magick ritual, jerk-off, bi-play, bondage, cruising, flirting, putting out, peeping-in.
www.sex-maniacs-ball.com

London Fetish Fair (UK)
Monthly fetish market in London at which you can buy leather products, bondage systems and reading material.
Tel: 0207 916 8360
http://lff.nixnet.com/FairInfo.htm

Exotic Erotic Ball (US)
San Fransisco ball that has been running for nearly 20 years.
www.exoticeroticball.net

SM

BDSM-Online UK/US/Australia
Information on BD and SM, including health, seniors and disability. Not a porn site.
www.bdsm-online.com

Informed Consent (US)
Deals with issues of consent in sexual relationships relating to sado-masochistic bondage. No pornographic images.
www.informedconsent.co.uk

Sexuality (US)
A social and educational organisation whose purpose is to promote understanding and appreciation for the many forms of adult intimate relationships and consensual sexual expression.
www.sexuality.org

ABIS (Australia)
BD and SM information site with everything from safety tips to personal ads. No porn.
www.master.webcentral.com.au/abis/

Piercing

British Body Piercing Association (UK)
Committed to promotion, advancement, health and safety, education and dissemination of information about body piercing.
Tel: 01458 831 666
www.profound-piercing.co.uk

Association of Professional Piercers (US)
Organises professional piercers, unites members and provides education and quality standards for body piercing.
Tel: 1888 515 4APP
www.safepiercing.org

The Piercing Urge (Australia)
Piercing studio, will undertake a full range of facial, body and genital piercing.
Melbourne: Tel: 03 9530 2244
Sydney: Tel: 02 9360 3179
www.thepiercingurge.com.au

Reading Lists

Body image

Body Outlaws
(Airlift Books, 2000), ed. Ophira Edut.
Collection of writing about women's body-image in Western societies.

Big Big Love
(Greenery Press, 2000), Hanne Blank.
A source book on sex for people of size and those who love them.

Twentieth Century Sexuality
(Blackwell 1995), Angus McLaren.
An historical overview.

Sexualia
(Konemann, 2001), Clifford Bishop, Xenia Osthelder.
A look at sex from prehistory to cyberspace.

The body

Why We Love and Lust
(Harper Collins 1997), Dr Theresa L Crenshaw.
How our sex hormones influence our relationships.

The Health Encyclopedia
(Bloomsbury 2001), Dr Robert Youngson.
Medical reference book.

The brain

The Sexual Brain
(MA Institute of Technology, 1993), Simon LeVay.
Examines the biological routes of human sexuality.

Women's anatomy

The Clitoral Truth
(Seven Stories Press 2000), Rebecca Chalker.
A guide to the clitoris.

The G-Spot
(Dell Publishing 1981), Alice Kahn Ladas, Beverly Whipple, John D. Perry.
How to find it and stimulate it.

Women's Bodies, Women's Wisdom
(Judy Piatkus 1995)
A guide to women's health and wellbeing.

Men's anatomy

Out in the Open
(North Atlantic Books 1999), R Louis Schultz.
An anatomical guide to the male pelvis.

Sexual beginnings

Deal with it
(Pocket Books, 1999), Esther Drill, Heather Macdonald, Rebecca Odes.
Aims to help adolescent girls; full of honest information and valuable resources.

All About Sex
(Three Rivers Press 1997), ed. Ronald Filiberti Moglia, Jon Knowles.
A family resource on sex and sexuality.

Sexuality

Cassell's Pink Directory
(Cassell 1994.)
Guide to lesbian and gay organisations in the UK and Eire.

Gay and Lesbian Online
(Alyson, 1998), Jeff Dawson.
Guide to cruising the gay and lesbian web.

Lesbian Sex
(Spinster Ink 1984), JoAnne Loulan.
Written for lesbians by lesbians.

Savage Love
(Fusion Press 2000), Dan Savage.
Straight answers from a gay sex columnist.

Pomosexuals
(Cleis Press 1997), Carol Queen.
Aims to challenge assumptions about gender and sexuality.

The Erotic Impulse
(Tarcher/Putnam 1992), ed David Steinberg.
Collection of essays, poems and writing on eroticism.

Understanding Gender Dysphoria
(Mind, 1998), George Stewart.
This booklet gives insights into gender identity and gender dysphoria and its causes, as well as sources of further help and advice.

The New Male Sexuality
(Bantam Books, 1999), Bernie Zilbergeld.
The truth about men, sex and pleasure.

Men and Sex
(Harper Collins 1995), Bernard Zilbergeld.
An examination of male sexuality.

Men Like Us
(Ballantine 2000), Daniel Wolfe.
A complete guide to gay men's sexual, physical and emotional well-being.

The Hite Report on Male Sexuality
(Random House 1982), Shere Hite.
How men feel about love, sex and relationships.

The Hite Report: A Nationwide Study of Female Sexuality
(Collier Macmillan.1976), Shere Hite.
Ground-breaking cultural interpretation of female sexuality.

Female's Desire
(Paladin Books 1985), Rosalind Coward.
A collection of essays examining cultural representations of female sexuality.

Coming out

Coming Out to Parents : A Two-Way Survival Guide for Lesbians and Gay Men and Their Parents
(Pilgrim Press, 1993), Mary V. Borhek.
A book for those wishing to come out, including sections on reconciling sexuality with spiritual belief.

Solo sex

Sex for One
(Three Rivers Press 1996), Betty Dodson.
About the joy of self-loving.

The Joy of Solo Sex
(Factor Press 1997), Dr Harold Litten.

First Person Sexual
(Down There Press, 1996)
Women and men write about self-pleasuring – 45 anecdotes.

Sex

Sex Tips for Straight Women from Gay Men
(Harper Collins 1997), Dan Anderson, Maggie Berman.

Human Sexuality
(Garland Publishing 1994), Vern L Bullough, Bonnie Bullough.

The Magic of Sex
(Dorling KIndersley 2001), Dr Miriam Stoppard.
A book for women who want to learn about men, and men who want to learn about women.

Sex: A Man's Guide
(Rodale Press 1996), Stefan Bechtel, Laurence Roy Stains.

Barefoot Doctor's Handbook for Modern Lovers
(Judy Piatkus 2000)
A guide to sex that employs ancient Taoist methods.

Sex for Beginners
(Writers and Readers Publishing 1994),
Errol Selkirk.
Examines human sexuality from a historical, biological and cultural standpoint.

The Guide to Living with HIV Infections
(John Hopkins University Press, 1998),
John Barlett MD and Ann K. Finkbeiner.

The Art of Kissing
(St Martin's Press 1995), William Cane.
Answers common questions on kissing.

A Complete Guide to Kissing
(Macmillan 1997), Nick Fisher.
A look at why people kiss, and what kind of kisses are on offer.

How to Give Her Absolute Pleasure
(Broadway Books 2000), Lou Paget.
Explicit techniques for straight men.

A Hand in the Bush
(Greenery Press 1997), Deborah Addington.
On vaginal fisting.

Stimulating men

The New Good Vibrations Guide to Sex
(Cleis Press 1997) Cathy Winks, Anne Seamans.
By the women who own Good Vibrations, a sex shop in San Francisco.

Playbook for Men About Sex
(Down There Press, 1981), Joani Blank.

How to Make His Wildest Dreams Come True
(Signet Books 1996), Graham Masterton.
Advice for women on having sex with men.

How to be a Great Lover
(Broadway Books, 1999), Lou Paget.
Explicit techniques for straight women.

Doing It
(Conari Press 2001), Isadora Alman.
To help real people have really good sex.

The New Joy of Gay Sex
(Harper Collins 1993), Dr Charles Silverstein, Felice Picano.
About safer gay sex and addresses emotional aspects of sex.

The Joy of Sex
(Reed International, first published 1972),
Alex Comfort.

Anal Pleasure and Health
(Down There Press, 1998), Jack Morin.
Research-based guide for men and women on anal stimulation and pleasure.

Ultimate Guide to Anal Sex for Women
(Cleis Press, 1997), Tristan Taormino.

The Big O
(Piatkus Books, 2001), Lou Paget.
Handbook devoted to orgasms.

The Multi-Orgasmic Man
(Harper Collins 1997), Mantak Chia, Douglas Abrams.
A guide for men to multiple orgasms.

Extended Sexual Orgasm
(Warner Books 2001), Alan P. Brauer, Donna J. Brauer.
A guide to extending sexual pleasure.

Becoming Orgasmic
(Judy Piatkus 1996), Julia R. Heiman, Joseph LoPiccolo.
A sexual and personal growth programme for women.

Hot Sex: How to do it.
(Corgi Books 1998), Tracey Cox.

Better sex

Tricks: More Than 125 Ways to Make Good Sex Better
(Greenery Press 1996), Jay Wiseman.
Tips for improving your sex life, including safer-sex advice and games.

Safer Planet Sex
(1994), Tuppy Owens.
A guide to safer-sex practices around the world.

Anal Pleasure and Health, A Guide For Men And Women
(Down There Press), Jack Movin.

Clitoral Truth – The Secret World At Your Fingertip
(Seven Stories Press), Rebecca Chalker.

Orgasm

The Technology of Orgasm
(John Hopkins Unversity Press 1999),
Rachel P Maines.
'Hysteria, the vibrator and women's orgasm'.

The Book of the Penis
(Grove Press 1999), Maggie Poley.

Sex as play

Cunt, A Declaration of Independence
(Seal Press), Inag Muscio.

Deviant Desires: Incredibly Strange Sex
(Juno Books), Katherine Gates.

SM 101 – An Introduction to S and M
(Greenery Press), Jay Wiseman.

Sex Tips from a Dominatrix
(Harper Collins 1999), Patricia Payne.
Step-by-step instructions on mood, decoration, outfits and techniques.

Encyclopedia of Unusual Sex Practices
(Abacus 1995), Brenda Love.

The Art of Sensual Female Dominance
(Citadel Press Book, 1999), Claudia Varrin.

A Guide for Women: The Topping Book
(Greenery Press 1995), Dossie Easton and Catherine A. Liszt. A guide to S&M – 'getting good at being bad'.

The Bottoming Book
(Greenery Press 1995), Dossie Easton and Catherine A. Liszt.
How to get terrible things done to you by wonderful people.

Come Hither: A Commonsense Guide to Kinky Sex
(Fireside 2000), Dr Gloria G. Brame.
For those who have wondered about bondage, spanking or cross-dressing.

Harold Litten's Best Erotic Fantasies
(Factor Press 1999), Harold Litten.
A guide to understanding the sex in your head.

Secrets of Sexual Ecstasy
(Marlowe and Company 1997), Carlo De Paoli.
Pathways to erotic pleasure.

The Family Jewels : A Guide to Male Genital Play and Torment
(Greenery Press, 2001), Hardy Haberman, Fetish Diva Midori.

Sex toys

The Ultimate Guide to Strap-on Sex
(Cleis Press, 2000), Karlyn Lotney.
A complete resource for men and women.

Kinkycrafts
(Greenery Press 1998), Lady Green,
James Easton. Guide to do-it-yourself
kinky toys.

Ancient techniques

Great Moments in Sex
(Three Rivers Press 1999), Cheryl Rilly.
Fascinating facts, follies and foibles in
sexual history.

The Tao of Health, Sex and Longevity
(Pocket Books 2001), Daniel Reid.
A modern practical approach to an
ancient way.

The Kama Sutra
(Park Street Press 1994), Alain Danielou.
The world's oldest guide to pleasure and
sexual techniques.

The Mythology of Sex
(Labyrinth 1996), Sarah Denning.
An exploration of sexual customs
throughout history.

Sex and the internet

Sex: Adults only Edition
(The Good Web Guide, 2000), Matt and
Jenny Blythe.
A guide to sex on the net.

The Woman's Guide to Sex on the Web
(Harpers Collins 1999). Anne Semans,
Cathy Winks. Information on sex, sex
forums and cybersex.

The Good Sex Guide Abroad
(BCA 1995), Suzie Hayman.
Sex techniques from around the world.

Sex through life

The New Our Bodies Ourselves (UK)
(Boston Women's Health Book Collective,
1996), Angela Phillips and Jan Rakusen.
A health book by and for women.

Sexual Health for Men
(Perseus Publishing 2000), Richard F
Spark.
A book for men of all ages.

The Lesbian Health Book
(Seal Press 1997), ed Jocelyn White,
Marissa C Martinez.
Brings together doctors, healthcare
providers, activists and others from the
lesbian community to make healthcare
accessible and responsive to lesbians.

Relationships

**The Relate Guide to Sex in Loving
Relationships**
(Vermilion 1999), Sarah Litvinoff.
Examines the role of sex within a long-
term relationship.

Facing Co-dependence
(Harper Collins 1989), Pia Mellody.
A guide to understanding the origins of
co-dependency.

Contraception

Contraception
(Oxford University Press, 2000), Anne
Szarewski, John Guillebaud.
Aims to cut through the often conflicting
evidence on the efficiency and safety of
contraceptive devices to offer clear and
accurate advice.

Sex and pregnancy

The Mother's Guide to Sex
(Three Rivers Press 2001), Anne Semans,
Cathy Wink.
A guide to enjoying your sexuality
throughout motherhood.

Sex in mid- and later-life

Sex Over 50
(Reward Books 1999), Joel D. Book.
A no-nonsense guide to sex in mid- and
later-life.

The Relate Guide to Loving in Later Life
(Vermilion 2000), Marj Thoburn, Suzy Powling.
Details the emotional and physical
changes of later-life and provides
strategies for coping with them.

A Lifetime of Sex
(Rodale 1998), Stephen C George, Ken
Winston Caine.
Male sex through life.

Sexual dysfunction

For Women Only
(Virago 2001), Jennifer Berman, Laura
Berman.
A guide to overcoming sexual dysfunction
and reclaiming your sex life.

Impotence: a Guide for Men of All Ages
(Royal Society of Medicine Press Ltd
2001), Wallace Dinsmore, Philip Kell.
A guide to erectile dysfunction aimed
specifically at patients, providing
information on the condition and causes.

Food for Sex

The Natural Health Bible
(Vermilion 2001), Maryon Stewart, Alan
Stewart.
An A–Z guide to drug-free health.

Better Sex Naturally
(Harper Collins 2000), Chris D. Meletis.
A guide to herbs and other natural
supplements and how they can improve
your sex life.

Peak Performance
(Dell Publishing 1999), Deborah Mitchell.
Eating and exercise for increased
pleasure.

Sexual Nutrition
(Avery Publishing Group 1994), Dr Morton
Walker.
A guide to nutritionally improving,
enhancing and stimulating your sexual
appetite.

Natural Aphrodisiacs
(Element Books 2000), Fiona Marshall.
Aims to guide you towards promoting
sexual energy levels through nutrition.

Reduced mobility

Sexuality and Disabilities
(Haworth Press, 1993), eds Romel W.
Mackelprang, Deborah Valentine.

Psychological health

Coping with Anxiety and Depression
(Sheldon Press, 1996), Shirley Trickett.
Self-help guide for anyone who suffers
from depression and anxiety. It explains
how and why these conditions occur,
suggesting positive ways of coping.

Sexual compulsion

Facing Love Addiction
(Harper Collins 1992), Pia Mellody.
An examination of the intricate and
debilitating dynamics of co-addicted
relationships.

Index

Entries in bold refer to the sidebar quotes, entries in italic to the illustrations, and entries in bold italic to the main headings.